HERE FOR THE AFTERWORD? RIGHT WAY!

WANT TO READ THE MANGA? WRONG WAY!

Japanese books, including manga like this one,
are meant to be read from right to left.
So the front cover is actually the back cover, and vice versa.
To read this book, please flip it over
and start in the top right-hand corner.
Read the panels, and the bubbles in the panels,
from right to left,
then drop down to the next row and repeat.
It may make you dizzy at first, but forcing your brain to do things
backwards makes you smarter in the long run.
We swear.

Tropic of the Sea

Translation: Maya Rosewood
Production: Grace Lu
Anthony Quintessenza

First published in Japan in 2011 by Kodansha, Ltd., Tokyo
Publication rights for this English edition arranged through Kodansha, Ltd., Tokyo
English language version produced by Vertical, Inc.

Translation provided by Vertical, Inc., 2013
Published by Vertical, Inc., New York

Originally published in Japanese as *Shinsouban Kaikisen* by Kodansha, Ltd., 2011
Kaikisen first serialized in *Young Magazine*, Kodansha, Ltd., 1990

ISBN: 978-1-939130-06-8

Manufactured in Canada

First Edition

Vertical, Inc.
451 Park Avenue South
7th Floor
New York, NY 10016
www.vertical-inc.com

TROPIC OF THE SEA

Satoshi Kon

VERTICAL.

Contents

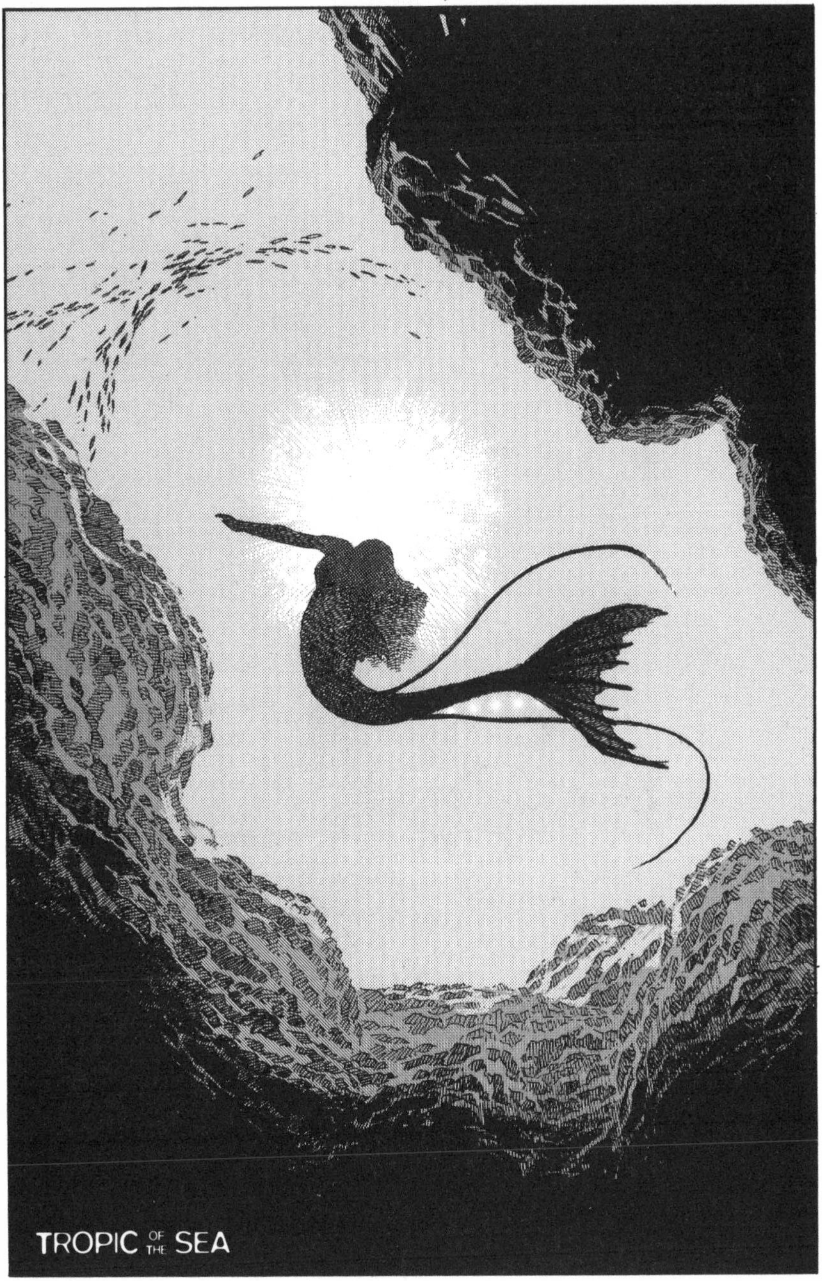
TROPIC OF THE SEA

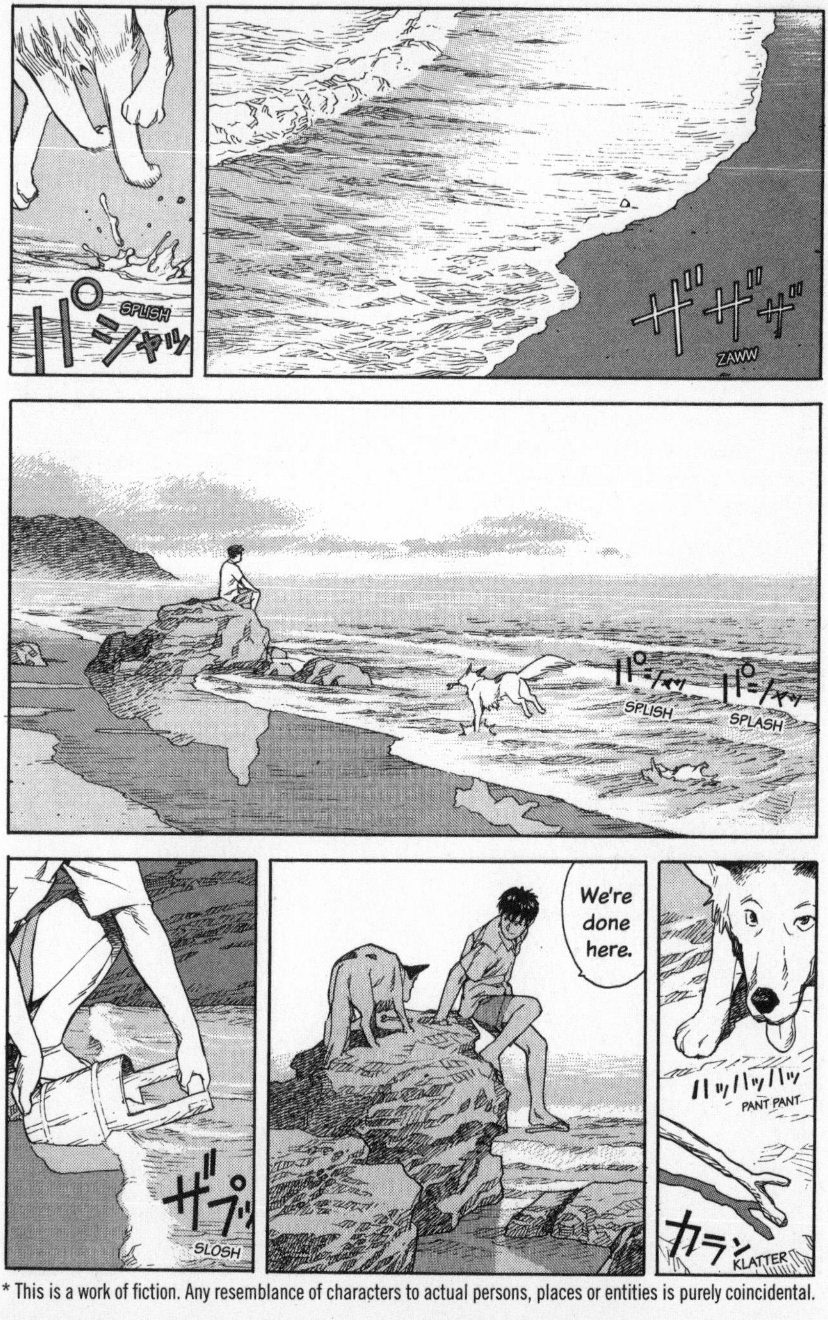
ザザザ
ZAWW
パシャッ
SPLISH
パシャッ
SPLASH
パシャッ
SPLISH
ハッハッハッ
PANT PANT
カラン
KLATTER
We're done here.
ザプッ
SLOSH

* This is a work of fiction. Any resemblance of characters to actual persons, places or entities is purely coincidental.

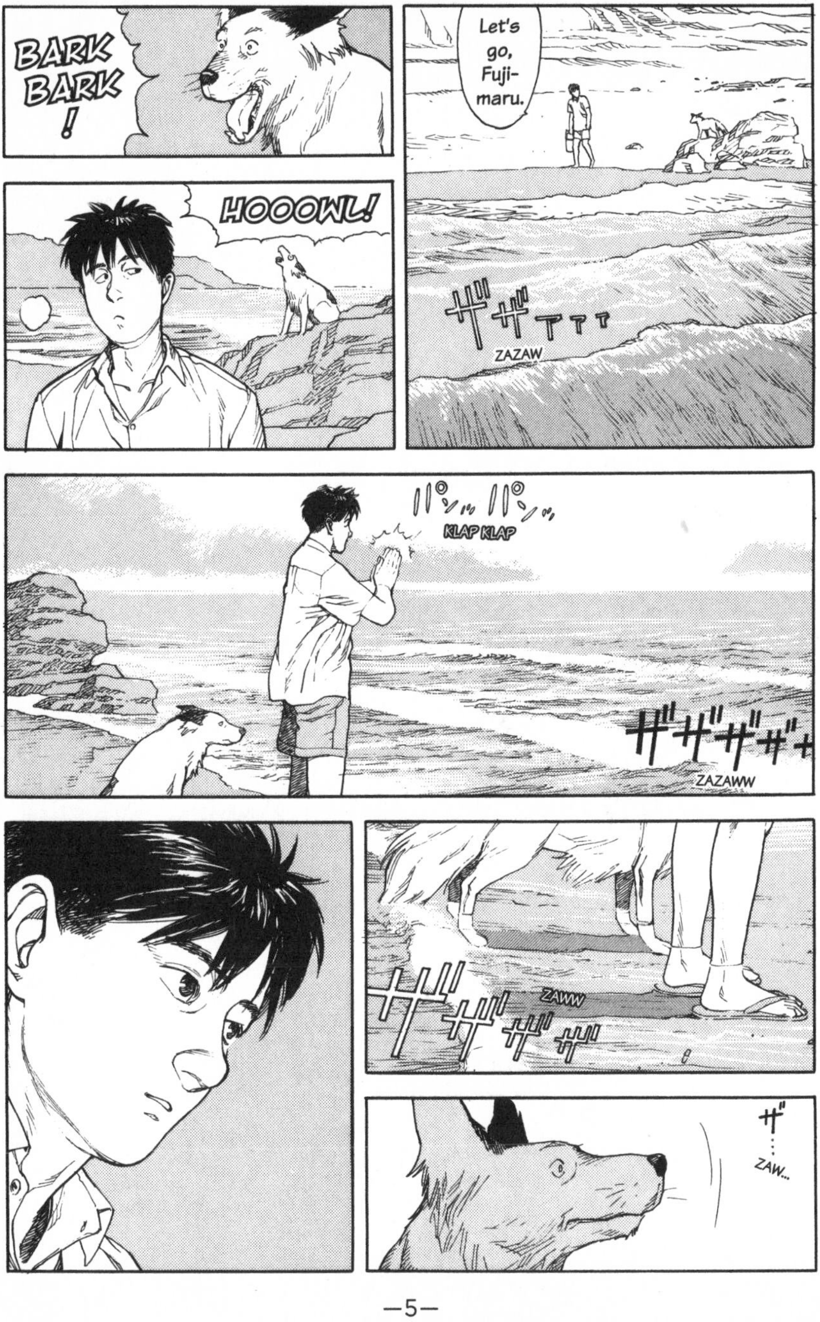

Let's go, Fuji-maru.
ZAZAW
BARK BARK !
HOOOWL!
KLAP KLAP
ZAZAWW
ZAWW
ZAW...

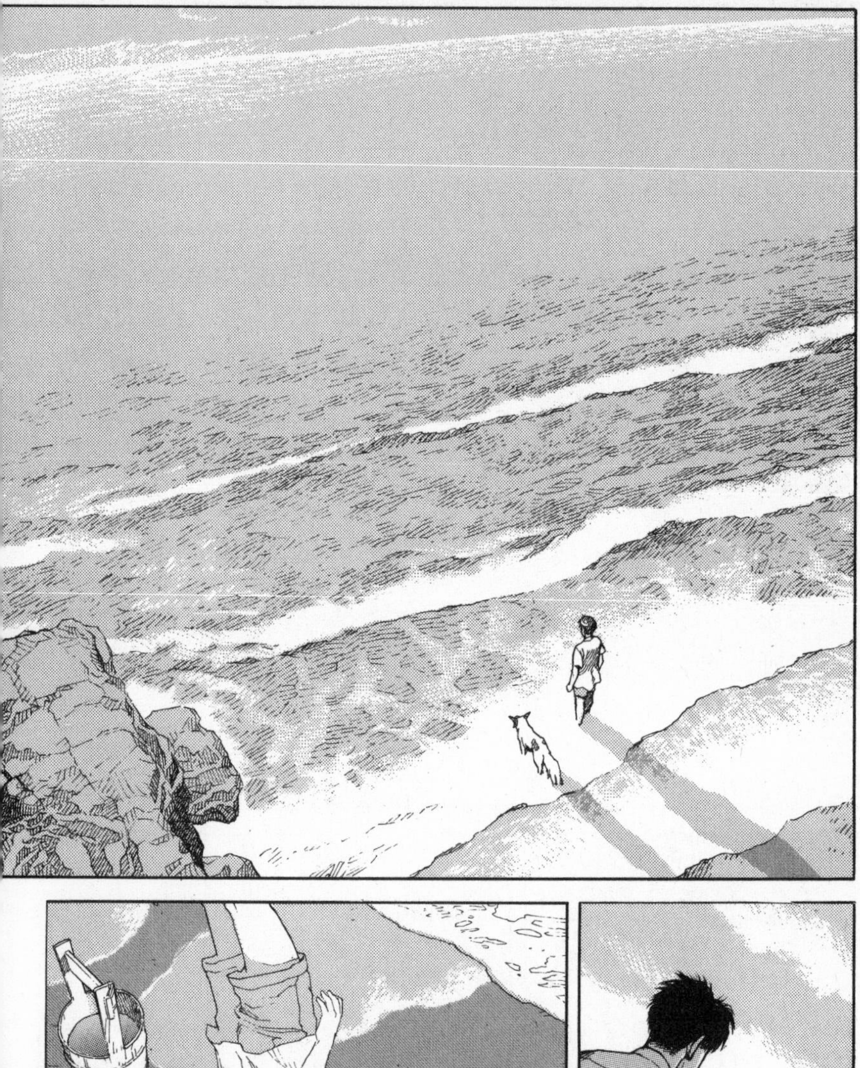

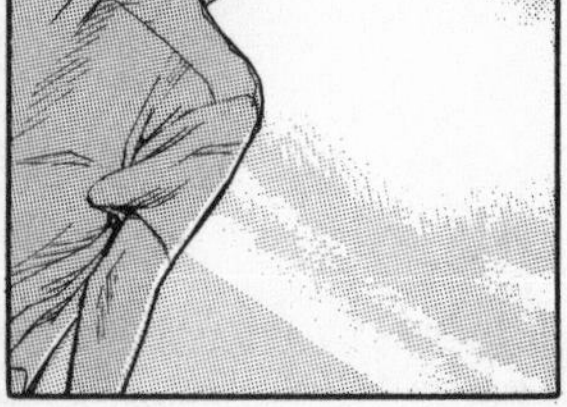

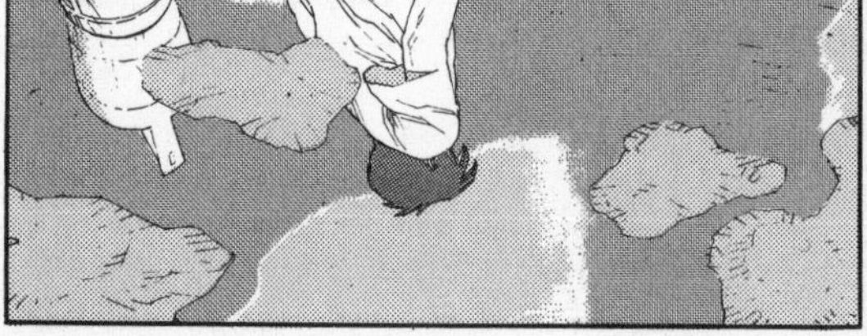

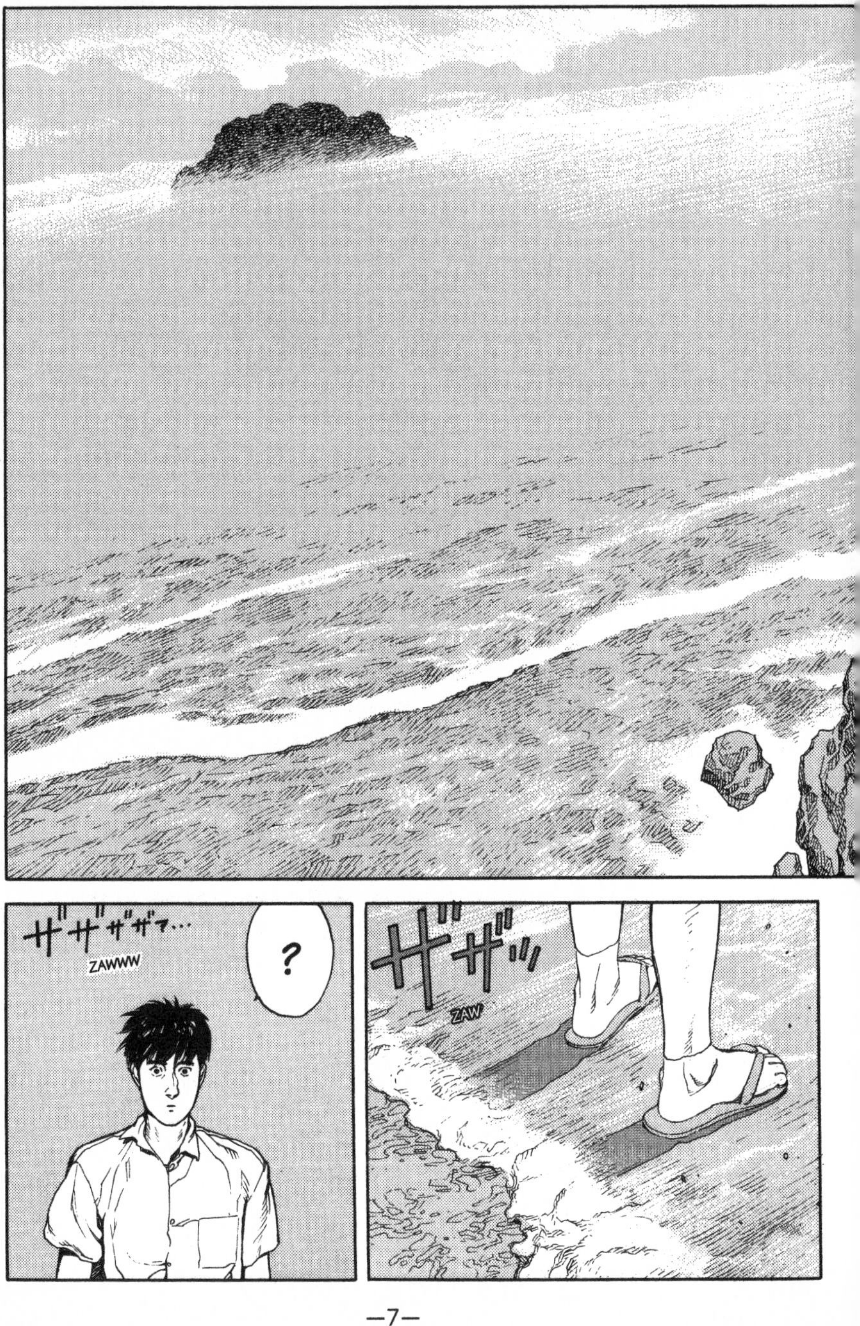
ザザッ
ZAW
?
ザザザザァ…
ZAWWW

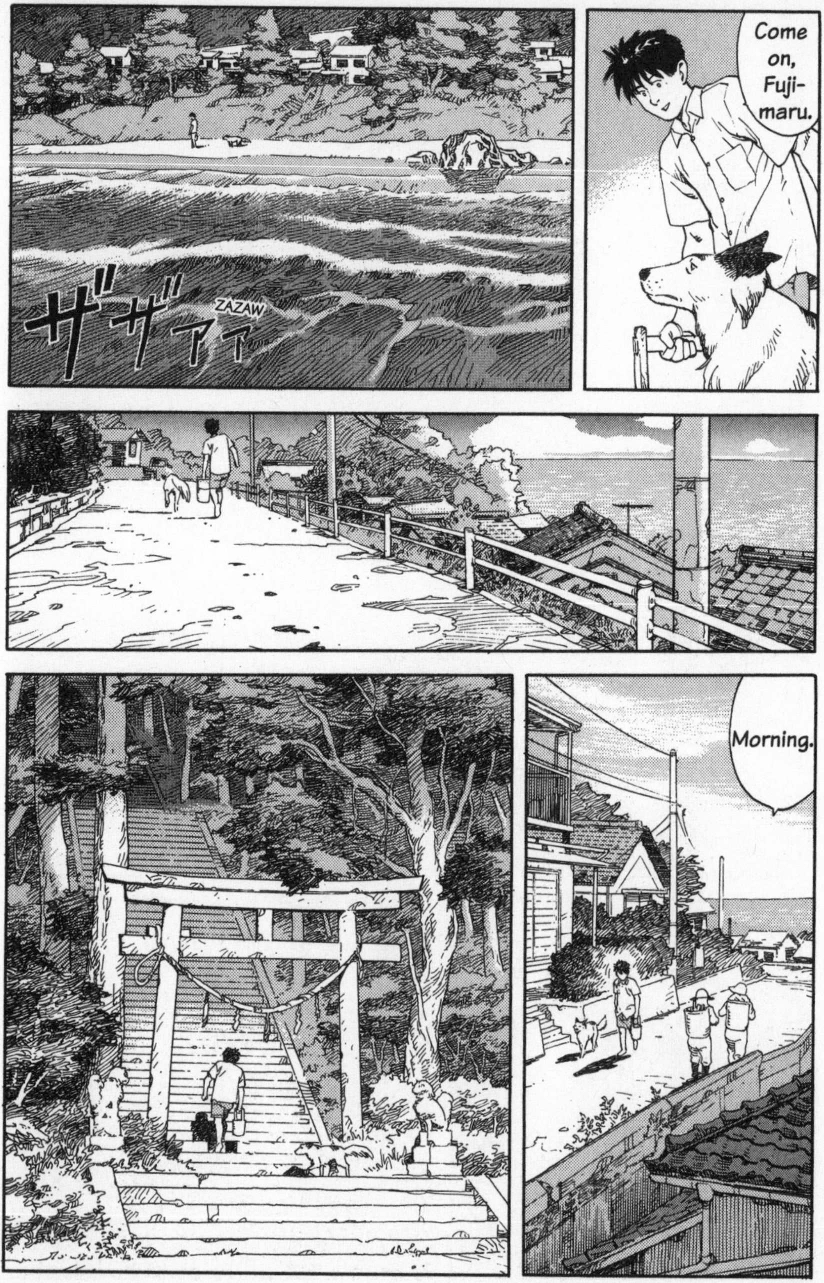
Come on, Fuji-maru.
ザザァ
ZAZAW
Morning.

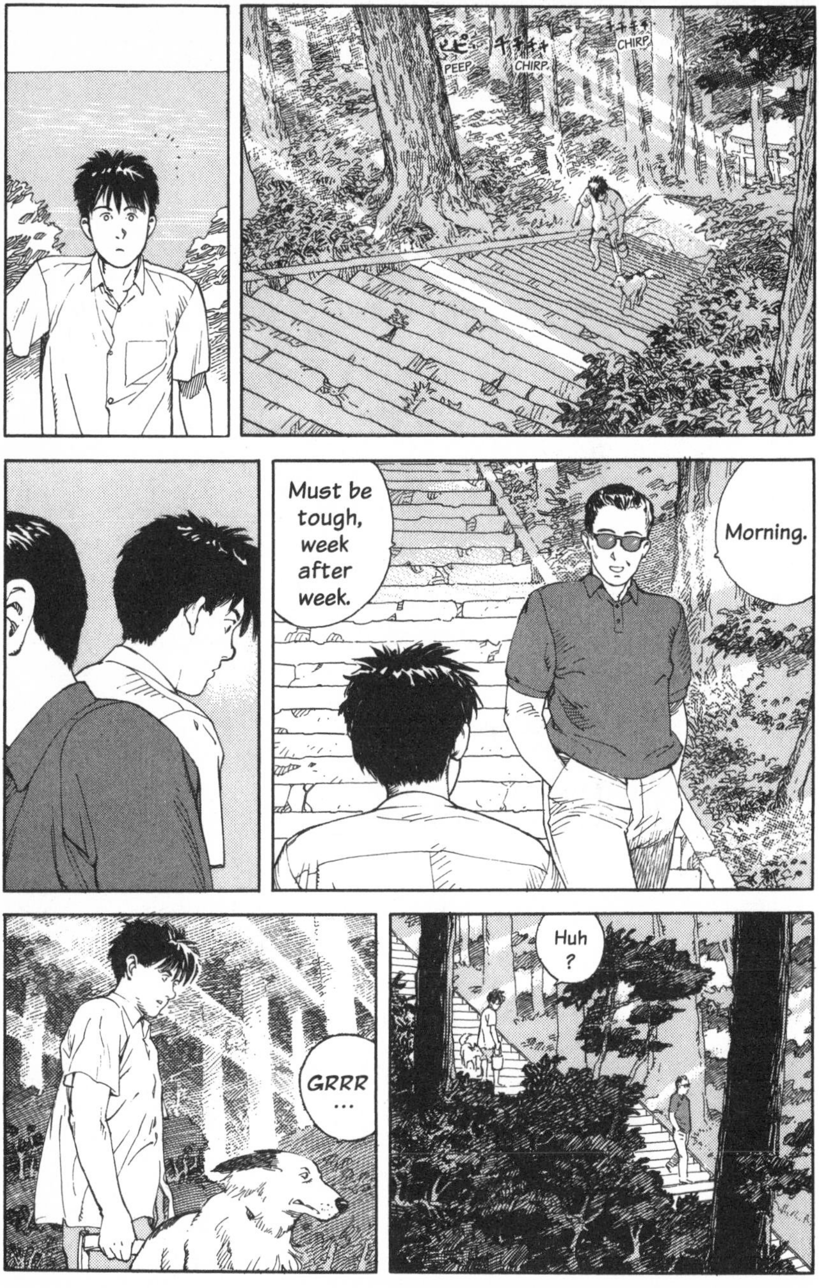

CHIRP
CHIRP
PEEP
Morning.
Must be tough, week after week.
Huh ?
GRRR ...

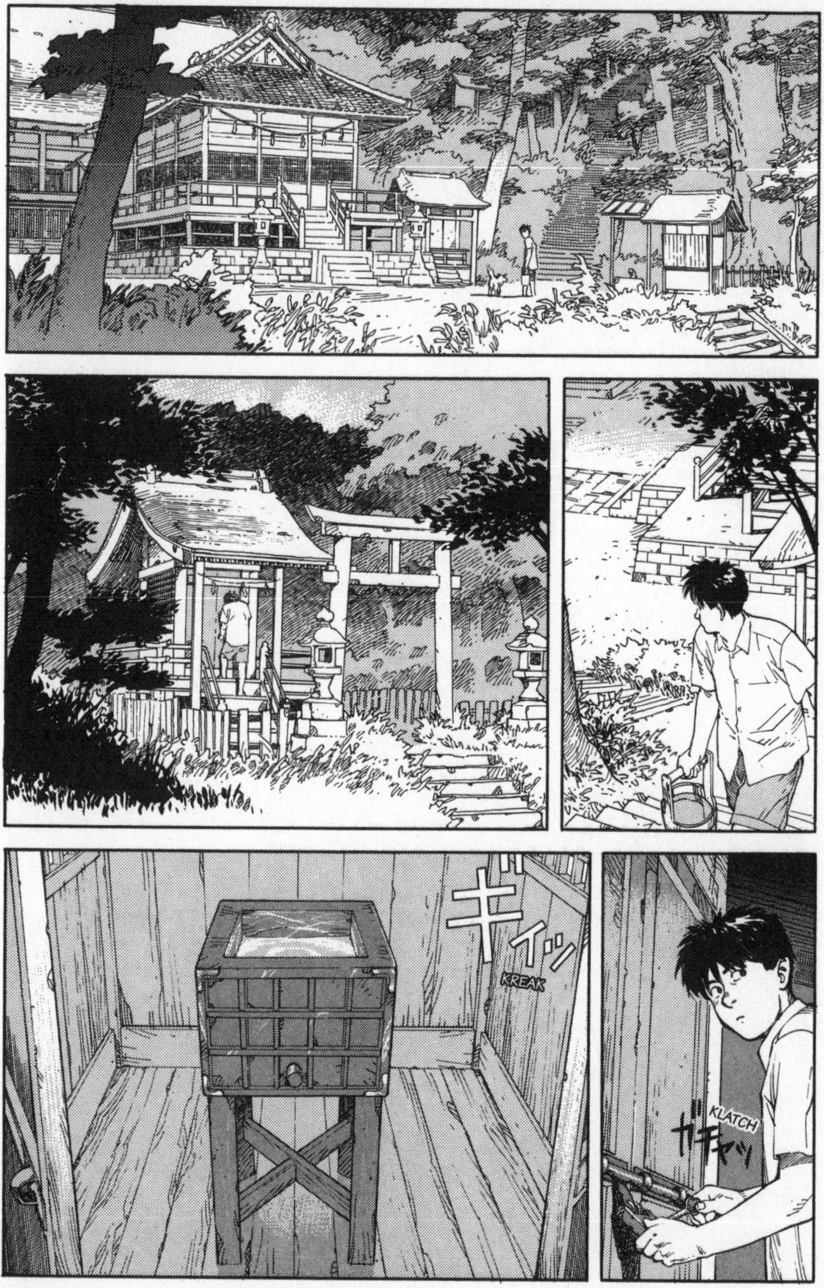
ガチャッ
KLATCH
ギィッ
KREAK

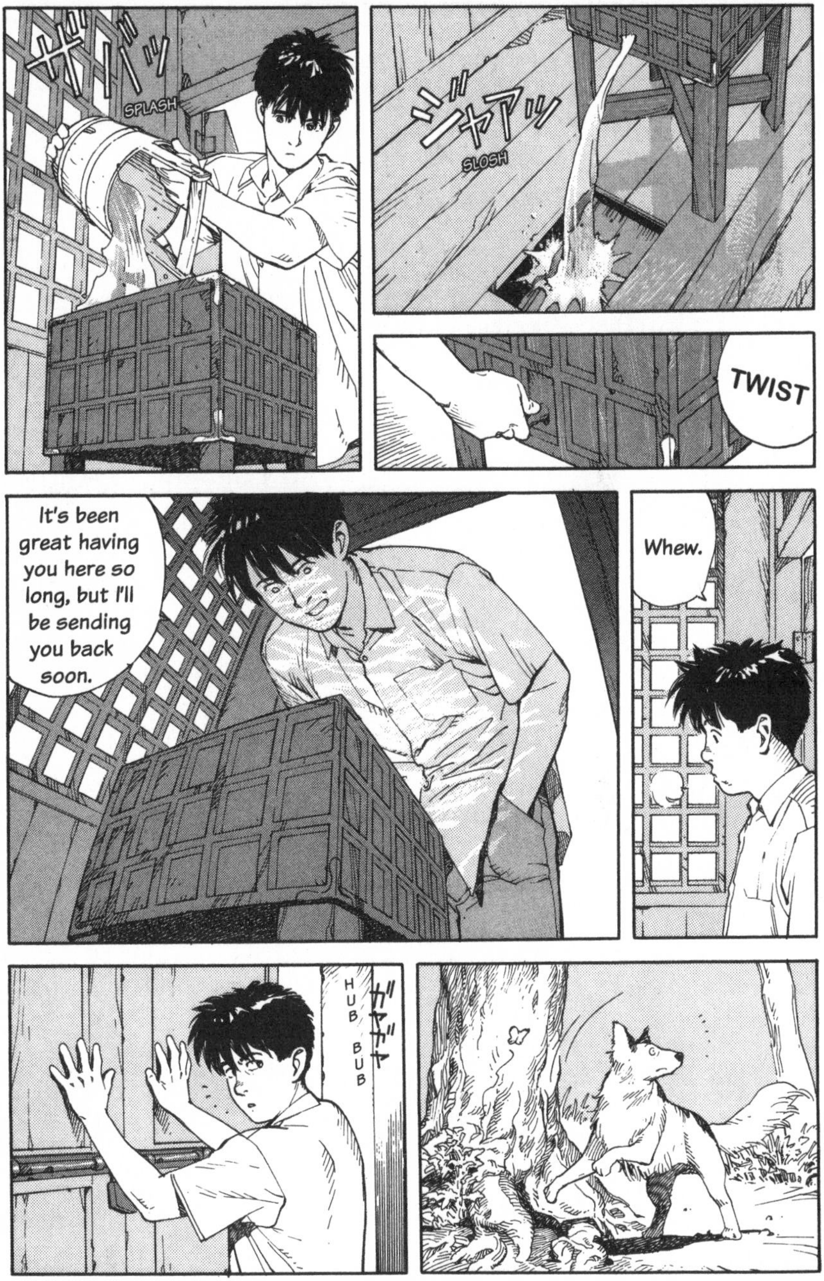
ジャアッ
SLOSH
TWIST
ザバッ
SPLASH
Whew.
It's been great having you here so long, but I'll be sending you back soon.
ガヤガヤ
HUB BUB

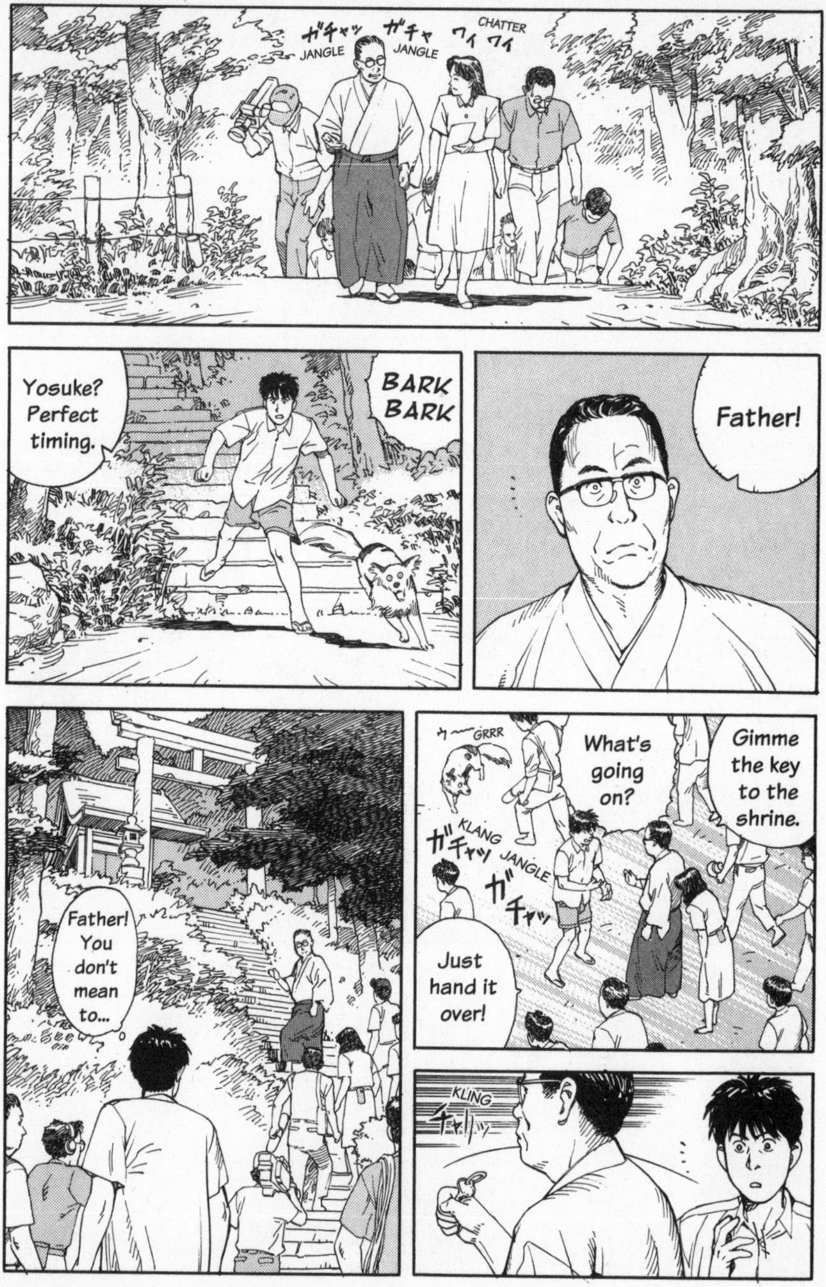
ワイワイ CHATTER
ガチャ JANGLE
ガチャッ JANGLE
Father!
BARK BARK
Yosuke? Perfect timing.
Gimme the key to the shrine.
What's going on?
ウ～ GRRR
ガチャッ KLANG
ガチャッ JANGLE
Just hand it over!
チャリッ KLING
Father! You don't mean to...

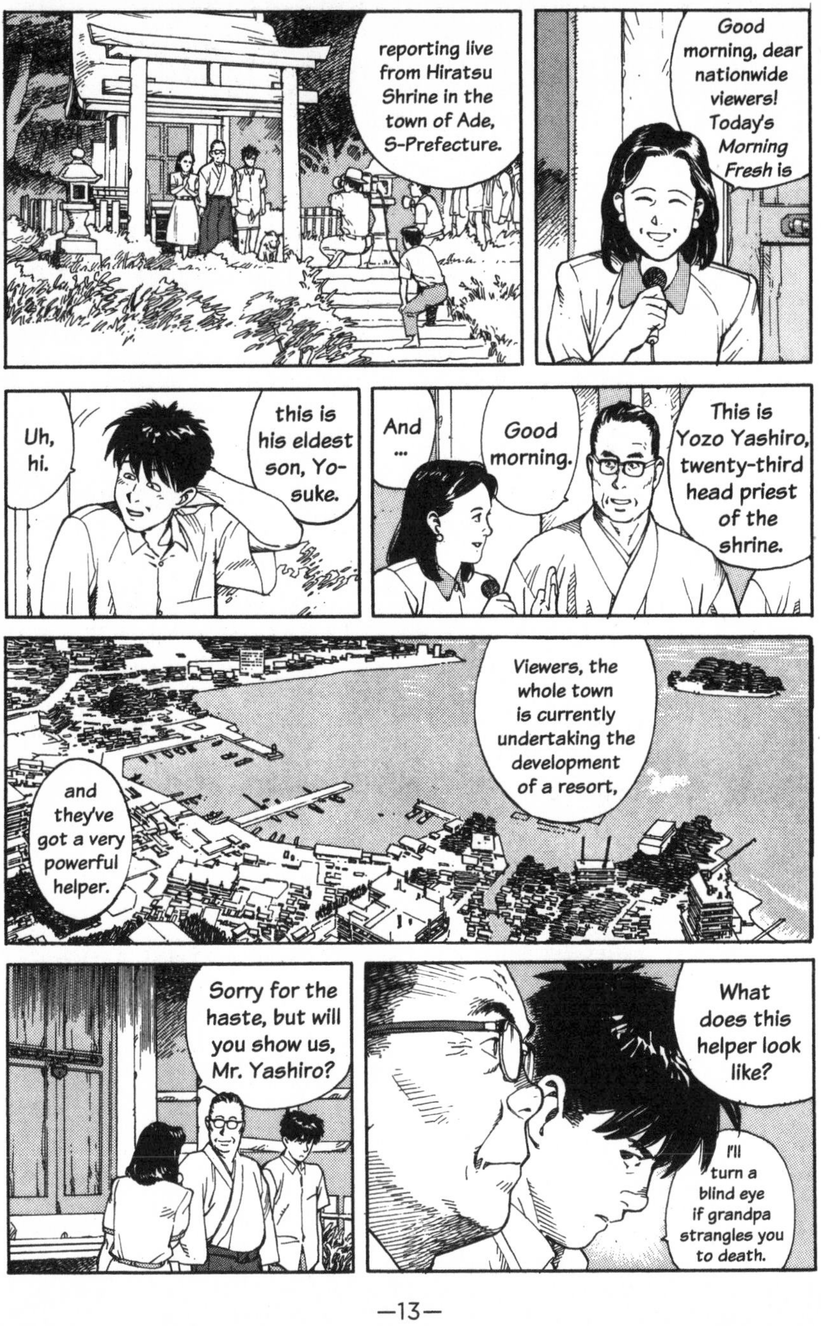
Good morning, dear nationwide viewers! Today's *Morning Fresh* is
reporting live from Hiratsu Shrine in the town of Ade, S-Prefecture.
This is Yozo Yashiro, twenty-third head priest of the shrine.
Good morning.
And ...
this is his eldest son, Yo-suke.
Uh, hi.
Viewers, the whole town is currently undertaking the development of a resort,
and they've got a very powerful helper.
What does this helper look like?
I'll turn a blind eye if grandpa strangles you to death.
Sorry for the haste, but will you show us, Mr. Yashiro?

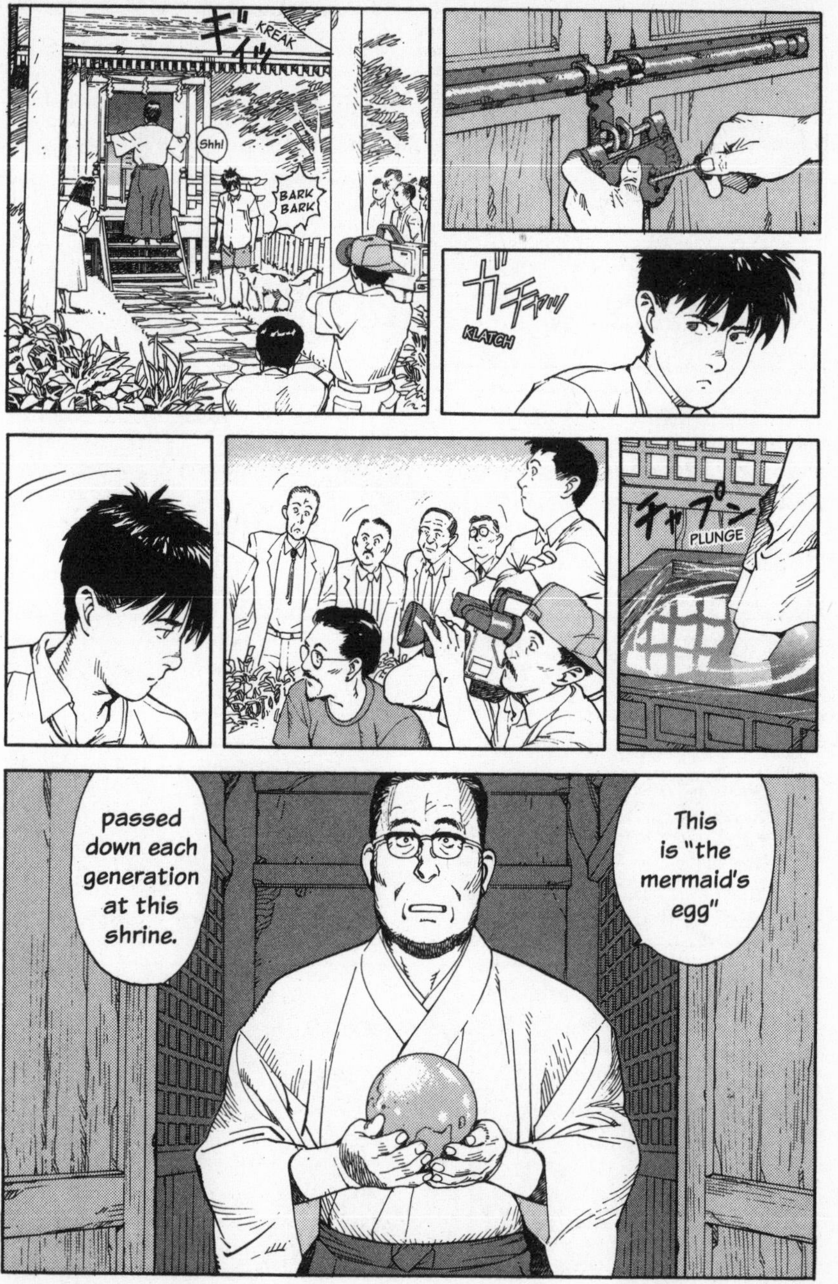
ガチャッ
KLATCH
ギィッ
KREAK
Shh!
BARK BARK
チャプン
PLUNGE
This is "the mermaid's egg"
passed down each generation at this shrine.

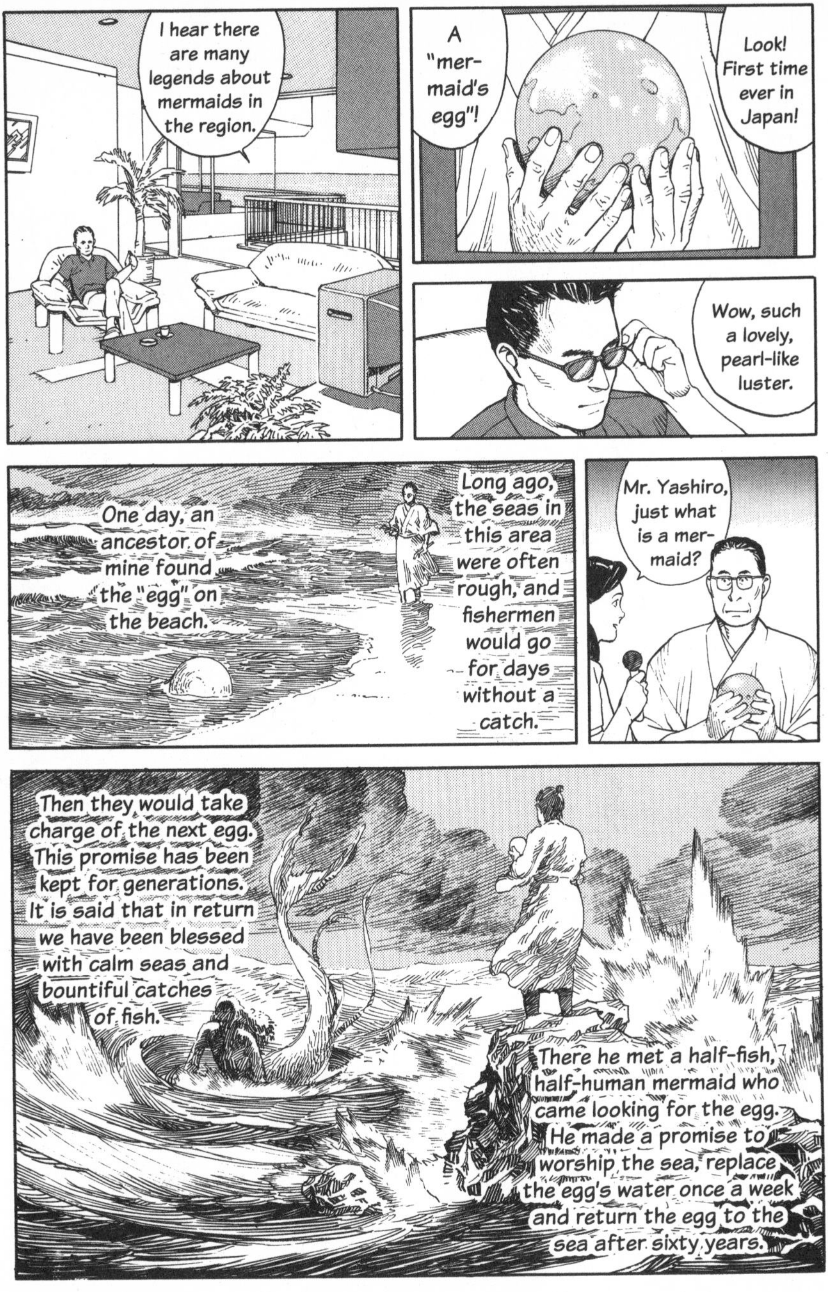

Look! First time ever in Japan!
A "mer-maid's egg"!
Wow, such a lovely, pearl-like luster.
I hear there are many legends about mermaids in the region.
Mr. Yashiro, just what is a mer-maid?
Long ago, the seas in this area were often rough, and fishermen would go for days without a catch.
One day, an ancestor of mine found the "egg" on the beach.
There he met a half-fish, half-human mermaid who came looking for the egg. He made a promise to worship the sea, replace the egg's water once a week and return the egg to the sea after sixty years.
Then they would take charge of the next egg. This promise has been kept for generations. It is said that in return we have been blessed with calm seas and bountiful catches of fish.

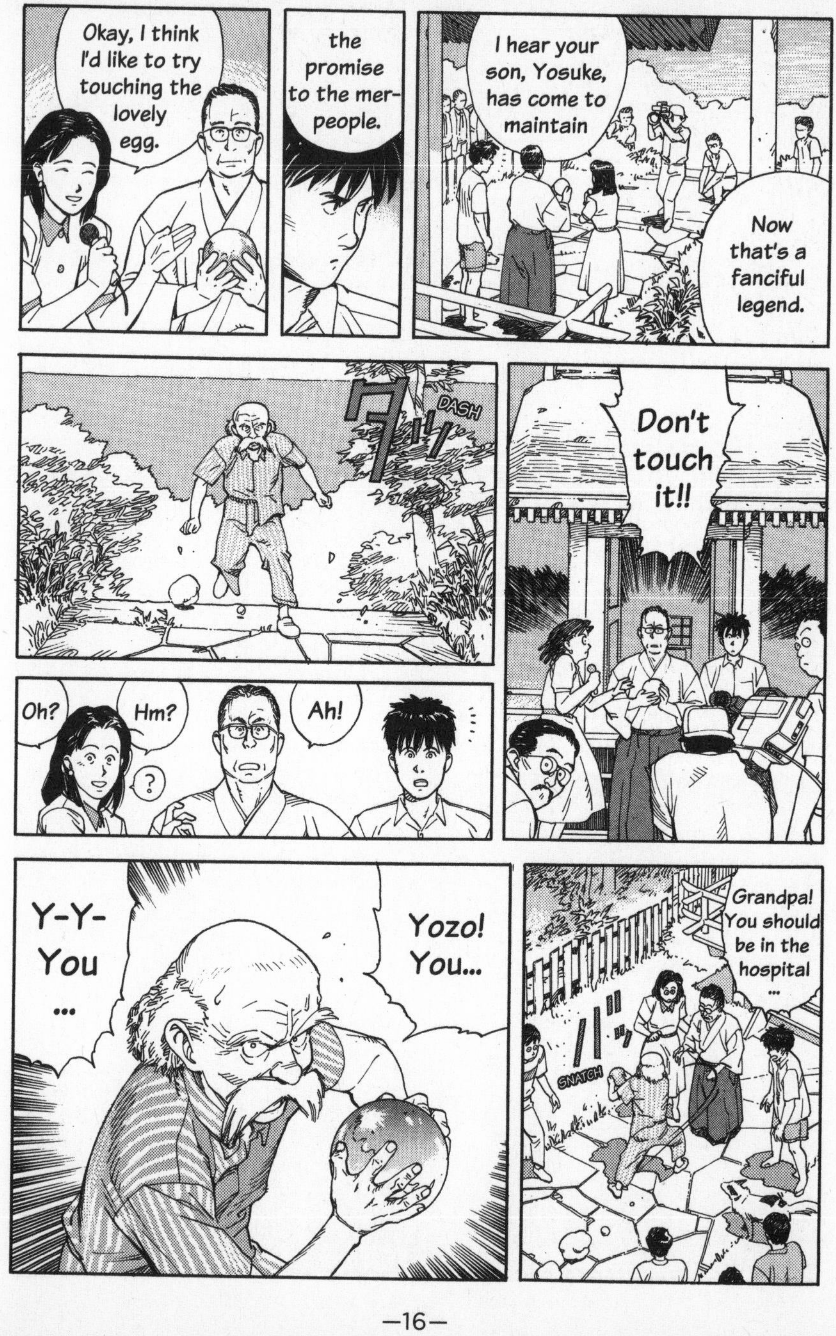
Now that's a fanciful legend.
I hear your son, Yosuke, has come to maintain
the promise to the mer-people.
Okay, I think I'd like to try touching the lovely egg.
Don't touch it!!
DASH
Ah!
Hm?
Oh?
?
Grandpa! You should be in the hospital ...
SNATCH
Yozo! You...
Y-Y- You ...

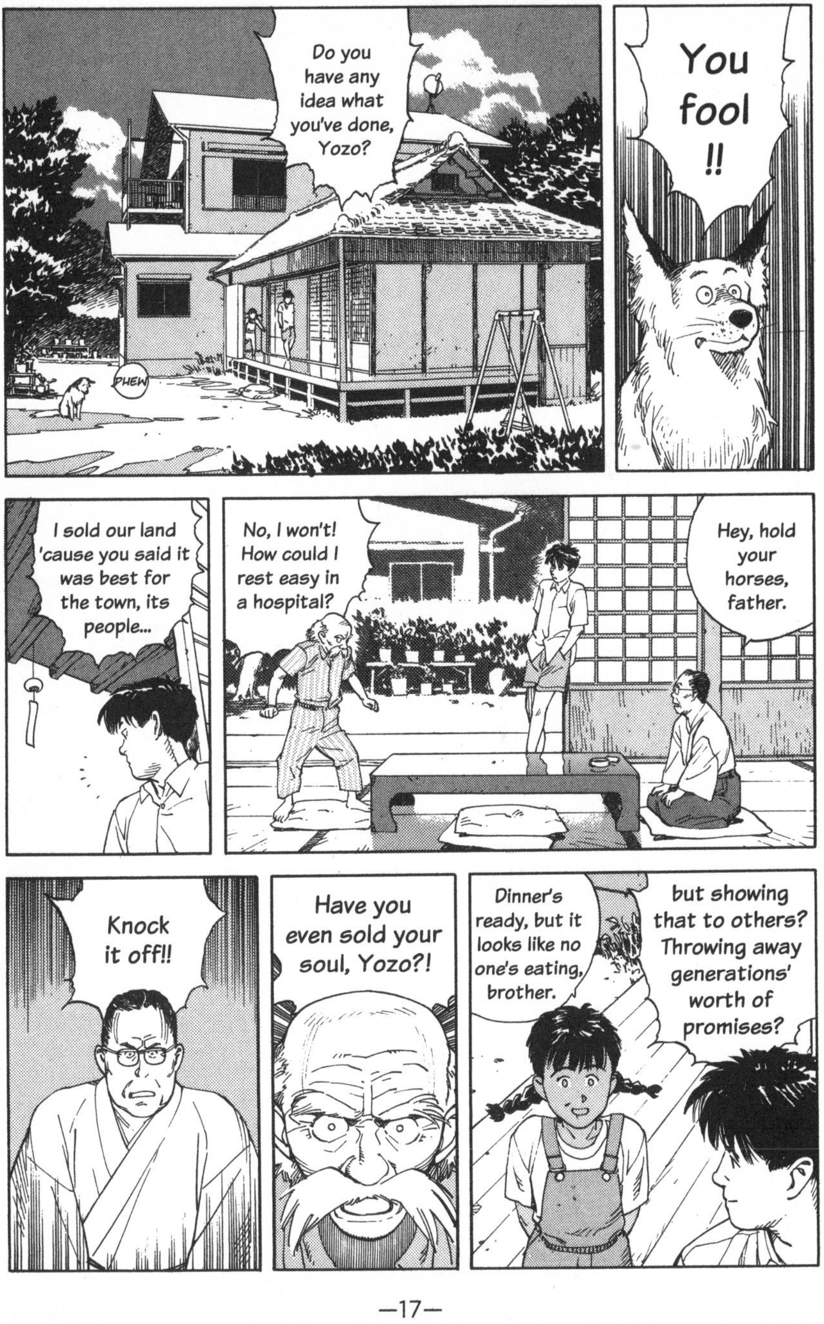
You fool !!
Do you have any idea what you've done, Yozo?
PHEW
Hey, hold your horses, father.
No, I won't! How could I rest easy in a hospital?
I sold our land 'cause you said it was best for the town, its people...
but showing that to others? Throwing away generations' worth of promises?
Dinner's ready, but it looks like no one's eating, brother.
Have you even sold your soul, Yozo?!
Knock it off!!

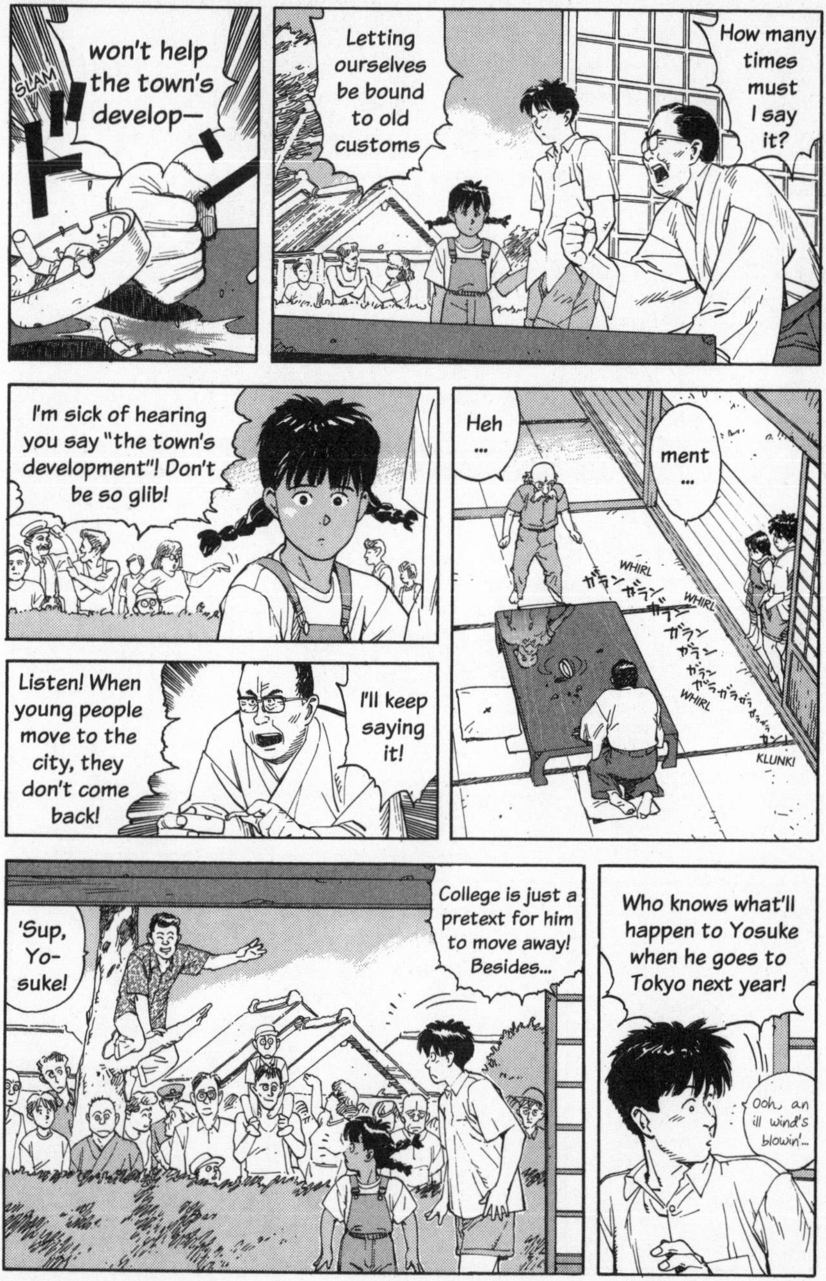
How many times must I say it?
Letting ourselves be bound to old customs
won't help the town's develop—
SLAM
ment ...
Heh ...
WHIRL
WHIRL
WHIRL
KLUNK!
I'm sick of hearing you say "the town's development"! Don't be so glib!
I'll keep saying it!
Listen! When young people move to the city, they don't come back!
Who knows what'll happen to Yosuke when he goes to Tokyo next year!
Ooh, an ill wind's blowin'...
College is just a pretext for him to move away! Besides...
'Sup, Yo-suke!

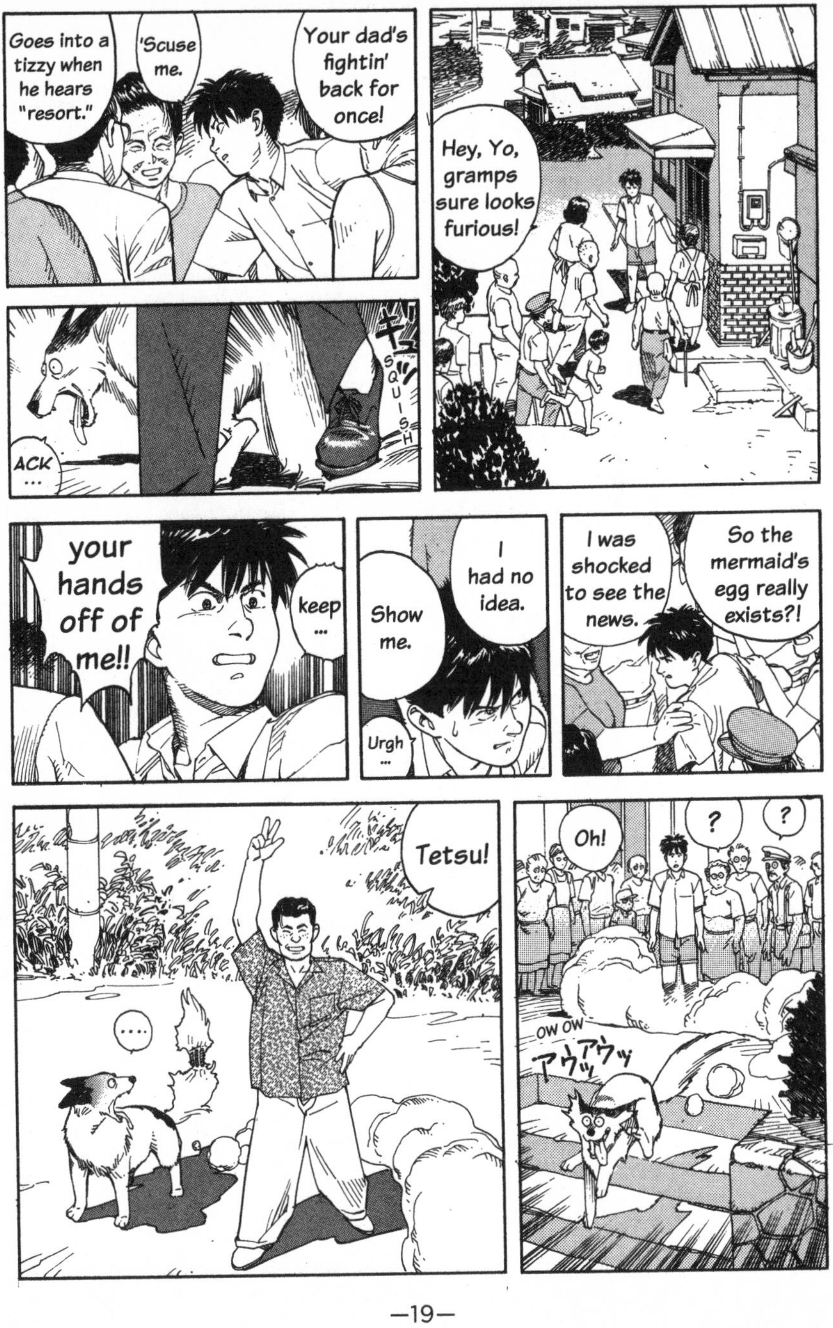

Hey, Yo, gramps sure looks furious!
Your dad's fightin' back for once!
'Scuse me.
Goes into a tizzy when he hears "resort."
SQUISH
ACK ...
So the mermaid's egg really exists?!
I was shocked to see the news.
I had no idea.
Show me.
Urgh ...
keep ...
your hands off of me!!
?
?
Oh!
OW OW
アウッアウッ
Tetsu!
....

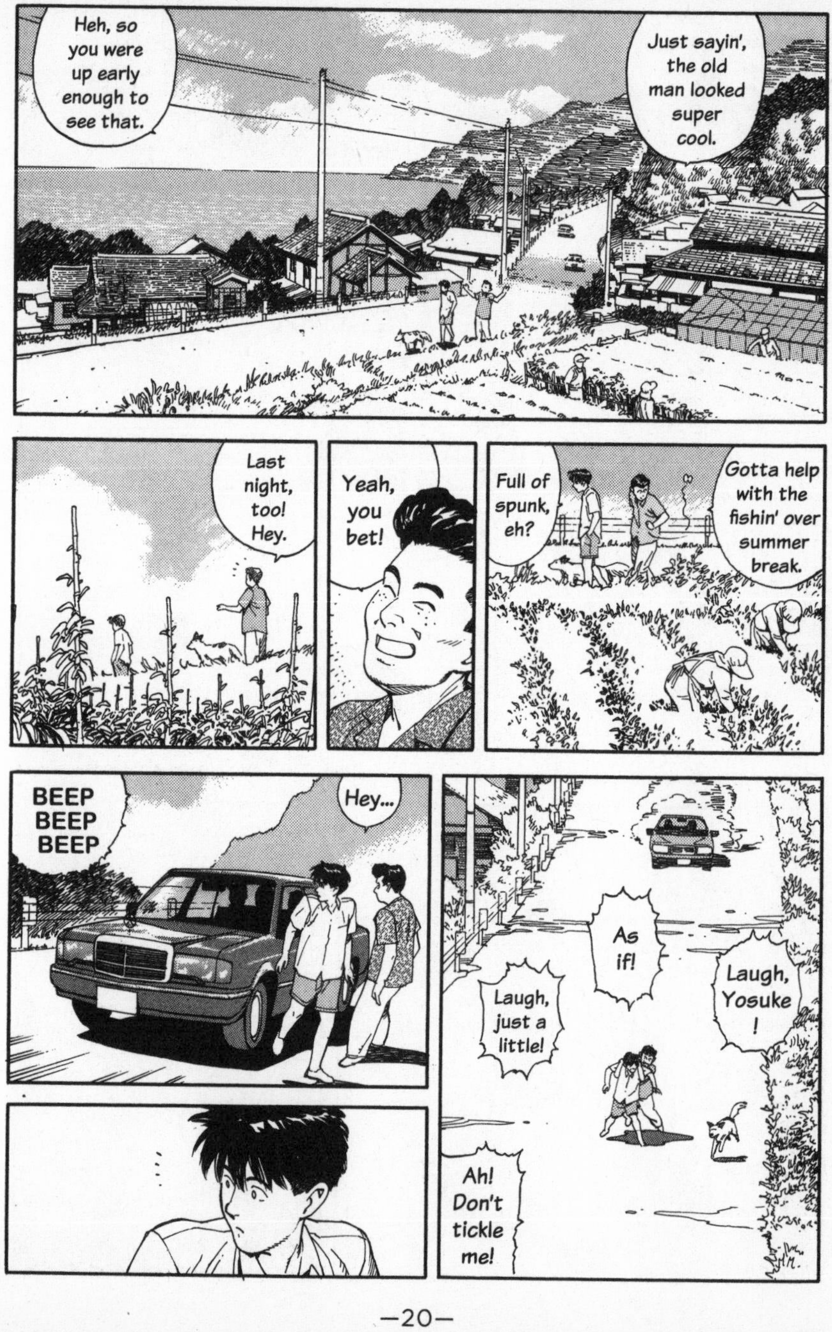
Just sayin', the old man looked super cool.
Heh, so you were up early enough to see that.
Gotta help with the fishin' over summer break.
Full of spunk, eh?
Yeah, you bet!
Last night, too! Hey.
Laugh, Yosuke!
As if!
Laugh, just a little!
Ah! Don't tickle me!
Hey...
BEEP BEEP BEEP

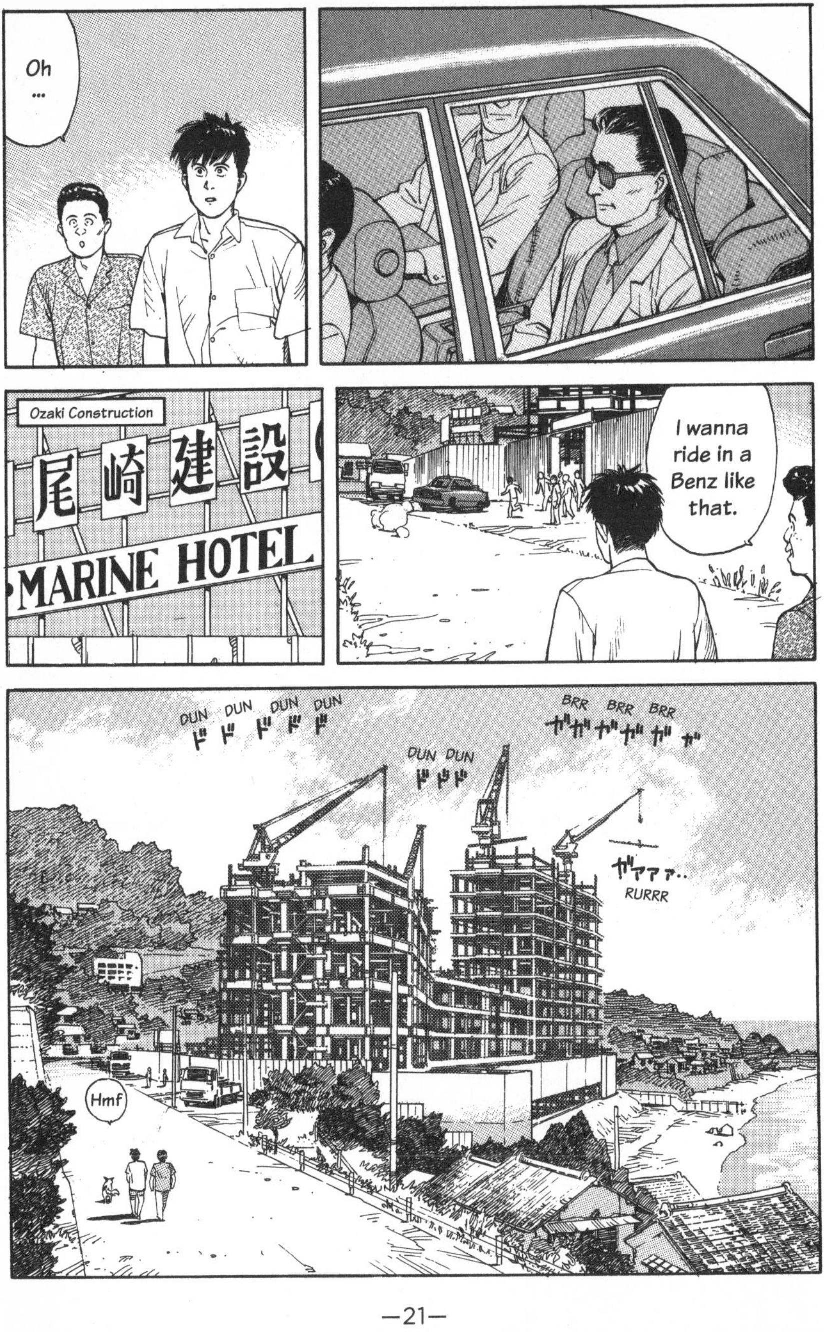
Oh ...
I wanna ride in a Benz like that.
Ozaki Construction
尾崎建設
MARINE HOTEL
BRR BRR BRR
ガガガガガガ
DUN DUN DUN DUN
ドドドドド
DUN DUN
ドドド
ガァァァ..
RURRR
Hmf

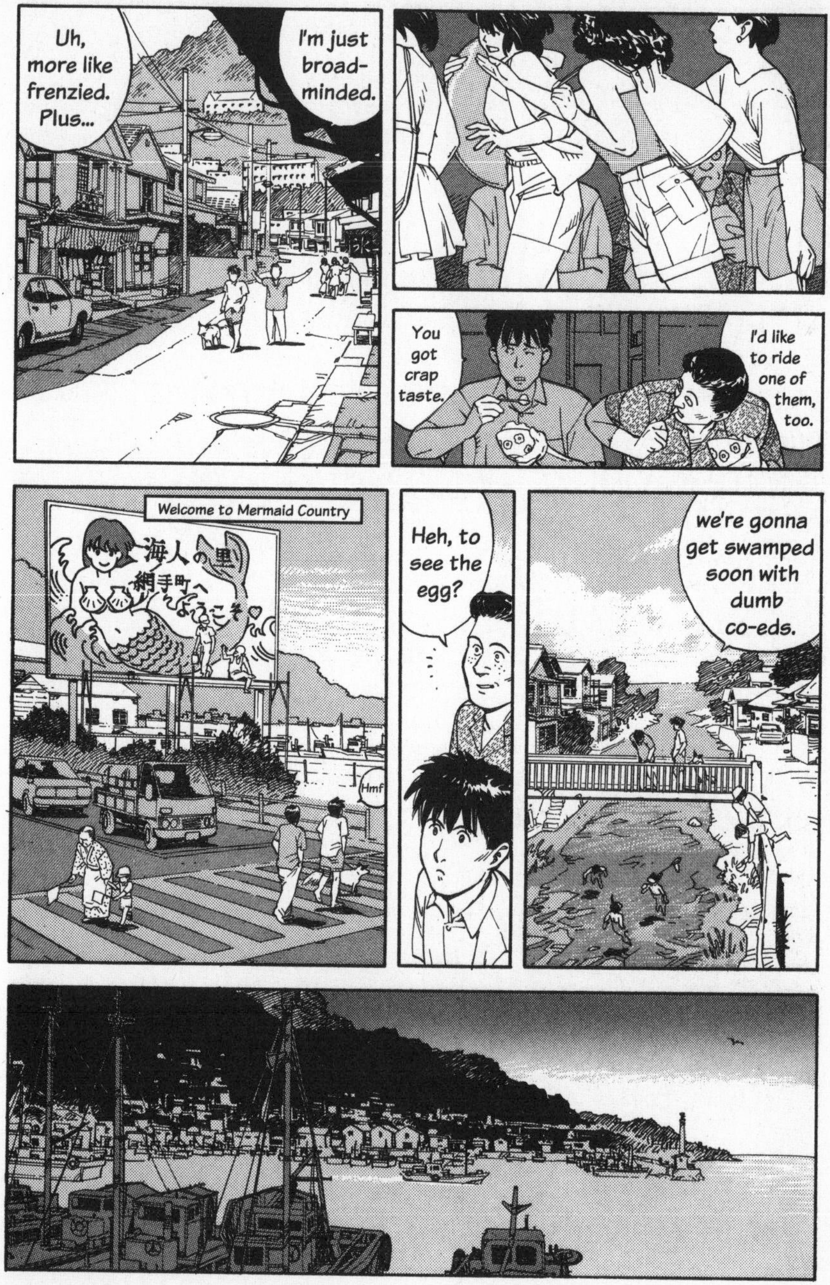
I'd like to ride one of them, too.
You got crap taste.
I'm just broad-minded.
Uh, more like frenzied. Plus...
we're gonna get swamped soon with dumb co-eds.
Heh, to see the egg?
Welcome to Mermaid Country
海人の里
網手町へようこそ
Hmf

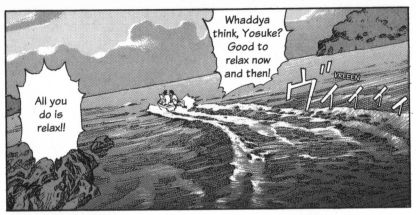

Whaddya think, Yosuke? Good to relax now and then!
VREEEN
All you do is relax!!
Gettin' all worked up over entrance exams...
Moron. It's the last stretch.
Sea Jaguar
Since last year?
Aren't you busy, too? With prep for the Mermaid Festival?
PIP
Yeah, it's comin' up. We've got the egg this year so it might get flashy!
"Mermaid country" my ass.
Ha ha, you suck! You're outta practice.
SPLISH

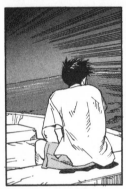

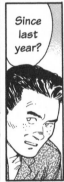

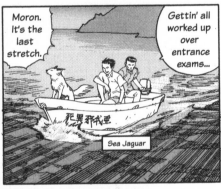

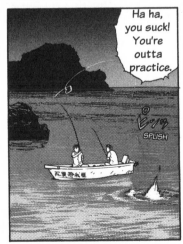

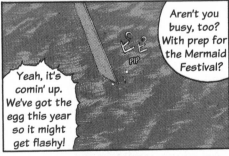

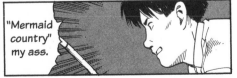

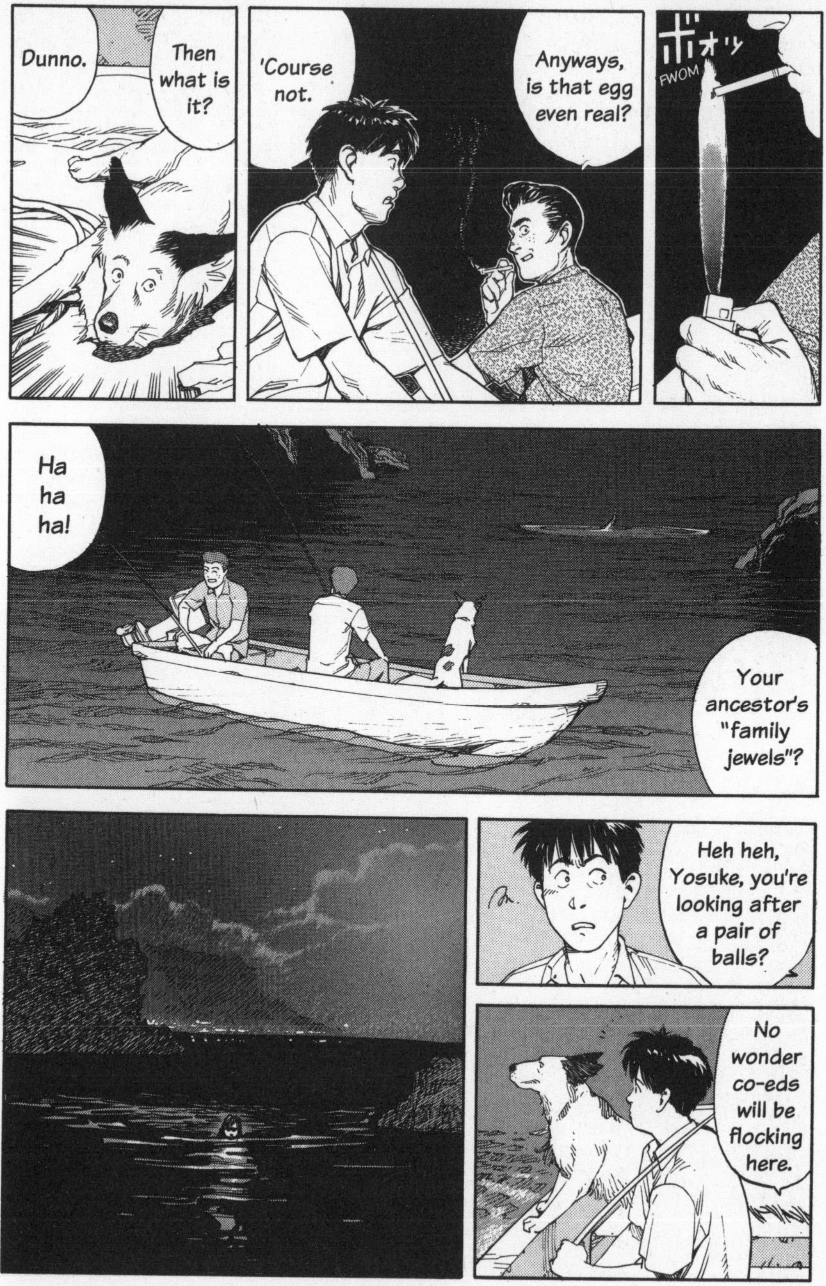

ボオッ
FWOM
Anyways, is that egg even real?
'Course not.
Then what is it?
Dunno.
Your ancestor's "family jewels"?
Ha ha ha!
Heh heh, Yosuke, you're looking after a pair of balls?
No wonder co-eds will be flocking here.

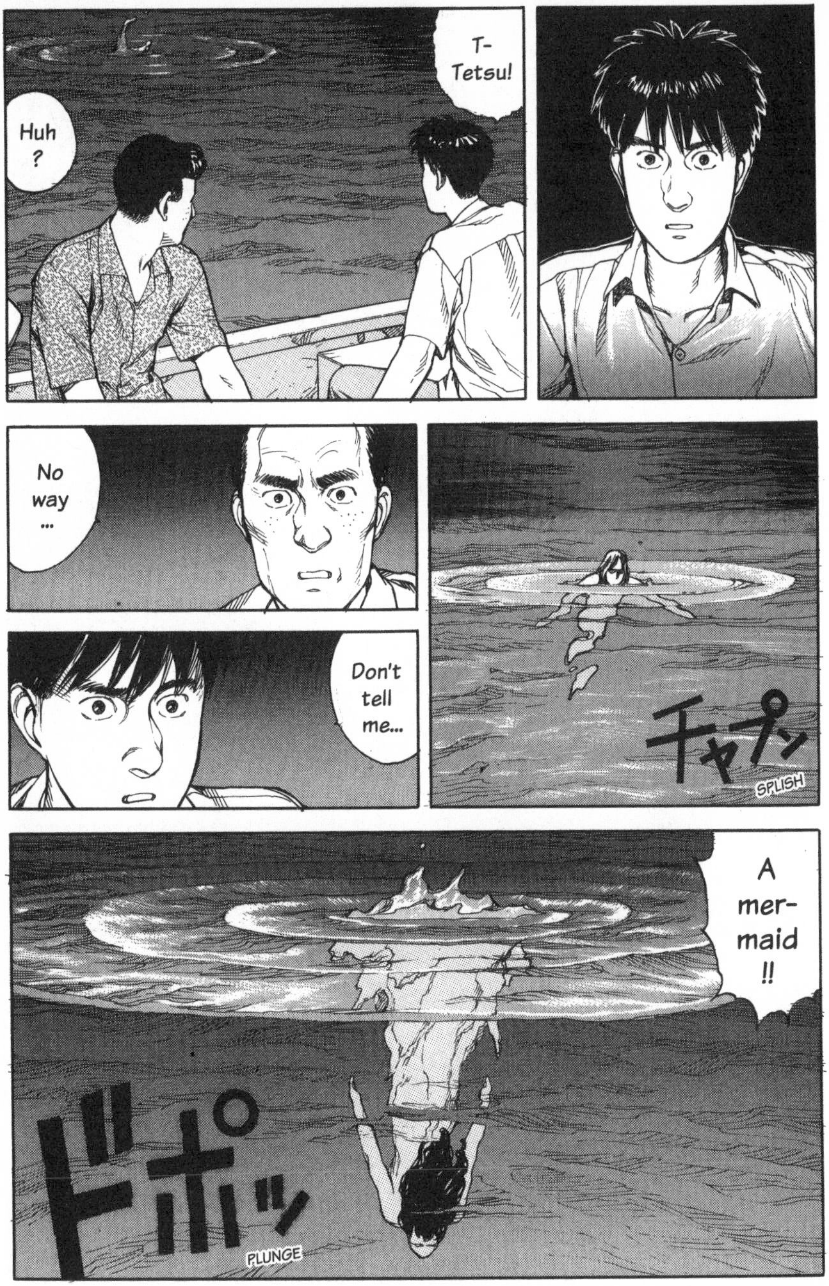
T- Tetsu!
Huh ?
チャプン
SPLISH
No way ...
Don't tell me...
A mer- maid !!
ドポッ
PLUNGE

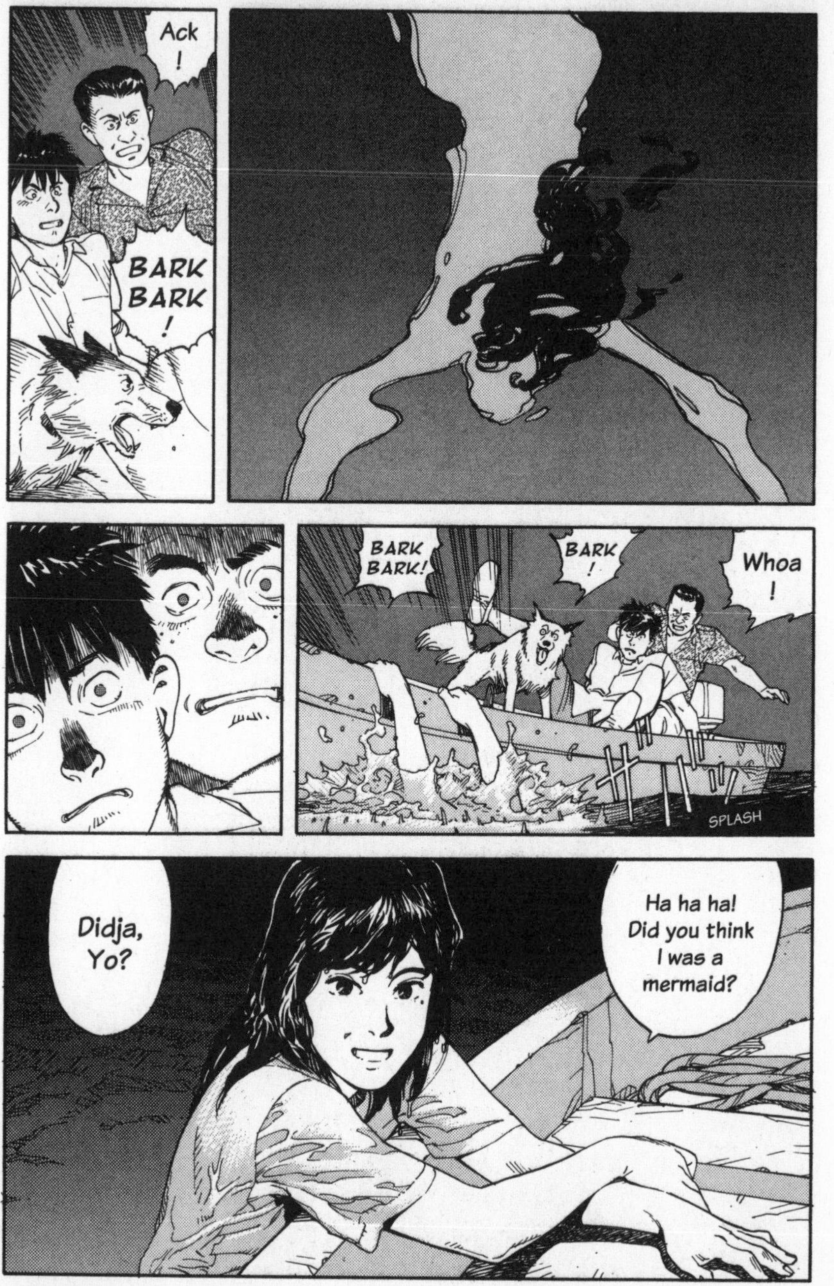
Ack !
BARK BARK !
Whoa !
BARK !
BARK BARK!
SPLASH
Ha ha ha! Did you think I was a mermaid?
Didja, Yo?

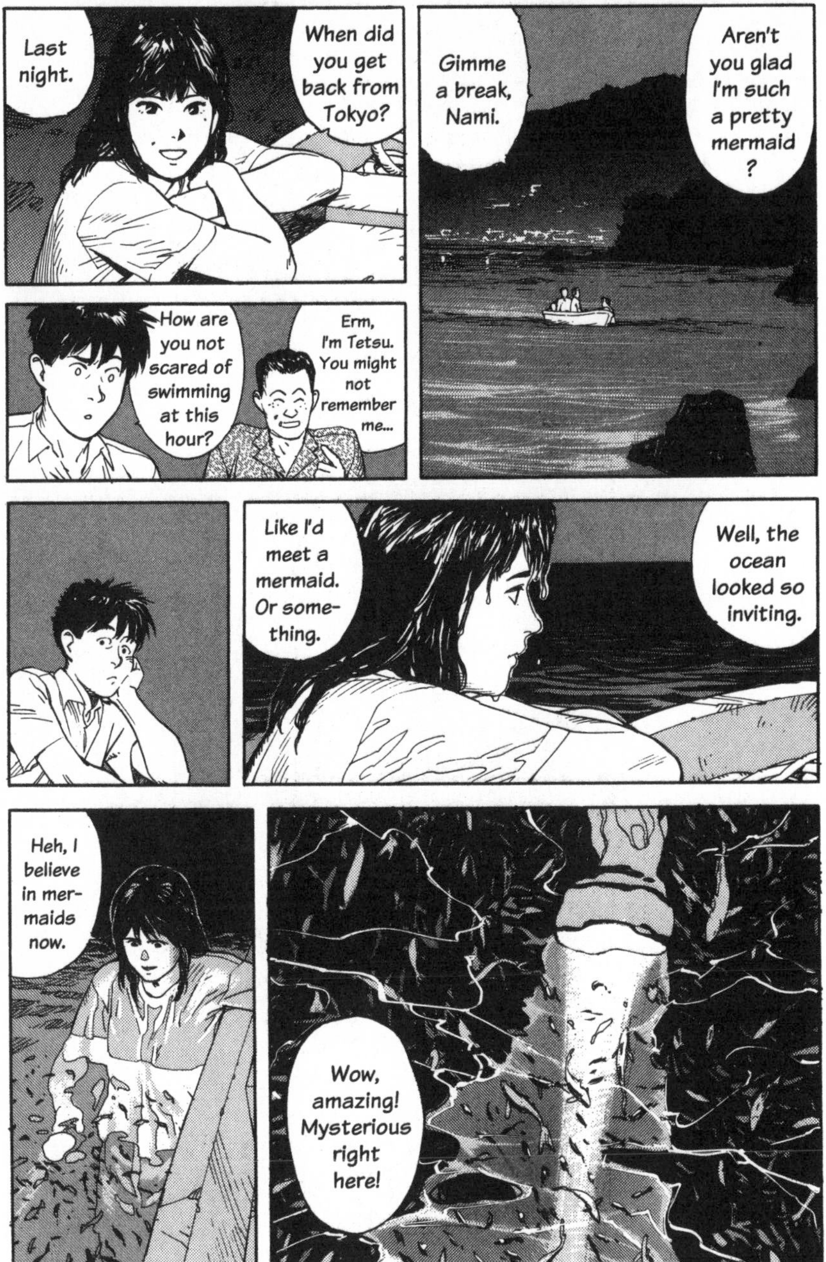
Aren't you glad I'm such a pretty mermaid?
Gimme a break, Nami.
When did you get back from Tokyo?
Last night.
Erm, I'm Tetsu. You might not remember me...
How are you not scared of swimming at this hour?
Well, the ocean looked so inviting.
Like I'd meet a mermaid. Or something.
Wow, amazing! Mysterious right here!
Heh, I believe in mermaids now.

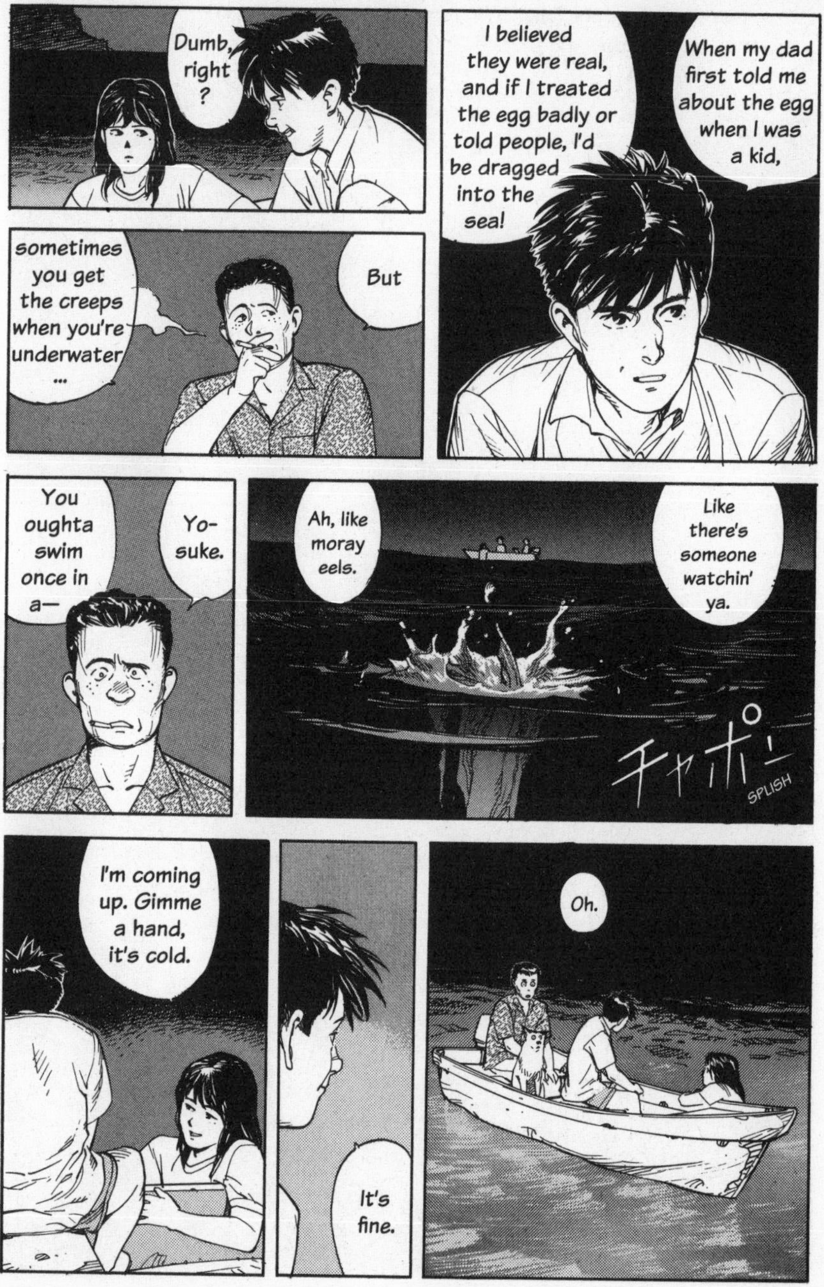
When my dad first told me about the egg when I was a kid,
I believed they were real, and if I treated the egg badly or told people, I'd be dragged into the sea!
Dumb, right?
But
sometimes you get the creeps when you're underwater ...
Like there's someone watchin' ya.
Ah, like moray eels.
チャポー
SPLISH
Yo-suke.
You oughta swim once in a—
Oh.
It's fine.
I'm coming up. Gimme a hand, it's cold.

Ah!

カチャ ッ
KLATTER

PLISH

チャボッ
SPLASH

I'm so sorry!

Don't worry, it was cheap.

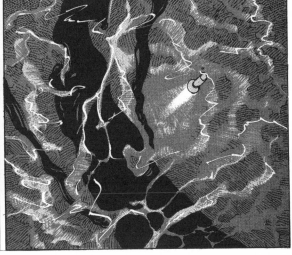

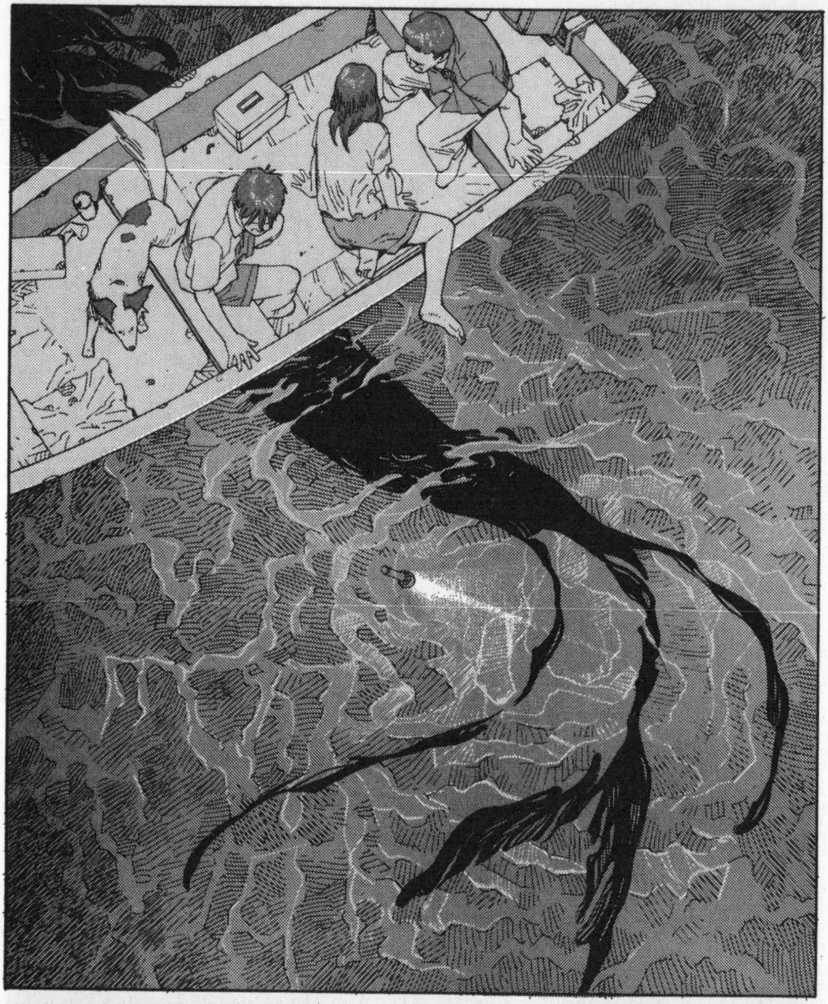

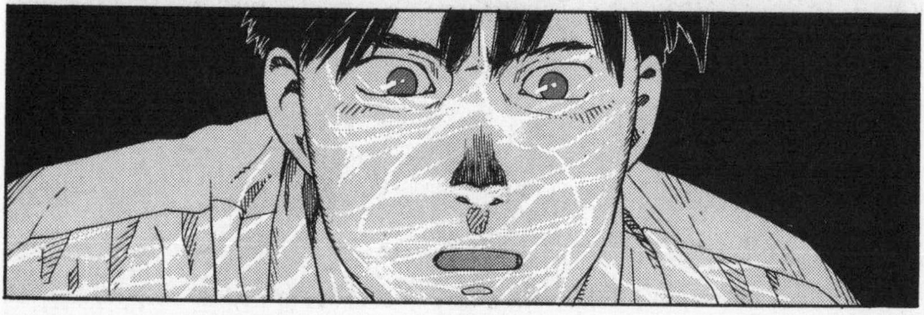

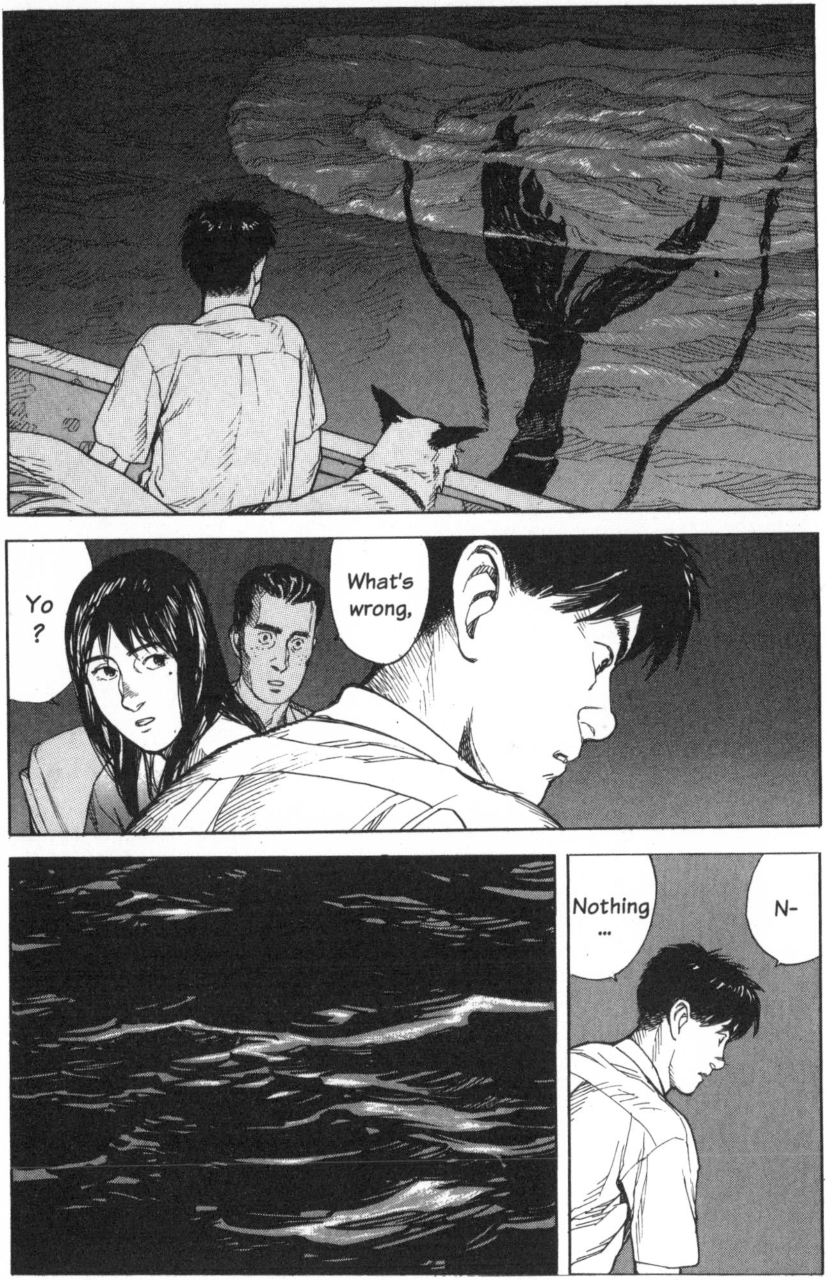
What's wrong,
Yo?
N-
Nothing ...

ポン
PAT

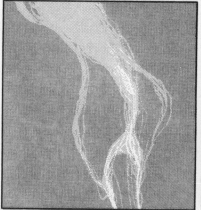

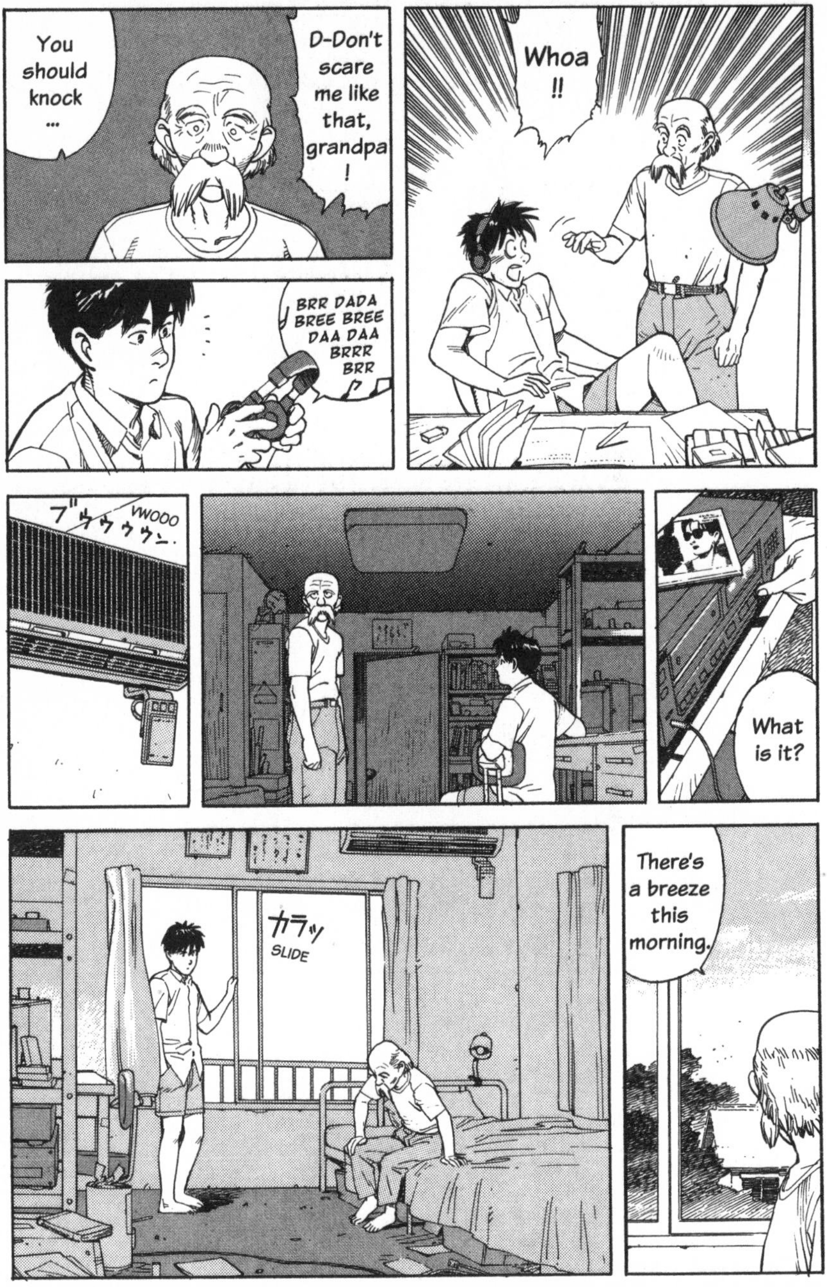
Whoa !!
D-Don't scare me like that, grandpa!
You should knock ...
BRR DADA BREE BREE DAA DAA BRRR BRR
What is it?
ブウウウウン
VWOOO
There's a breeze this morning.
カラッ
SLIDE

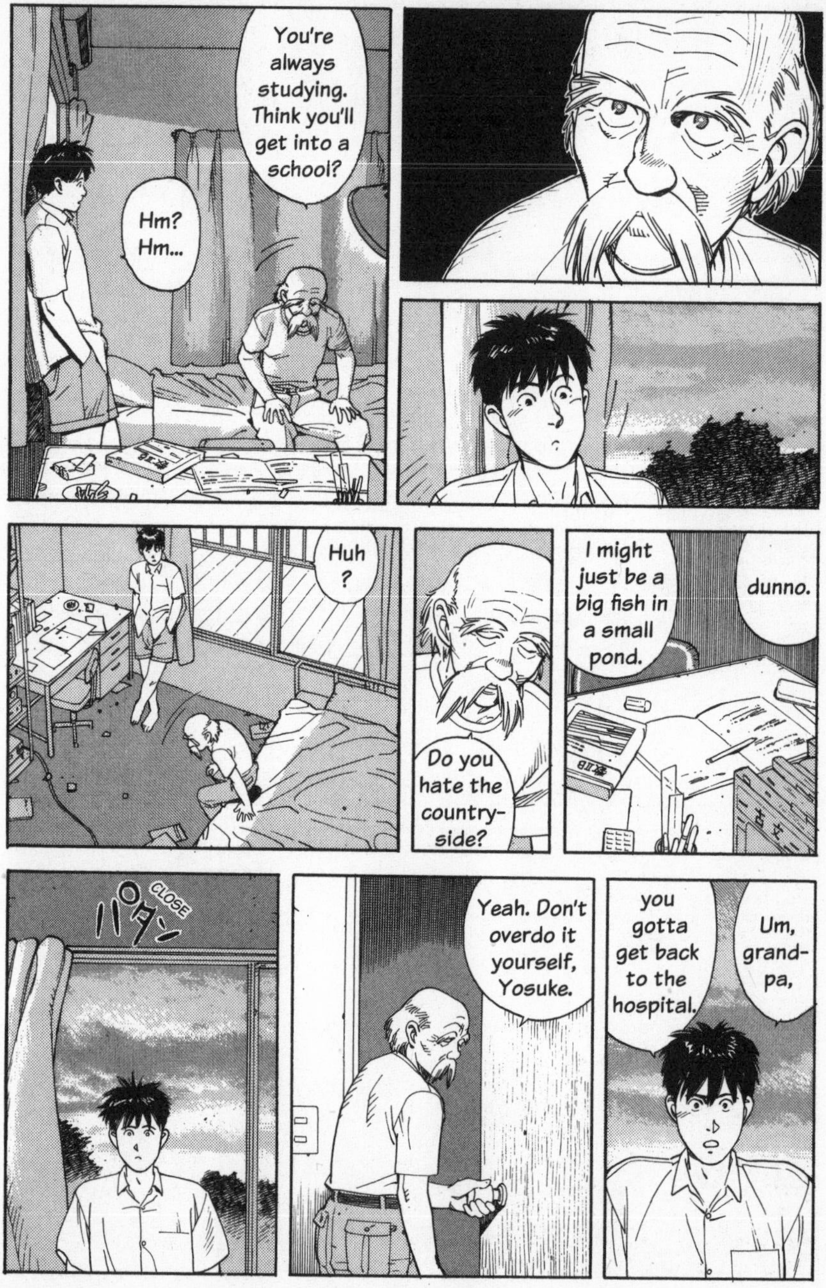
You're always studying. Think you'll get into a school?
Hm? Hm...
dunno.
I might just be a big fish in a small pond.
Do you hate the country-side?
Huh?
Um, grand-pa,
you gotta get back to the hospital.
Yeah. Don't overdo it yourself, Yosuke.
パタン
CLOSE

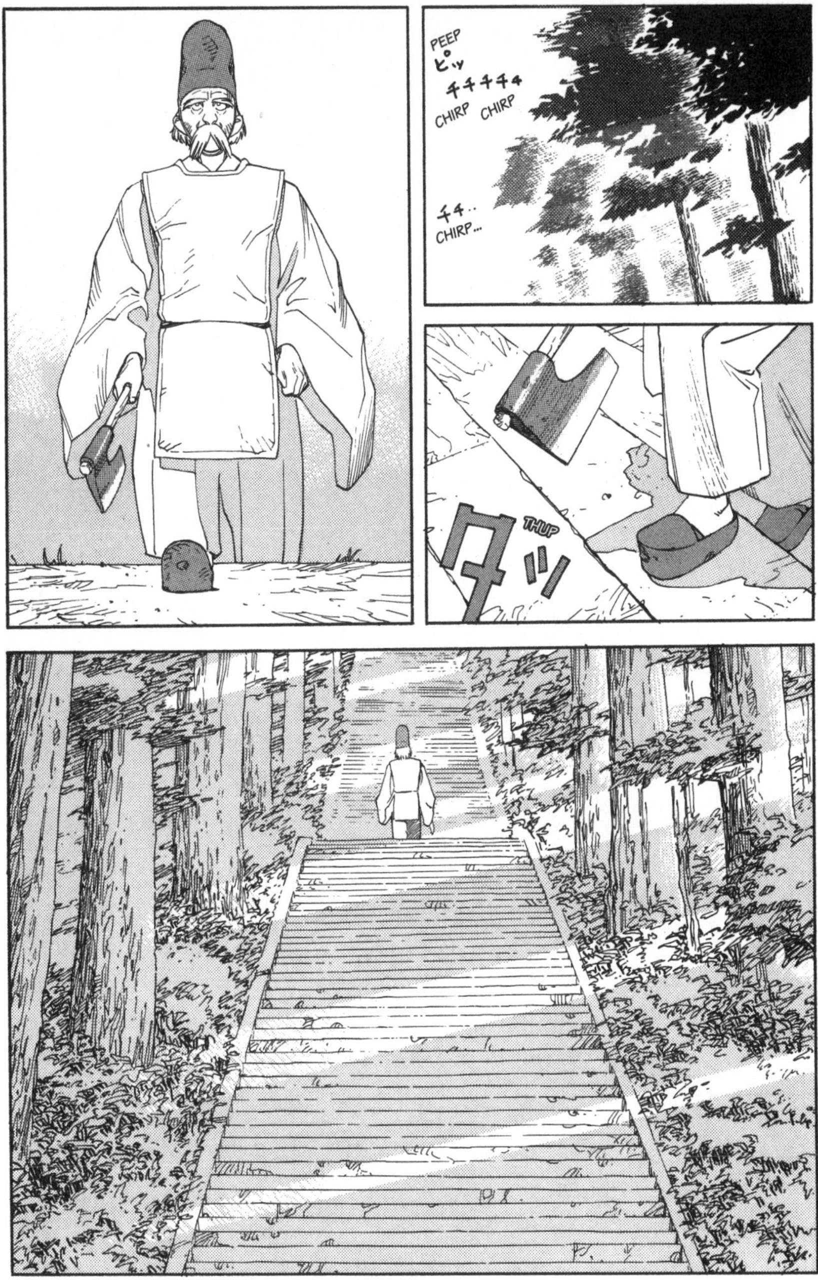
PEEP
ピッ
チチチチ
CHIRP CHIRP
チチ..
CHIRP...
タッ
THUP

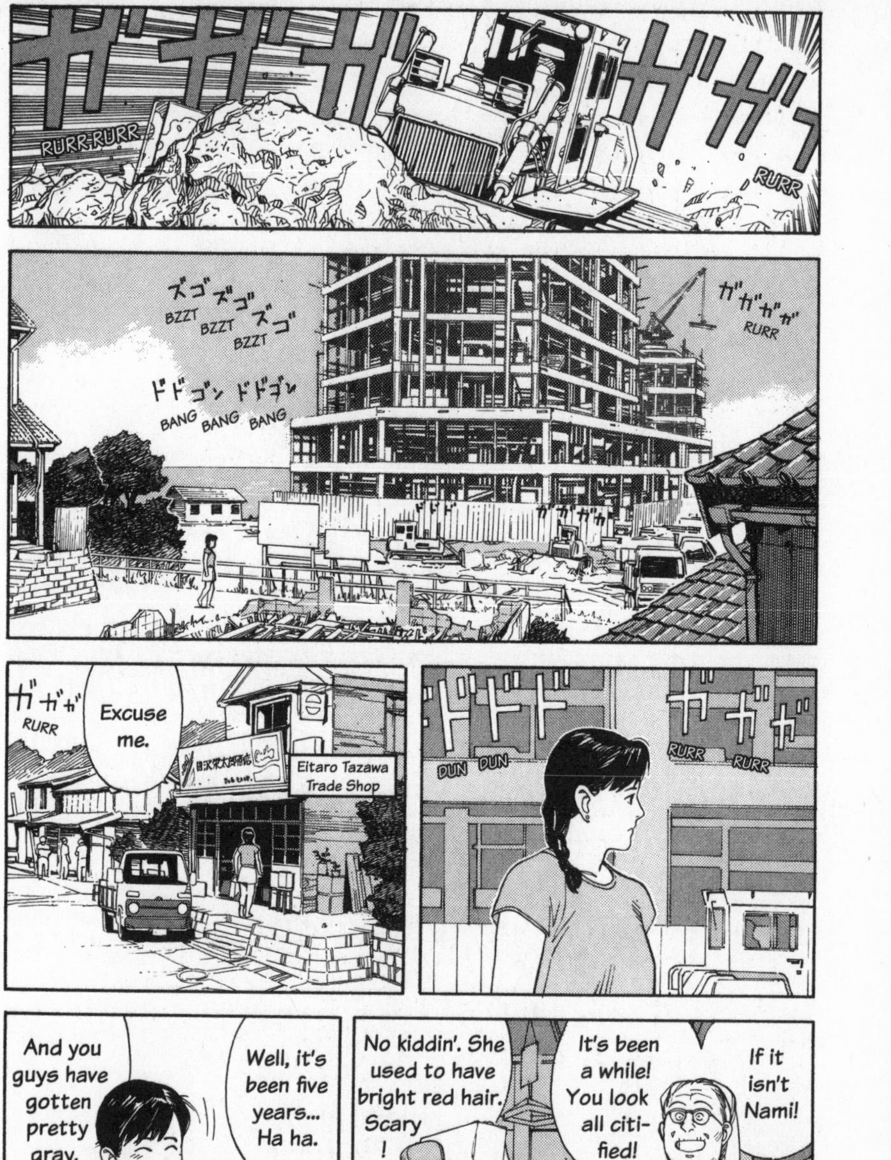
RURR
RURR-RURR
RURR
BZZT BZZT BZZT
BANG BANG BANG
RURR RURR
DUN DUN
Excuse me.
Eitaro Tazawa Trade Shop
RURR
If it isn't Nami!
It's been a while! You look all citified!
No kiddin'. She used to have bright red hair. Scary!
Well, it's been five years... Ha ha.
And you guys have gotten pretty gray.

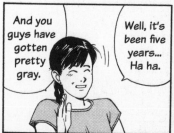

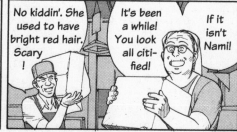

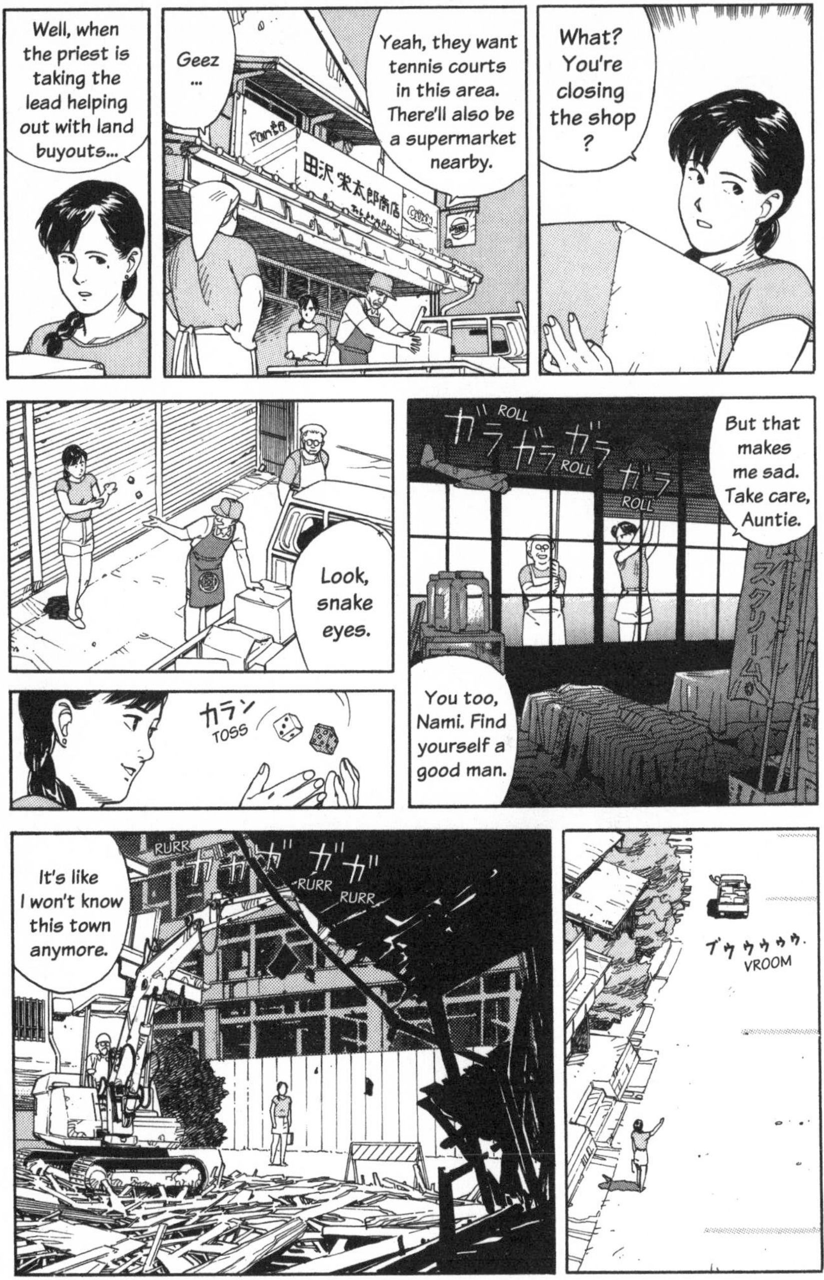
What? You're closing the shop?
Yeah, they want tennis courts in this area. There'll also be a supermarket nearby.
Geez ...
田沢栄太郎商店
Fanta
Well, when the priest is taking the lead helping out with land buyouts...
ガラ ROLL
ガラ ROLL
ガラ
ガラ ROLL
But that makes me sad. Take care, Auntie.
You too, Nami. Find yourself a good man.
Look, snake eyes.
カラン TOSS
ブウウウウ VROOM
ガガガガ RURR RURR RURR
It's like I won't know this town anymore.

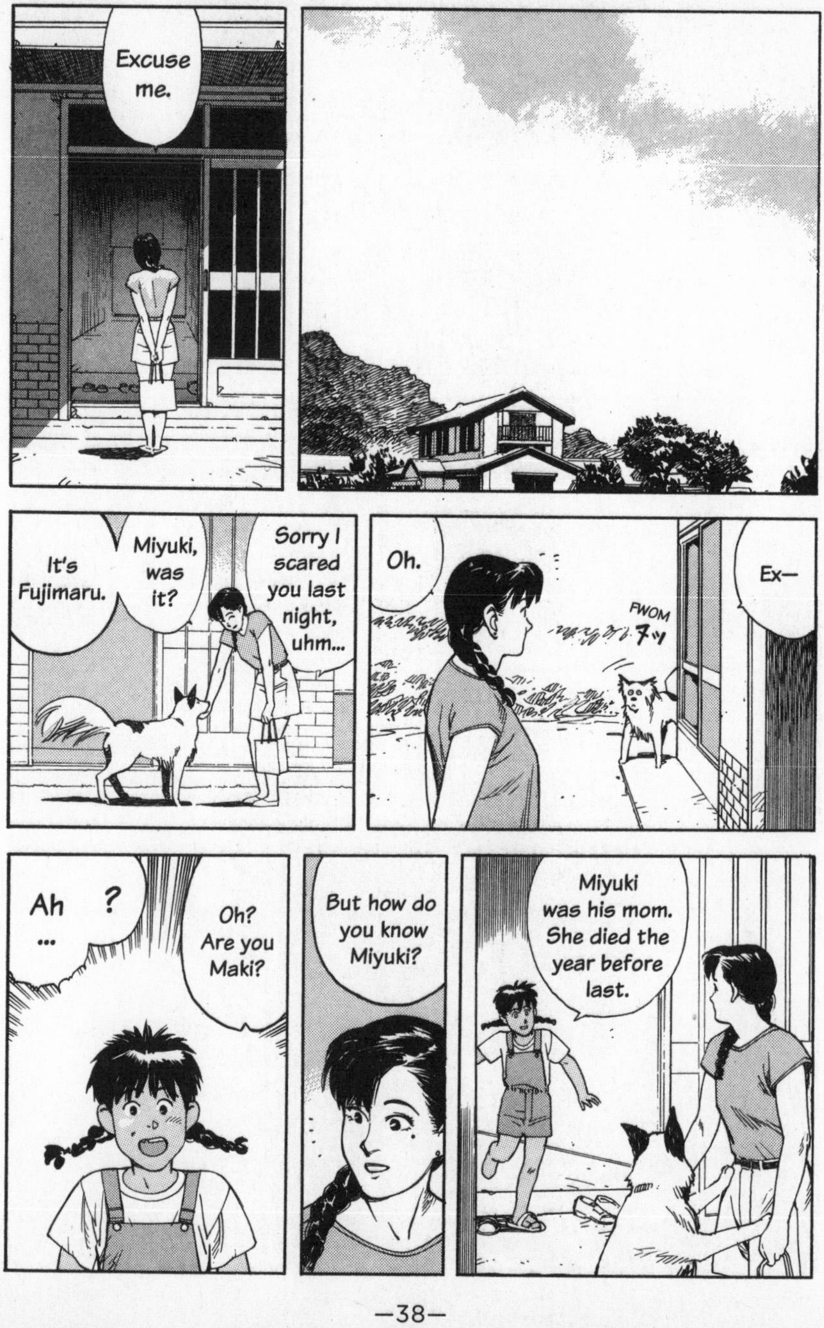

Excuse me.
Ex—
FWOM
フッ
Oh.
Sorry I scared you last night, uhm...
Miyuki, was it?
It's Fujimaru.
Miyuki was his mom. She died the year before last.
But how do you know Miyuki?
Oh? Are you Maki?
Ah ... ?

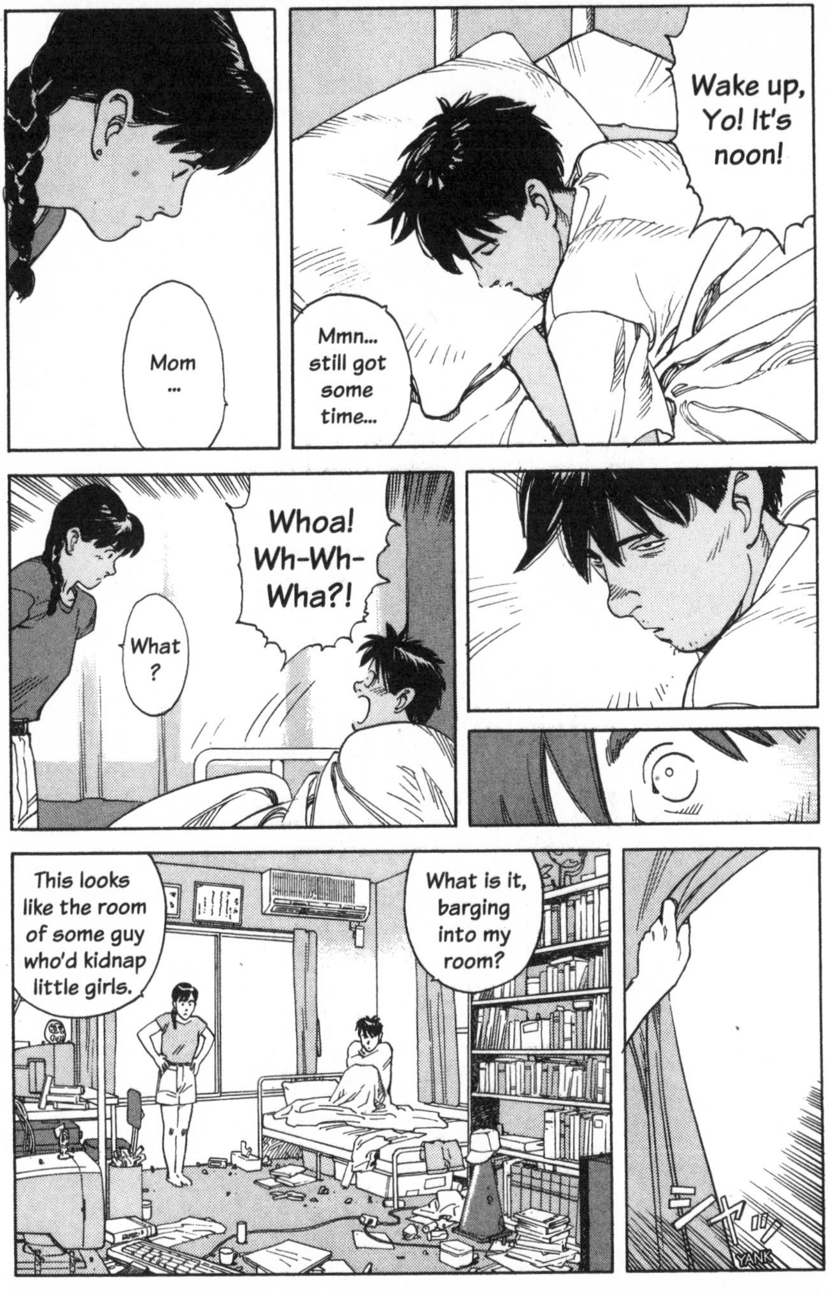

Wake up, Yo! It's noon!
Mmn... still got some time...
Mom ...
Whoa! Wh-Wh-Wha?!
What ?
YANK
What is it, barging into my room?
This looks like the room of some guy who'd kidnap little girls.

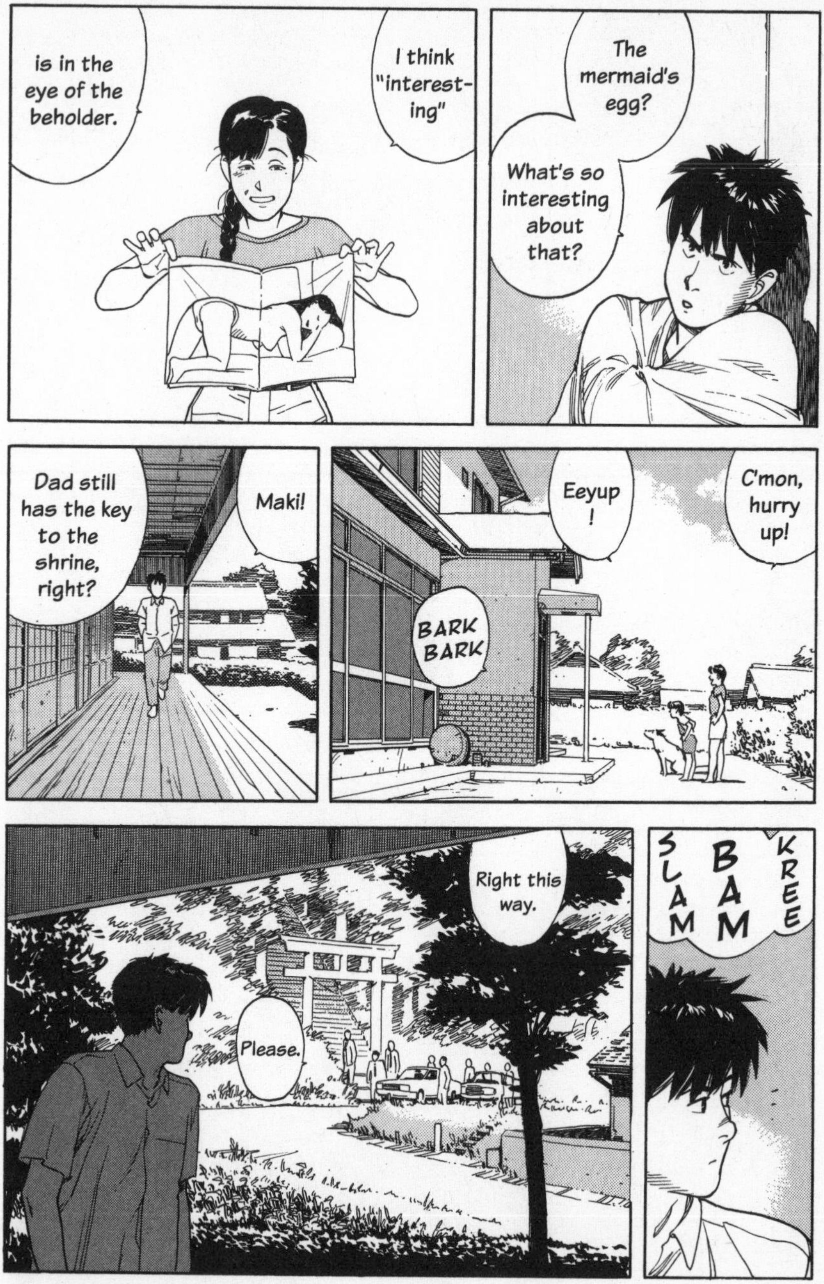

The mermaid's egg?
What's so interesting about that?
I think "interest-ing"
is in the eye of the beholder.
C'mon, hurry up!
Eeyup!
BARK BARK
Maki!
Dad still has the key to the shrine, right?
KREE
BAM
SLAM
Right this way.
Please.

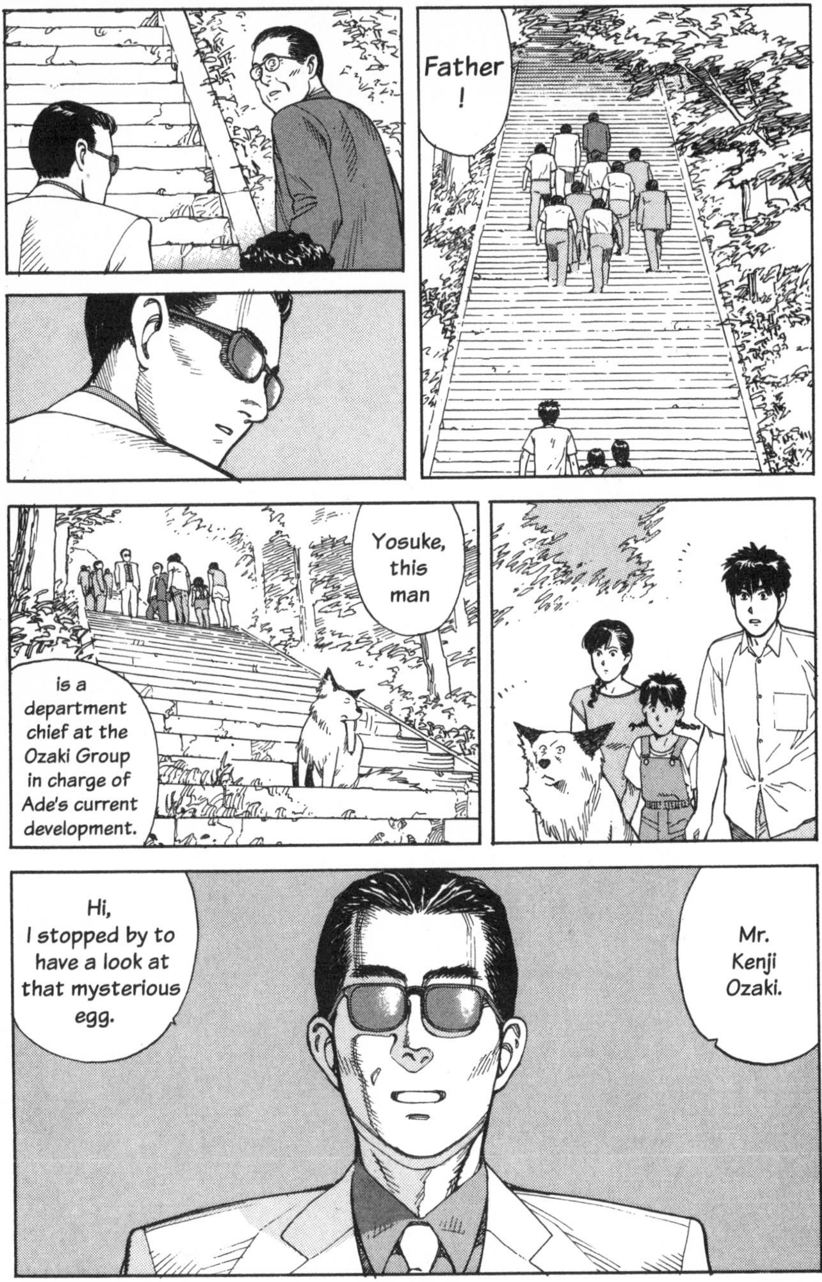
Father !
Yosuke, this man
is a department chief at the Ozaki Group in charge of Ade's current development.
Mr. Kenji Ozaki.
Hi, I stopped by to have a look at that mysterious egg.

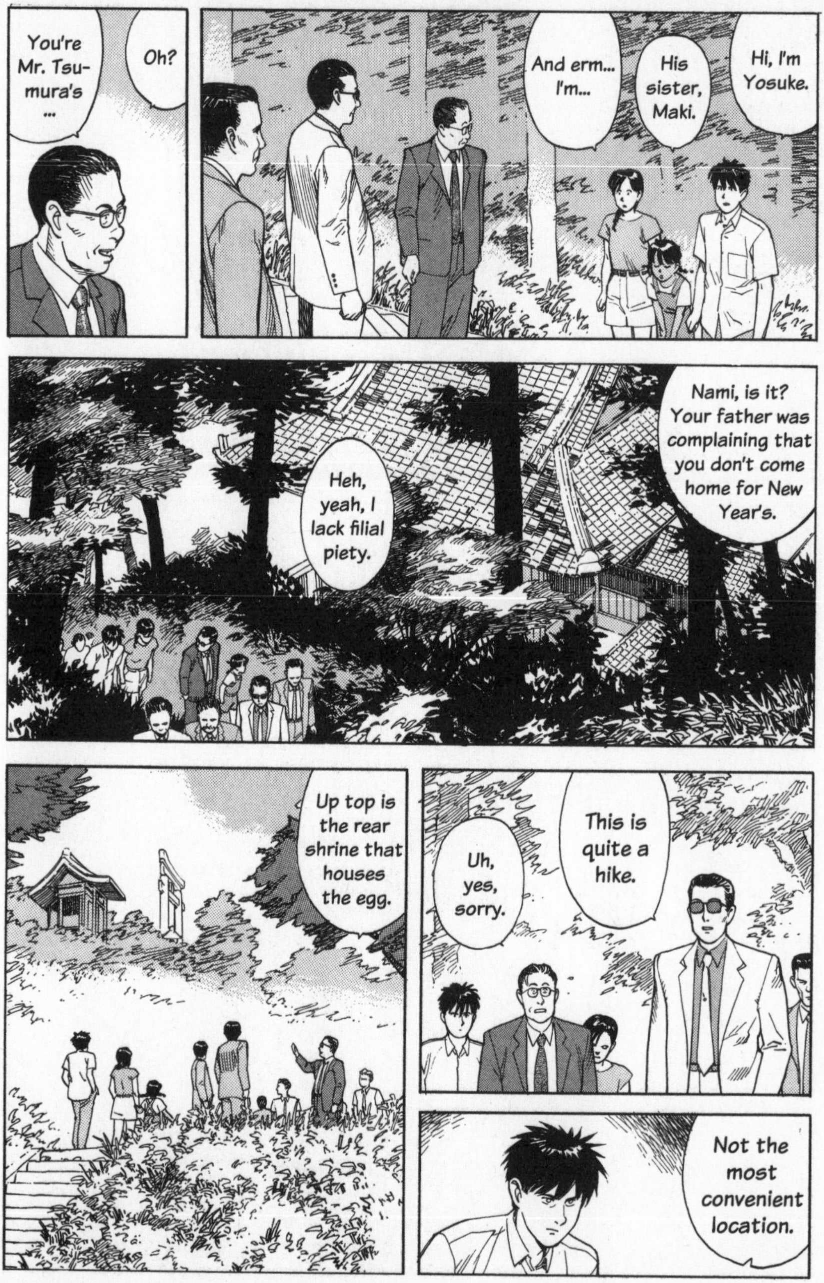
Hi, I'm Yosuke.
His sister, Maki.
And erm... I'm...
Oh?
You're Mr. Tsumura's ...
Nami, is it? Your father was complaining that you don't come home for New Year's.
Heh, yeah, I lack filial piety.
This is quite a hike.
Uh, yes, sorry.
Not the most convenient location.
Up top is the rear shrine that houses the egg.

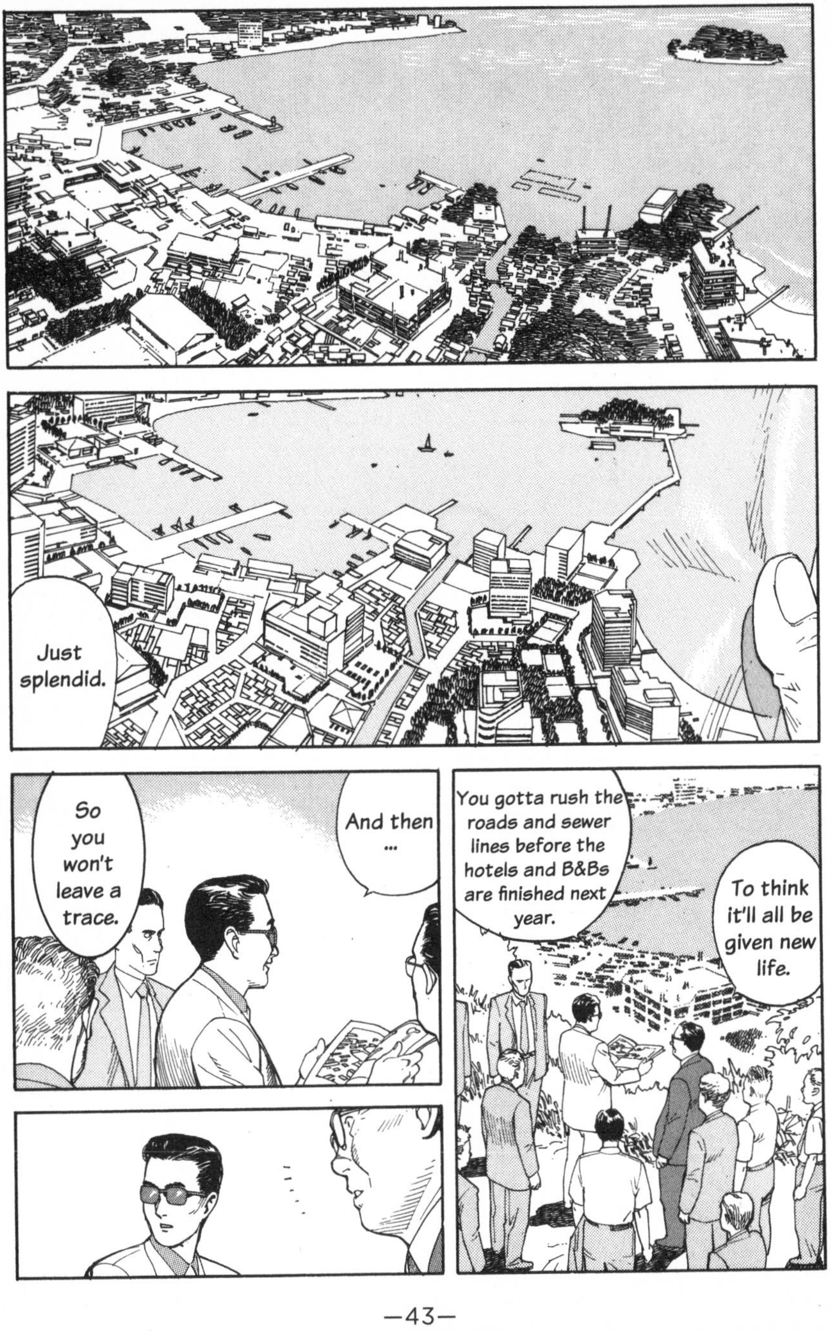
Just splendid.
You gotta rush the roads and sewer lines before the hotels and B&Bs are finished next year.
To think it'll all be given new life.
And then ...
So you won't leave a trace.

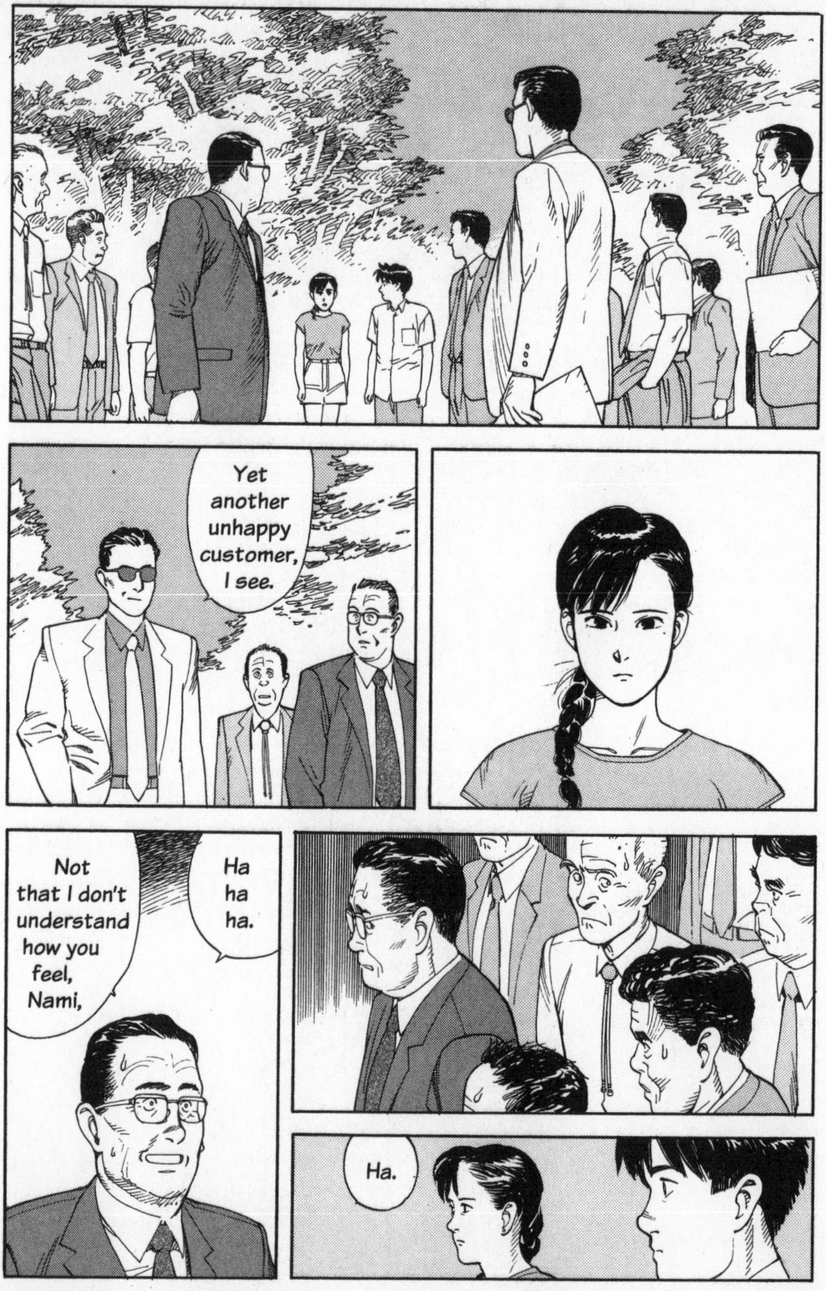
Yet another unhappy customer, I see.
Ha.
Ha ha ha.
Not that I don't understand how you feel, Nami,

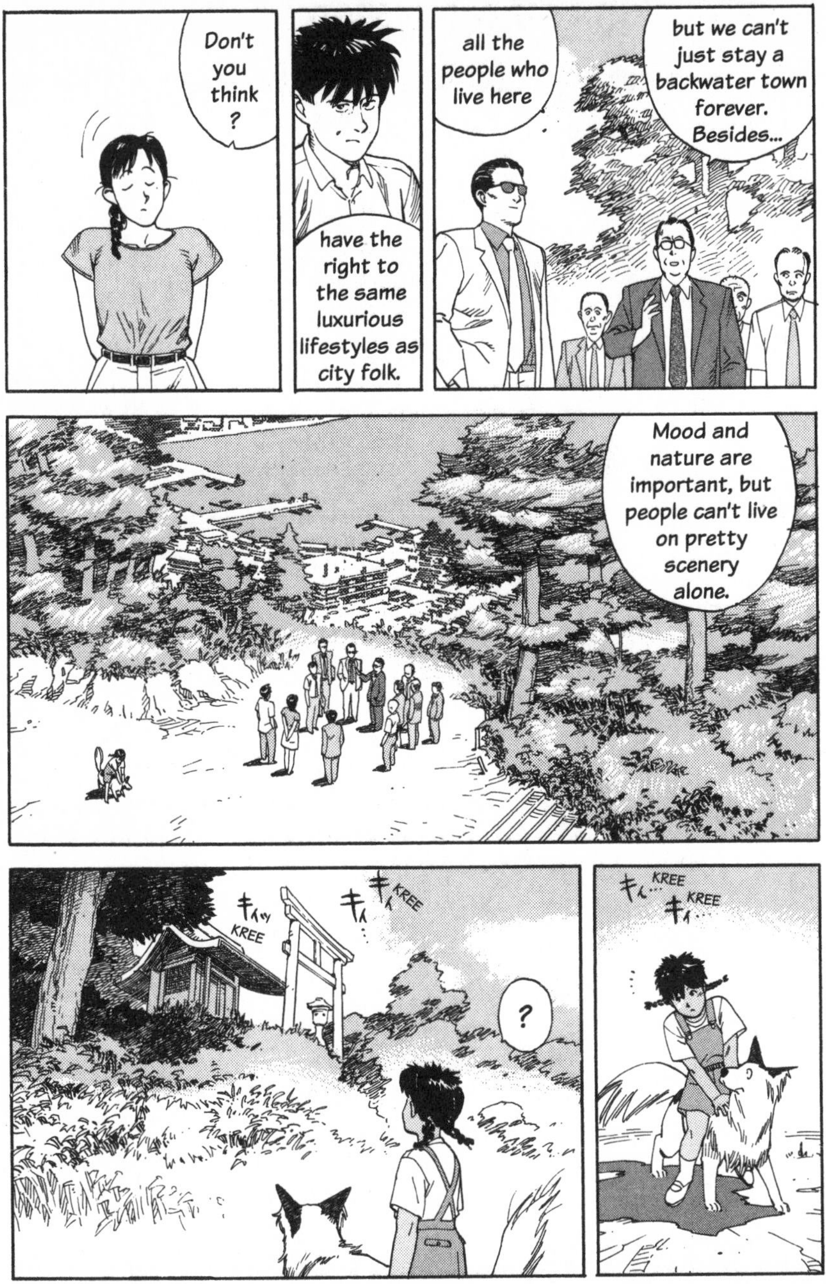
but we can't just stay a backwater town forever. Besides...
all the people who live here
have the right to the same luxurious lifestyles as city folk.
Don't you think?
Mood and nature are important, but people can't live on pretty scenery alone.
キん… KREE
キィ… KREE
キィ KREE
キィ…
キィッ KREE
?

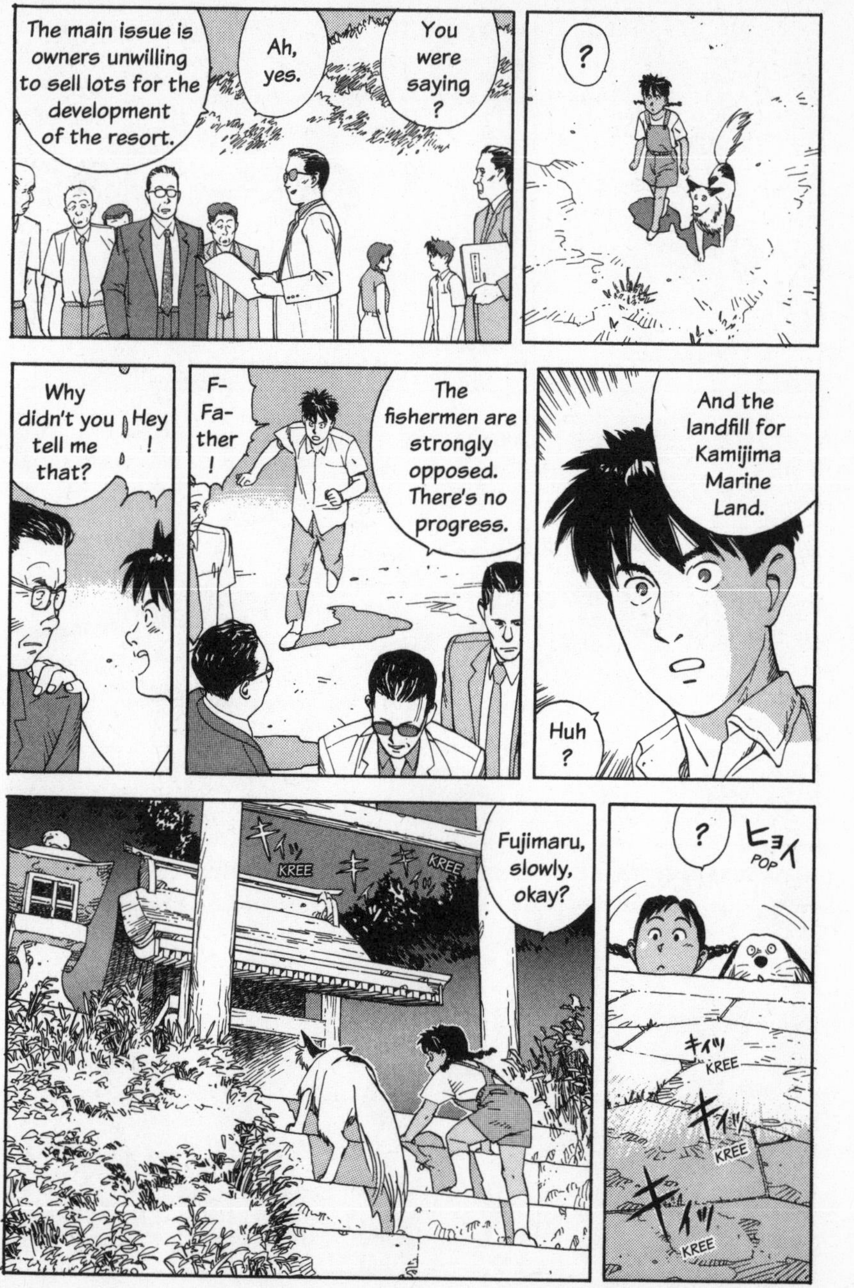
?
You were saying?
Ah, yes.
The main issue is owners unwilling to sell lots for the development of the resort.
And the landfill for Kamijima Marine Land.
Huh?
The fishermen are strongly opposed. There's no progress.
F- Fa- ther!
Hey!
Why didn't you tell me that?
?
ヒョイ
POP
キィッ
KREE
キィッ
KREE
キィッ
KREE
Fujimaru, slowly, okay?
キィッ
KREE
キィッ
KREE

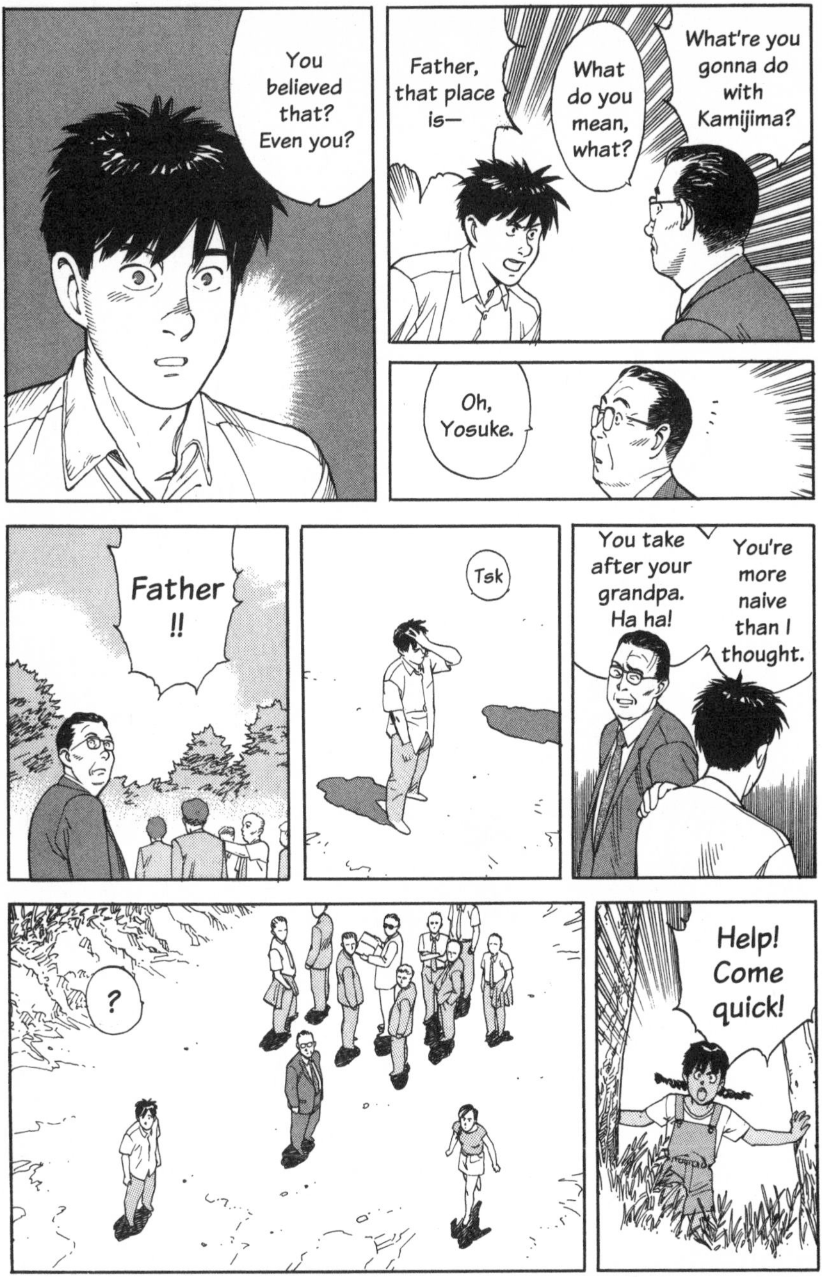
What're you gonna do with Kamijima?
What do you mean, what?
Father, that place is—
Oh, Yosuke.
You believed that? Even you?
You're more naive than I thought.
You take after your grandpa. Ha ha!
Tsk
Father !!
Help! Come quick!
?

What's going on?

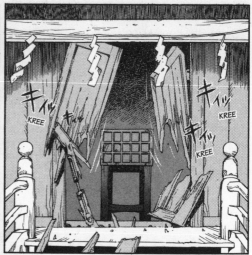

KREE
KREE
KREE
KREE

!

...

The egg didn't up and walk back to the ocean itself, did it?

Grandpa!!

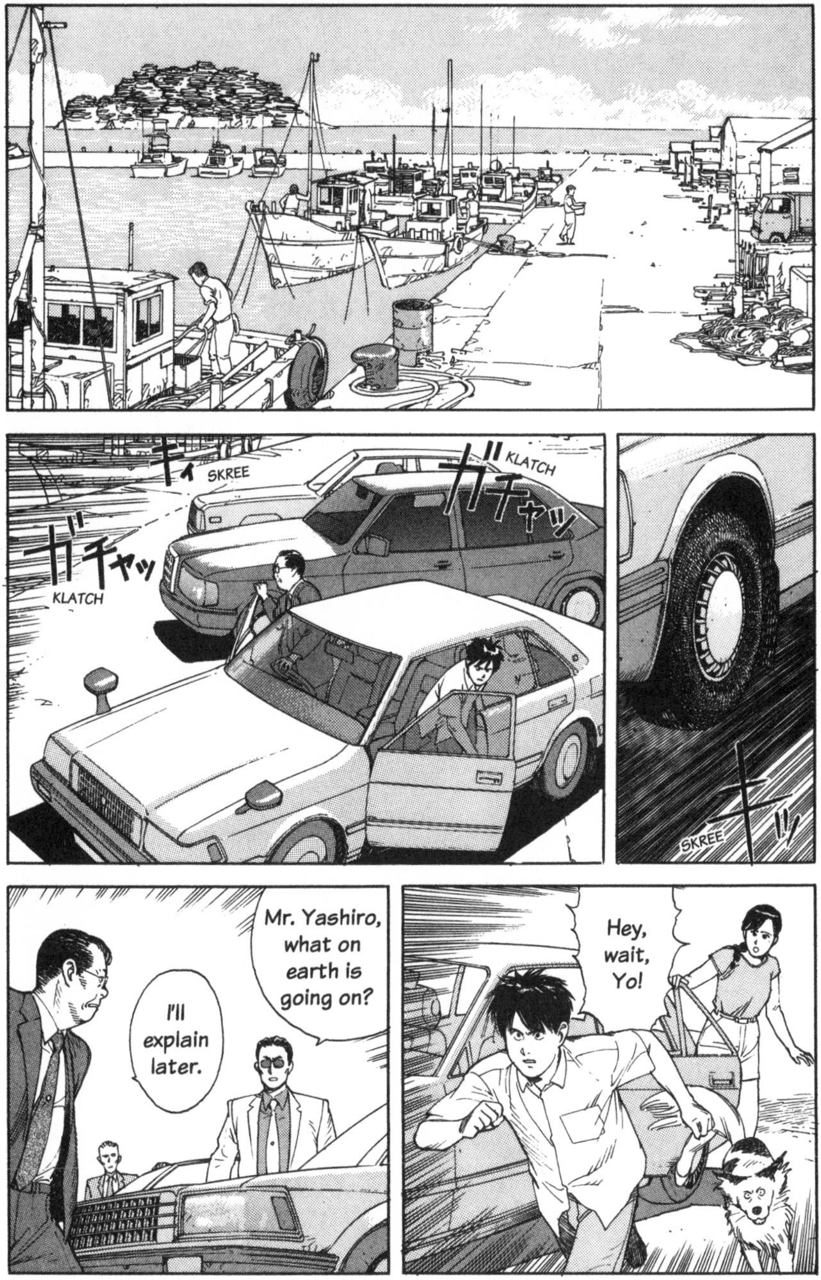
キッ
SKREE
ガチャッ
KLATCH
キィ
SKREE
ガチャッ
KLATCH
Hey, wait, Yo!
Mr. Yashiro, what on earth is going on?
I'll explain later.

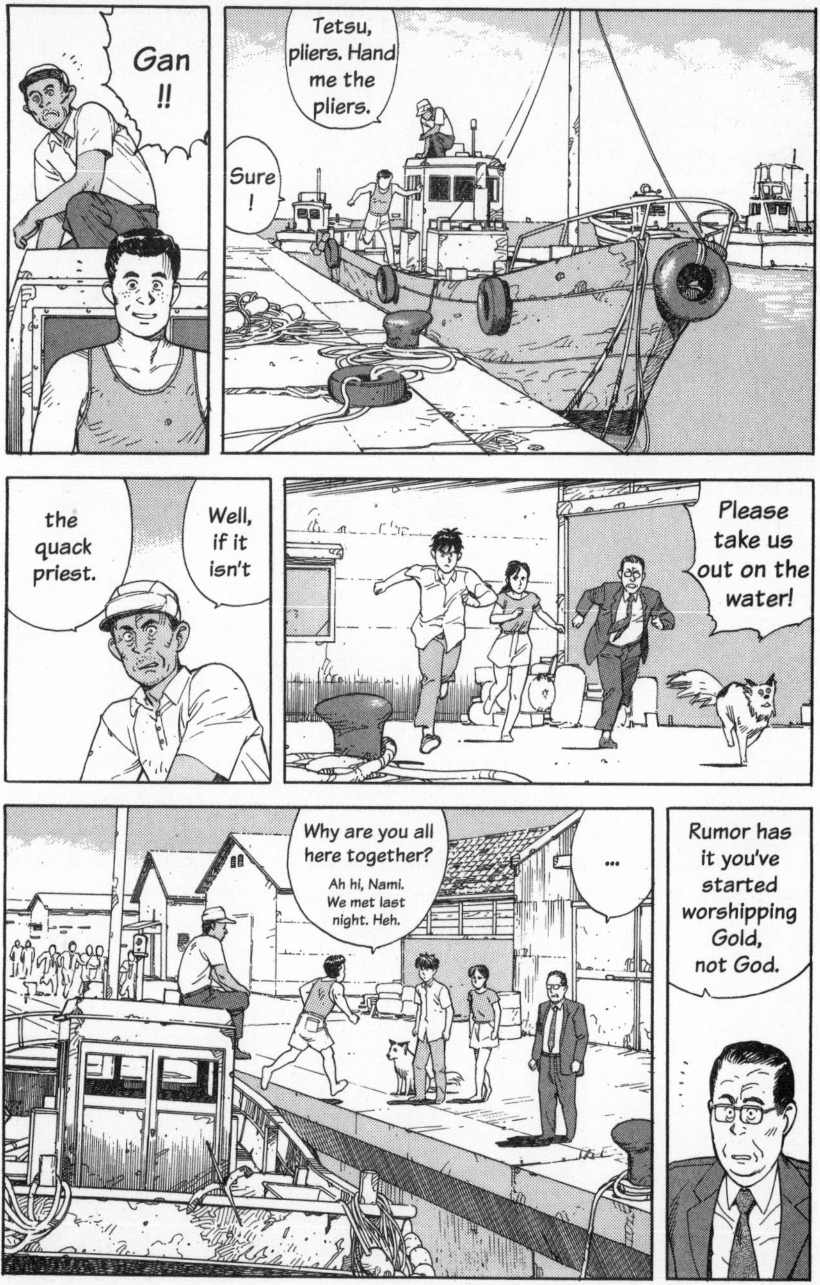
Tetsu, pliers. Hand me the pliers.
Sure!
Gan!!
Please take us out on the water!
Well, if it isn't
the quack priest.
Rumor has it you've started worshipping Gold, not God.
...
Why are you all here together?
Ah hi, Nami. We met last night. Heh.

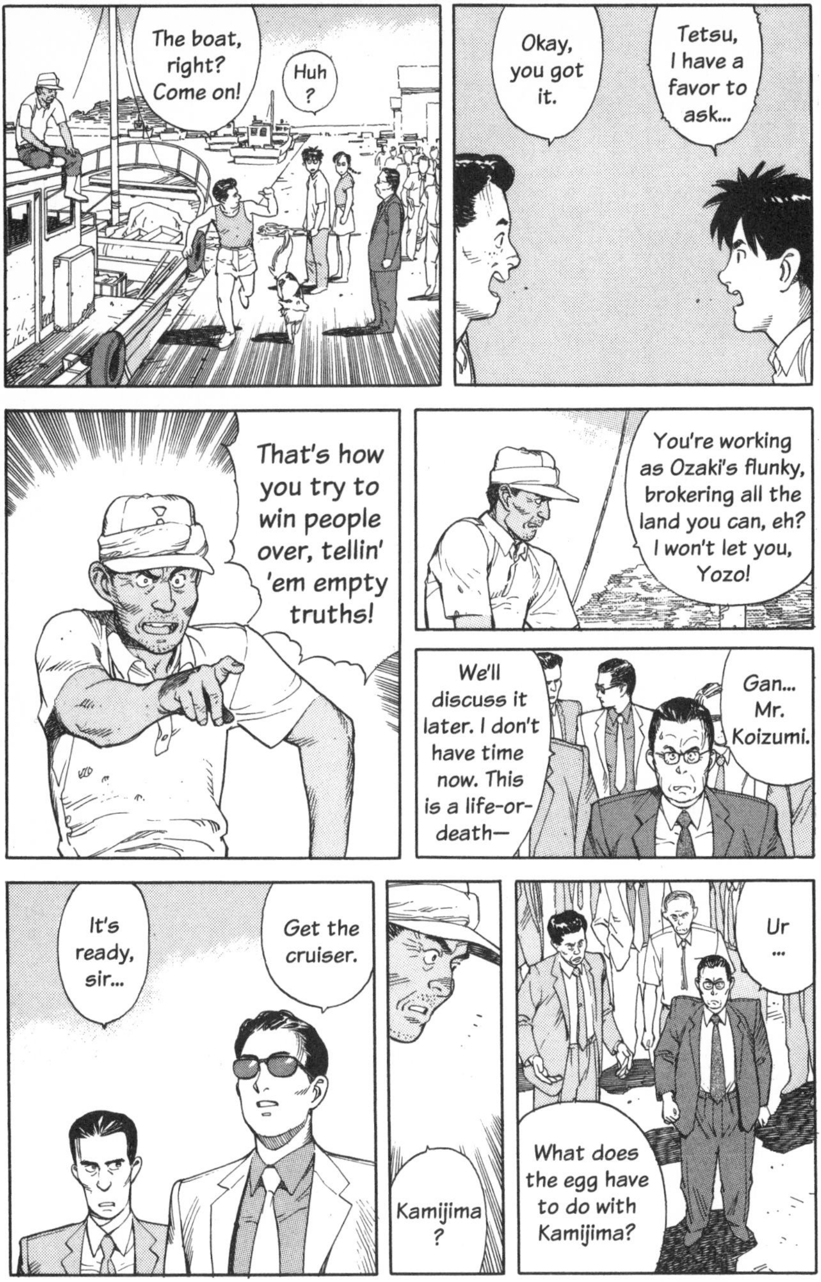
Tetsu, I have a favor to ask...
Okay, you got it.
Huh ?
The boat, right? Come on!
You're working as Ozaki's flunky, brokering all the land you can, eh? I won't let you, Yozo!
Gan... Mr. Koizumi.
We'll discuss it later. I don't have time now. This is a life-or-death—
That's how you try to win people over, tellin' 'em empty truths!
Ur ...
What does the egg have to do with Kamijima?
Kamijima ?
Get the cruiser.
It's ready, sir...

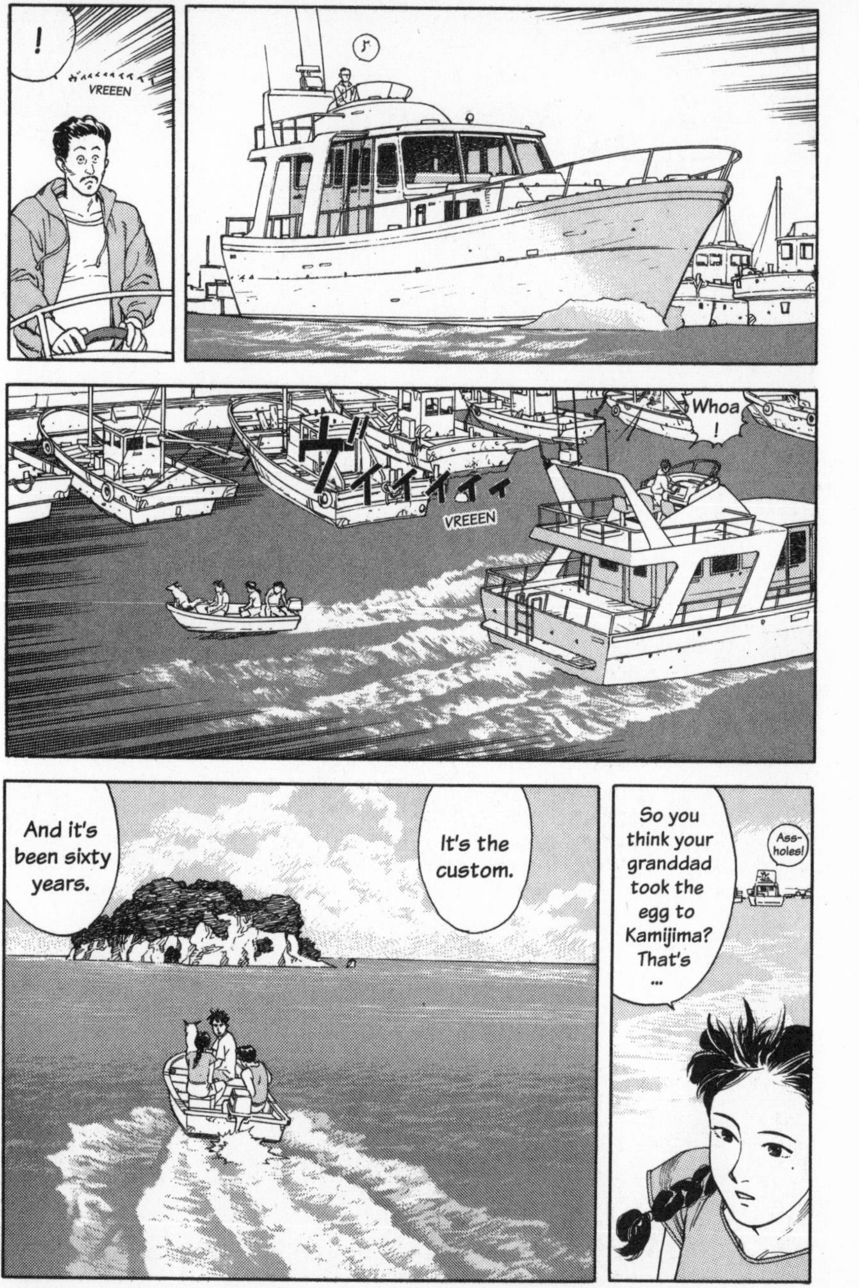
!
VREEN
Whoa !
VREEEN
So you think your granddad took the egg to Kamijima? That's ...
Ass-holes!
It's the custom.
And it's been sixty years.

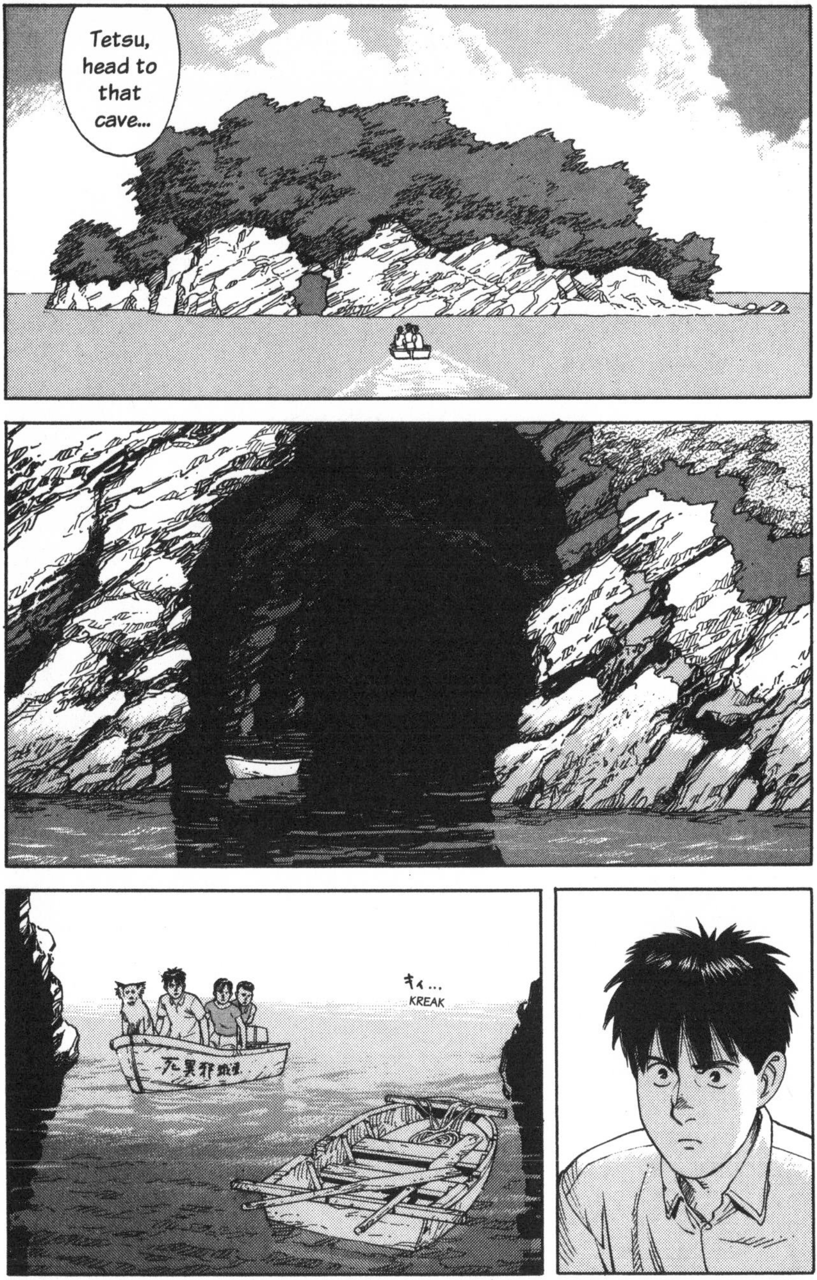
Tetsu, head to that cave...
キィ…
KREAK

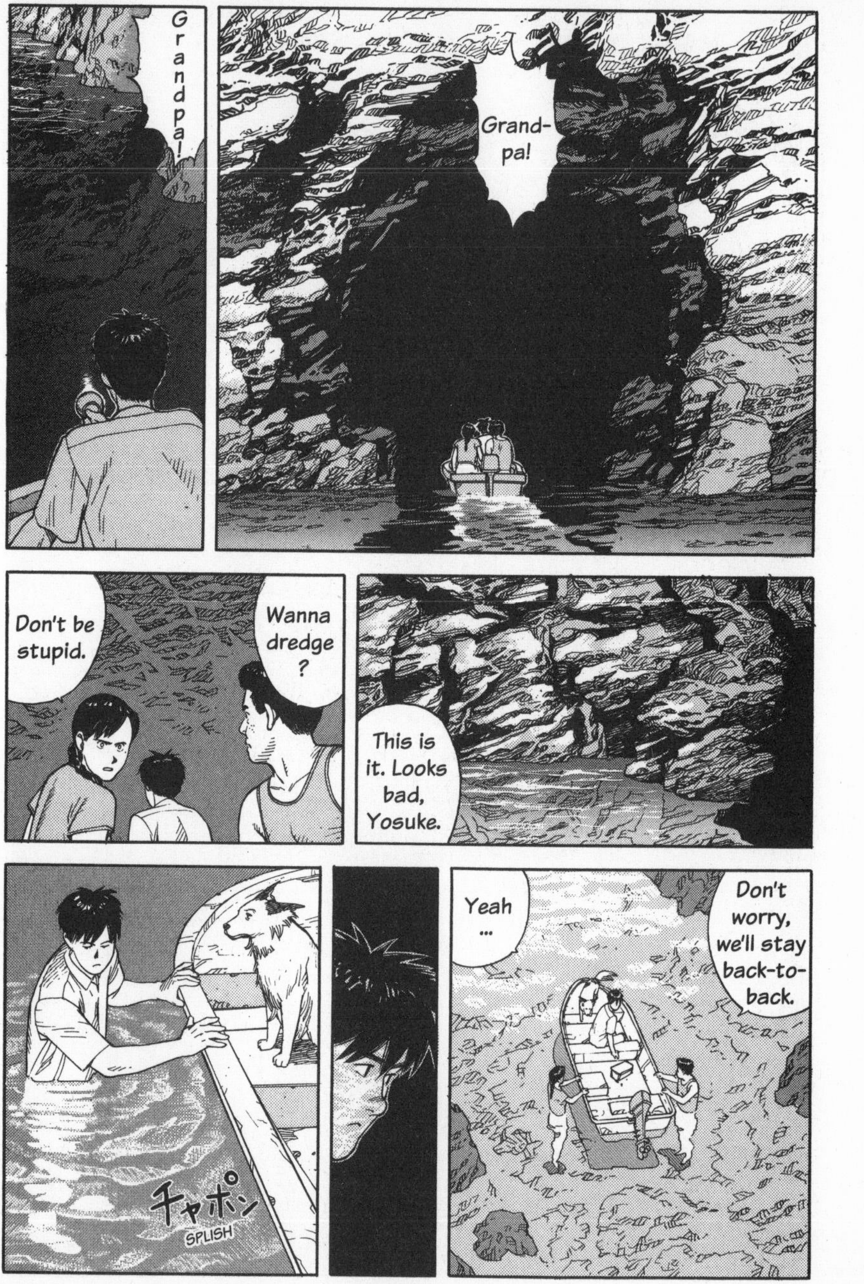
Grand-pa!
Grandpa!
This is it. Looks bad, Yosuke.
Wanna dredge?
Don't be stupid.
Don't worry, we'll stay back-to-back.
Yeah ...
チャポン
SPLISH

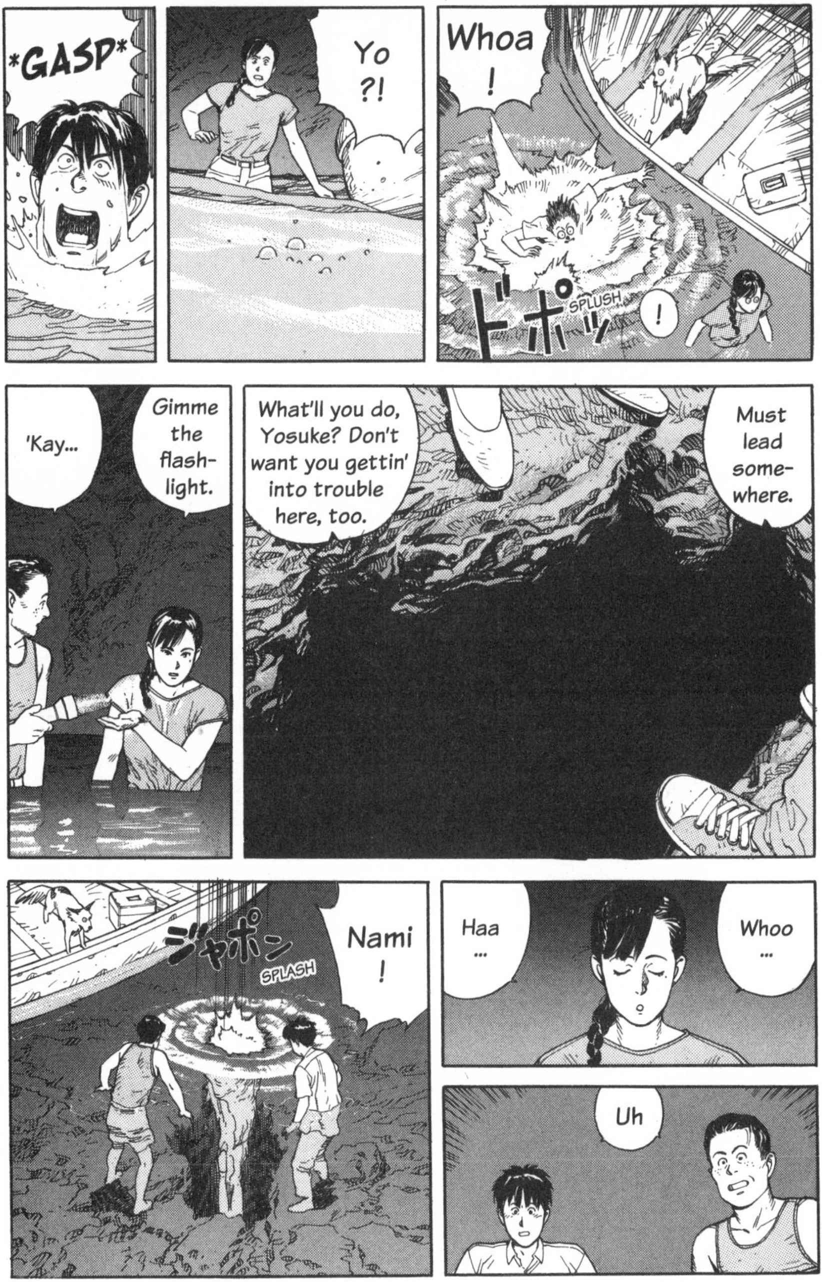
Whoa
!
ドボッ
SPLUSH
!
Yo
?!
GASP
Must lead some-where.
What'll you do, Yosuke? Don't want you gettin' into trouble here, too.
Gimme the flash-light.
'Kay...
Whoo
...
Haa
...
Uh
Nami
!
ジャポン
SPLASH

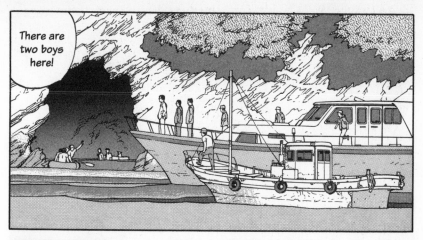

There are two boys here!
It's Yosuke. I'll go in.
Help them out.
Hey !!
No entry permitted! Move along!
Ah! Ch-Chief!!
S-So terribly sorry.
Shit. "Construction postponed" my ass. They do as they please.

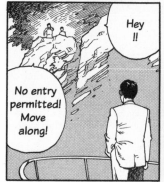

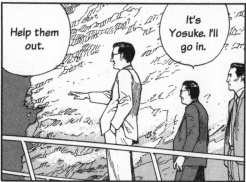

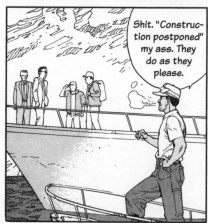

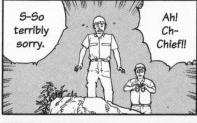

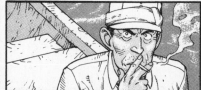

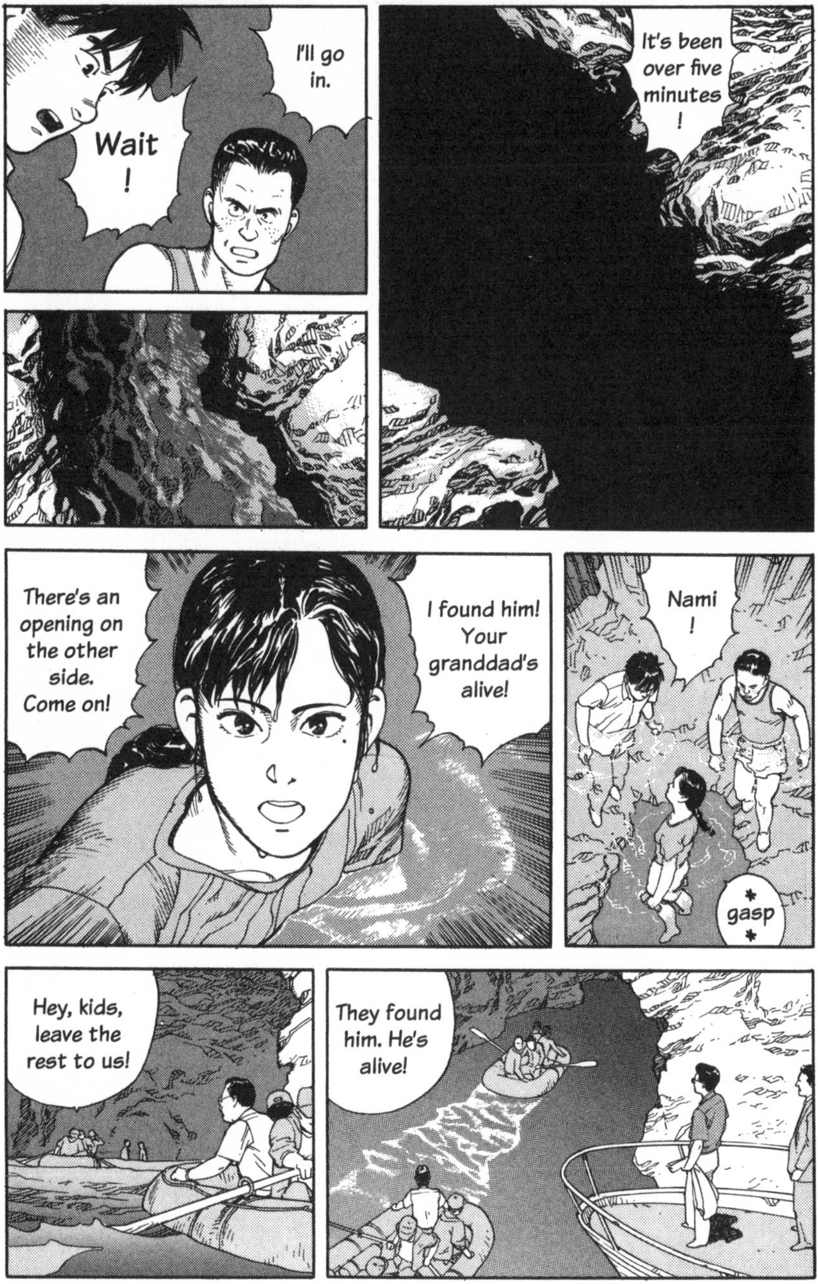
It's been over five minutes!
I'll go in.
Wait!
Nami!
* gasp *
I found him! Your granddad's alive!
There's an opening on the other side. Come on!
They found him. He's alive!
Hey, kids, leave the rest to us!

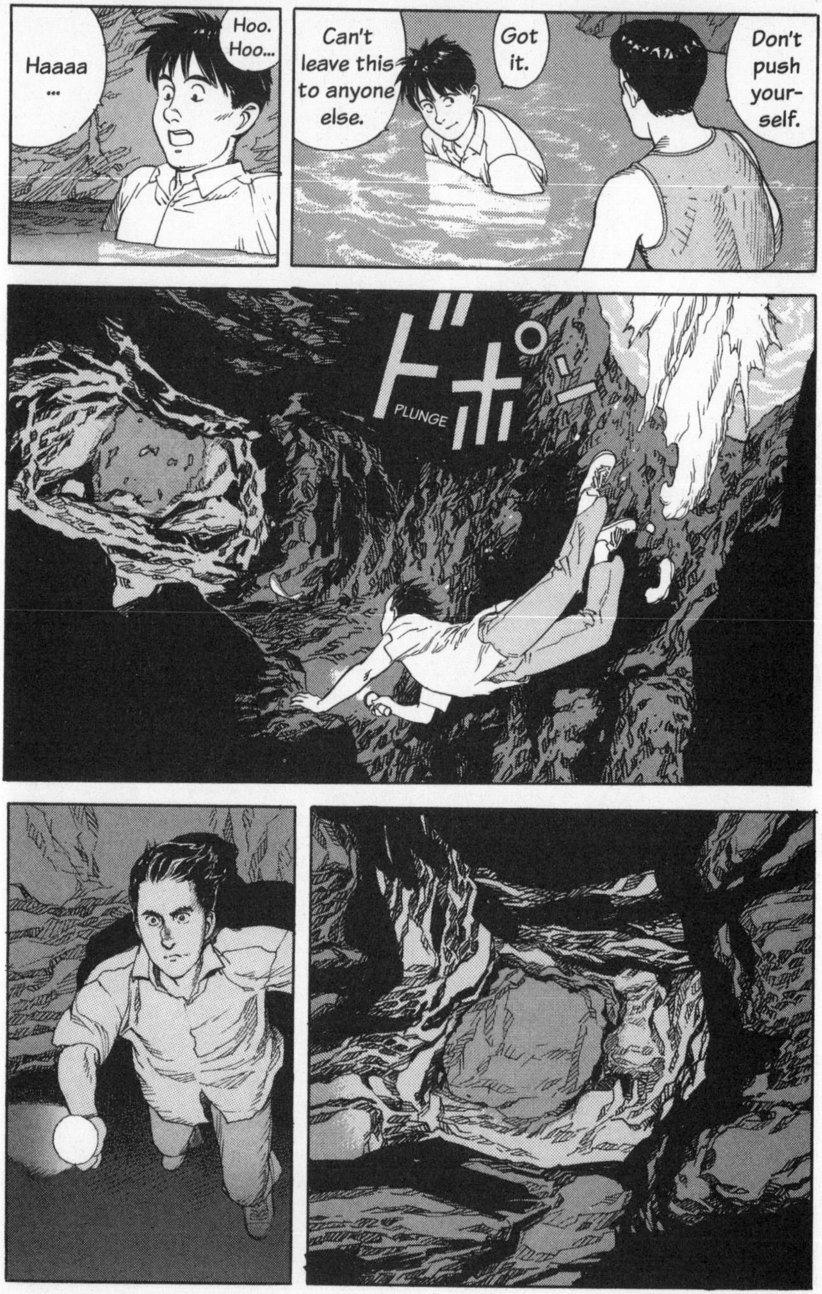
Don't push your-self.
Got it.
Can't leave this to anyone else.
Hoo. Hoo...
Haaaa ...
ドポー
PLUNGE

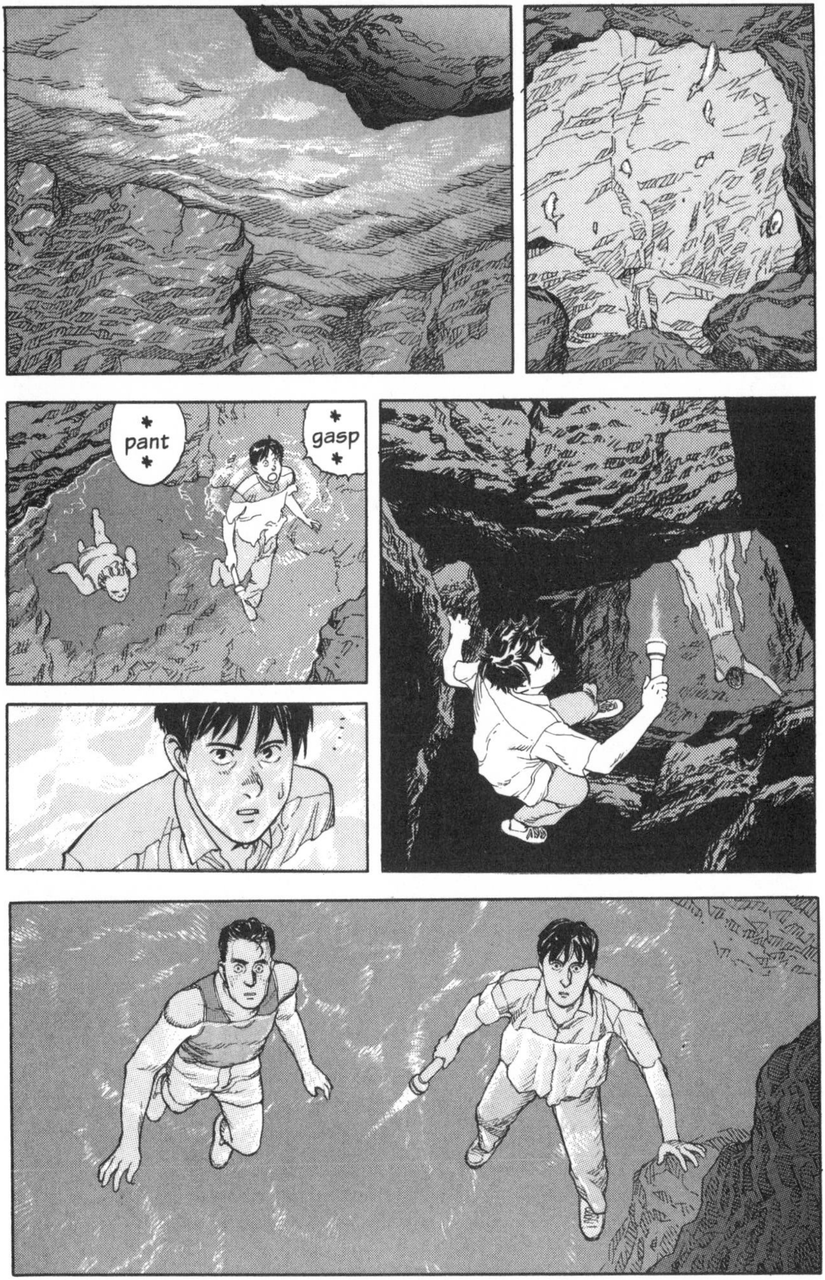
gasp
pant

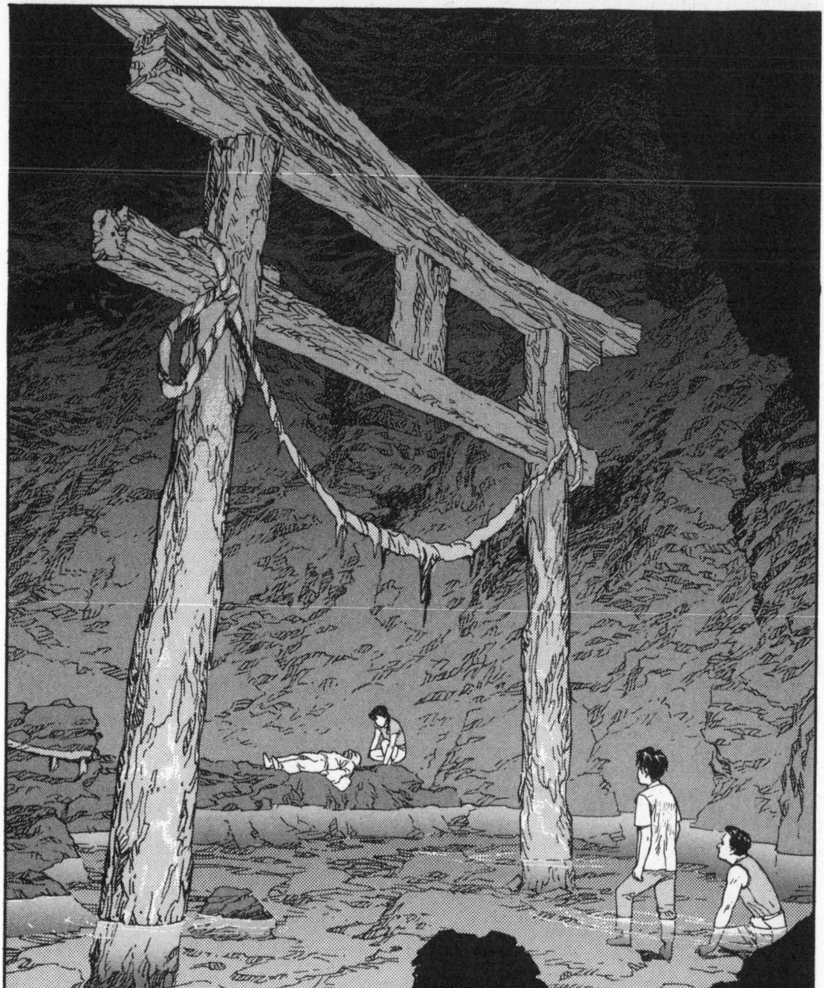

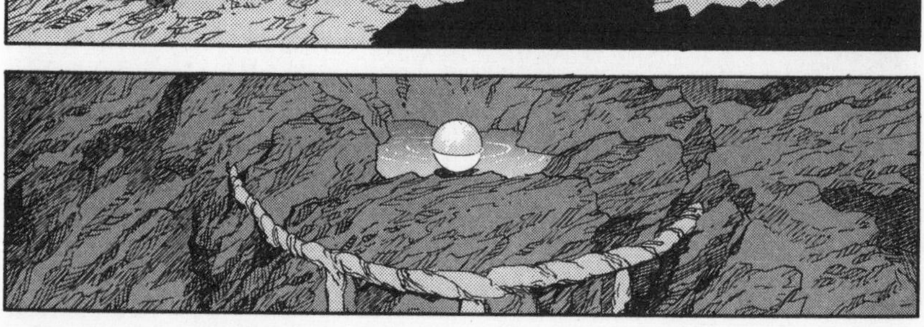

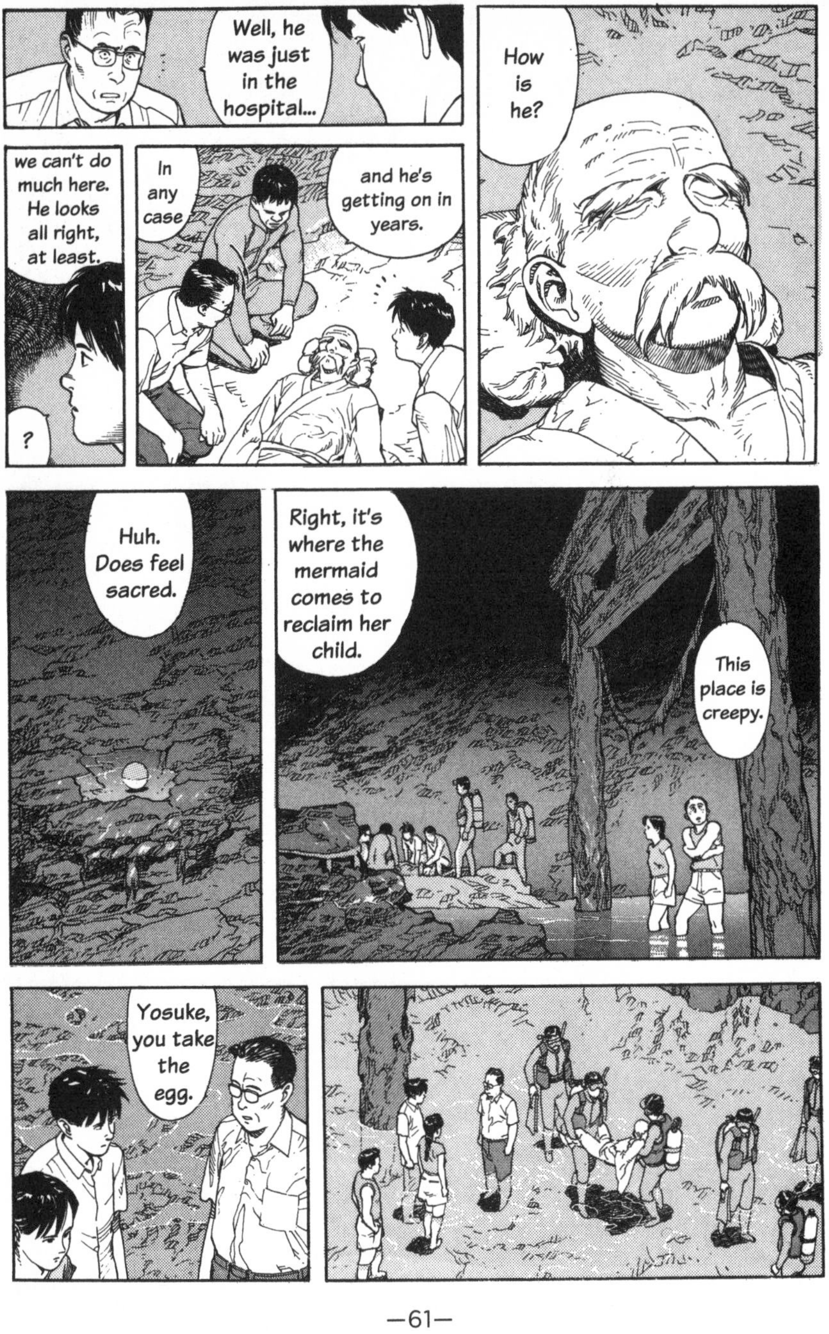
How is he?
Well, he was just in the hospital...
and he's getting on in years.
In any case
we can't do much here. He looks all right, at least.
?
Right, it's where the mermaid comes to reclaim her child.
This place is creepy.
Huh. Does feel sacred.
Yosuke, you take the egg.

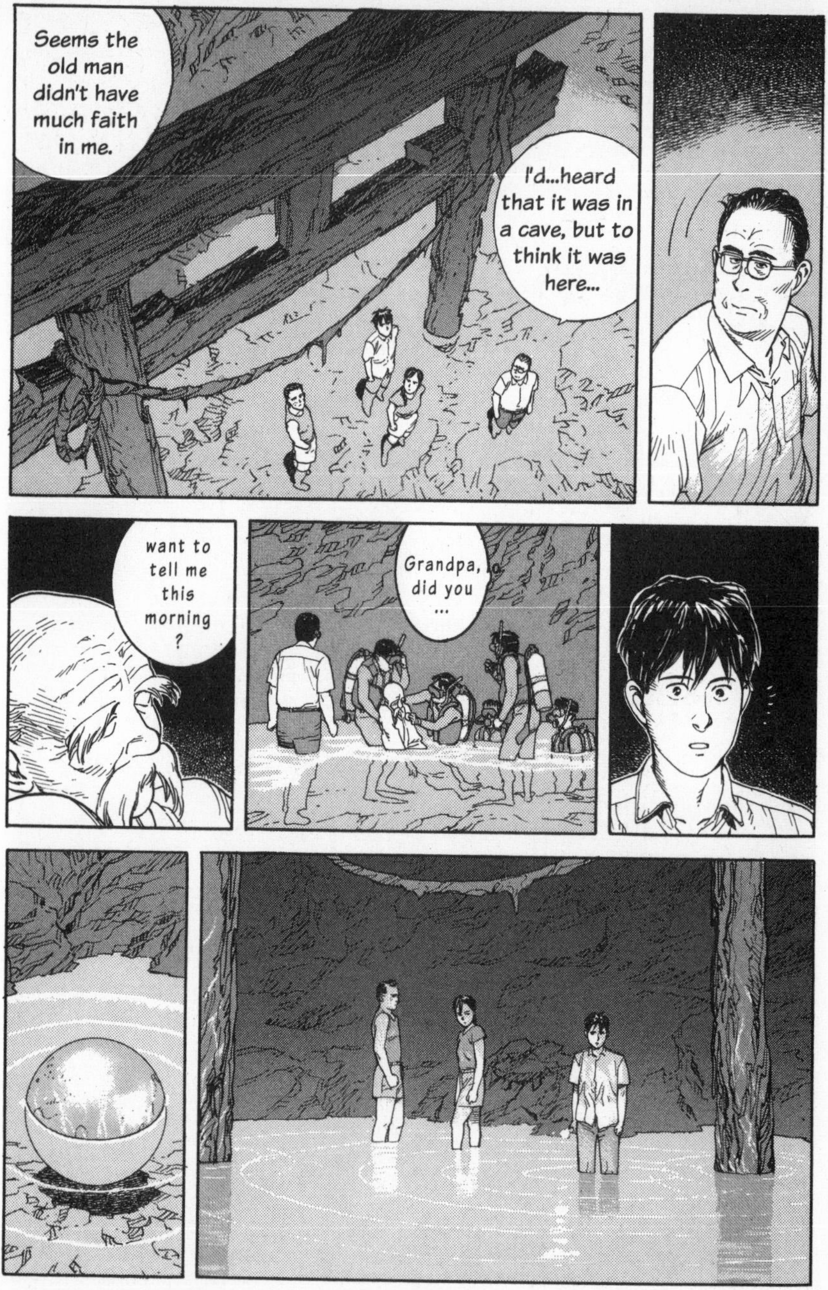
I'd...heard that it was in a cave, but to think it was here...
Seems the old man didn't have much faith in me.
Grandpa, did you ...
want to tell me this morning ?

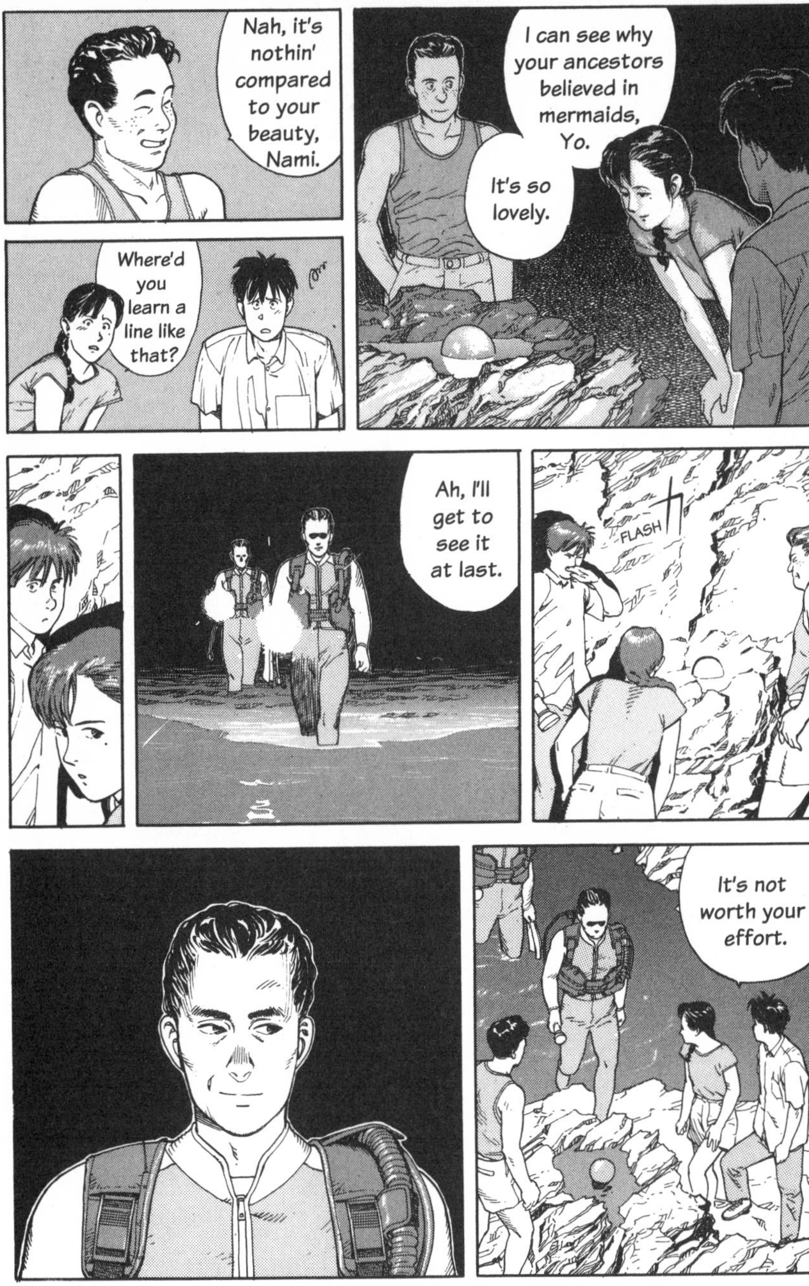
I can see why your ancestors believed in mermaids, Yo.
It's so lovely.
Nah, it's nothin' compared to your beauty, Nami.
Where'd you learn a line like that?
FLASH
Ah, I'll get to see it at last.
It's not worth your effort.

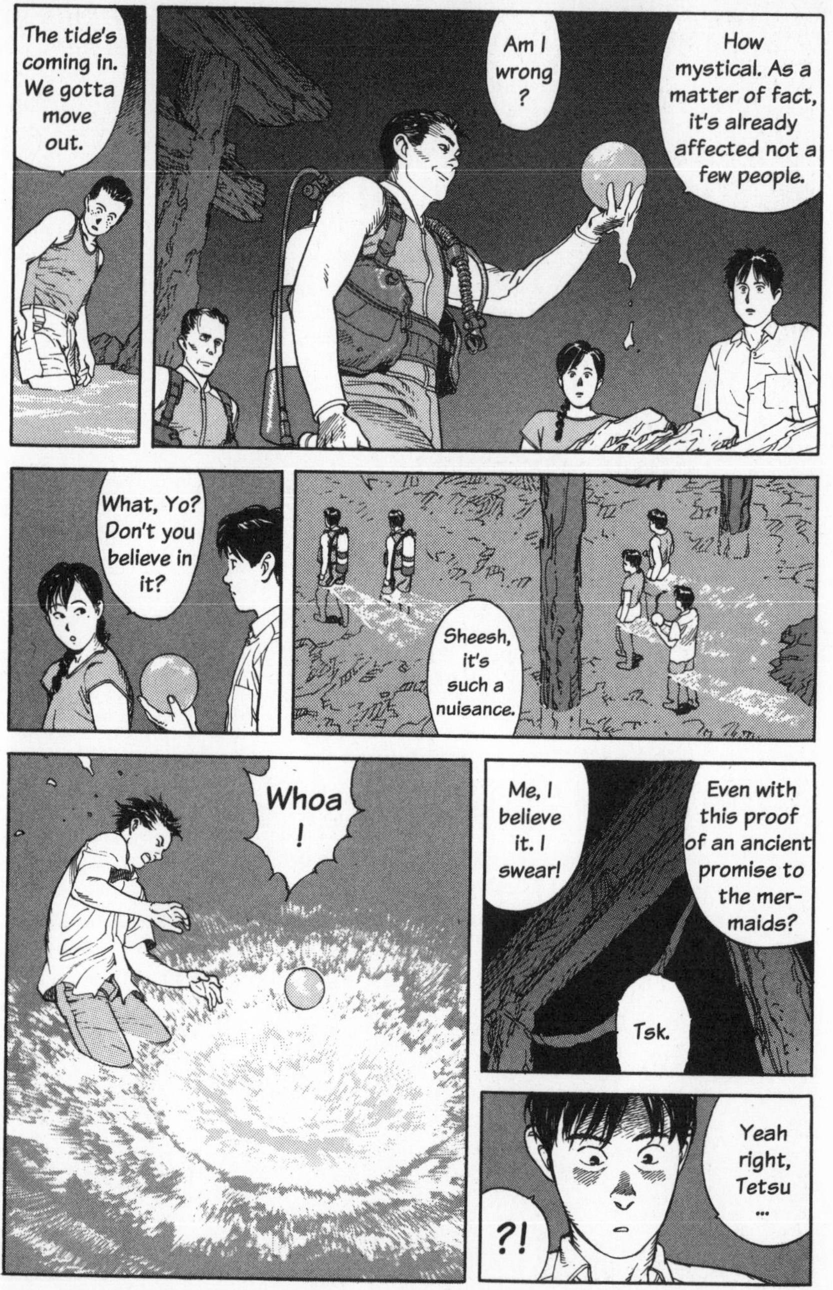
How mystical. As a matter of fact, it's already affected not a few people.
Am I wrong?
The tide's coming in. We gotta move out.
Sheesh, it's such a nuisance.
What, Yo? Don't you believe in it?
Even with this proof of an ancient promise to the mer-maids?
Me, I believe it. I swear!
Tsk.
Yeah right, Tetsu ...
?!
Whoa!

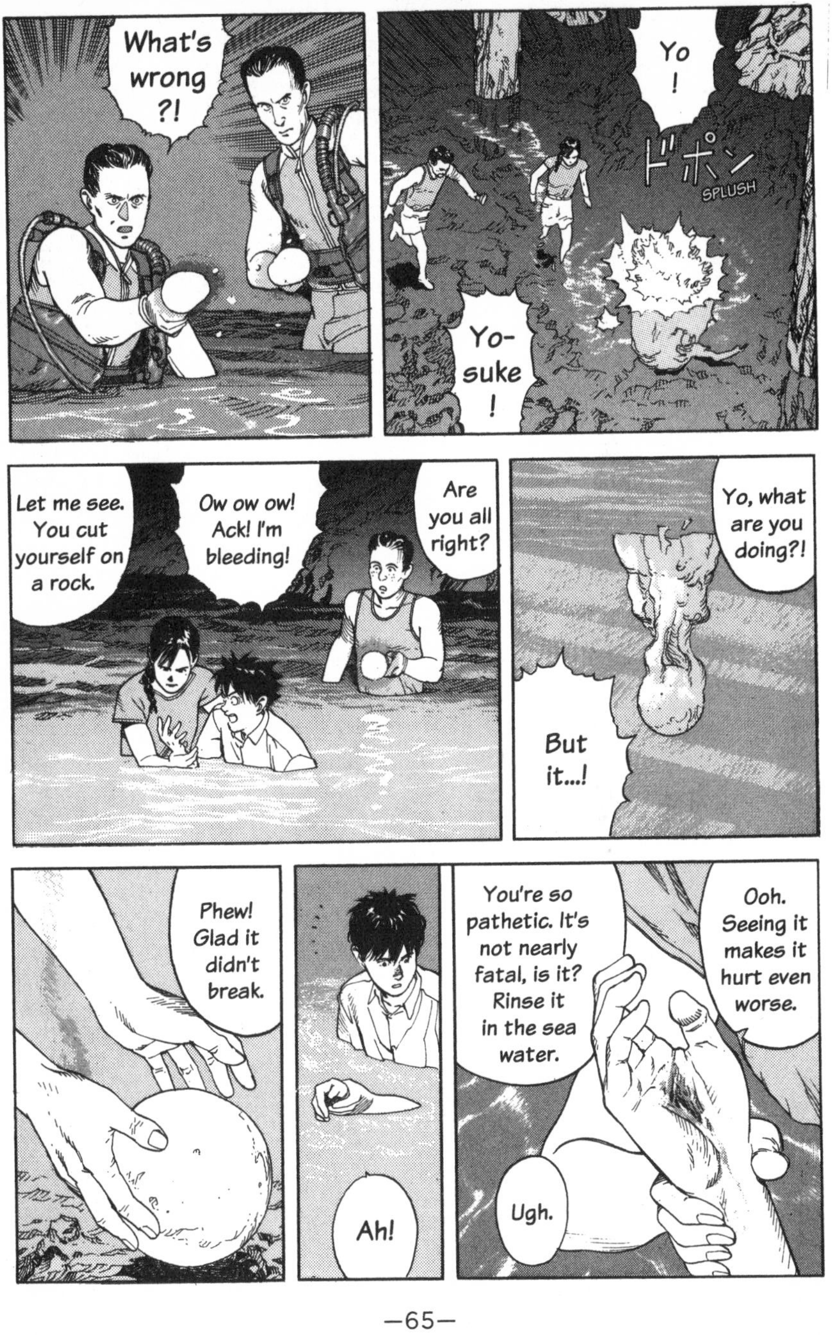

Yo!
ドポン
SPLUSH
Yo-suke!
What's wrong?!
Yo, what are you doing?!
But it...!
Are you all right?
Ow ow ow! Ack! I'm bleeding!
Let me see. You cut yourself on a rock.
Ooh. Seeing it makes it hurt even worse.
You're so pathetic. It's not nearly fatal, is it? Rinse it in the sea water.
Ugh.
Ah!
Phew! Glad it didn't break.

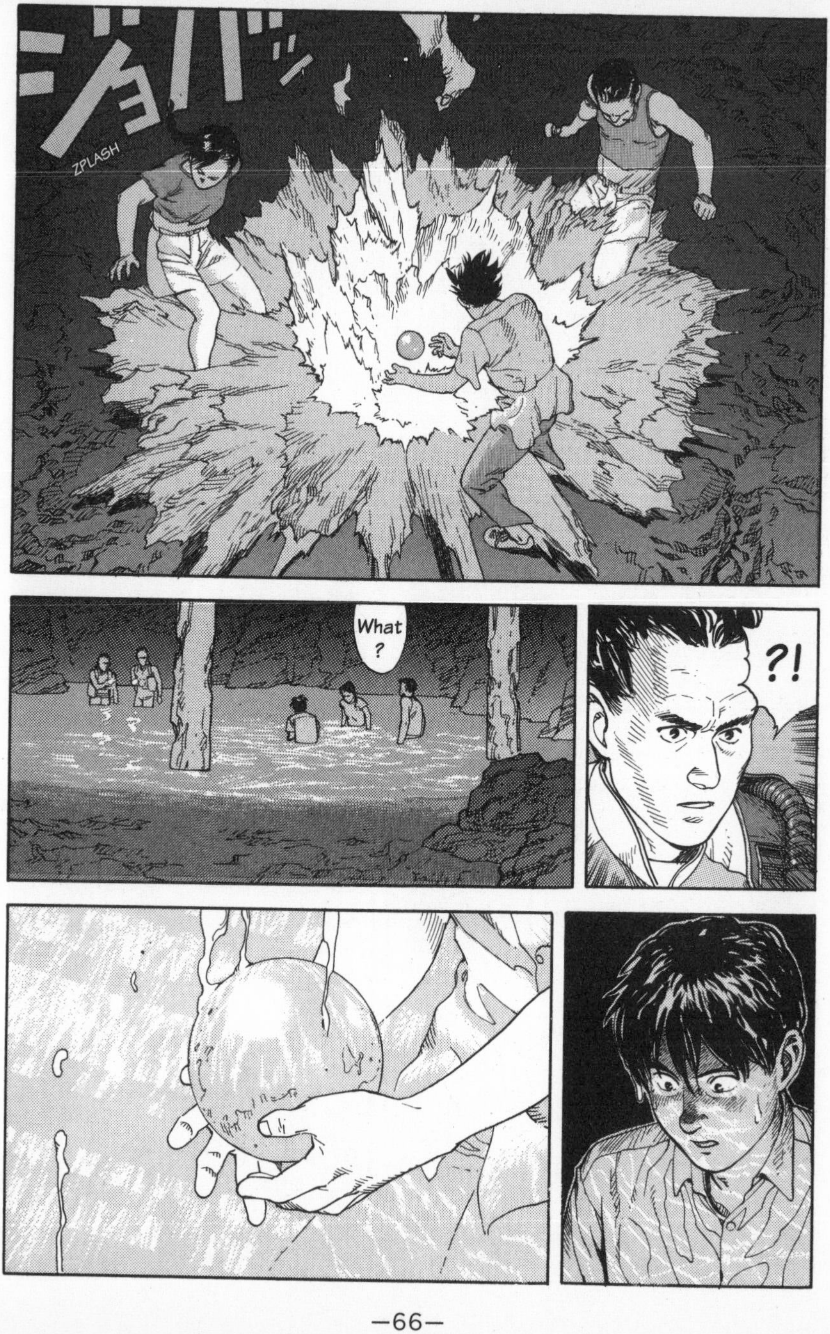
ジョバッ
ZPLASH
?!
What ?

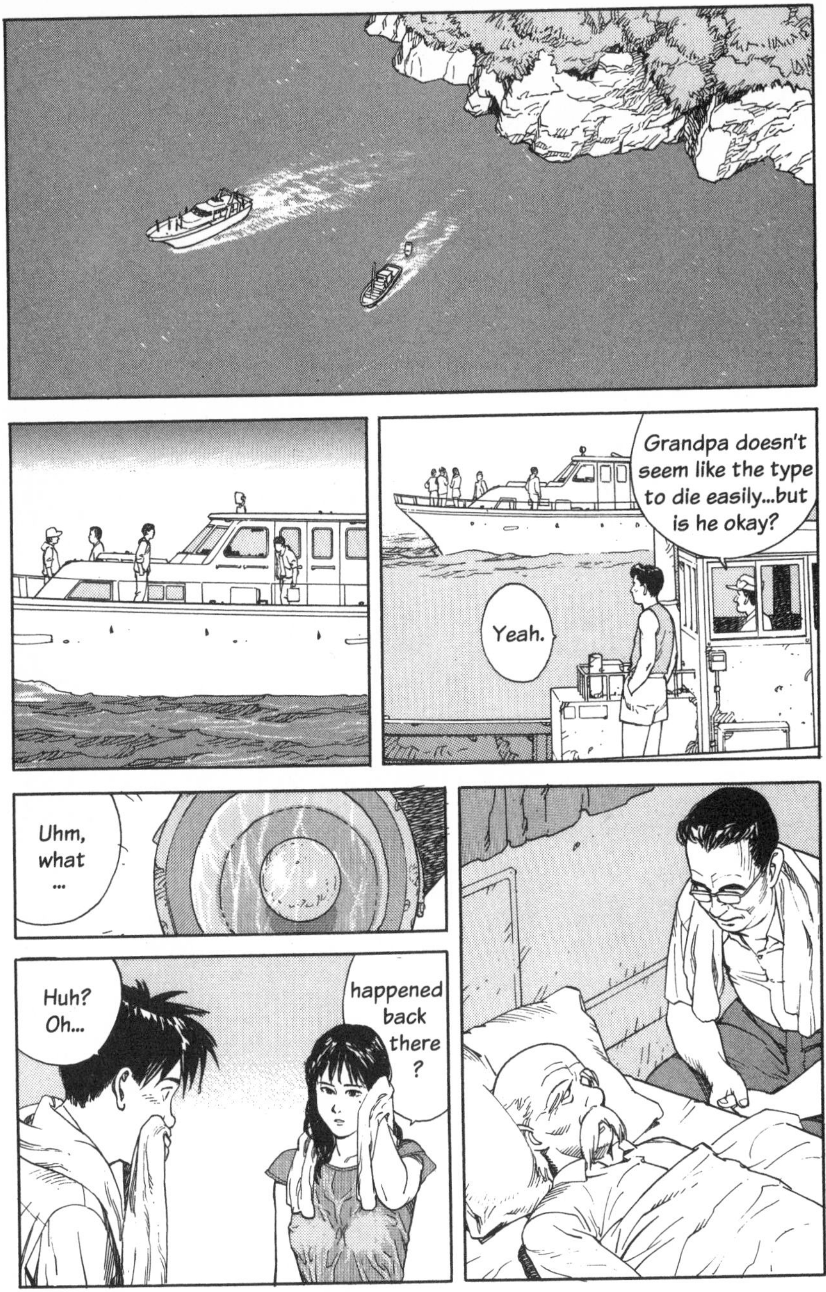
Grandpa doesn't seem like the type to die easily...but is he okay?
Yeah.
Uhm, what ...
happened back there ?
Huh? Oh...

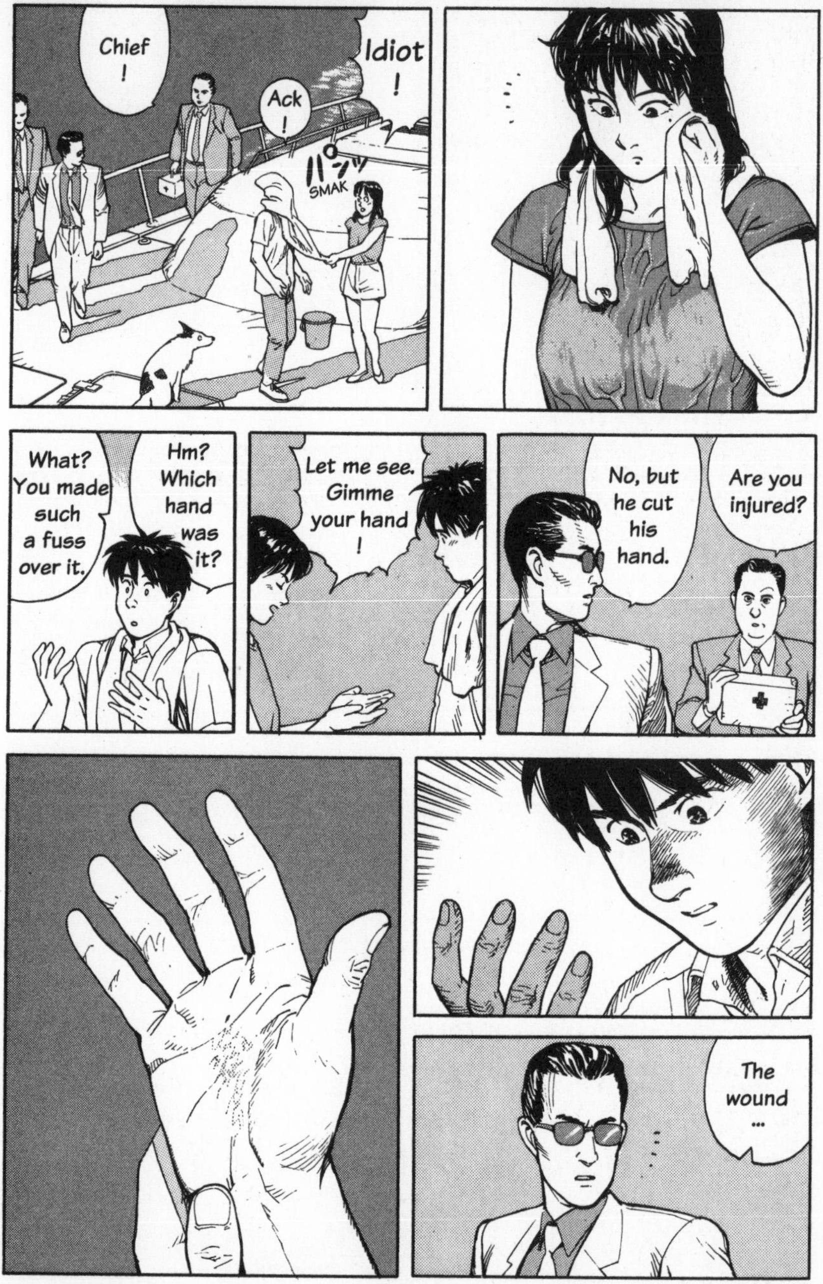
Idiot !
Chief !
Ack !
SMAK
Are you injured?
No, but he cut his hand.
Let me see. Gimme your hand !
Hm? Which hand was it?
What? You made such a fuss over it.
The wound ...

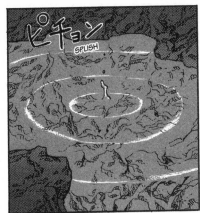

ピチョン
SPLISH

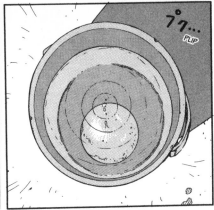

プク…
FLIP

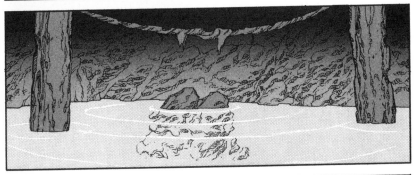

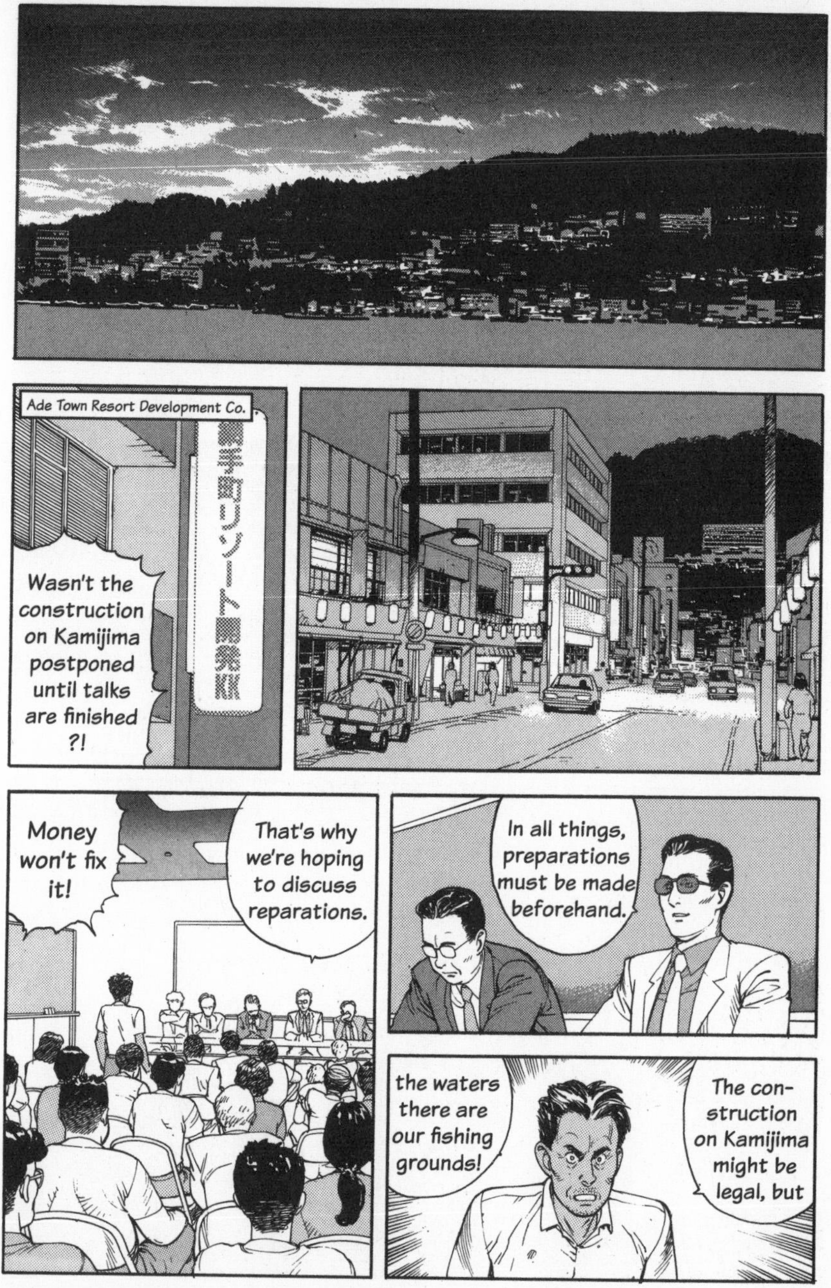
Ade Town Resort Development Co.
手町リゾート開発KK
Wasn't the construction on Kamijima postponed until talks are finished ?!
In all things, preparations must be made beforehand.
The con-struction on Kamijima might be legal, but
the waters there are our fishing grounds!
That's why we're hoping to discuss reparations.
Money won't fix it!

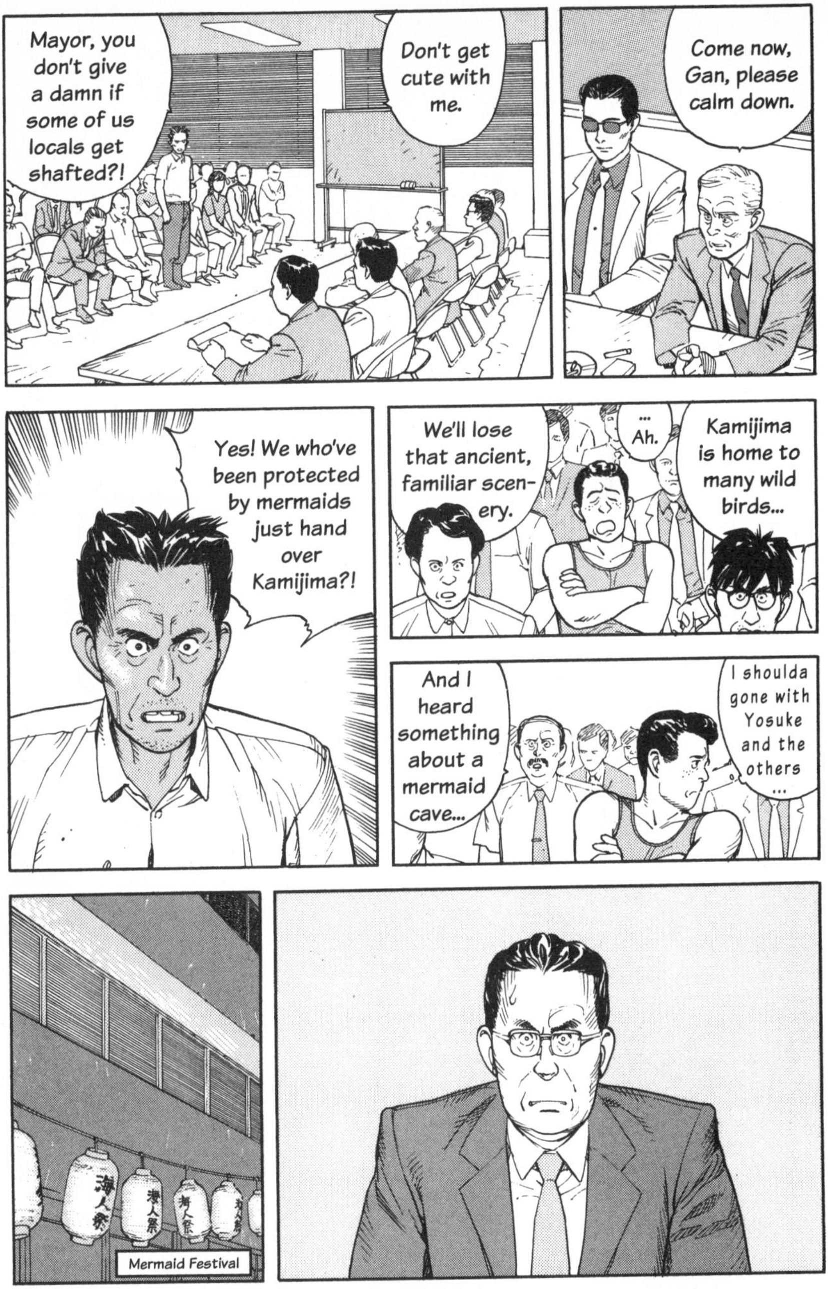
Come now, Gan, please calm down.
Don't get cute with me.
Mayor, you don't give a damn if some of us locals get shafted?!
Kamijima is home to many wild birds...
... Ah.
We'll lose that ancient, familiar scen-ery.
I shoulda gone with Yosuke and the others ...
And I heard something about a mermaid cave...
Yes! We who've been protected by mermaids just hand over Kamijima?!
Mermaid Festival

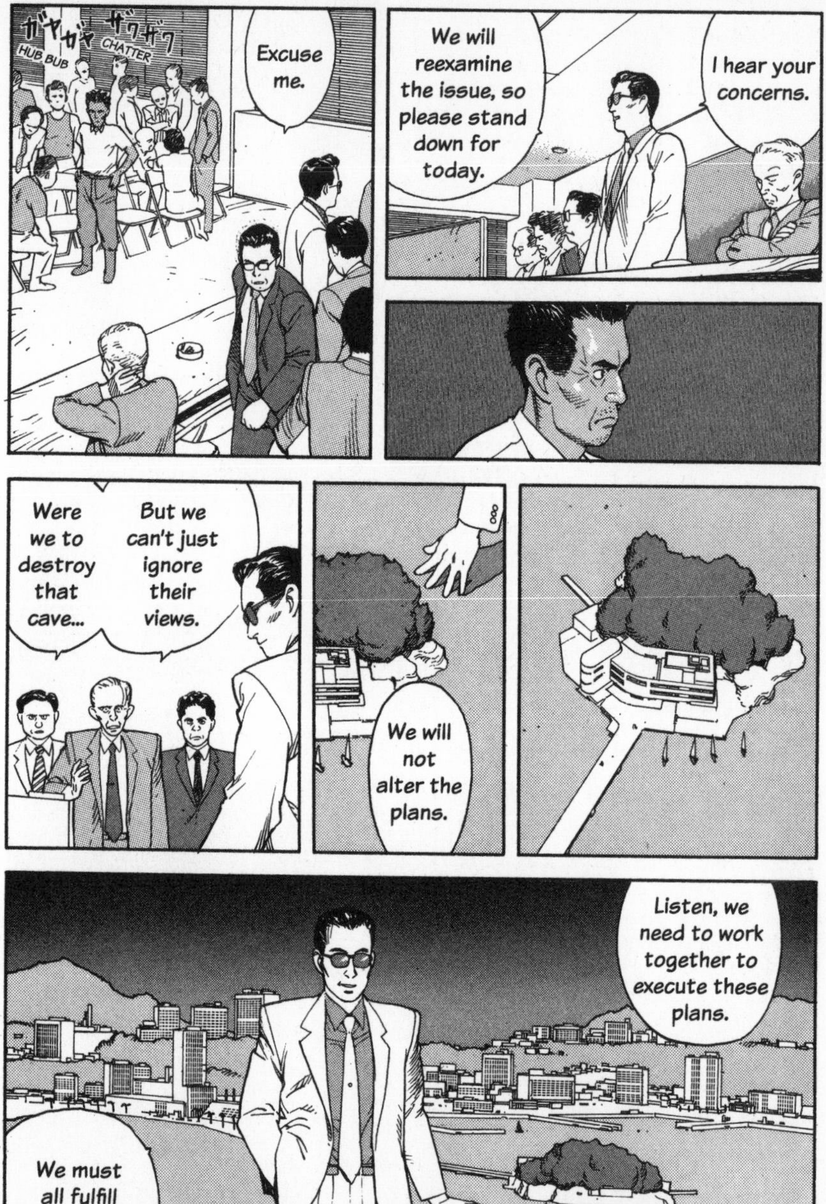
I hear your concerns.
We will reexamine the issue, so please stand down for today.
ザワザワ
CHATTER
ガヤガヤ
HUB BUB
Excuse me.
We will not alter the plans.
But we can't just ignore their views.
Were we to destroy that cave...
Listen, we need to work together to execute these plans.
We must all fulfill our duties.

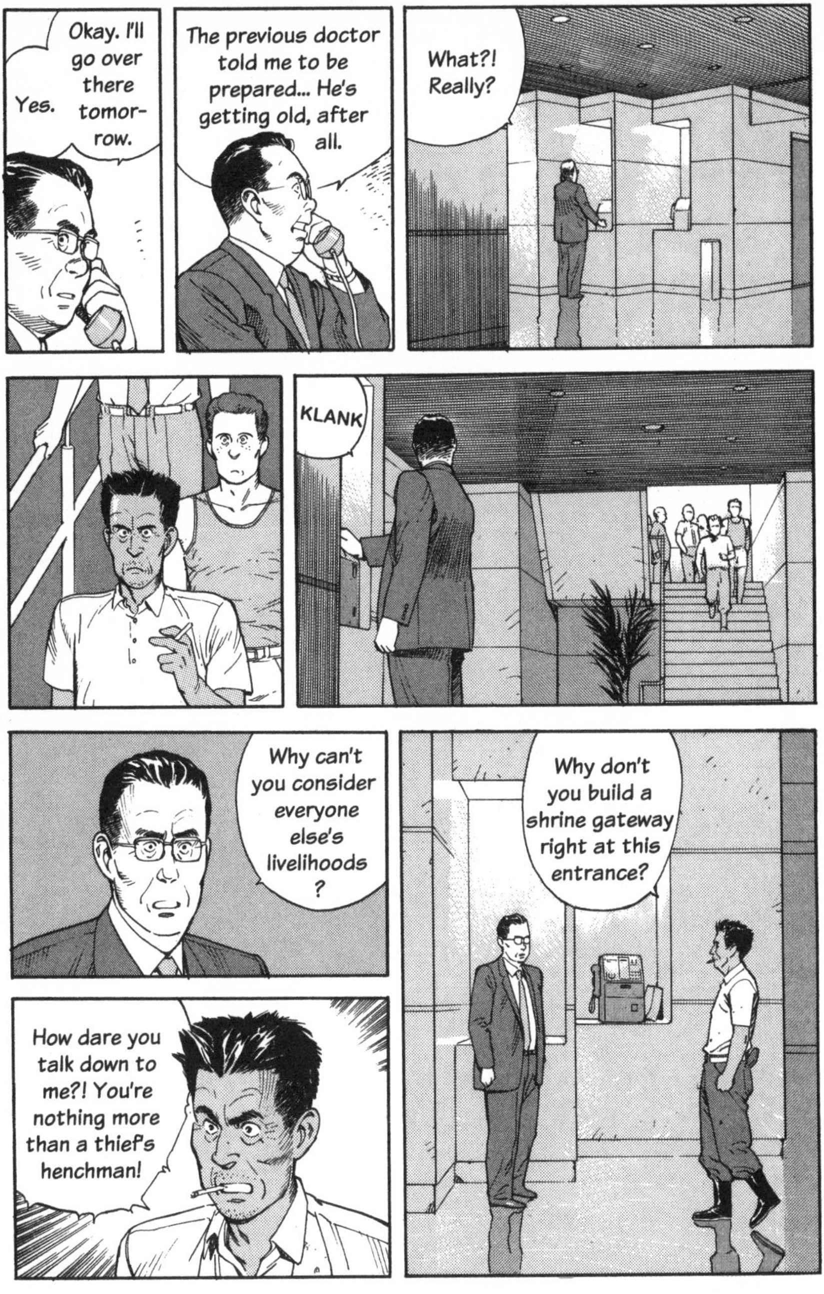
What?! Really?
The previous doctor told me to be prepared... He's getting old, after all.
Okay. I'll go over there tomorrow.
Yes.
KLANK
Why don't you build a shrine gateway right at this entrance?
Why can't you consider everyone else's livelihoods?
How dare you talk down to me?! You're nothing more than a thief's henchman!

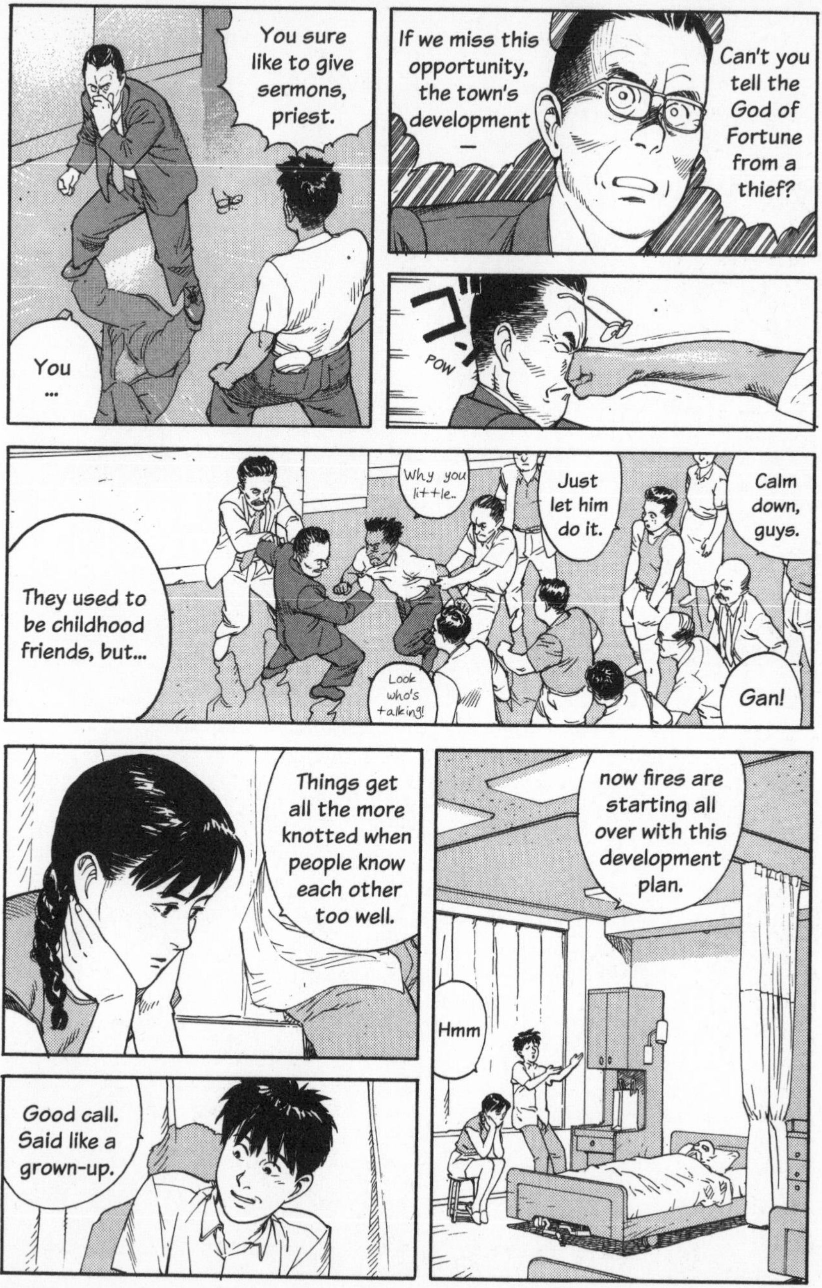

Can't you tell the God of Fortune from a thief?
If we miss this opportunity, the town's development —
POW
You sure like to give sermons, priest.
You ...
Calm down, guys.
Just let him do it.
Why you little..
Gan!
Look who's talking!
They used to be childhood friends, but...
now fires are starting all over with this development plan.
Hmm
Things get all the more knotted when people know each other too well.
Good call. Said like a grown-up.

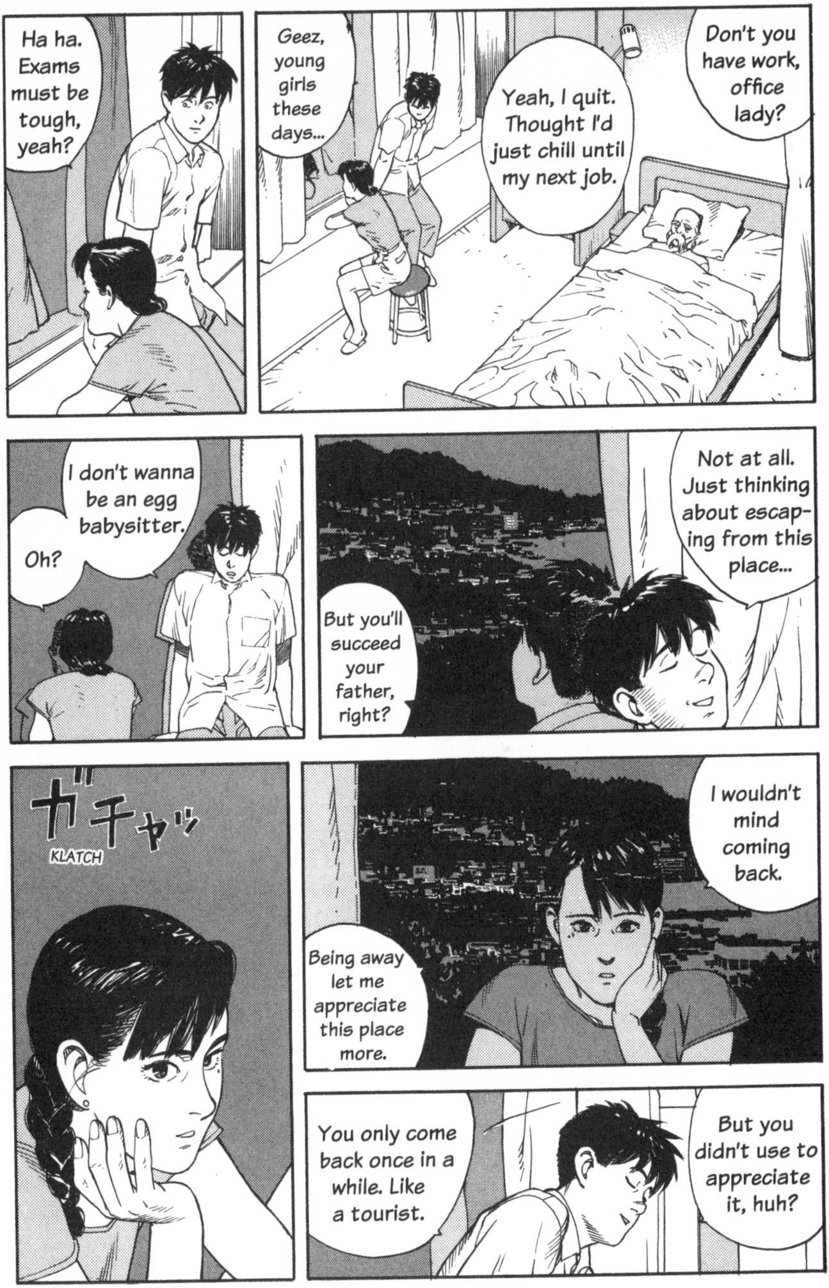
Don't you have work, office lady?
Yeah, I quit. Thought I'd just chill until my next job.
Geez, young girls these days...
Ha ha. Exams must be tough, yeah?
Not at all. Just thinking about escaping from this place...
But you'll succeed your father, right?
I don't wanna be an egg babysitter.
Oh?
I wouldn't mind coming back.
Being away let me appreciate this place more.
But you didn't use to appreciate it, huh?
You only come back once in a while. Like a tourist.
ガチャッ
KLATCH

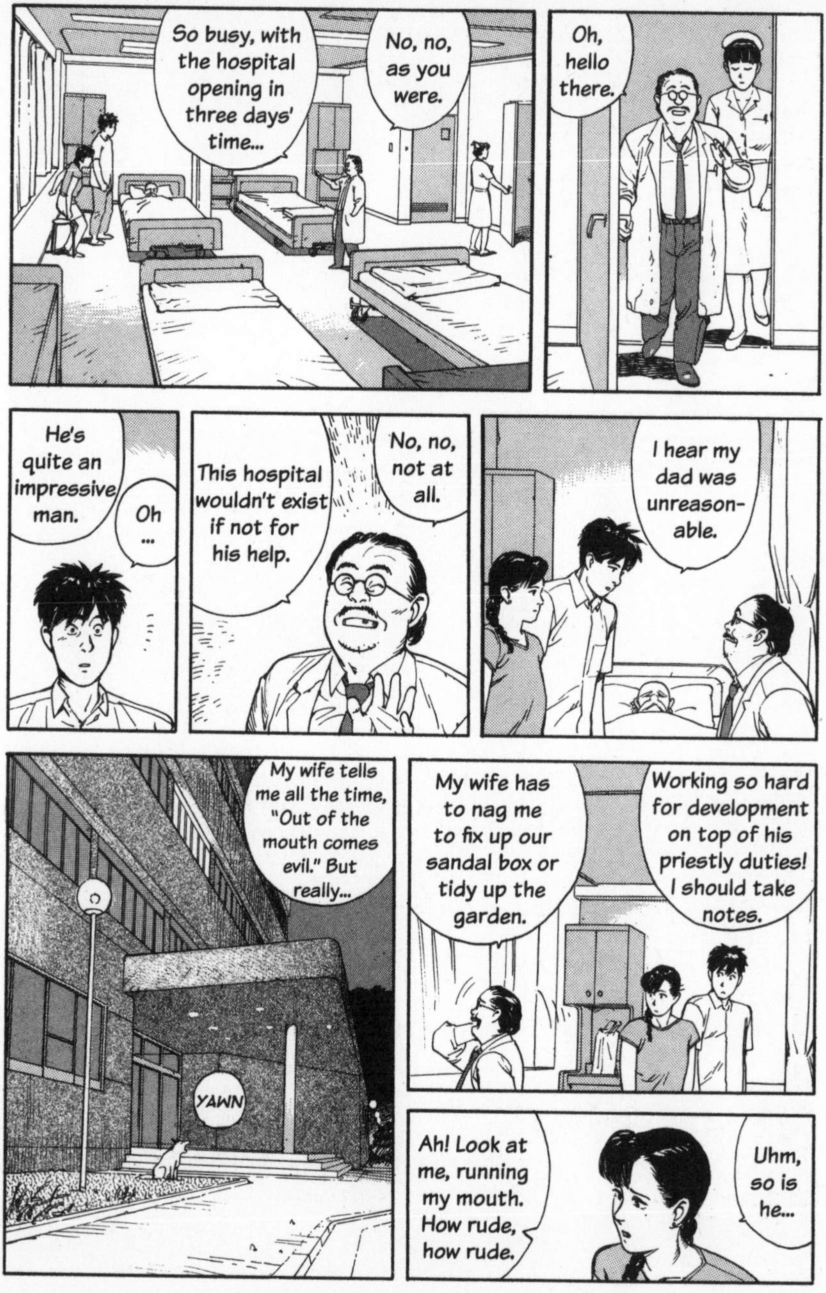
Oh, hello there.
No, no, as you were.
So busy, with the hospital opening in three days' time...
I hear my dad was unreason-able.
No, no, not at all.
This hospital wouldn't exist if not for his help.
Oh ...
He's quite an impressive man.
Working so hard for development on top of his priestly duties! I should take notes.
My wife has to nag me to fix up our sandal box or tidy up the garden.
Uhm, so is he...
Ah! Look at me, running my mouth. How rude, how rude.
My wife tells me all the time, "Out of the mouth comes evil." But really...
YAWN

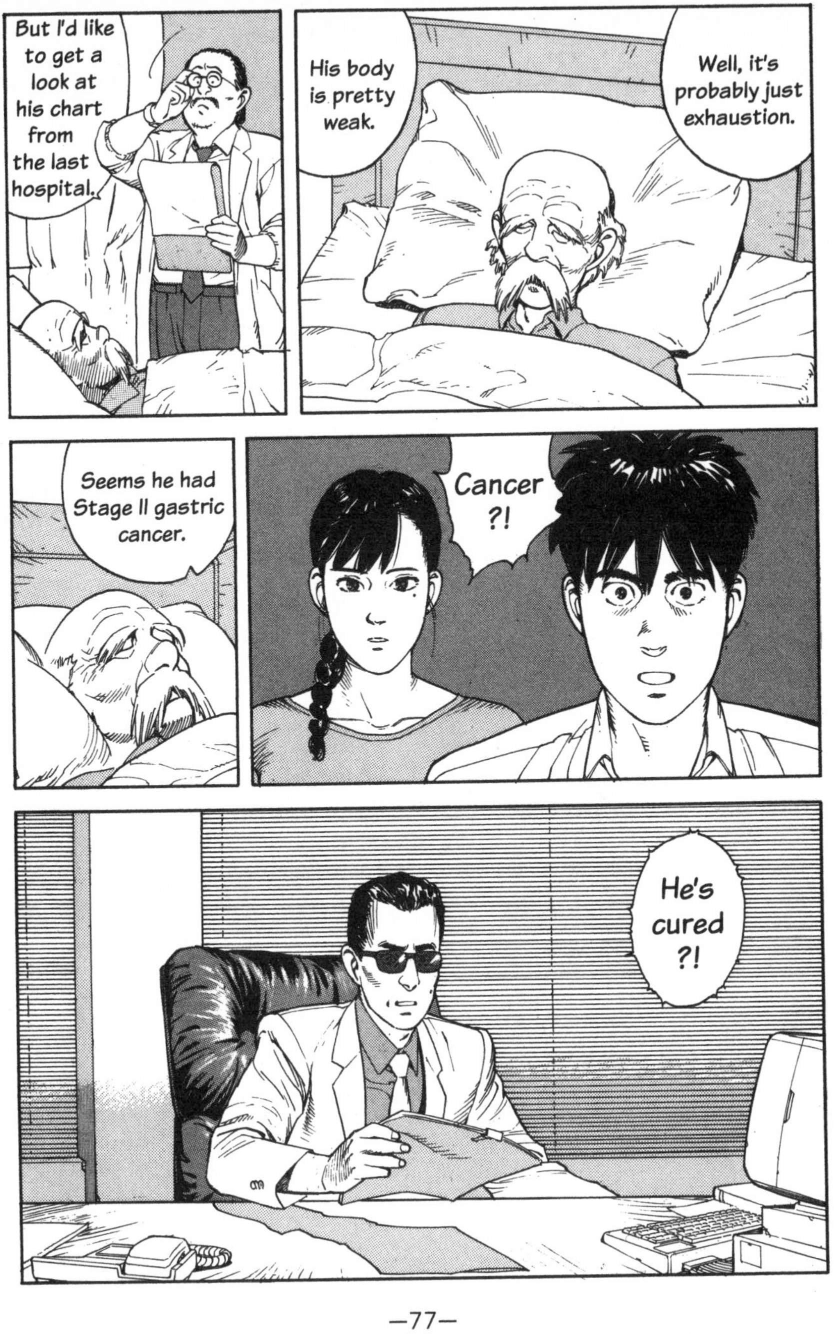
Well, it's probably just exhaustion.
His body is pretty weak.
But I'd like to get a look at his chart from the last hospital.
Cancer ?!
Seems he had Stage II gastric cancer.
He's cured ?!

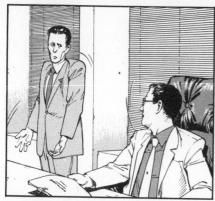

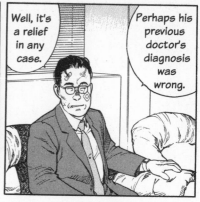

Perhaps his previous doctor's diagnosis was wrong.
Well, it's a relief in any case.
It's so heartening for us locals to have a major hospital.
It's all thanks to your assistance, Mr. Ozaki.
It is, it is.

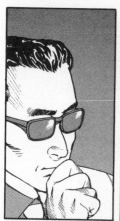

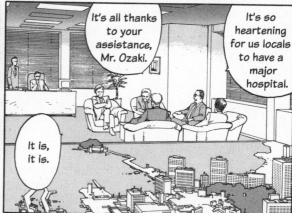

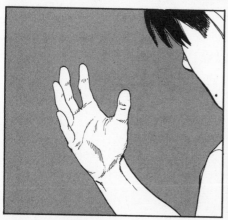

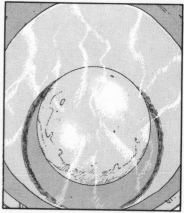

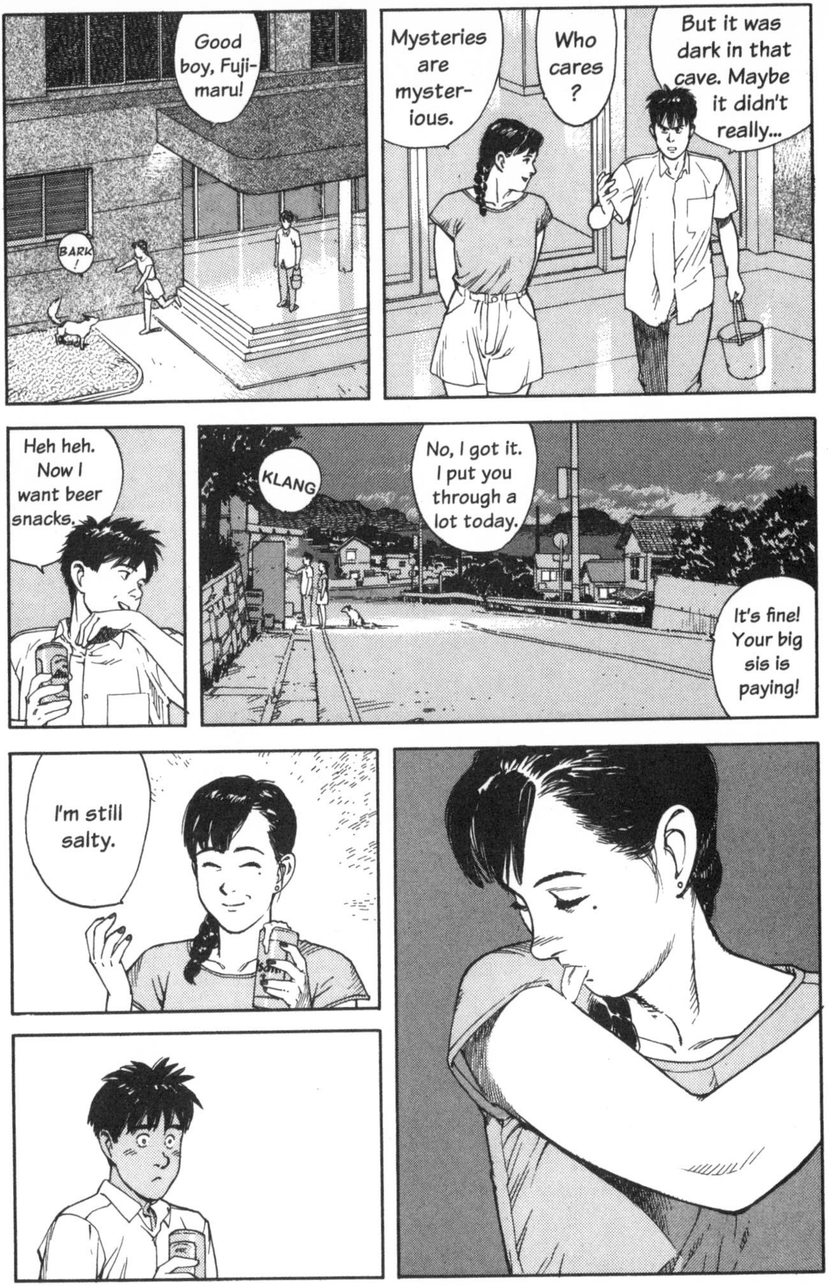
But it was dark in that cave. Maybe it didn't really...
Who cares?
Mysteries are mysterious.
Good boy, Fuji-maru!
BARK!
No, I got it. I put you through a lot today.
KLANG
It's fine! Your big sis is paying!
Heh heh. Now I want beer snacks.
I'm still salty.

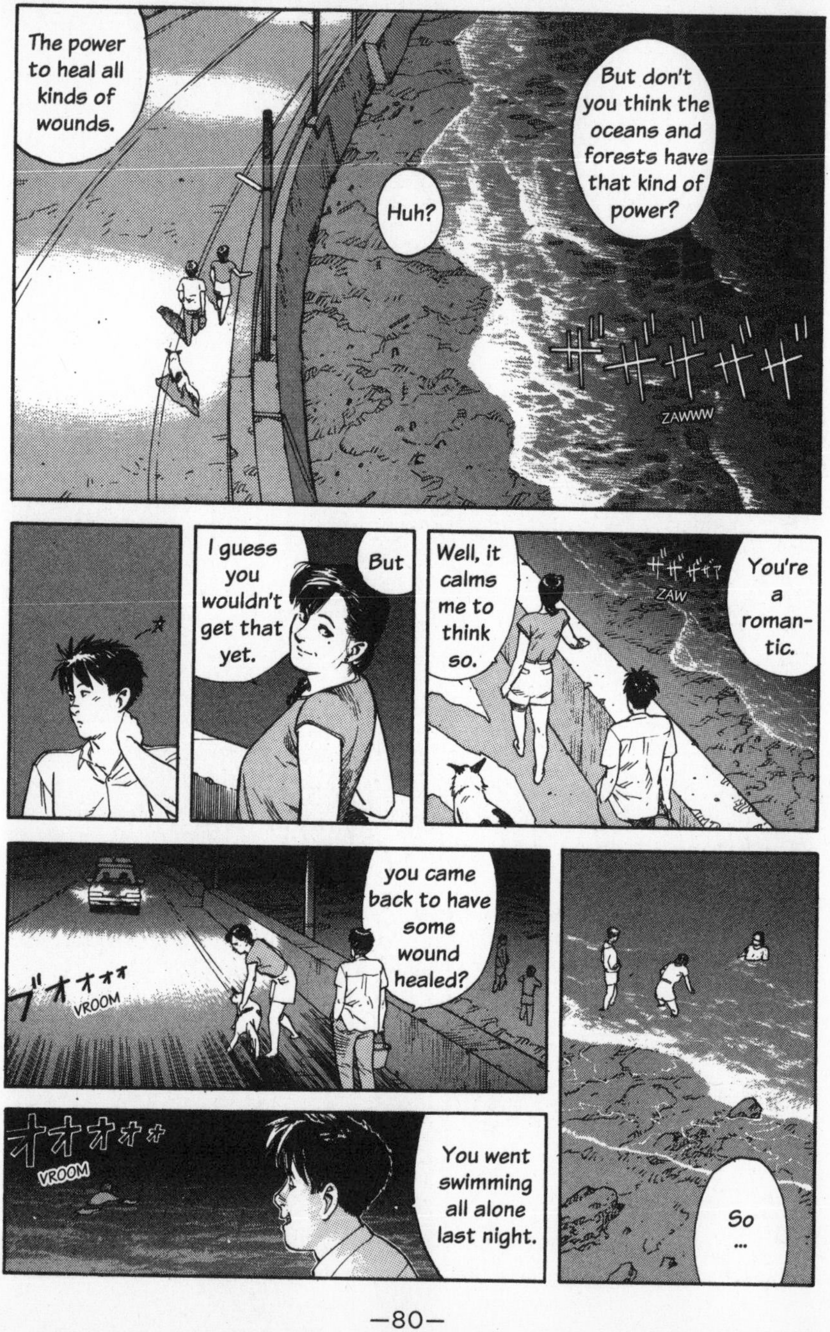
But don't you think the oceans and forests have that kind of power?
Huh?
The power to heal all kinds of wounds.
ザザザザザ
ZAWWW
You're a romantic.
ザザザァ
ZAW
Well, it calms me to think so.
But
I guess you wouldn't get that yet.
So ...
ブオオオオ
VROOM
you came back to have some wound healed?
オオオオォ
VROOM
You went swimming all alone last night.

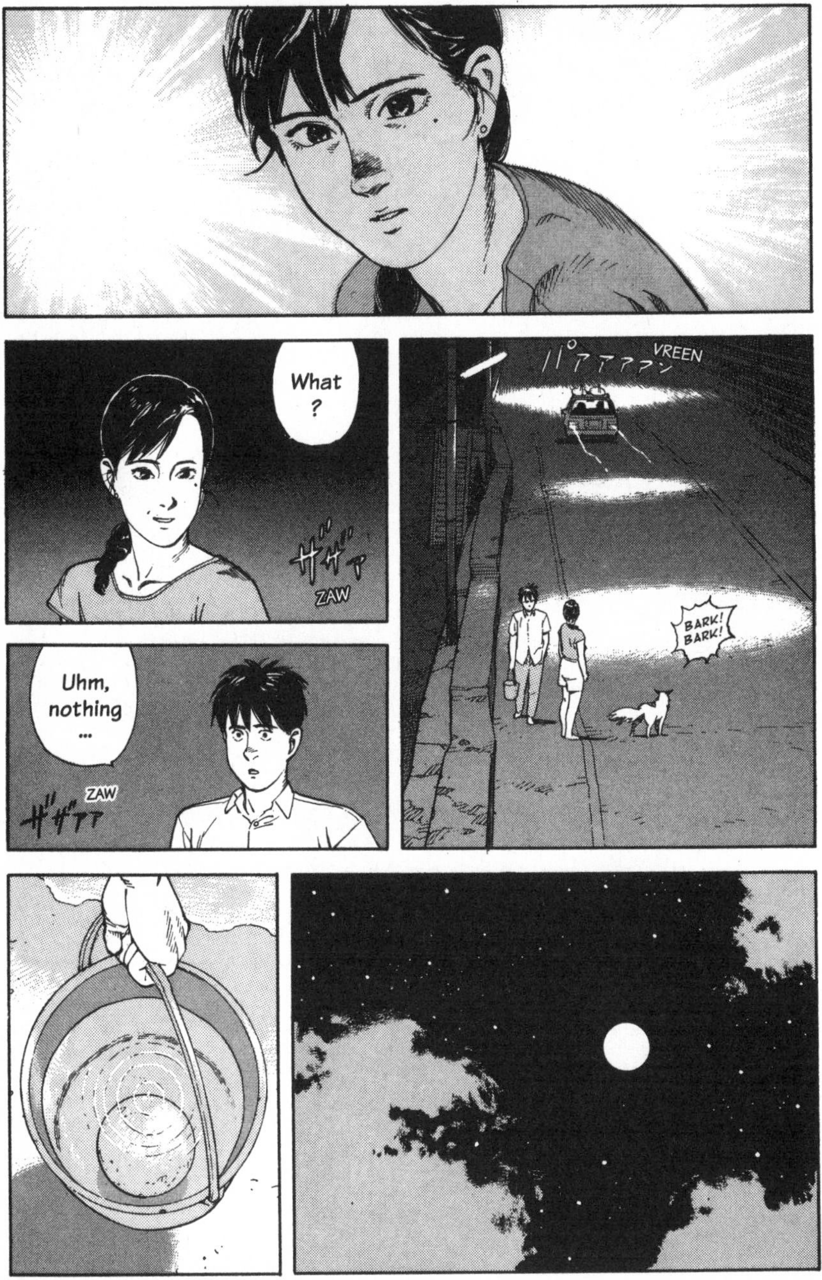
VREEN
BARK! BARK!
What?
ZAW
Uhm, nothing ...
ZAW

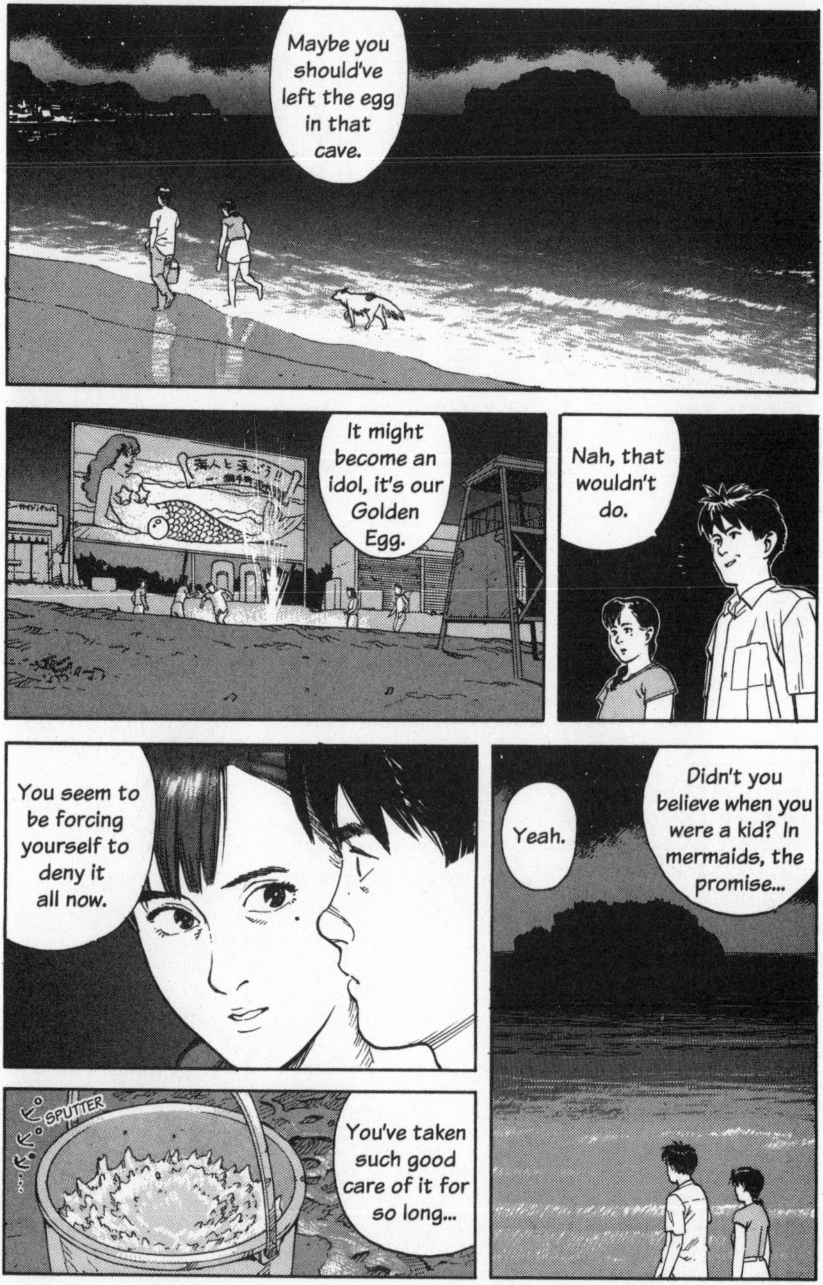
Maybe you should've left the egg in that cave.
Nah, that wouldn't do.
It might become an idol, it's our Golden Egg.
Didn't you believe when you were a kid? In mermaids, the promise...
Yeah.
You seem to be forcing yourself to deny it all now.
SPUTTER
You've taken such good care of it for so long...

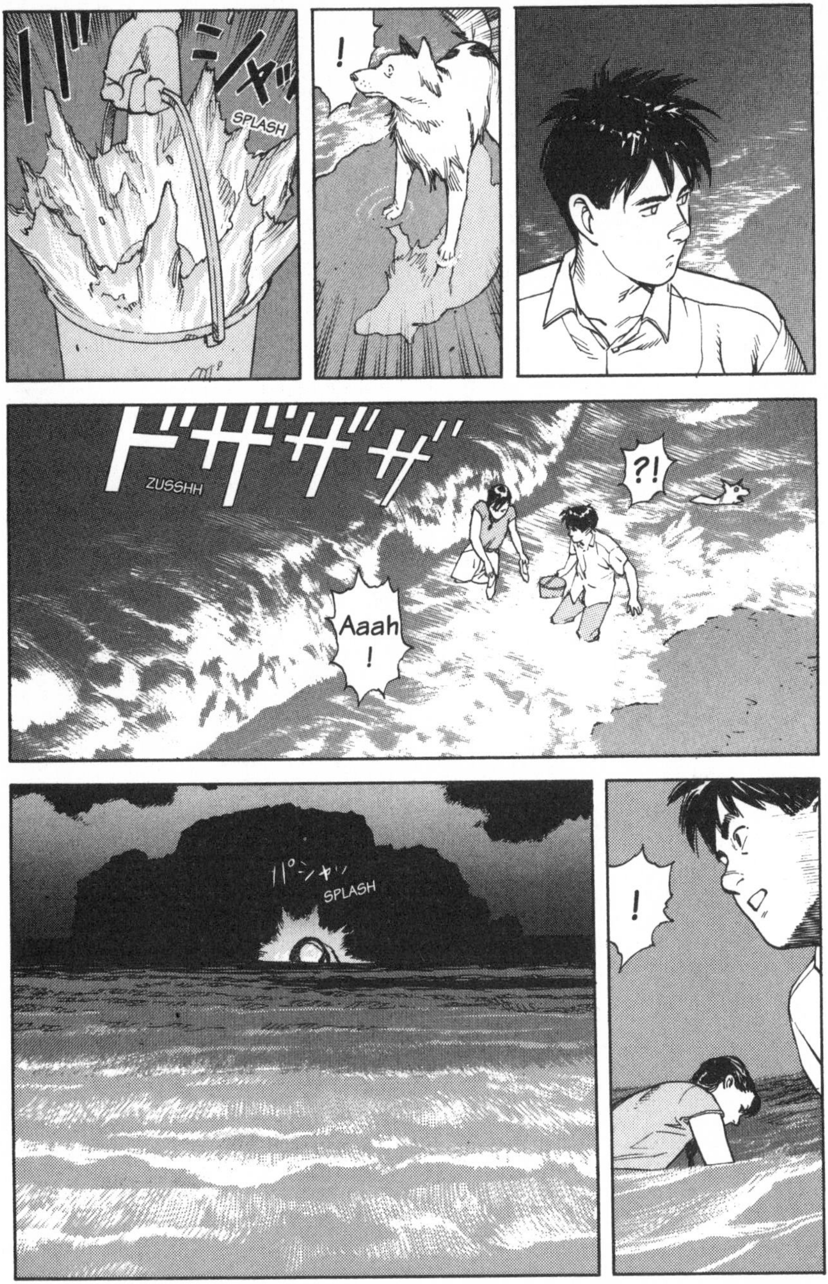
!
バシャッ
SPLASH
?!
ドザザザ
ZUSSHH
Aaah !
!
パシャッ
SPLASH

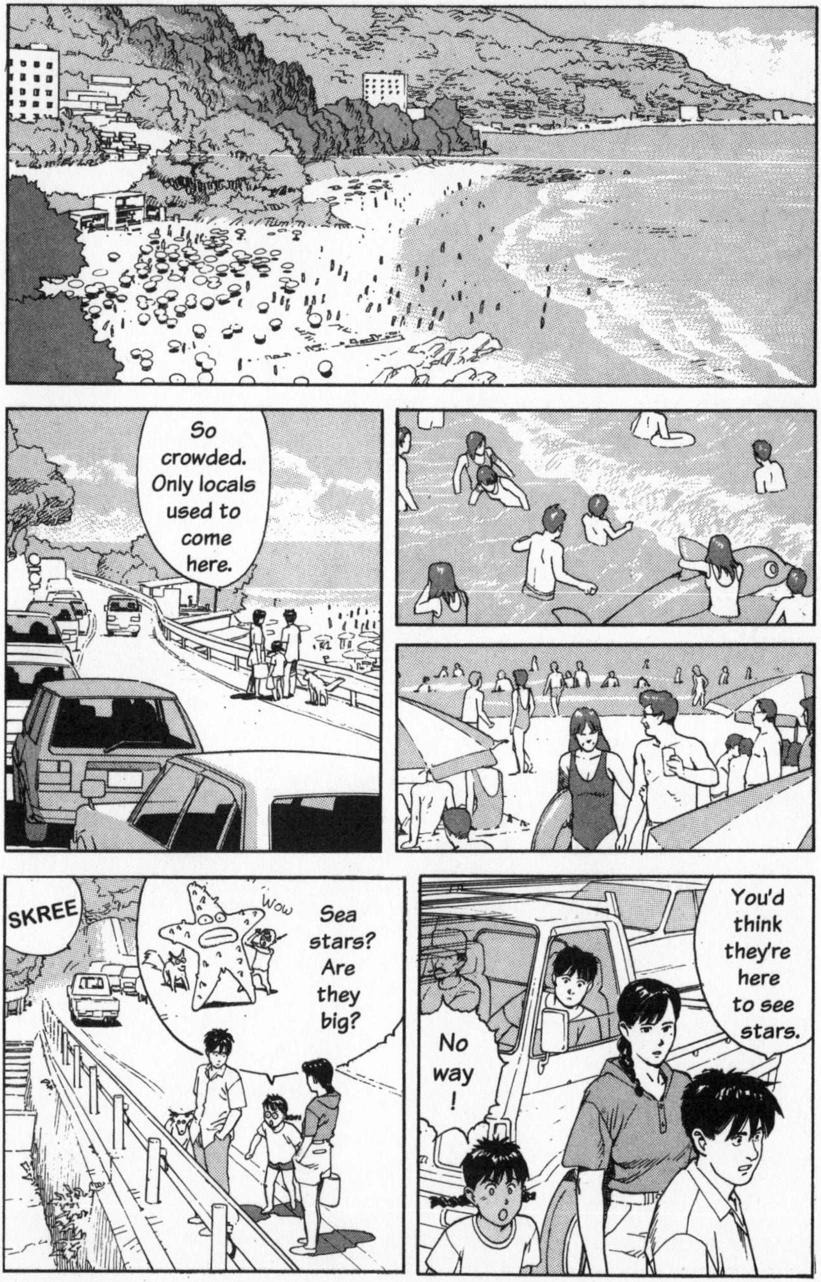
So crowded. Only locals used to come here.
You'd think they're here to see stars.
No way!
Sea stars? Are they big?
WOW
SKREE

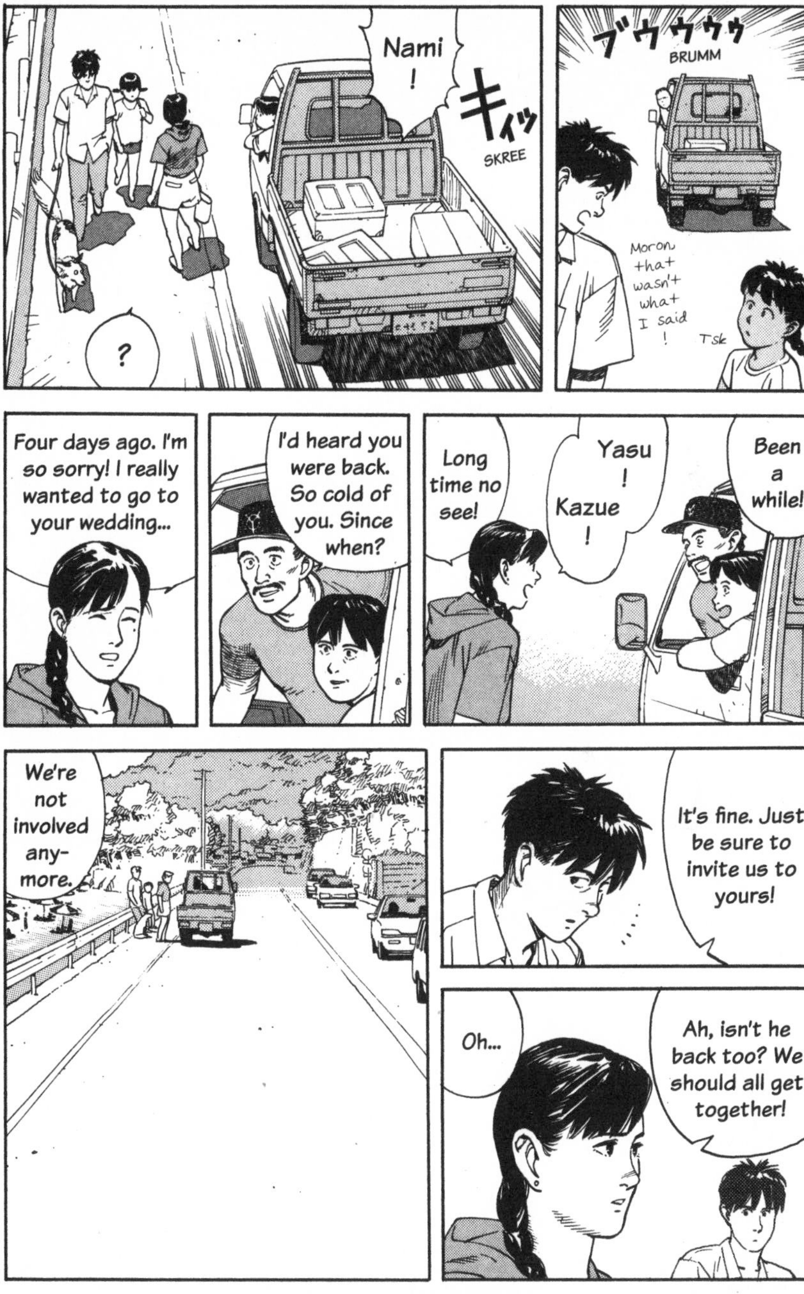
ブウウウウ
BRUMM
Moron, that wasn't what I said!
Tsk
Nami!
キイッ
SKREE
?
Been a while!
Yasu! Kazue!
Long time no see!
I'd heard you were back. So cold of you. Since when?
Four days ago. I'm so sorry! I really wanted to go to your wedding...
It's fine. Just be sure to invite us to yours!
Ah, isn't he back too? We should all get together!
Oh...
We're not involved anymore.

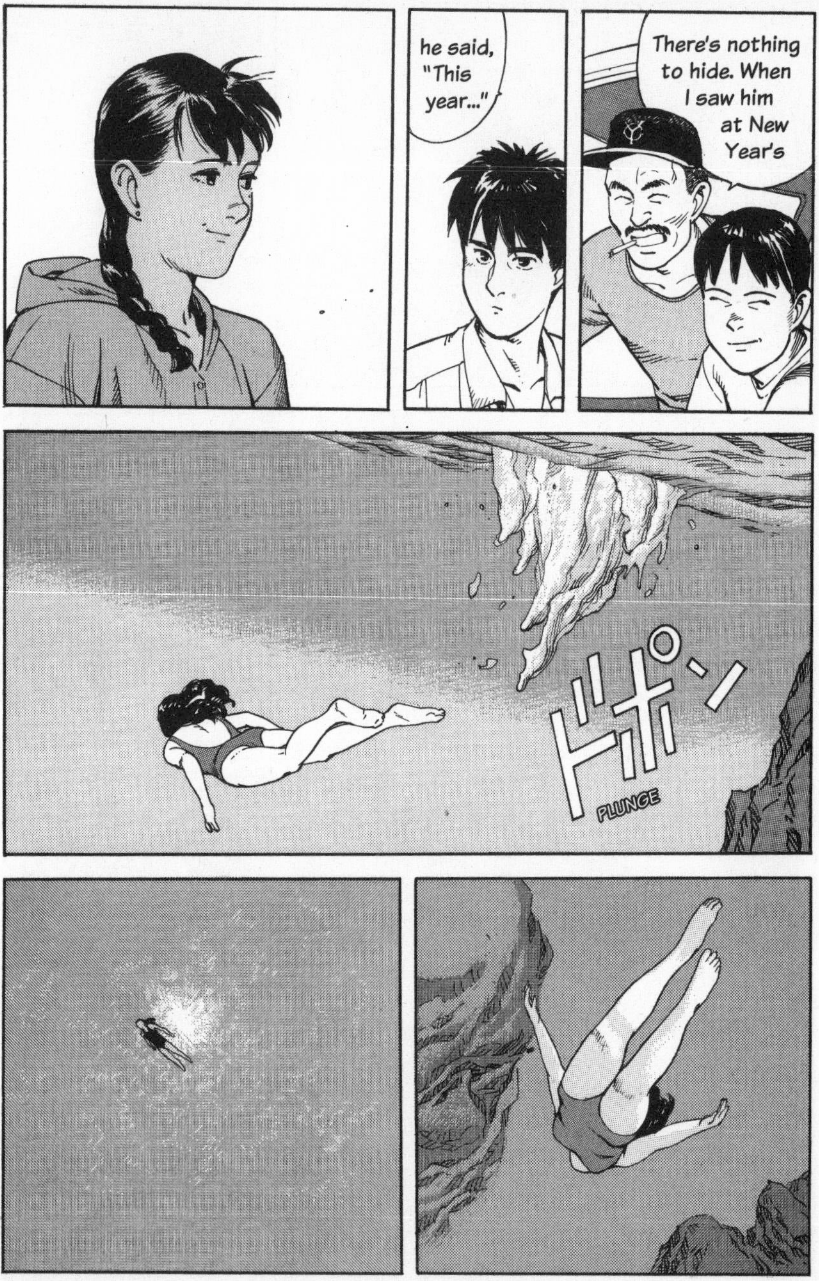
There's nothing to hide. When I saw him at New Year's
he said, "This year..."
ドポン
PLUNGE

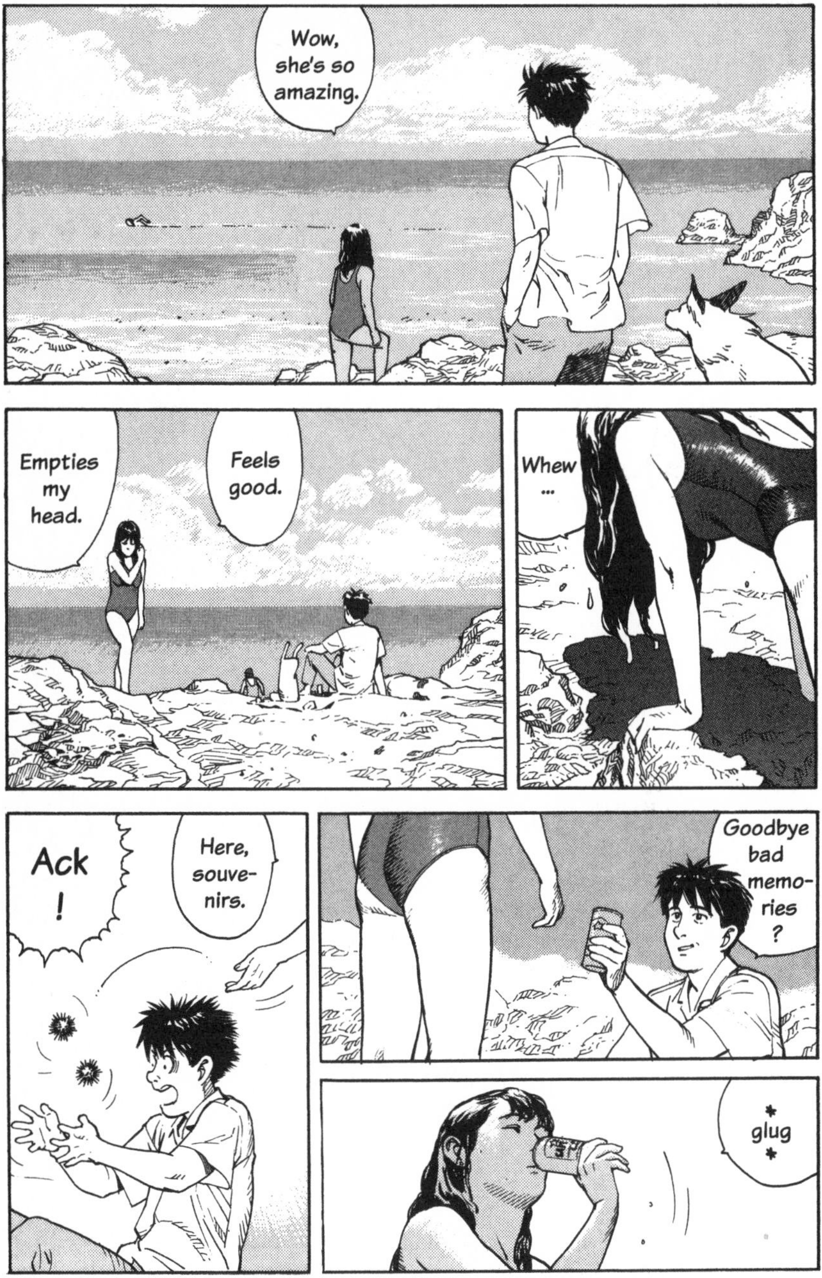
Wow, she's so amazing.
Whew ...
Feels good.
Empties my head.
Goodbye bad memories?
* glug *
Here, souvenirs.
Ack !

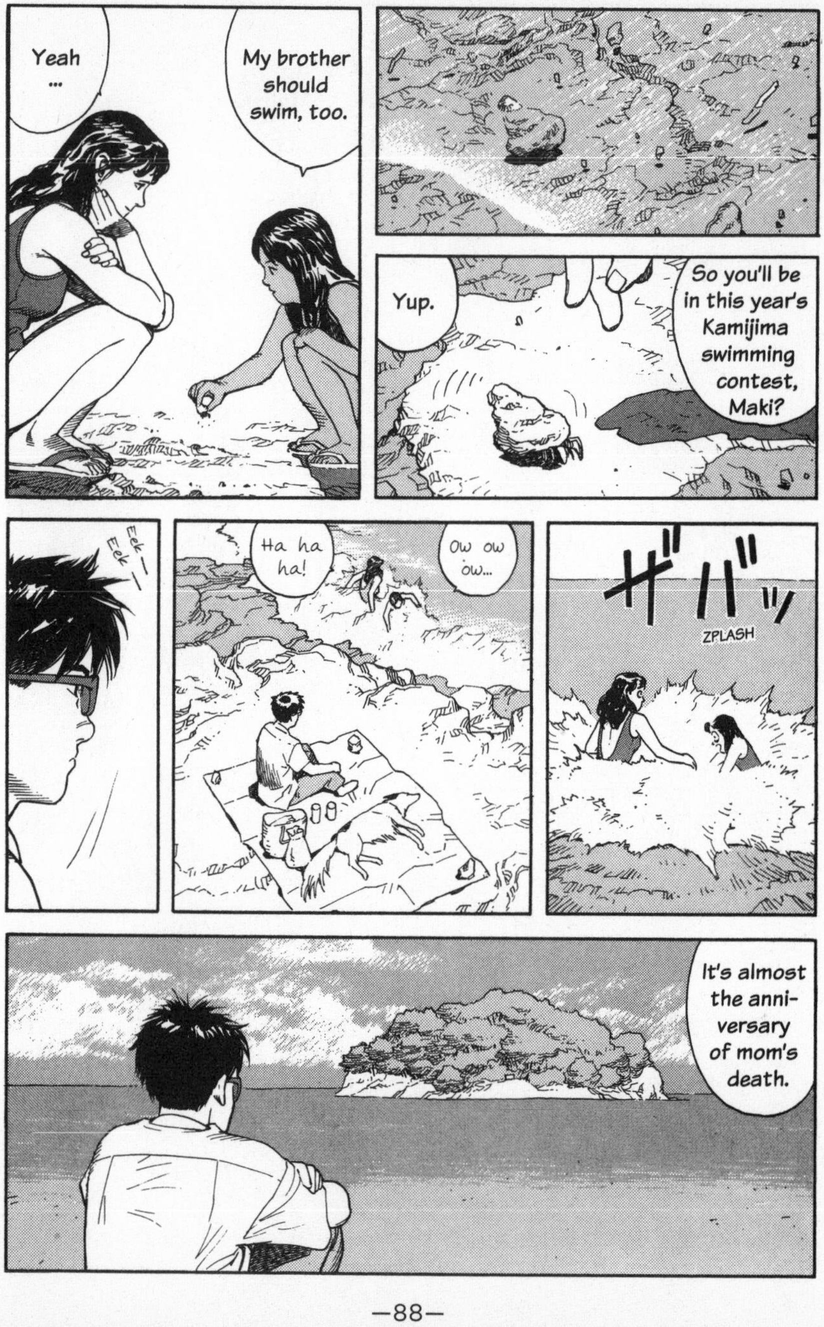
So you'll be in this year's Kamijima swimming contest, Maki?
Yup.
My brother should swim, too.
Yeah ...
ザバッ
ZPLASH
Ow ow ow...
Ha ha ha!
Eek — Eek —
It's almost the anni-versary of mom's death.

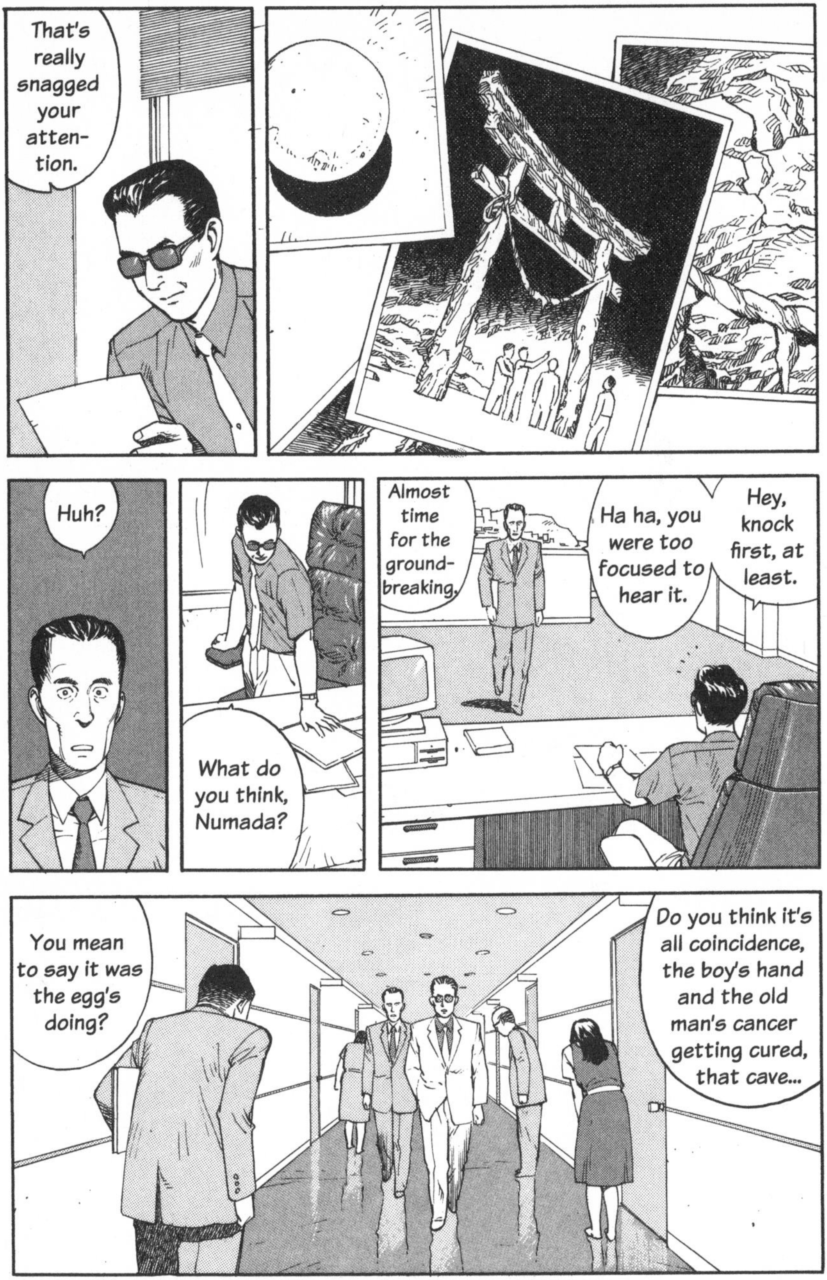
That's really snagged your attention.
Hey, knock first, at least.
Ha ha, you were too focused to hear it.
Almost time for the ground-breaking.
What do you think, Numada?
Huh?
Do you think it's all coincidence, the boy's hand and the old man's cancer getting cured, that cave...
You mean to say it was the egg's doing?

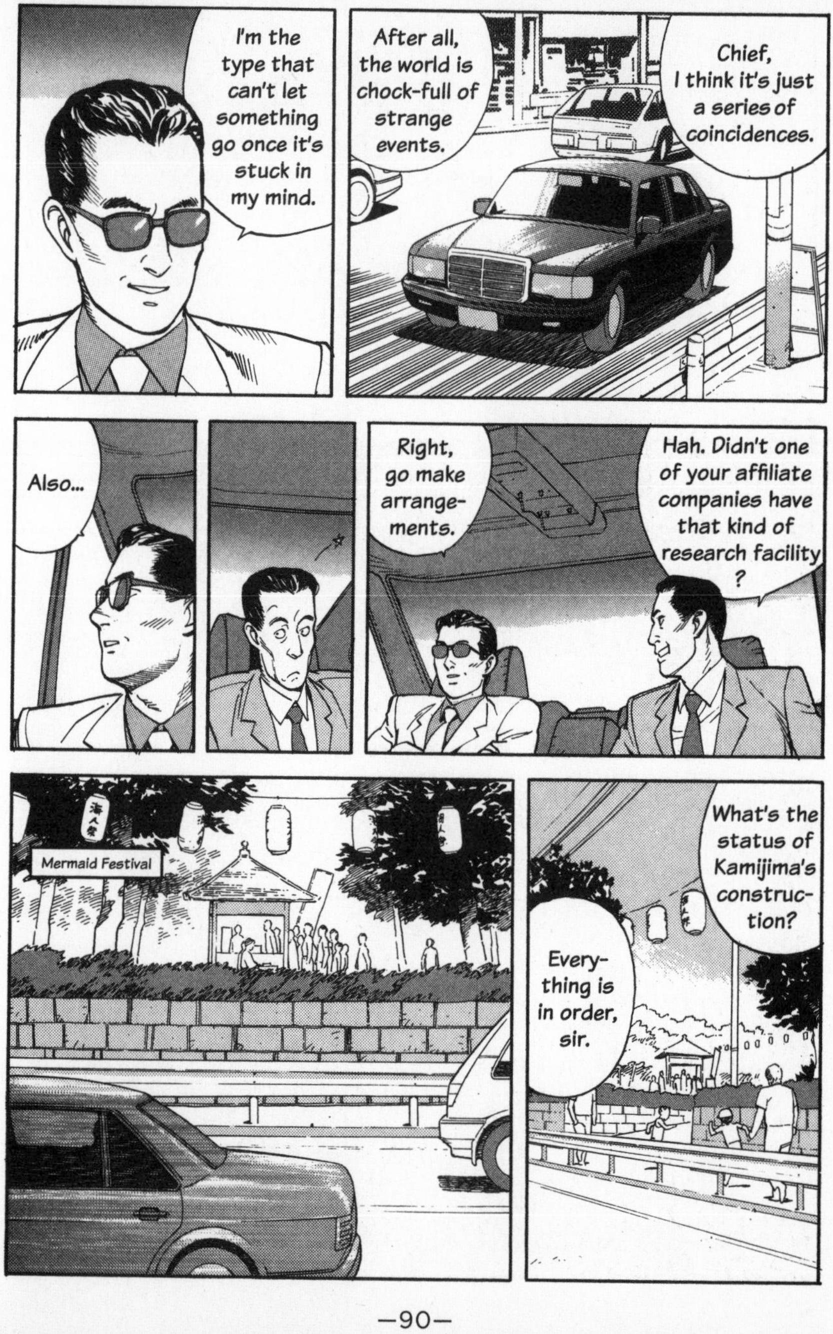
Chief, I think it's just a series of coincidences.
After all, the world is chock-full of strange events.
I'm the type that can't let something go once it's stuck in my mind.
Hah. Didn't one of your affiliate companies have that kind of research facility?
Right, go make arrangements.
Also...
What's the status of Kamijima's construction?
Every-thing is in order, sir.
Mermaid Festival

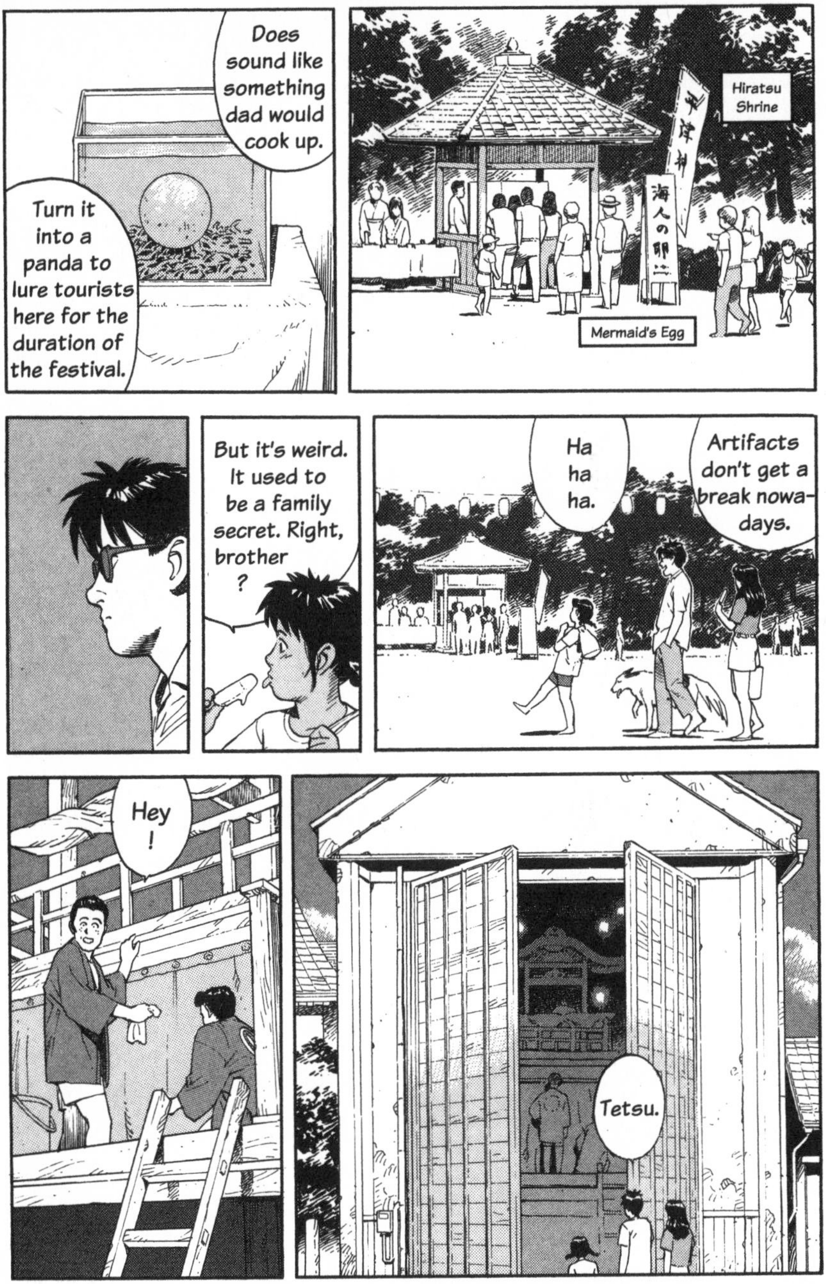
Hiratsu Shrine
Mermaid's Egg
Does sound like something dad would cook up.
Turn it into a panda to lure tourists here for the duration of the festival.
Artifacts don't get a break nowa-days.
Ha ha ha.
But it's weird. It used to be a family secret. Right, brother?
Tetsu.
Hey!

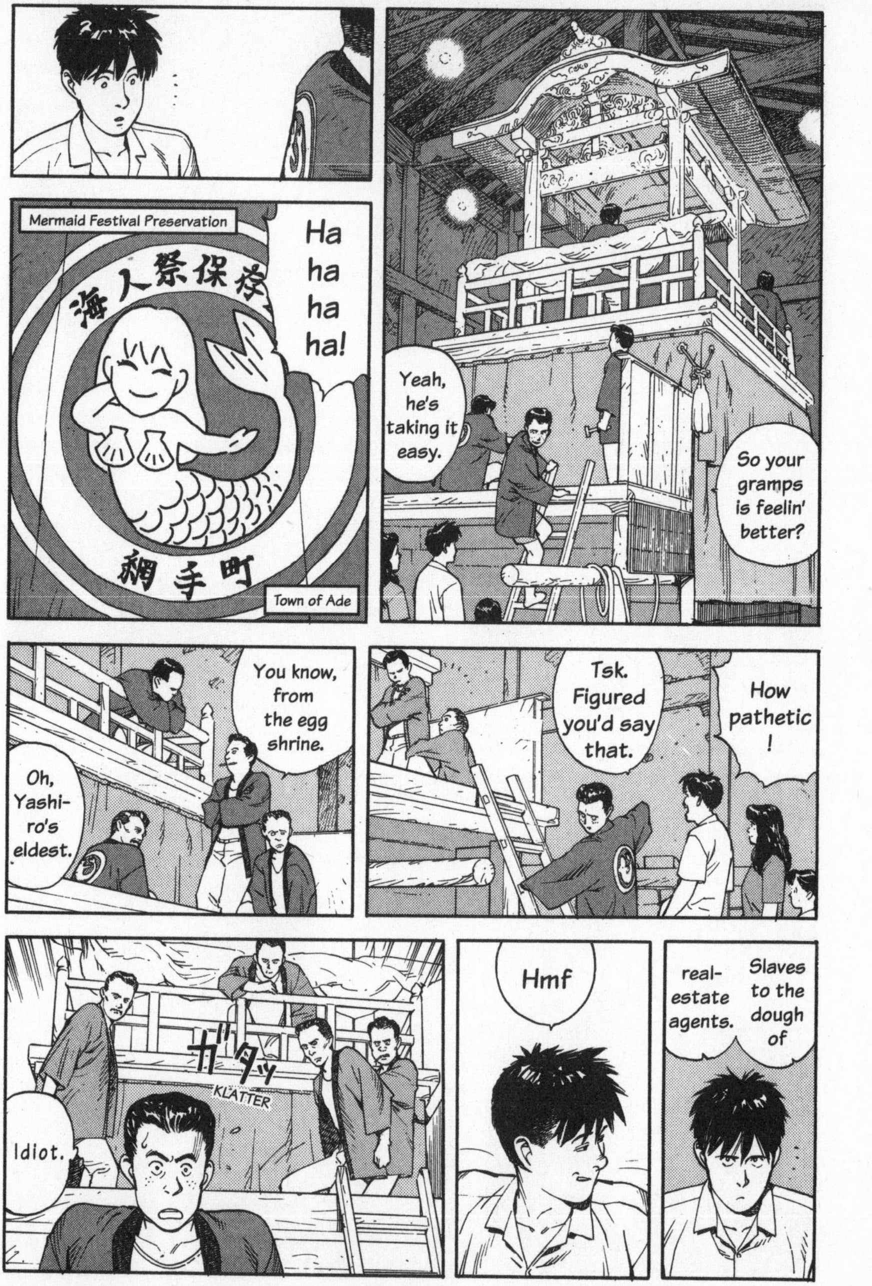

So your gramps is feelin' better?
Yeah, he's taking it easy.
......
Ha ha ha ha!
Mermaid Festival Preservation
海人祭保存
網手町
Town of Ade
How pathetic!
Tsk. Figured you'd say that.
You know, from the egg shrine.
Oh, Yashiro's eldest.
Slaves to the dough of real-estate agents.
Hmf
ガタッ
KLATTER
Idiot.

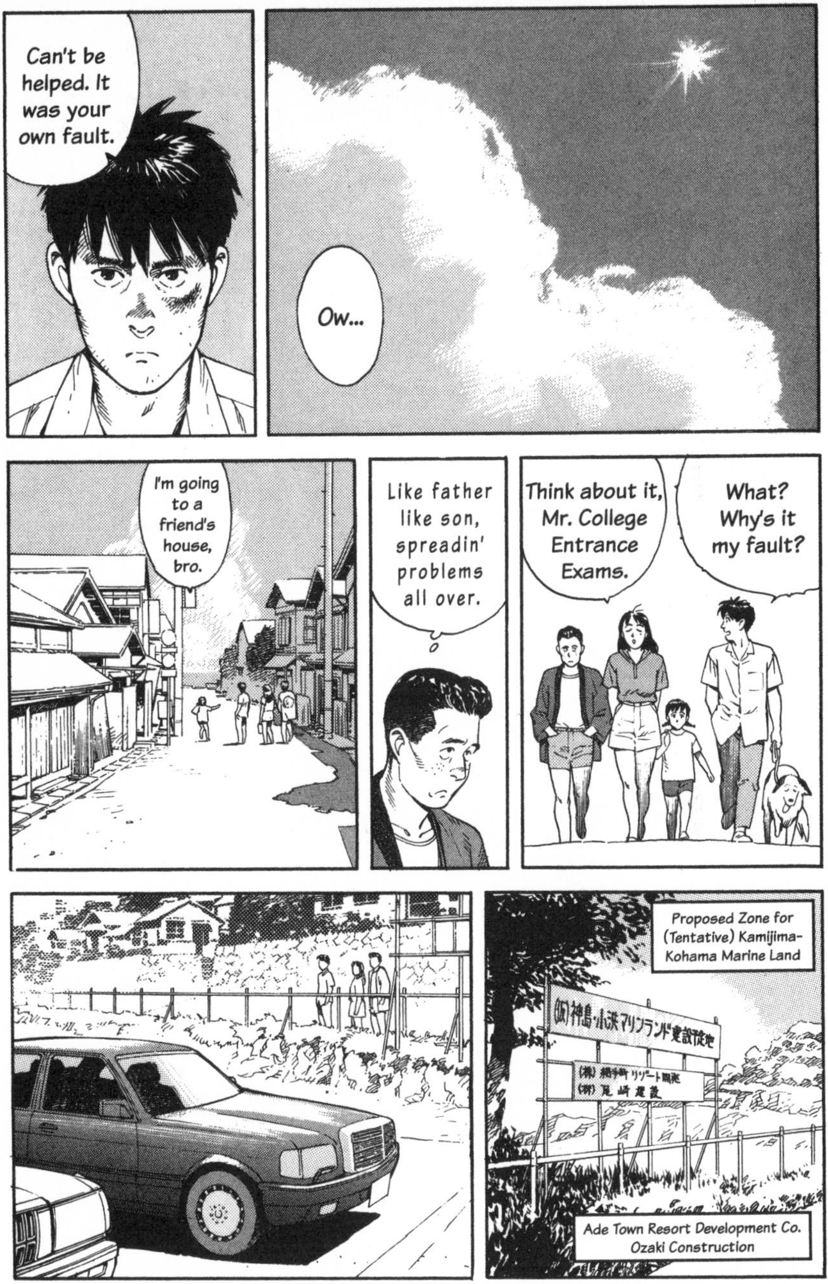
Ow...
Can't be helped. It was your own fault.
What? Why's it my fault?
Think about it, Mr. College Entrance Exams.
Like father like son, spreadin' problems all over.
I'm going to a friend's house, bro.
Proposed Zone for (Tentative) Kamijima-Kohama Marine Land
(仮)神島・小浜マリンランド建設予定地
Ade Town Resort Development Co.
Ozaki Construction

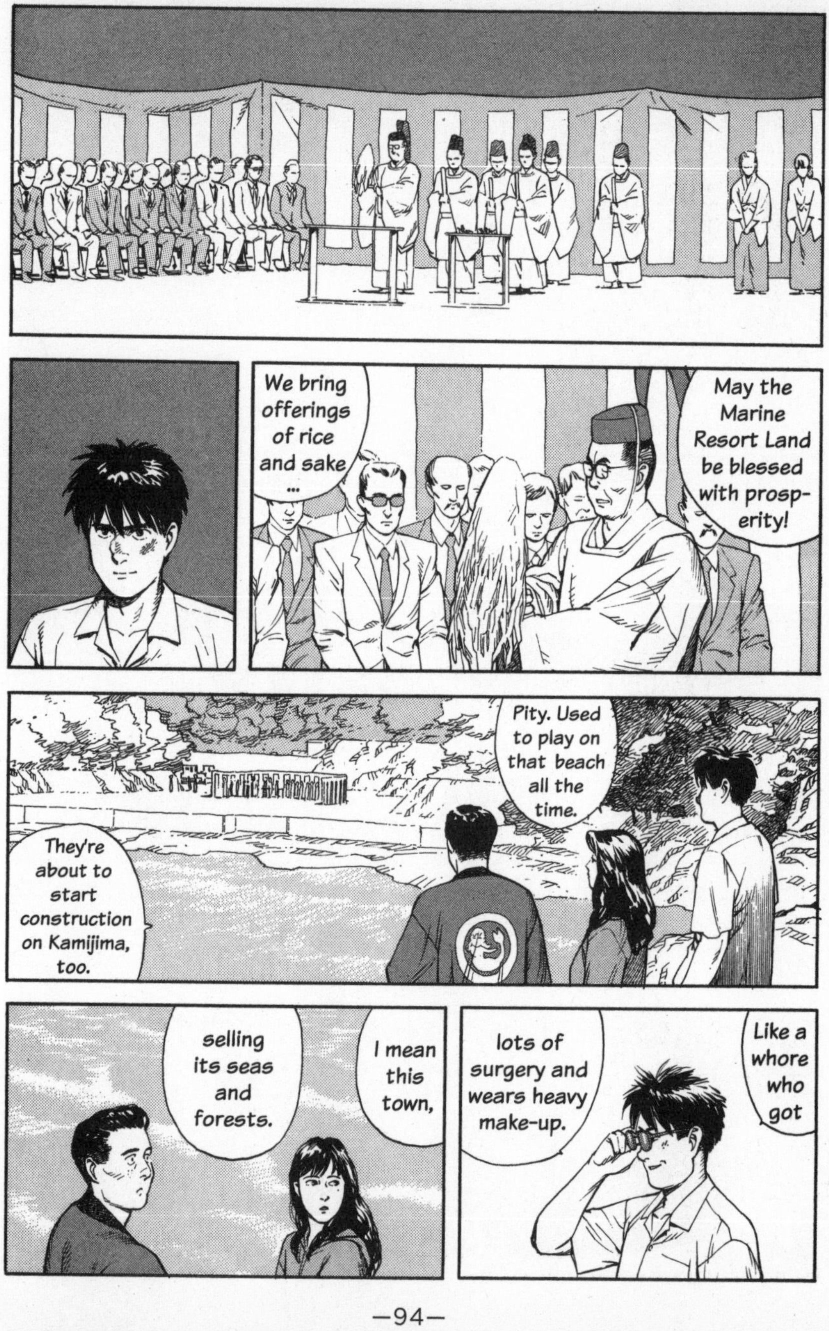
May the Marine Resort Land be blessed with prosperity!
We bring offerings of rice and sake ...
Pity. Used to play on that beach all the time.
They're about to start construction on Kamijima, too.
Like a whore who got
lots of surgery and wears heavy make-up.
I mean this town,
selling its seas and forests.

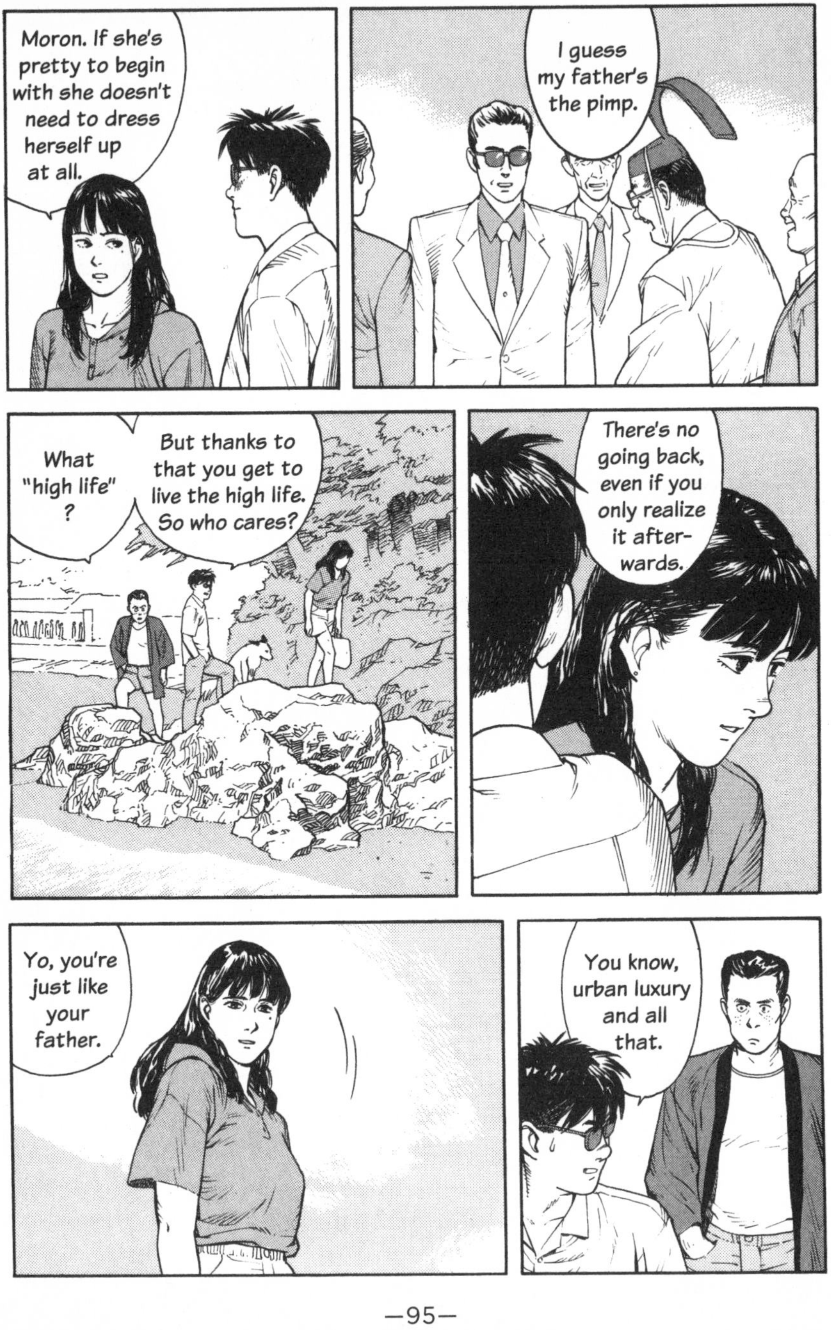
I guess my father's the pimp.
Moron. If she's pretty to begin with she doesn't need to dress herself up at all.
There's no going back, even if you only realize it after-wards.
But thanks to that you get to live the high life. So who cares?
What "high life"?
You know, urban luxury and all that.
Yo, you're just like your father.

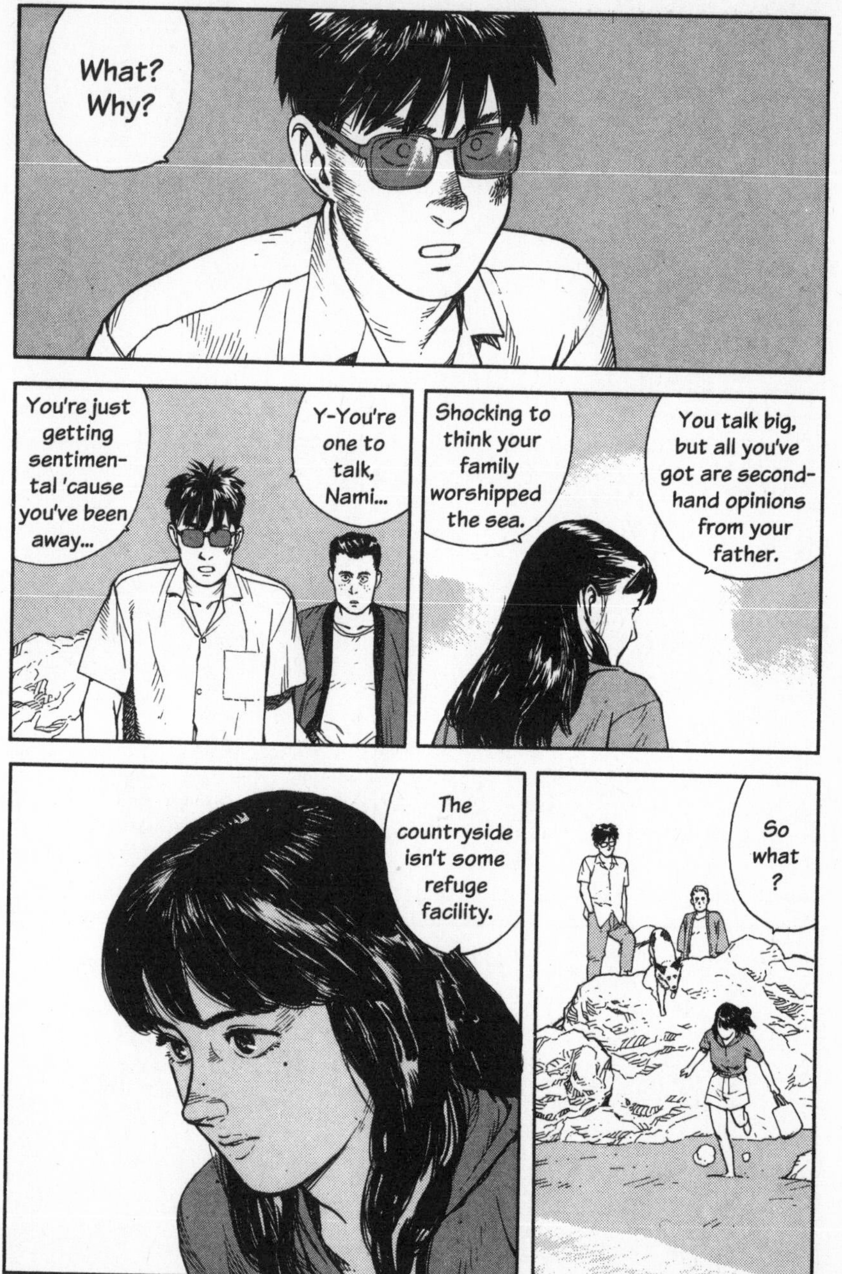
What? Why?
You talk big, but all you've got are second-hand opinions from your father.
Shocking to think your family worshipped the sea.
Y-You're one to talk, Nami...
You're just getting sentimental 'cause you've been away...
So what ?
The countryside isn't some refuge facility.

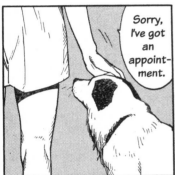

Sorry,
I've got
an
appoint-
ment.

Uh
...

I don't get
what just
happened
but I think
it's your
fault.

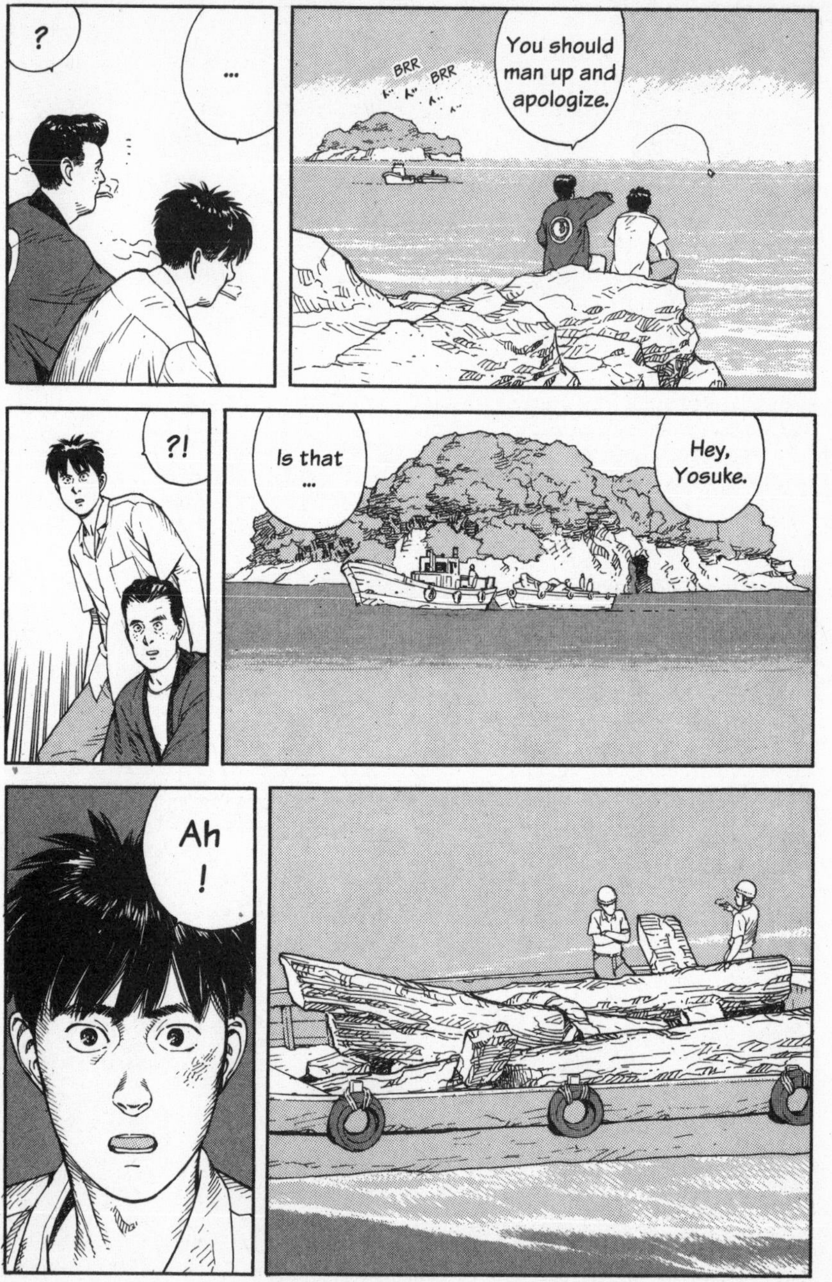
You should man up and apologize.
BRR
BRR
...
?
Hey, Yosuke.
Is that ...
?!
Ah !

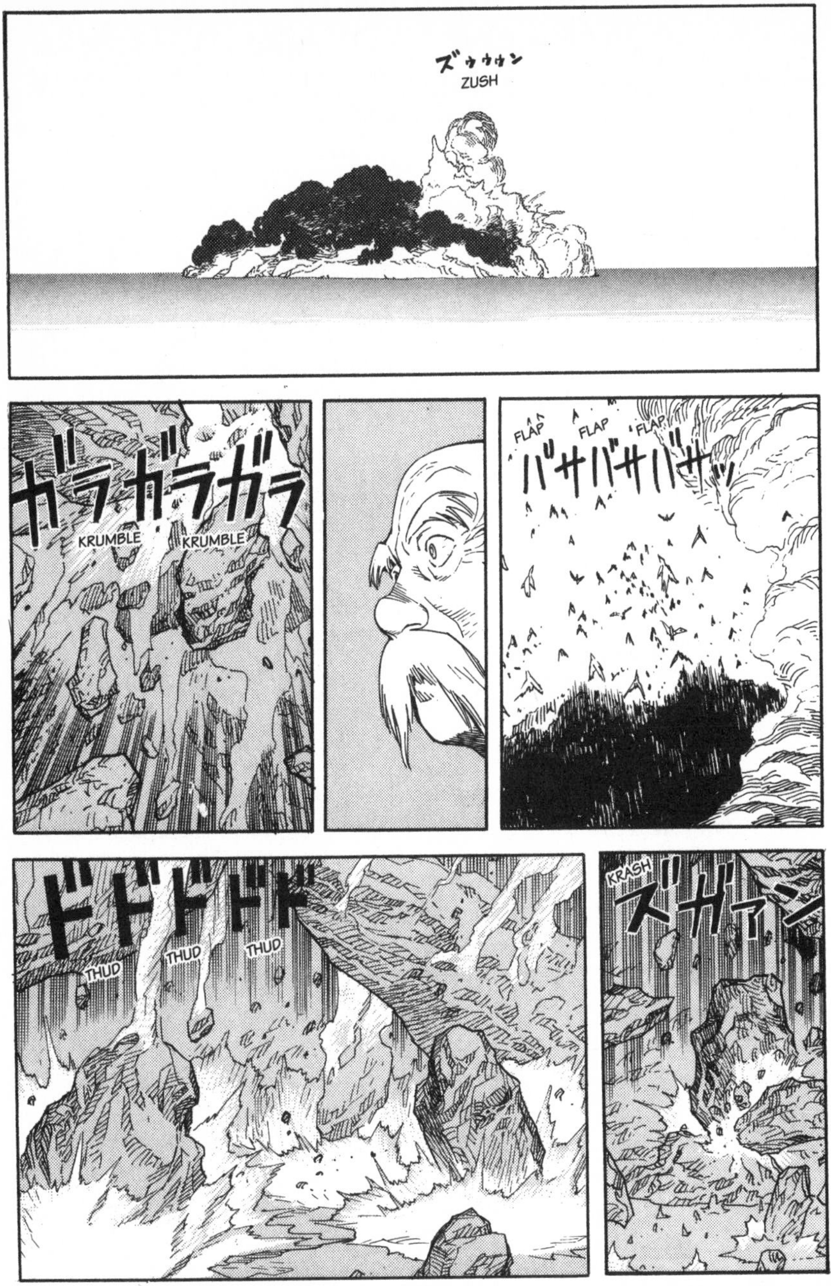
ズゥゥゥン
ZUSH
バサバサバサッ
FLAP FLAP FLAP
ガラガラガラ
KRUMBLE KRUMBLE
ズガァン
KRASH
ドドドドド
THUD THUD THUD

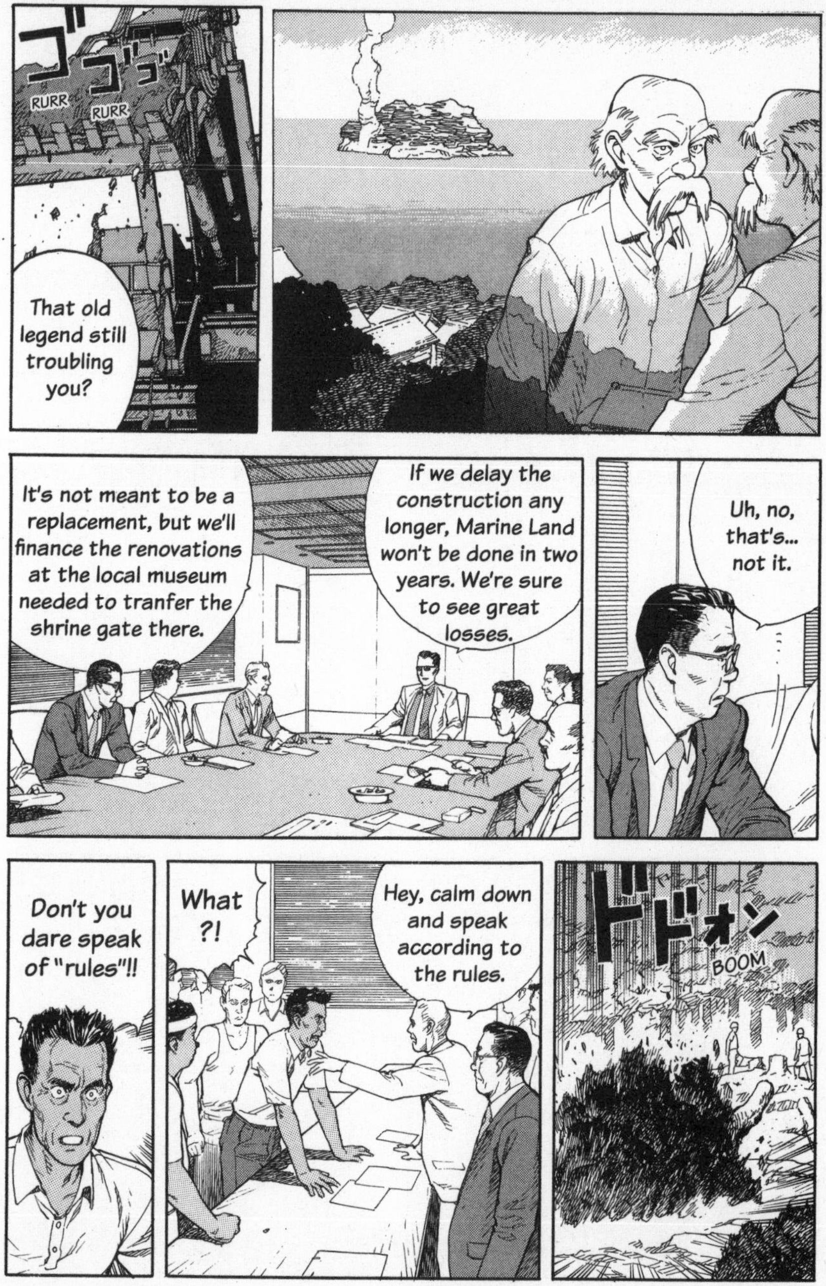
ゴゴゴ
RURR
RURR
That old legend still troubling you?
Uh, no, that's... not it.
If we delay the construction any longer, Marine Land won't be done in two years. We're sure to see great losses.
It's not meant to be a replacement, but we'll finance the renovations at the local museum needed to tranfer the shrine gate there.
ドドォン
BOOM
Hey, calm down and speak according to the rules.
What ?!
Don't you dare speak of "rules"!!

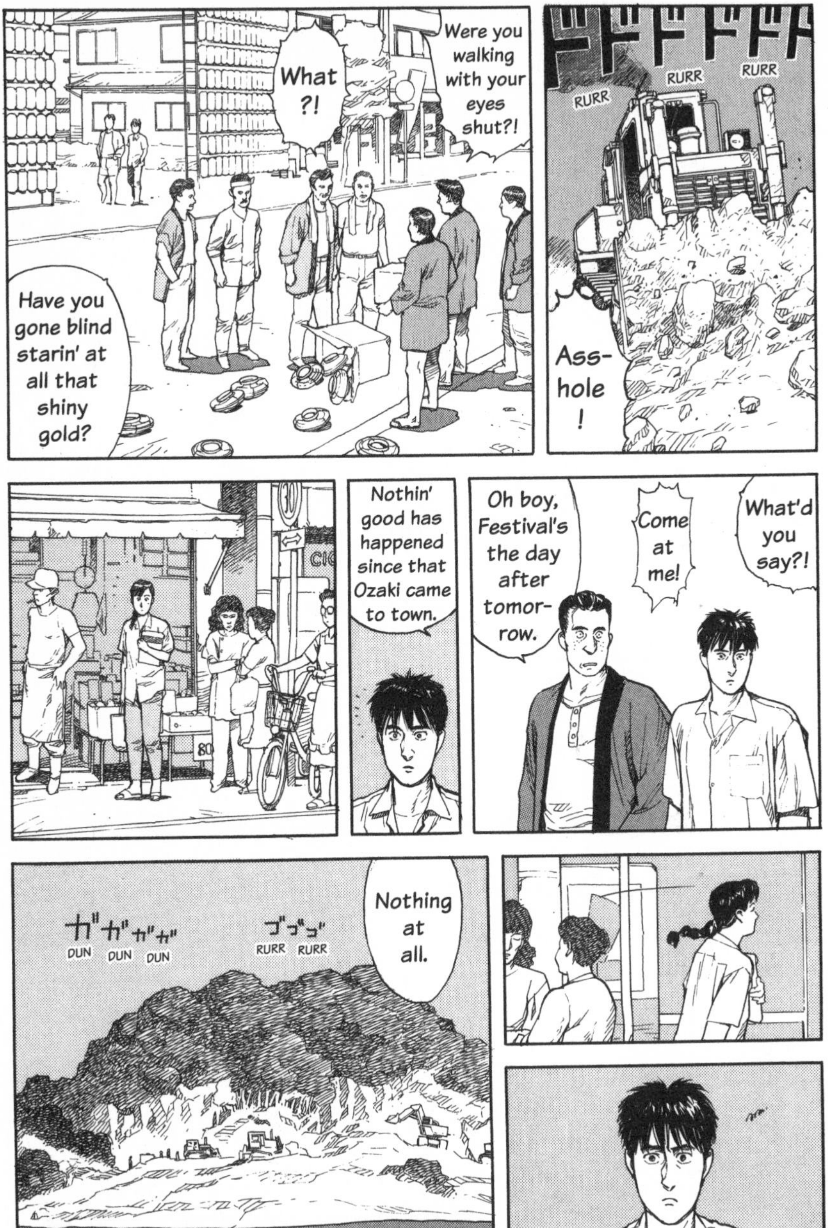
ドドドドド
RURR
RURR
RURR
Ass-hole!
Were you walking with your eyes shut?!
What?!
Have you gone blind starin' at all that shiny gold?
What'd you say?!
Come at me!
Oh boy, Festival's the day after tomorrow.
Nothin' good has happened since that Ozaki came to town.
80
Nothing at all.
ゴゴゴ
RURR RURR
ガガガガ
DUN DUN DUN

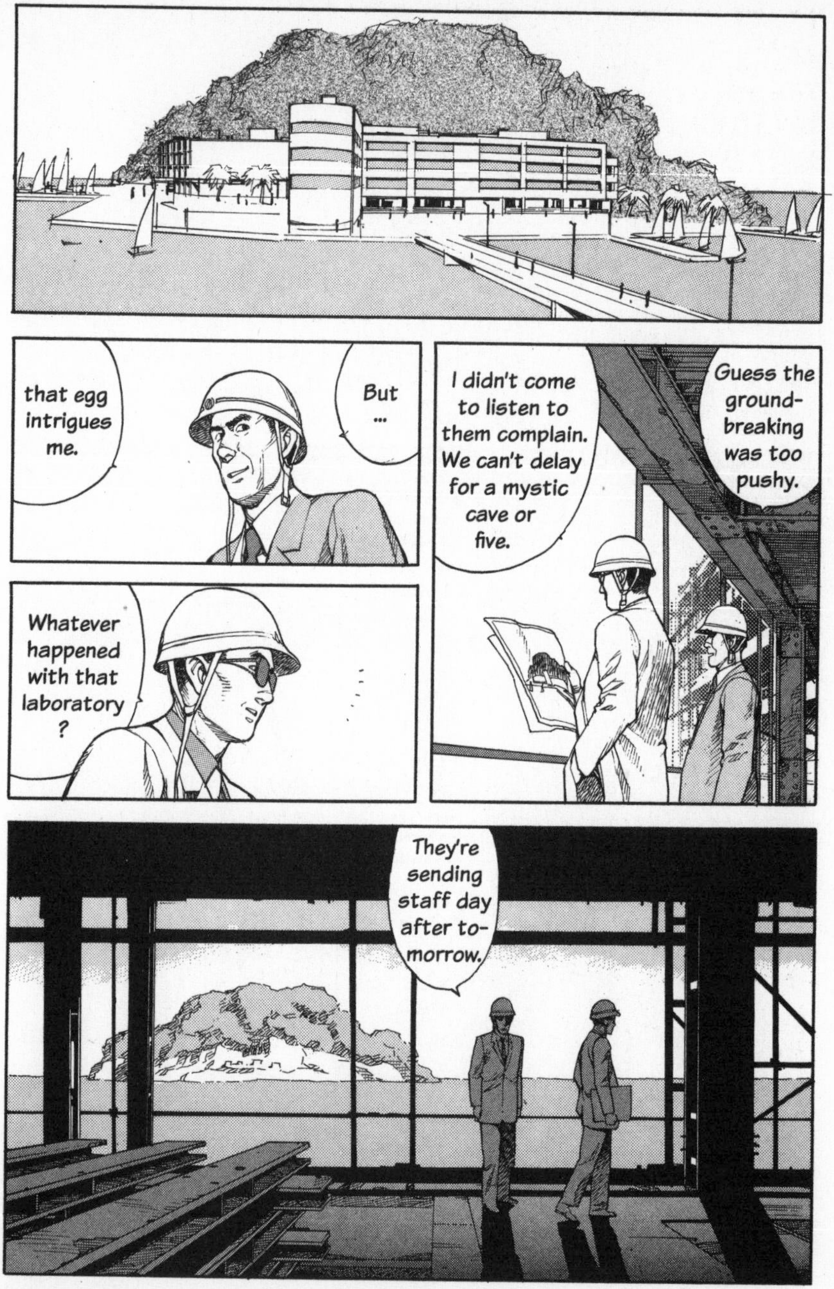
Guess the ground-breaking was too pushy.
I didn't come to listen to them complain. We can't delay for a mystic cave or five.
But ...
that egg intrigues me.
Whatever happened with that laboratory ?
They're sending staff day after to-morrow.

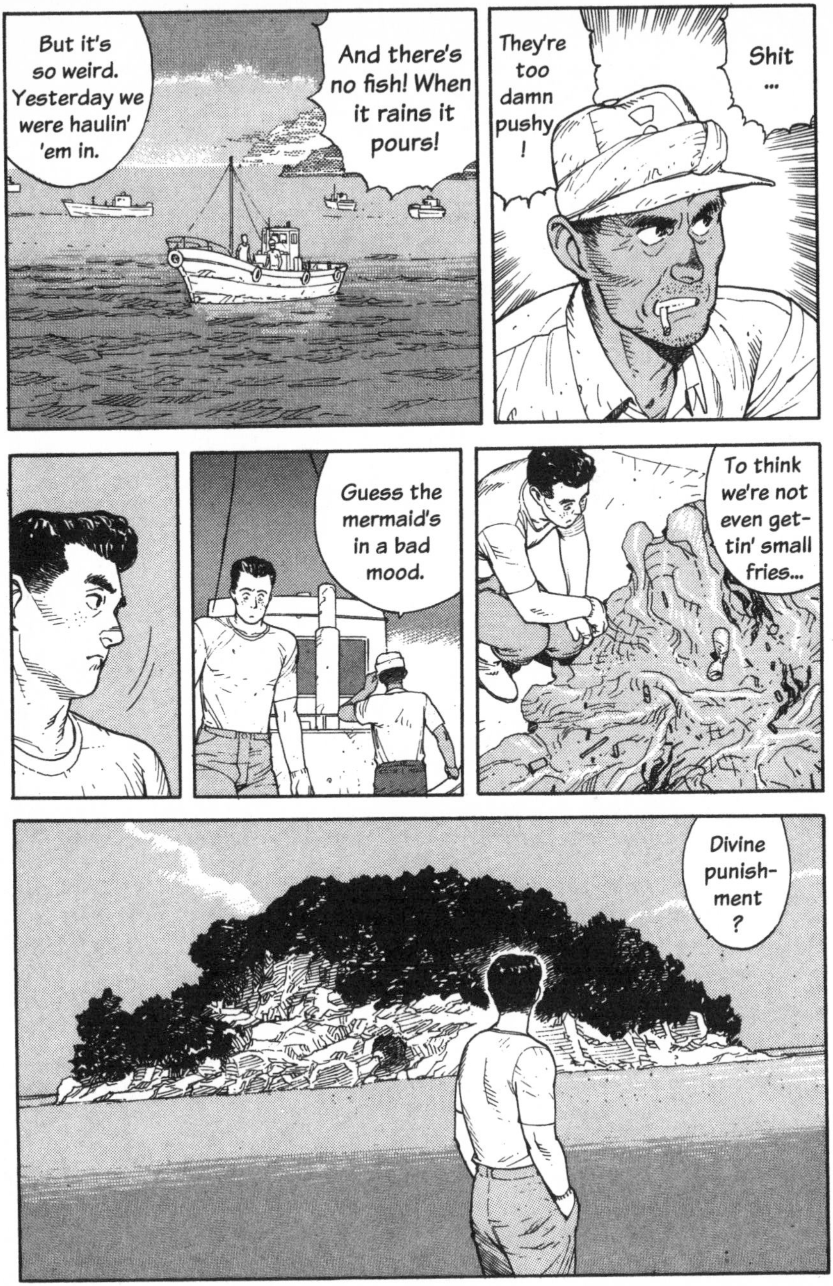
Shit ...
They're too damn pushy !
And there's no fish! When it rains it pours!
But it's so weird. Yesterday we were haulin' 'em in.
To think we're not even get-tin' small fries...
Guess the mermaid's in a bad mood.
Divine punish-ment ?

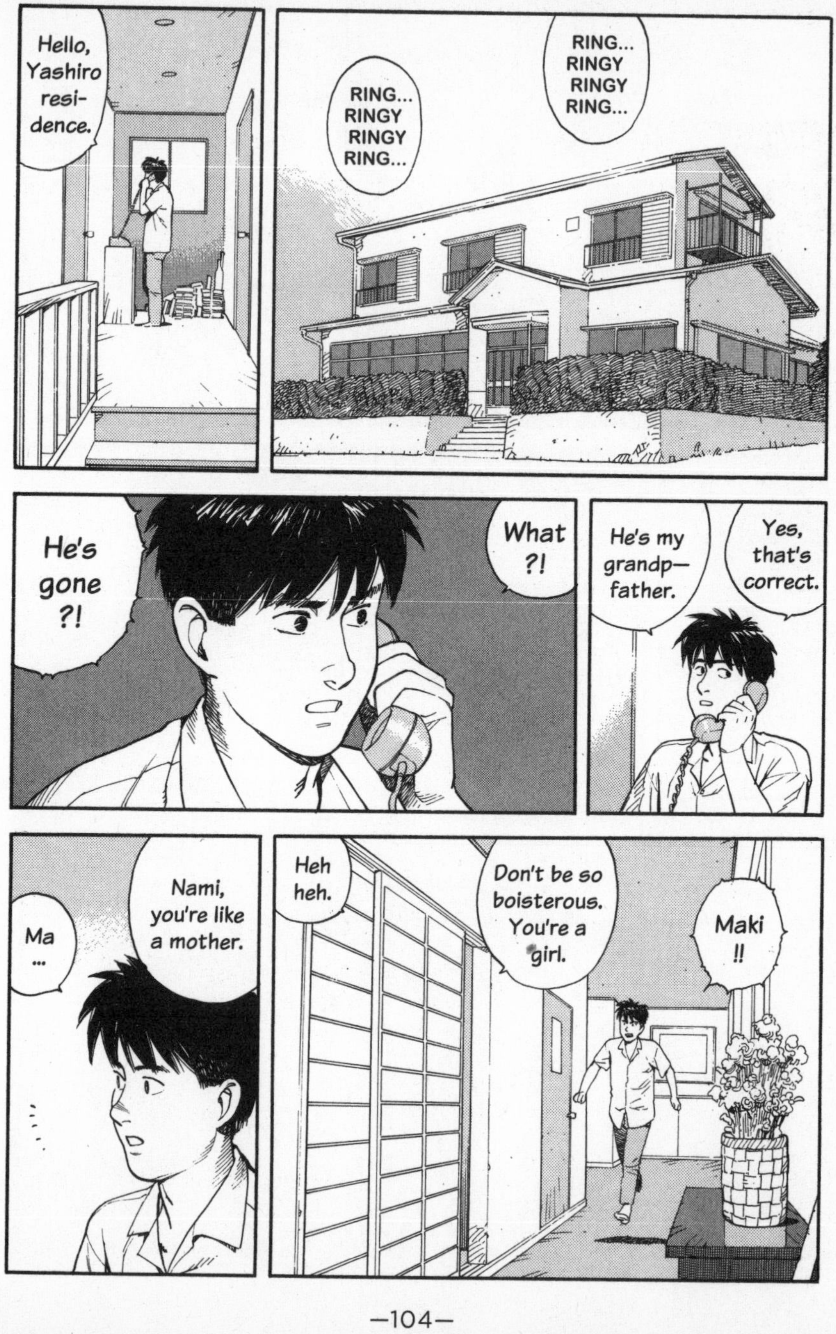
RING... RINGY RINGY RING...
RING... RINGY RINGY RING...
Hello, Yashiro resi- dence.
Yes, that's correct.
He's my grandp— father.
What ?!
He's gone ?!
Maki !!
Don't be so boisterous. You're a girl.
Heh heh.
Nami, you're like a mother.
Ma ...

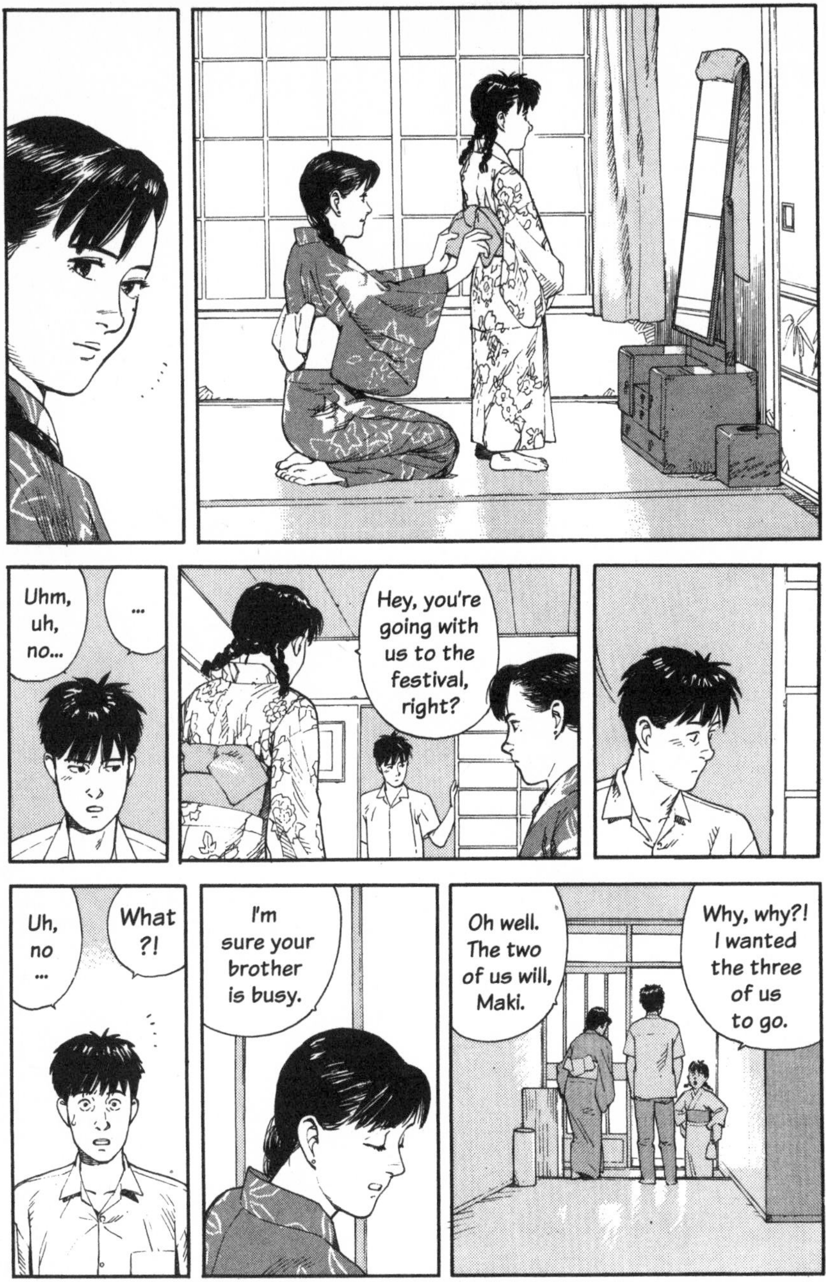
Hey, you're going with us to the festival, right?
...
Uhm, uh, no...
Why, why?! I wanted the three of us to go.
Oh well. The two of us will, Maki.
I'm sure your brother is busy.
What ?!
Uh, no ...

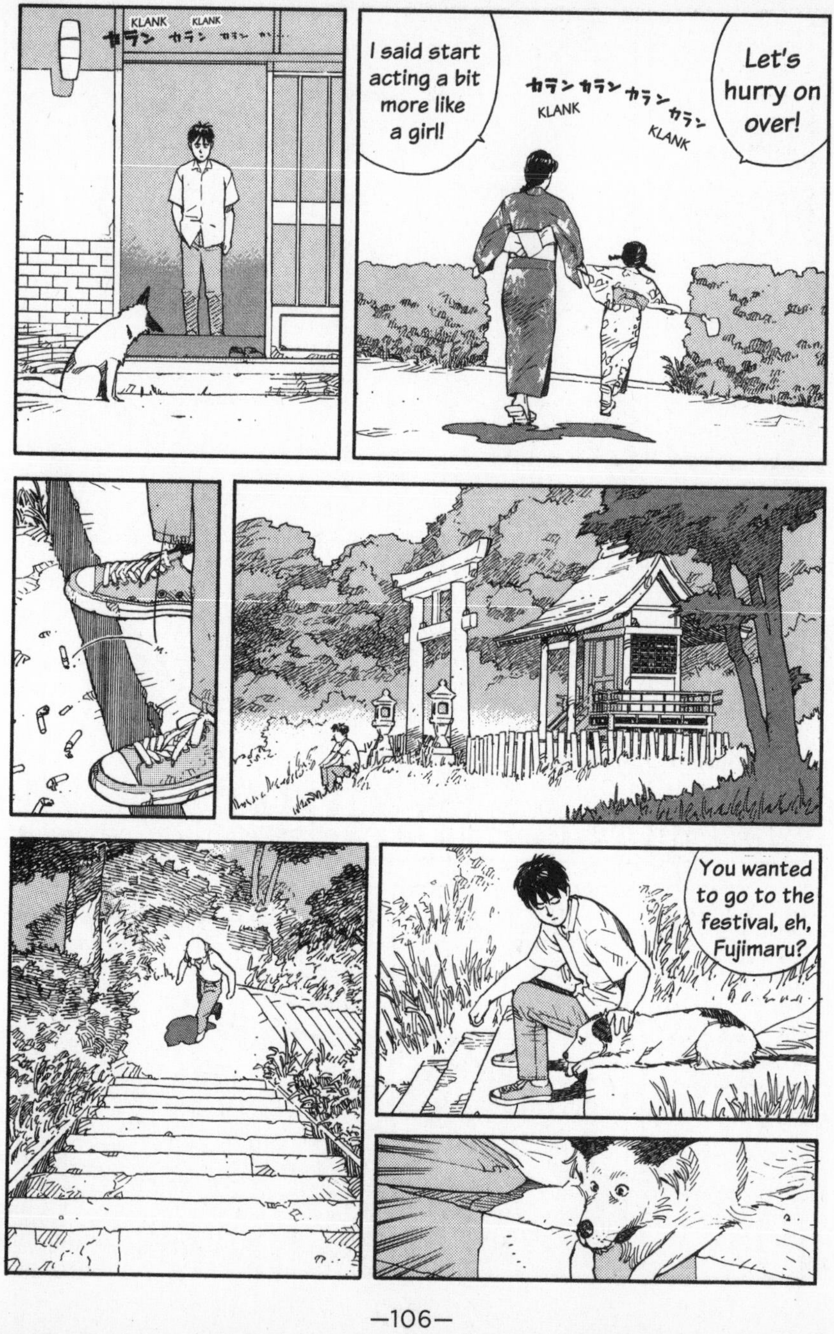
Let's hurry on over!
カラン カラン カラン カラン
KLANK
KLANK
I said start acting a bit more like a girl!
KLANK KLANK
カラン カラン
You wanted to go to the festival, eh, Fujimaru?

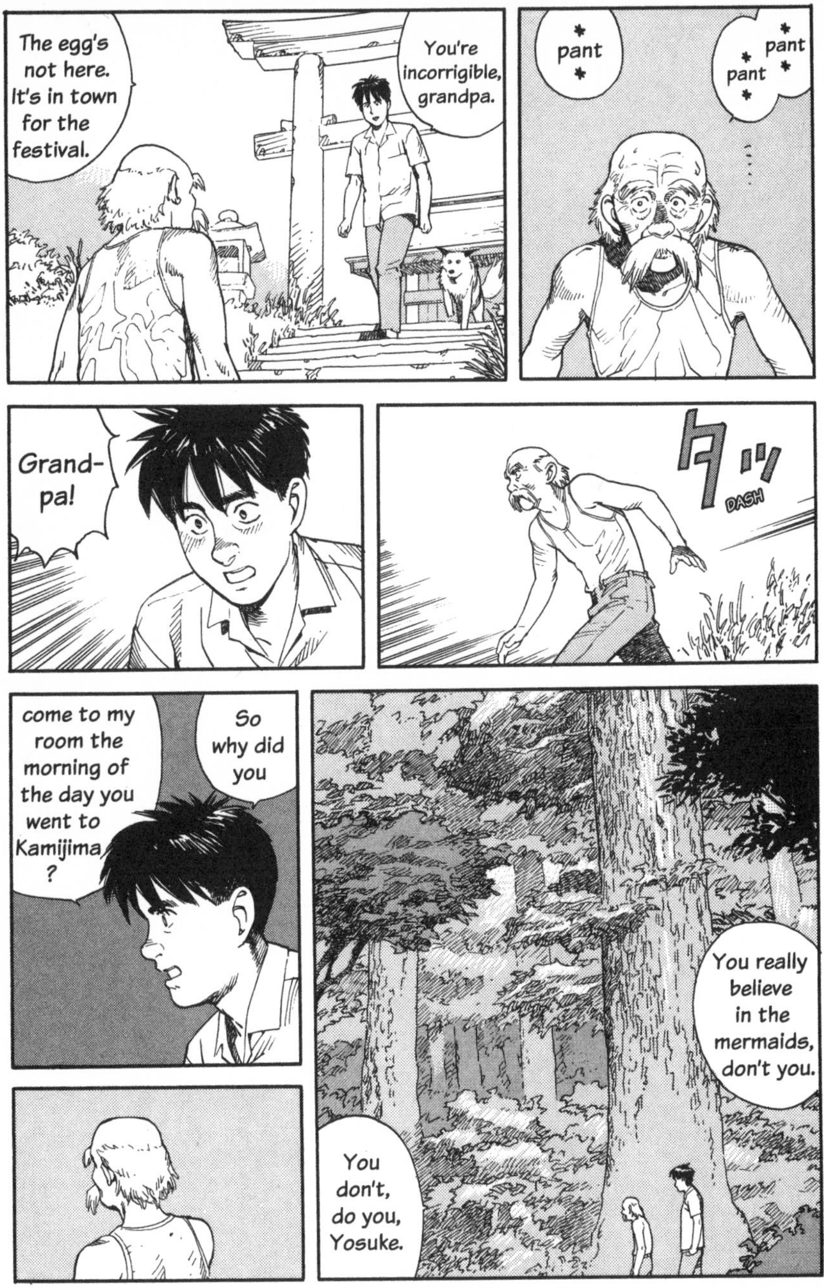

pant pant
pant
You're incorrigible, grandpa.
The egg's not here. It's in town for the festival.
タッ
DASH
Grand-pa!
You really believe in the mermaids, don't you.
You don't, do you, Yosuke.
So why did you
come to my room the morning of the day you went to Kamijima ?

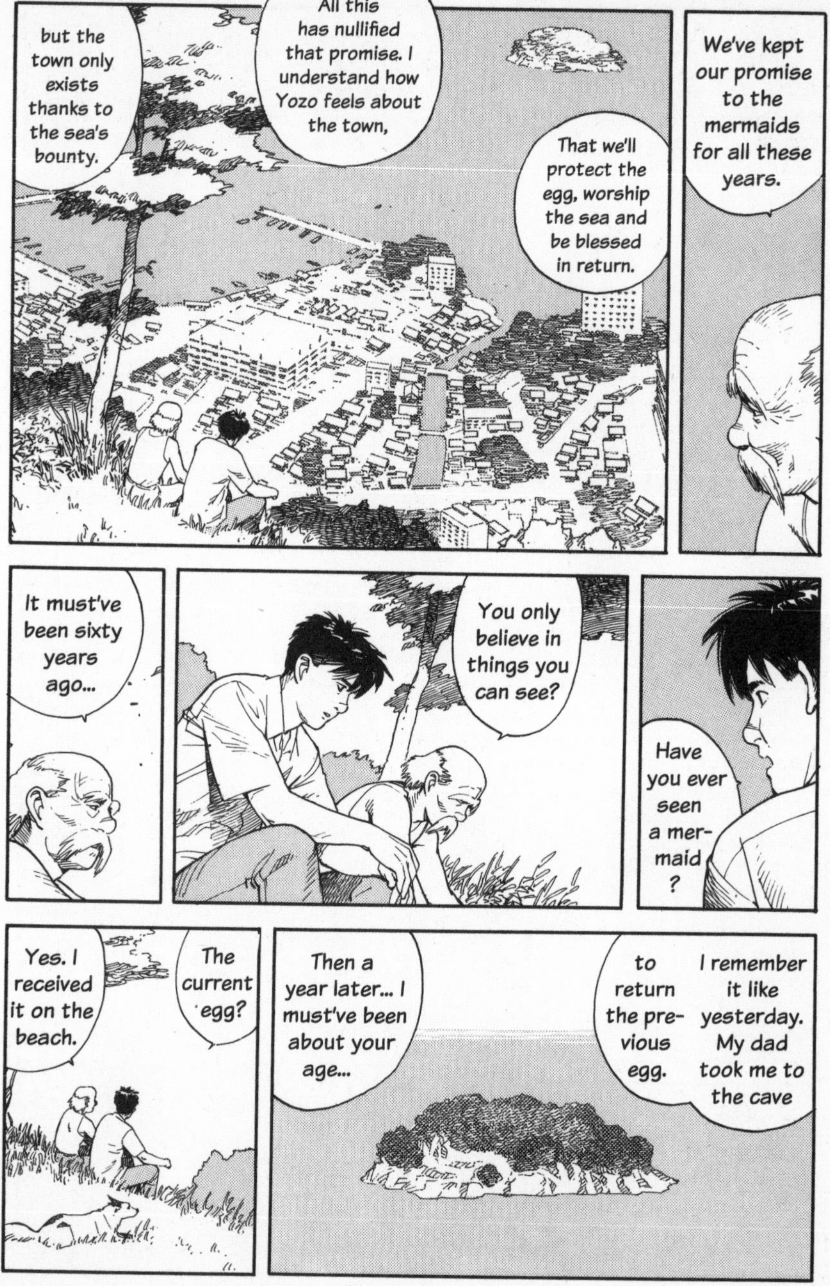
We've kept our promise to the mermaids for all these years.
That we'll protect the egg, worship the sea and be blessed in return.
All this has nullified that promise. I understand how Yozo feels about the town,
but the town only exists thanks to the sea's bounty.
Have you ever seen a mermaid?
You only believe in things you can see?
It must've been sixty years ago...
I remember it like yesterday. My dad took me to the cave
to return the previous egg.
Then a year later... I must've been about your age...
The current egg?
Yes. I received it on the beach.

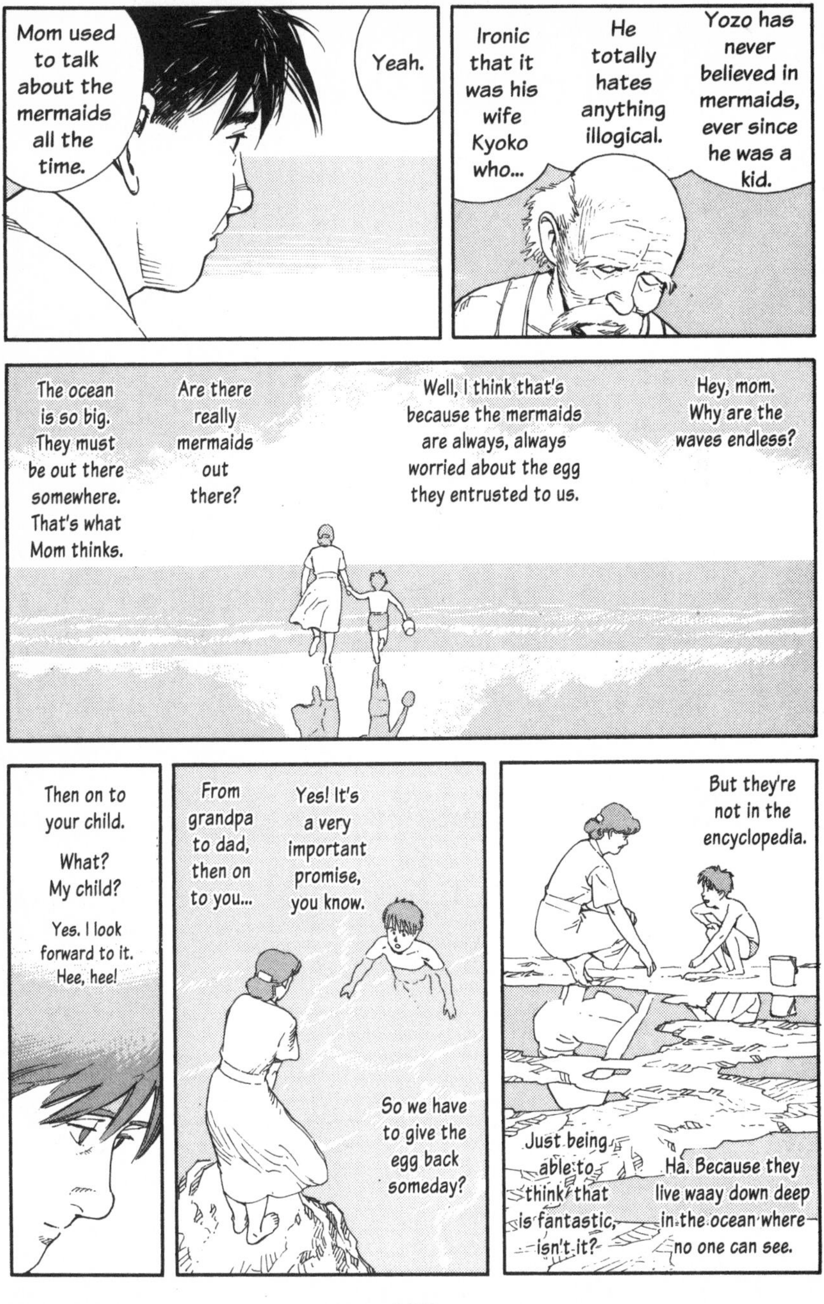

Yozo has never believed in mermaids, ever since he was a kid.
He totally hates anything illogical.
Ironic that it was his wife Kyoko who...
Yeah.
Mom used to talk about the mermaids all the time.
Hey, mom. Why are the waves endless?
Well, I think that's because the mermaids are always, always worried about the egg they entrusted to us.
Are there really mermaids out there?
The ocean is so big. They must be out there somewhere. That's what Mom thinks.
But they're not in the encyclopedia.
Ha. Because they live waay down deep in the ocean where no one can see.
Just being able to think that is fantastic, isn't it?
Yes! It's a very important promise, you know.
From grandpa to dad, then on to you...
So we have to give the egg back someday?
Then on to your child.
What? My child?
Yes. I look forward to it. Hee, hee!

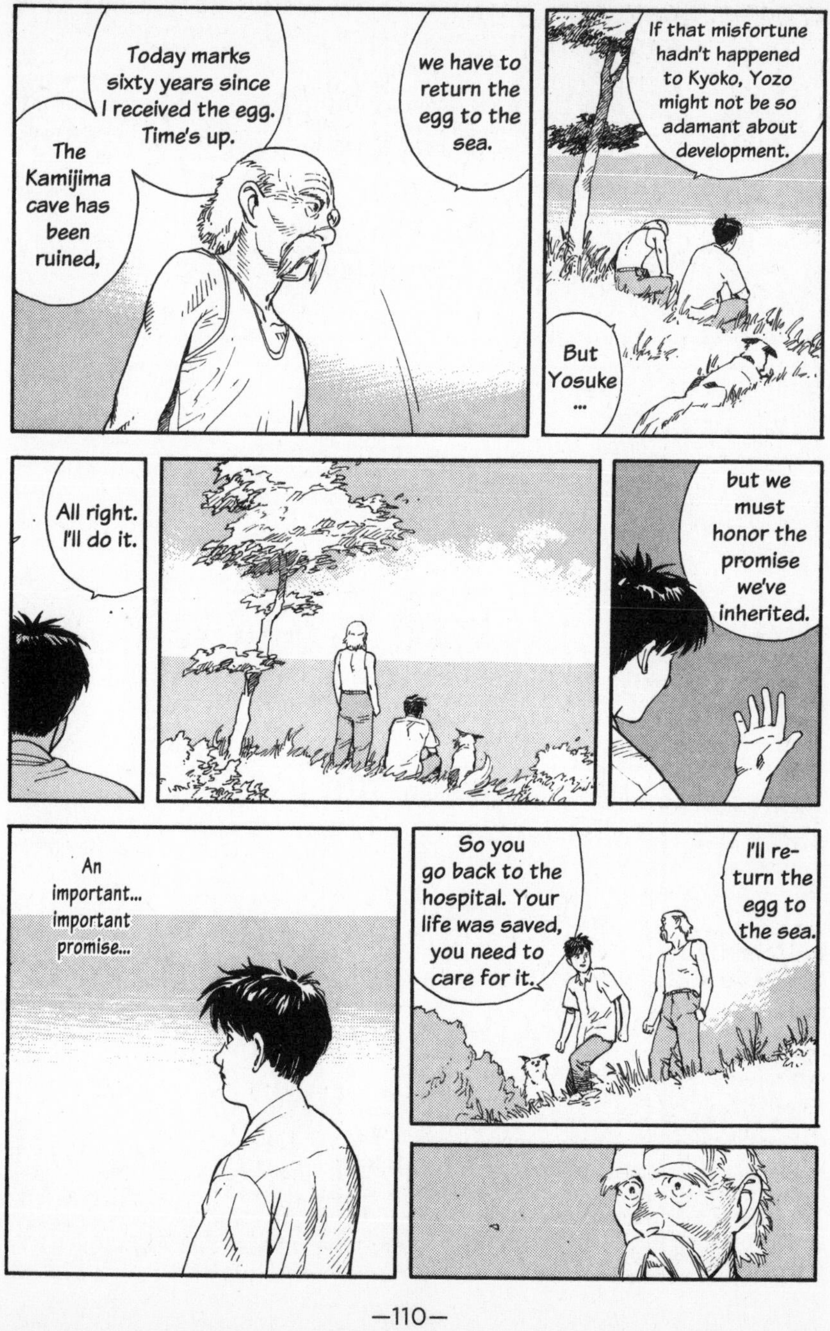
If that misfortune hadn't happened to Kyoko, Yozo might not be so adamant about development.
But Yosuke ...
Today marks sixty years since I received the egg. Time's up.
The Kamijima cave has been ruined,
we have to return the egg to the sea.
but we must honor the promise we've inherited.
All right. I'll do it.
I'll re-turn the egg to the sea.
So you go back to the hospital. Your life was saved, you need to care for it.
An important... important promise...

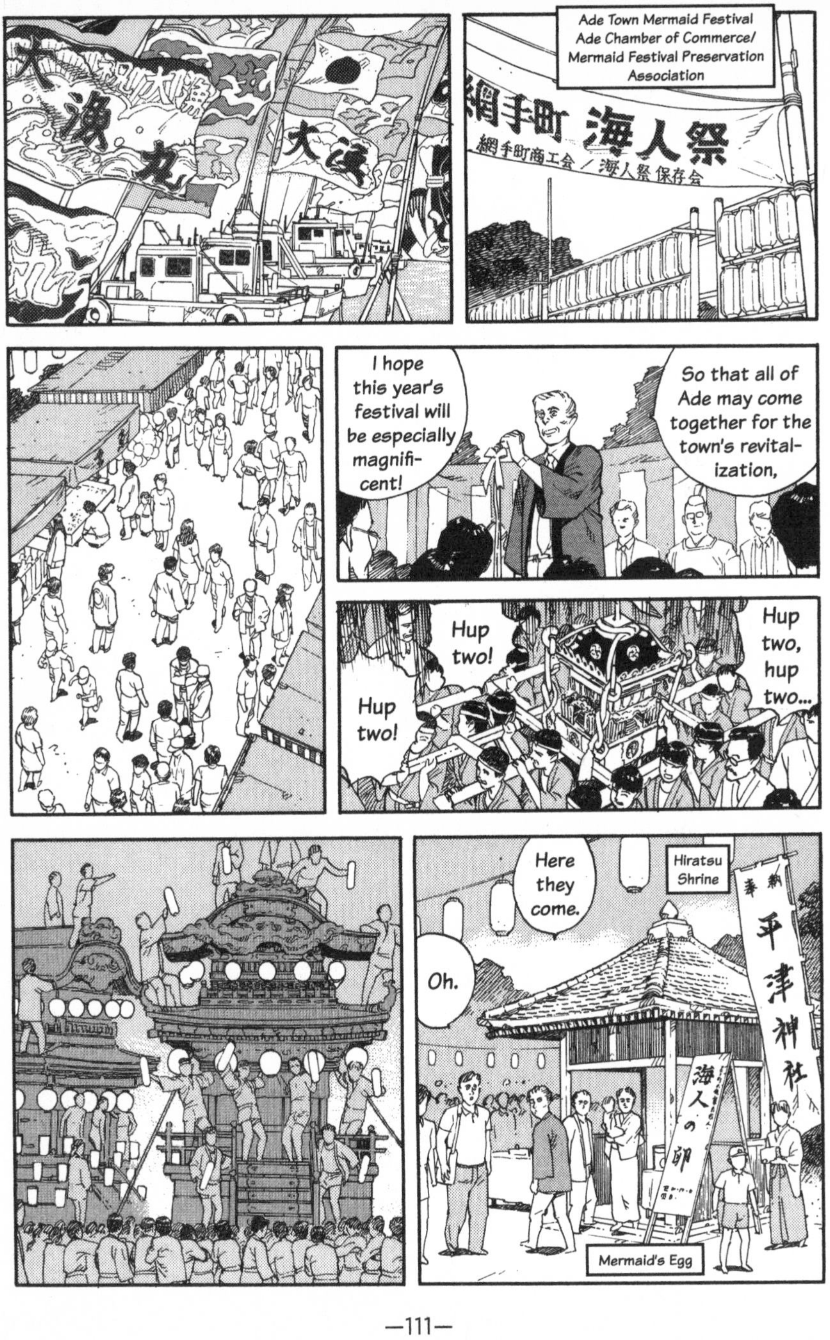
Ade Town Mermaid Festival
Ade Chamber of Commerce/
Mermaid Festival Preservation
Association
網手町 海人祭
網手町商工会／海人祭保存会
So that all of Ade may come together for the town's revital-ization,
I hope this year's festival will be especially magnifi-cent!
Hup two, hup two...
Hup two!
Hup two!
Hiratsu Shrine
奉納
平津神社
Here they come.
Oh.
海人の卵
Mermaid's Egg

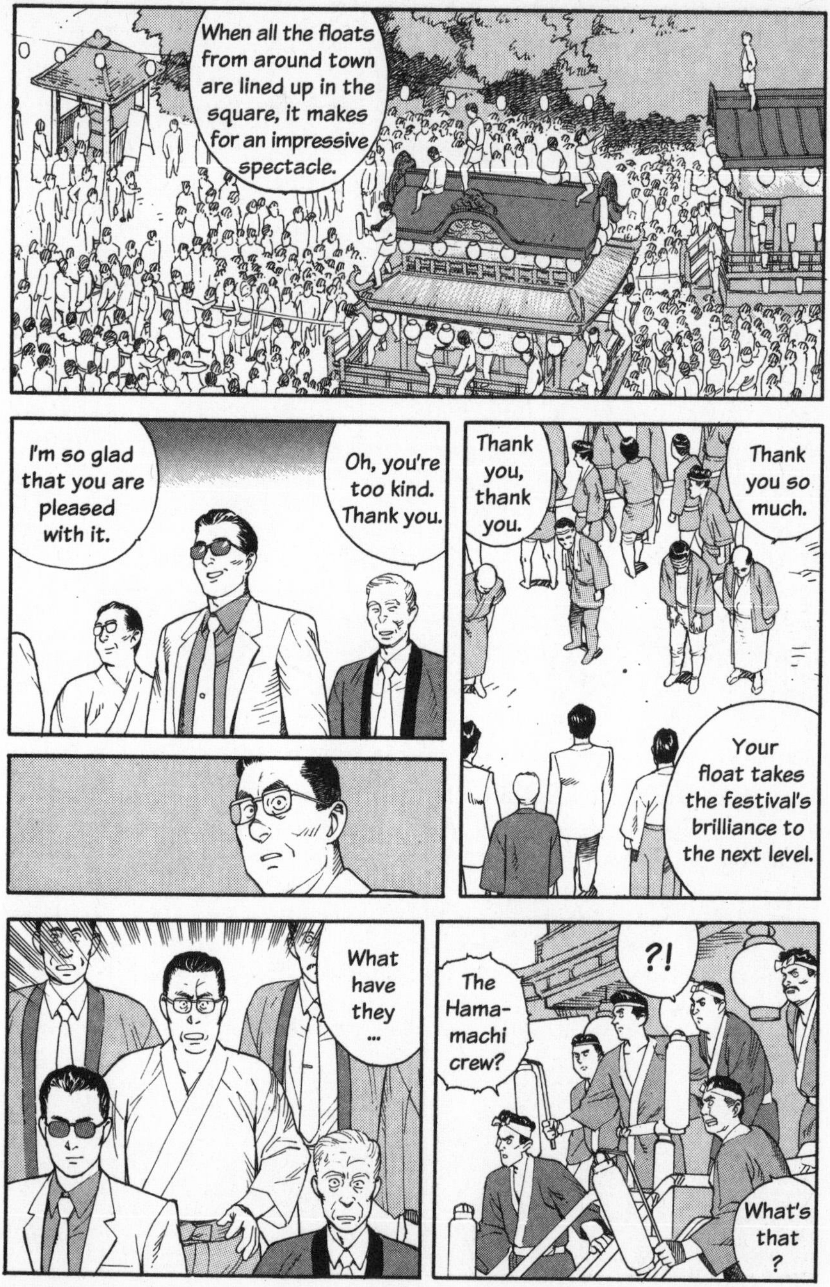
When all the floats from around town are lined up in the square, it makes for an impressive spectacle.
Thank you so much.
Thank you, thank you.
Your float takes the festival's brilliance to the next level.
Oh, you're too kind. Thank you.
I'm so glad that you are pleased with it.
?!
The Hamamachi crew?
What's that?
What have they ...

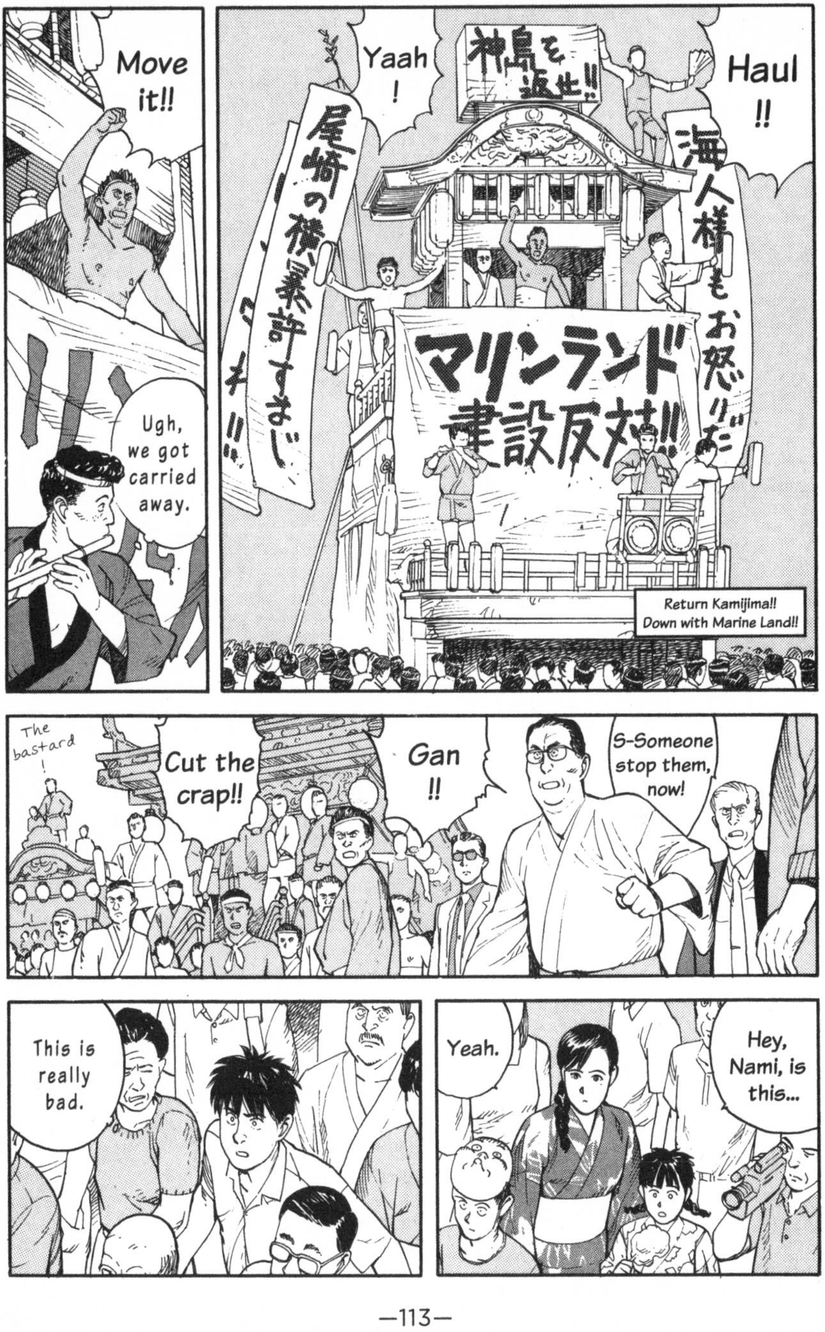
Haul!!
海人様もお怒りだ
神島を返せ!!
Yaah!
尾崎の横暴許すまじ
マリンランド建設反対!!
Return Kamijima!! Down with Marine Land!!
Move it!!
Ugh, we got carried away.
S-Someone stop them, now!
Gan!!
Cut the crap!!
The bastard!
Hey, Nami, is this...
Yeah.
This is really bad.

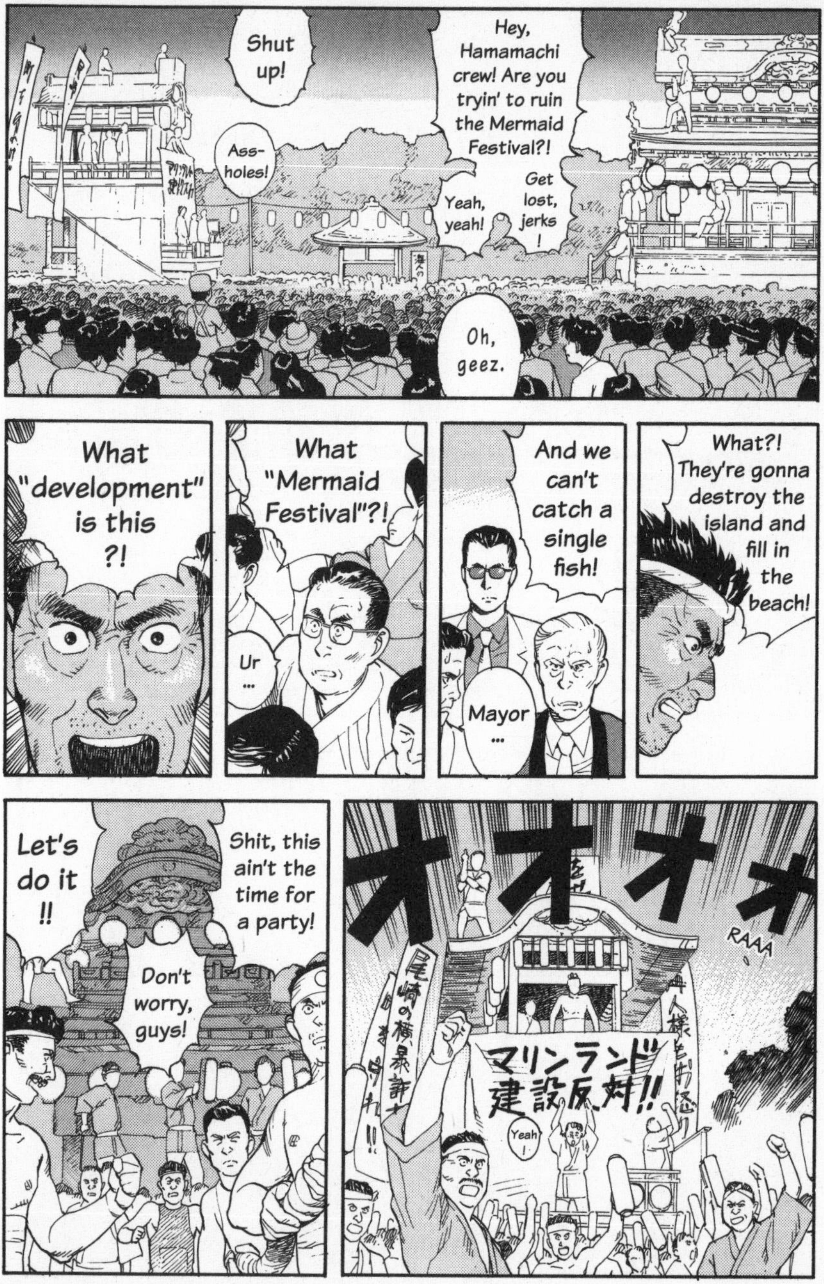

Hey, Hamamachi crew! Are you tryin' to ruin the Mermaid Festival?!
Shut up!
Get lost, jerks!
Yeah, yeah!
Ass-holes!
Oh, geez.
What?! They're gonna destroy the island and fill in the beach!
And we can't catch a single fish!
Mayor ...
What "Mermaid Festival"?!
Ur ...
What "development" is this ?!
オオオオ
RAAA
マリンランド建設反対!!
Yeah!
Shit, this ain't the time for a party!
Let's do it !!
Don't worry, guys!

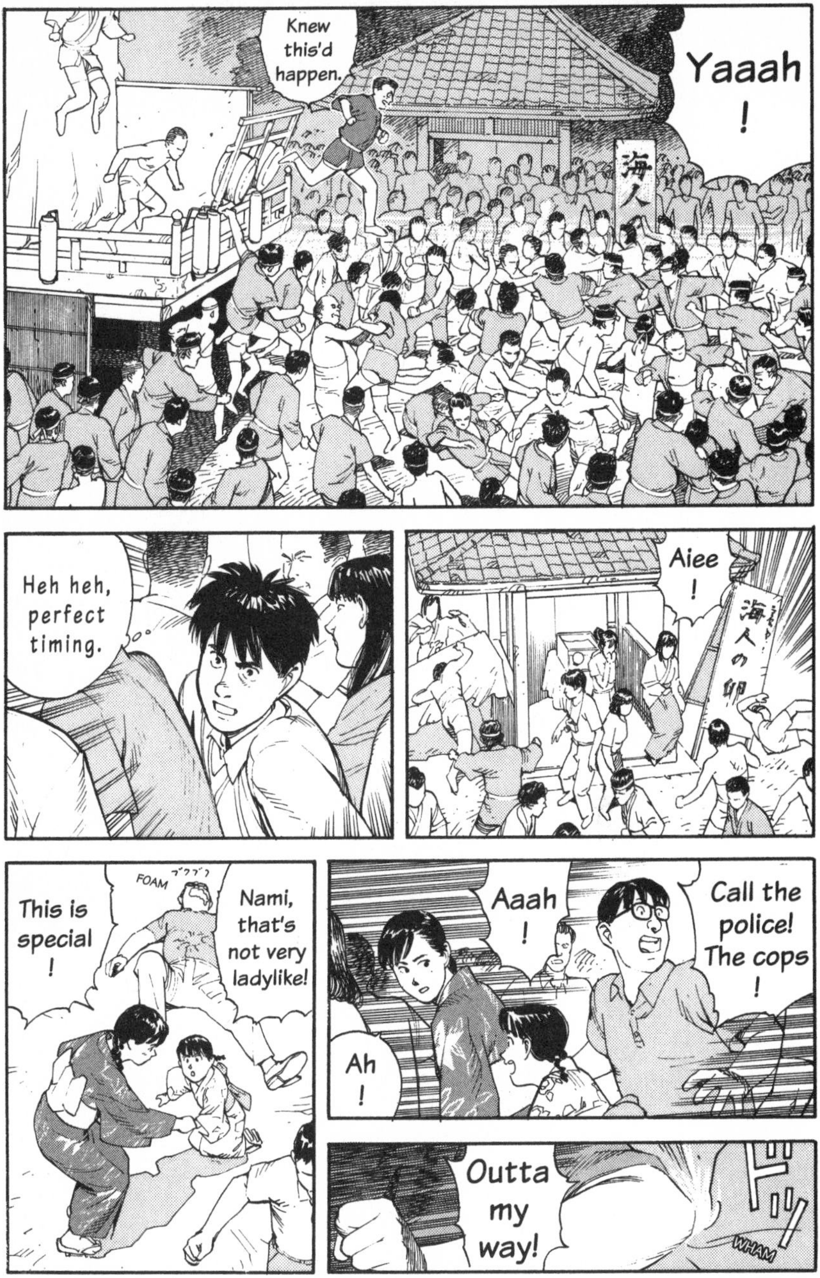
Yaaah !
海人
Knew this'd happen.
Aiee !
海人の卵
Heh heh, perfect timing.
Call the police! The cops !
Aaah !
Ah !
Outta my way!
WHAM
Nami, that's not very ladylike!
FOAM
This is special !

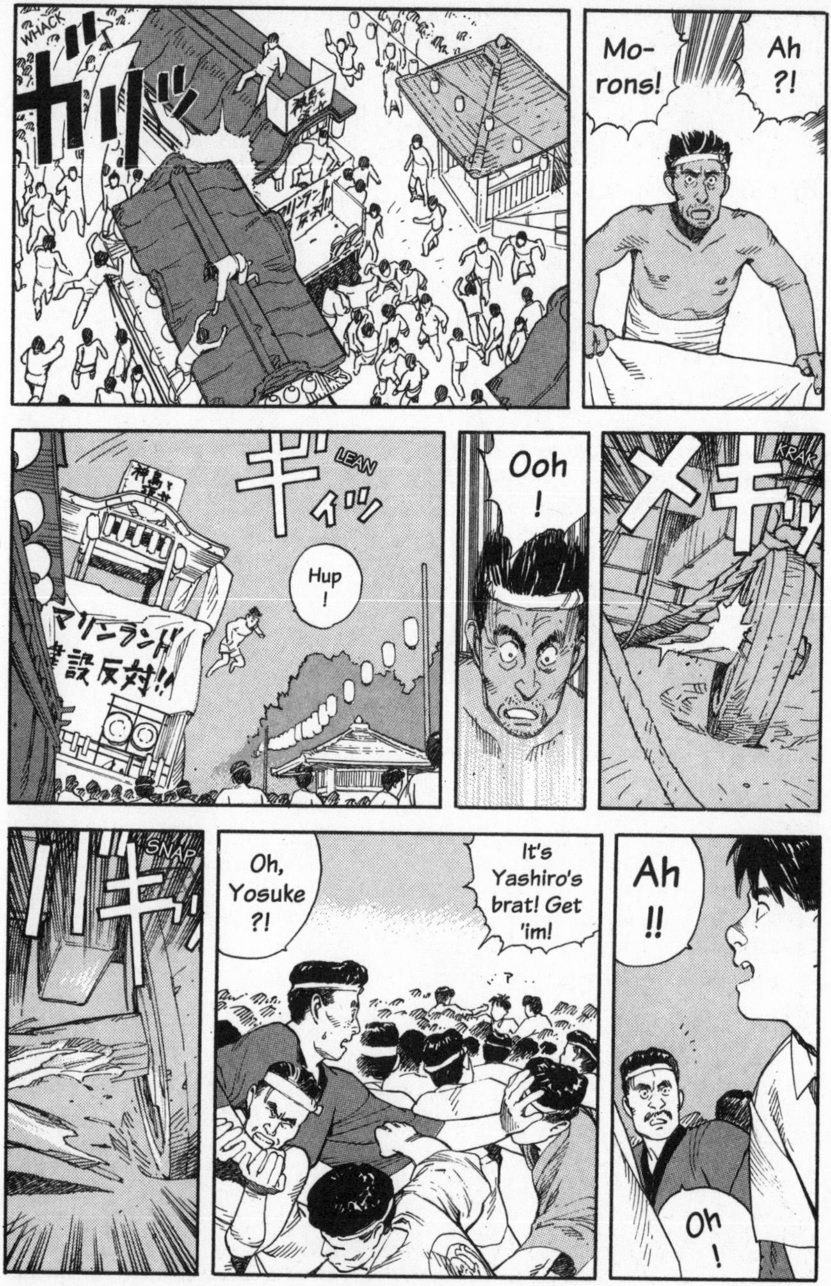
Ah ?!
Mo-rons!
ガリッ
WHACK
メキッ
KRAK
Ooh !
ギイッ
LEAN
Hup !
マリンランド建設反対!!
Ah !!
Oh !
It's Yashiro's brat! Get 'im!
Oh, Yosuke ?!
バキッ
SNAP

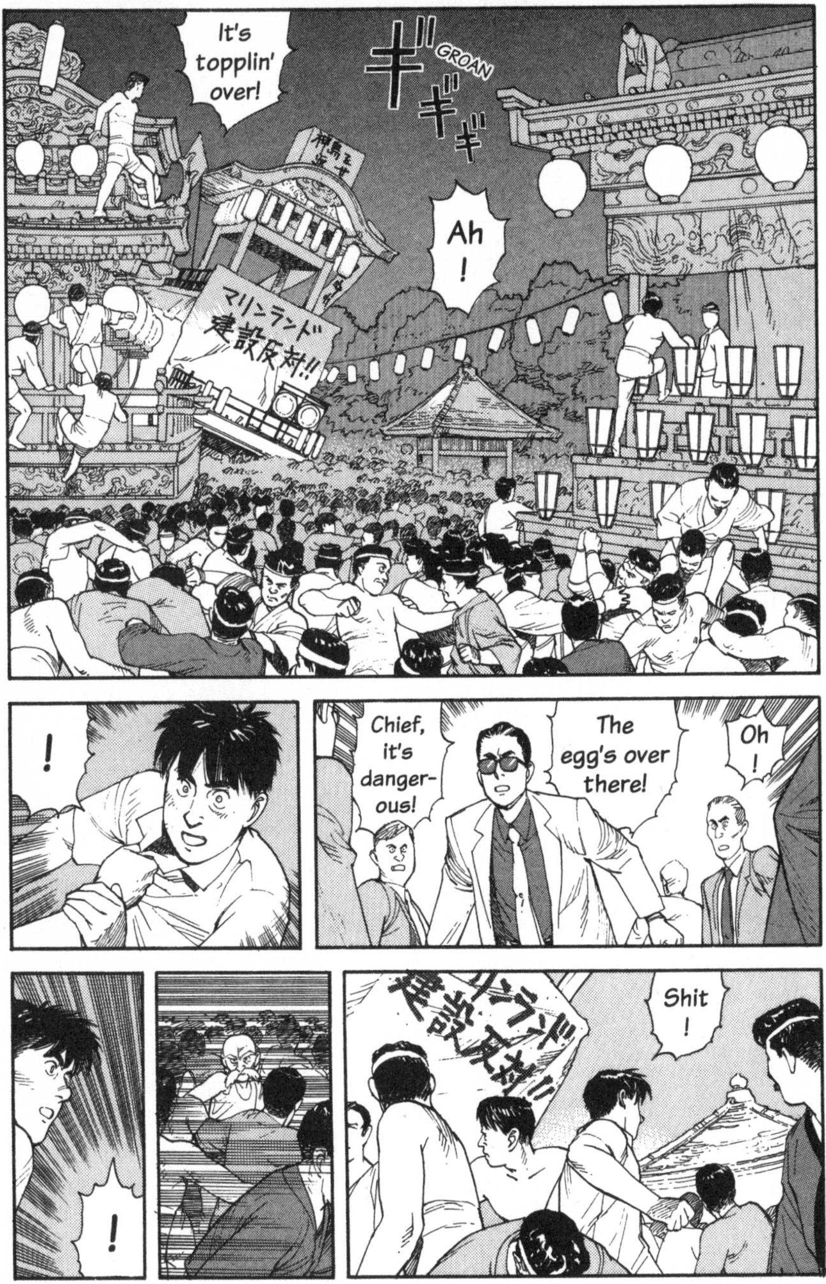
ギ
ギギ
GROAN
It's topplin' over!
Ah!
マリンランド建設反対!!
Oh!
The egg's over there!
Chief, it's danger-ous!
!
Shit!
!

KREAK

Grand-pa?!

KRASH

Ack

Whoa!

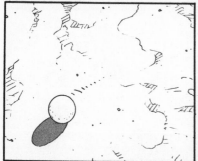

WHUMP

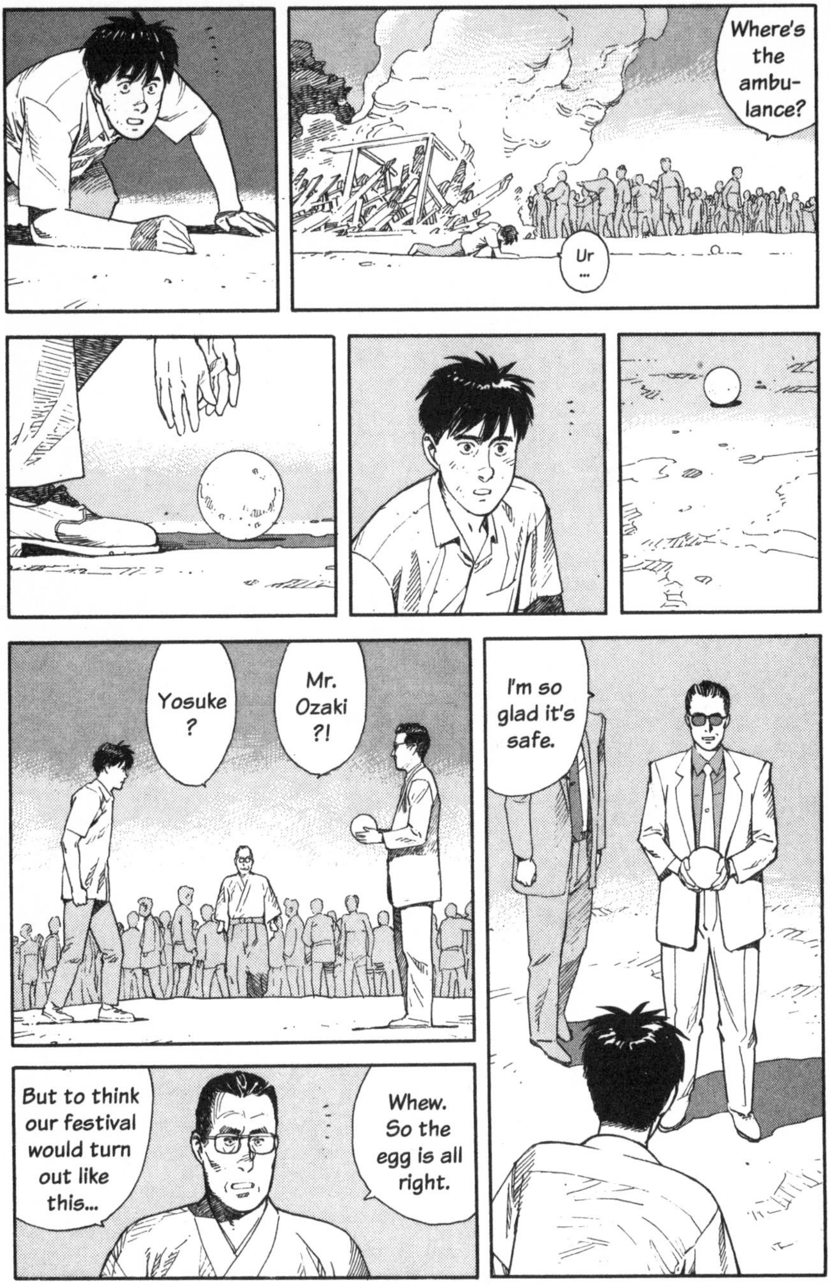
Where's the ambulance?
Ur ...
I'm so glad it's safe.
Mr. Ozaki ?!
Yosuke ?
Whew. So the egg is all right.
But to think our festival would turn out like this...

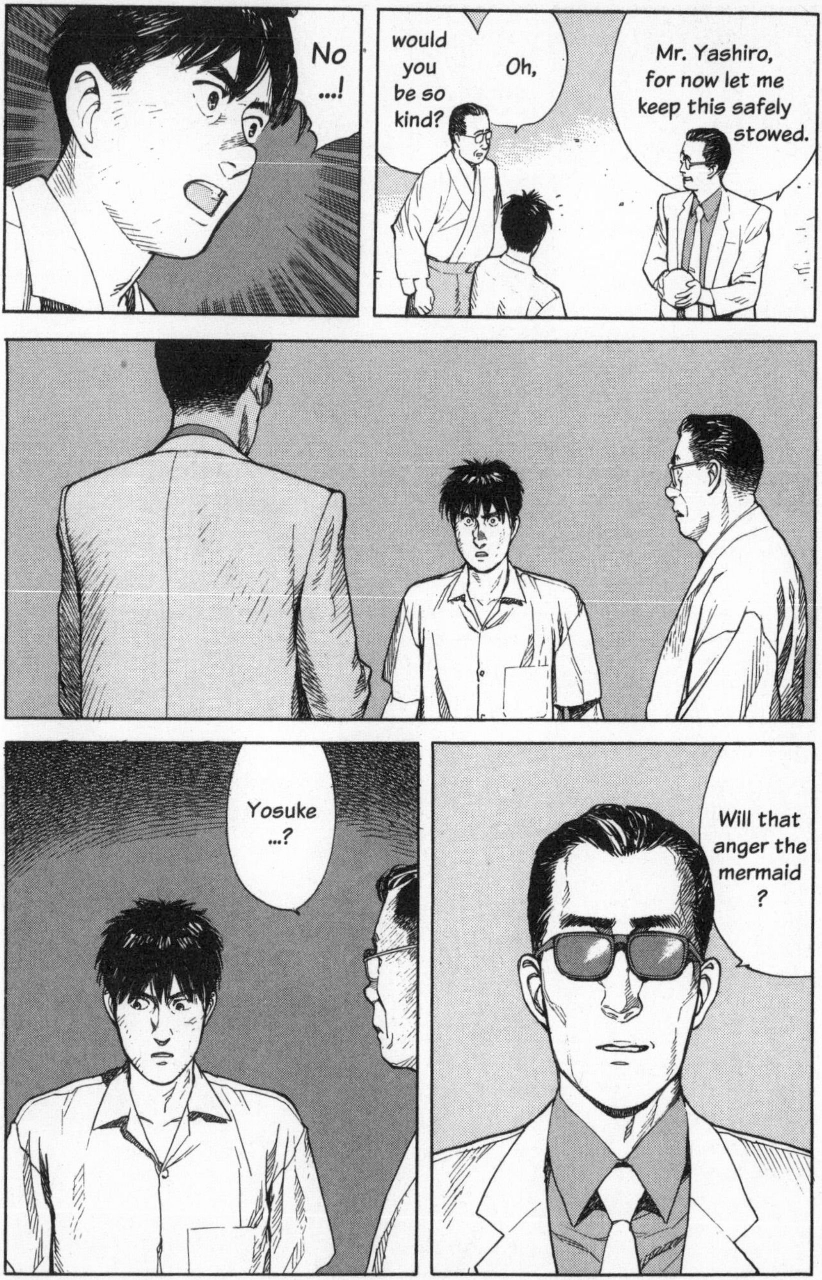
Mr. Yashiro, for now let me keep this safely stowed.
Oh,
would you be so kind?
No ...!
Will that anger the mermaid ?
Yosuke ...?

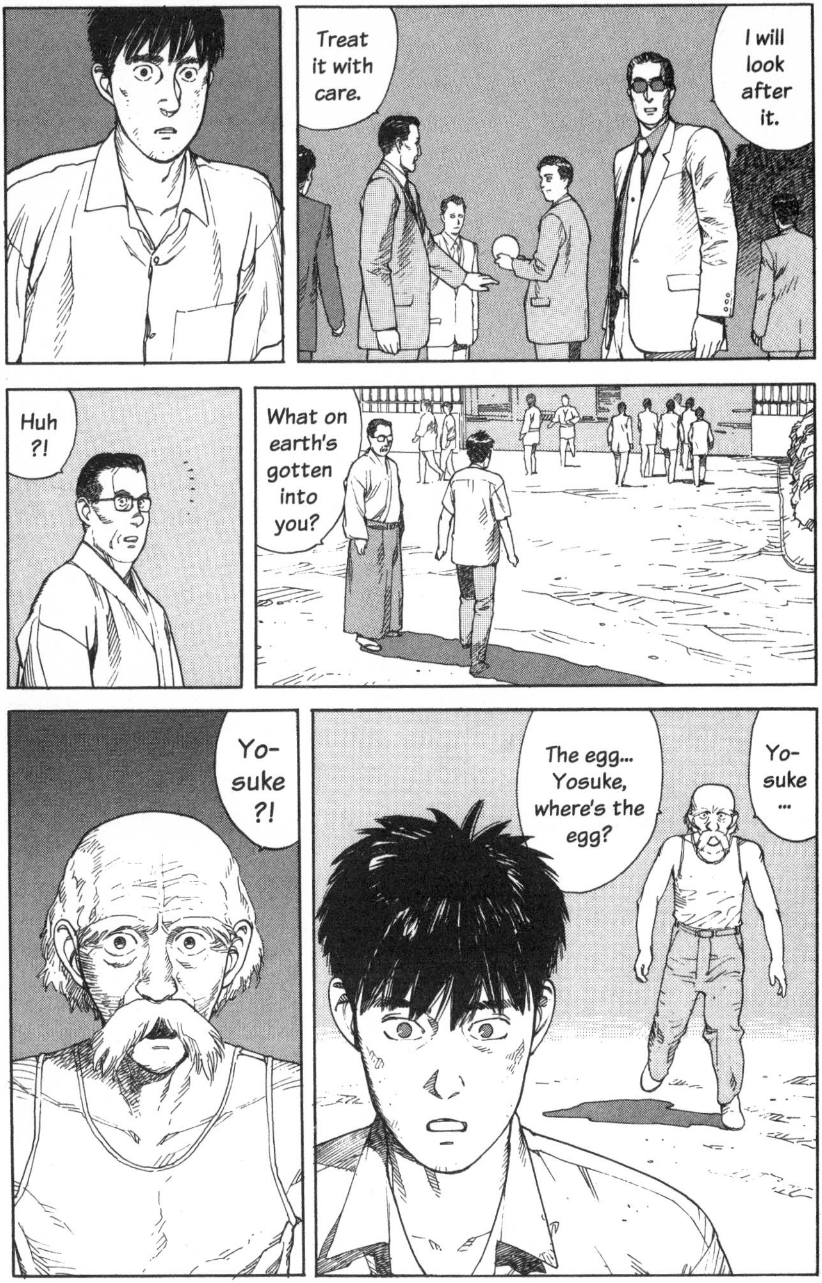
I will look after it.
Treat it with care.
What on earth's gotten into you?
Huh ?!
Yo-suke ...
The egg... Yosuke, where's the egg?
Yo-suke ?!

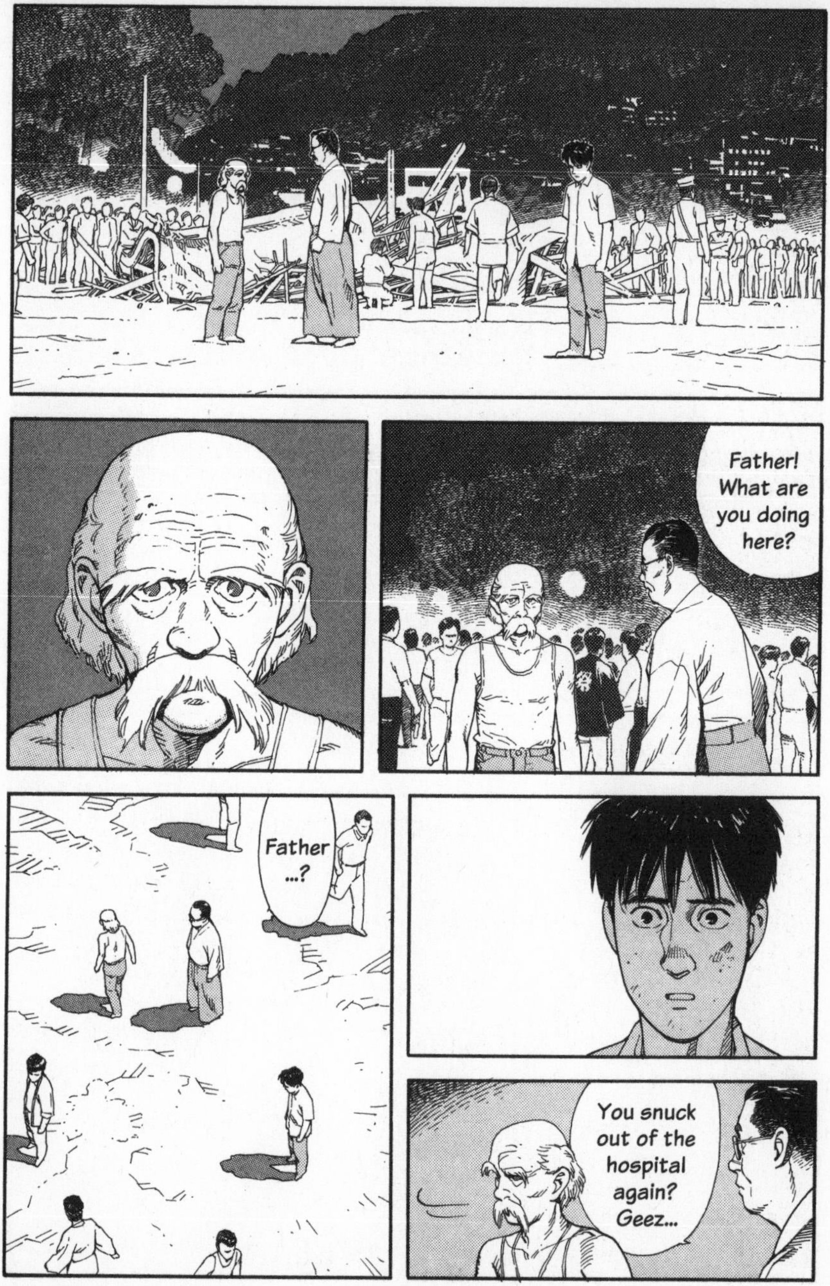
Father! What are you doing here?
You snuck out of the hospital again? Geez...
Father ...?

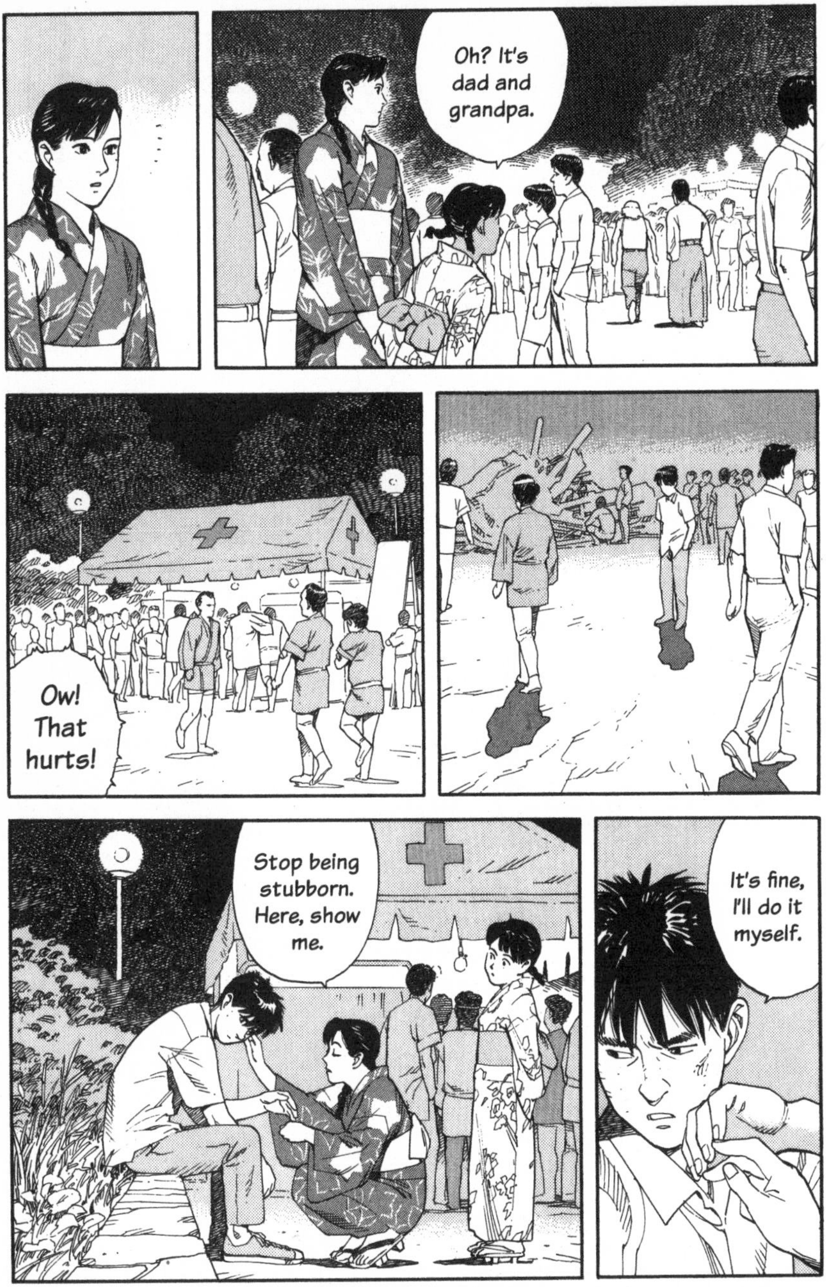
Oh? It's dad and grandpa.
Ow! That hurts!
It's fine, I'll do it myself.
Stop being stubborn. Here, show me.

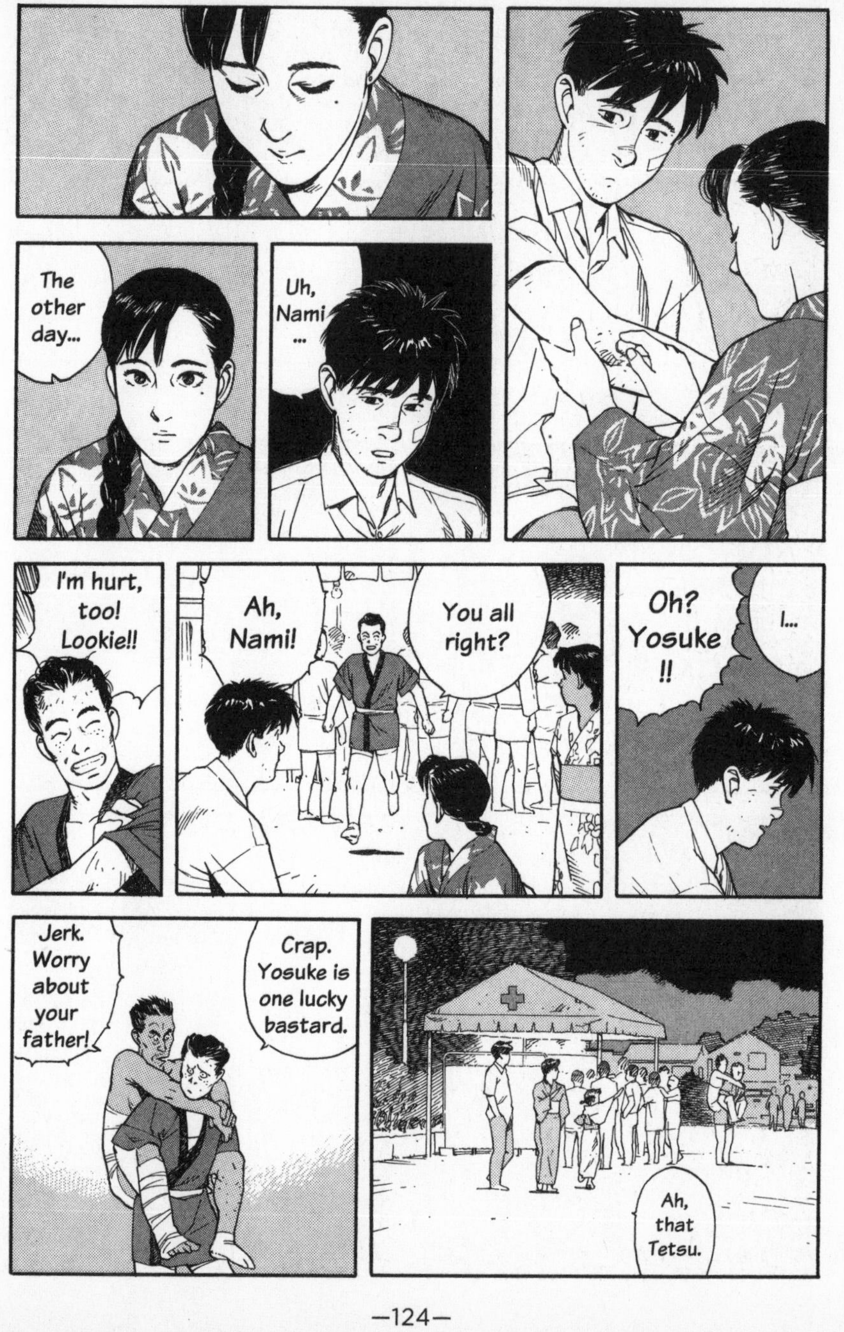
Uh, Nami...
The other day...
I...
Oh? Yosuke!!
You all right?
Ah, Nami!
I'm hurt, too! Lookie!!
Ah, that Tetsu.
Crap. Yosuke is one lucky bastard.
Jerk. Worry about your father!

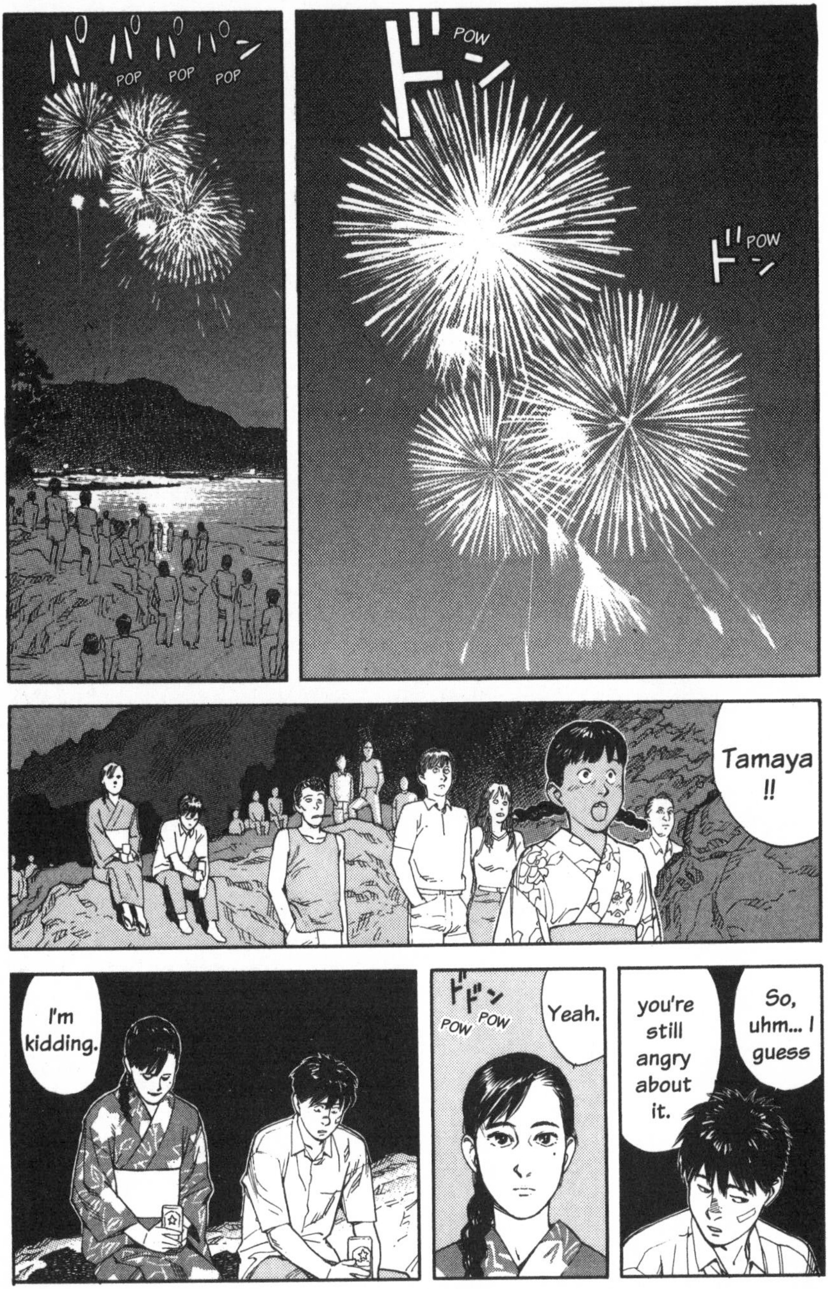
ドーン
POW
ドーン
POW
パパパパーン
POP POP POP
Tamaya !!
So, uhm... I guess
you're still angry about it.
Yeah.
ドドン
POW POW
I'm kidding.

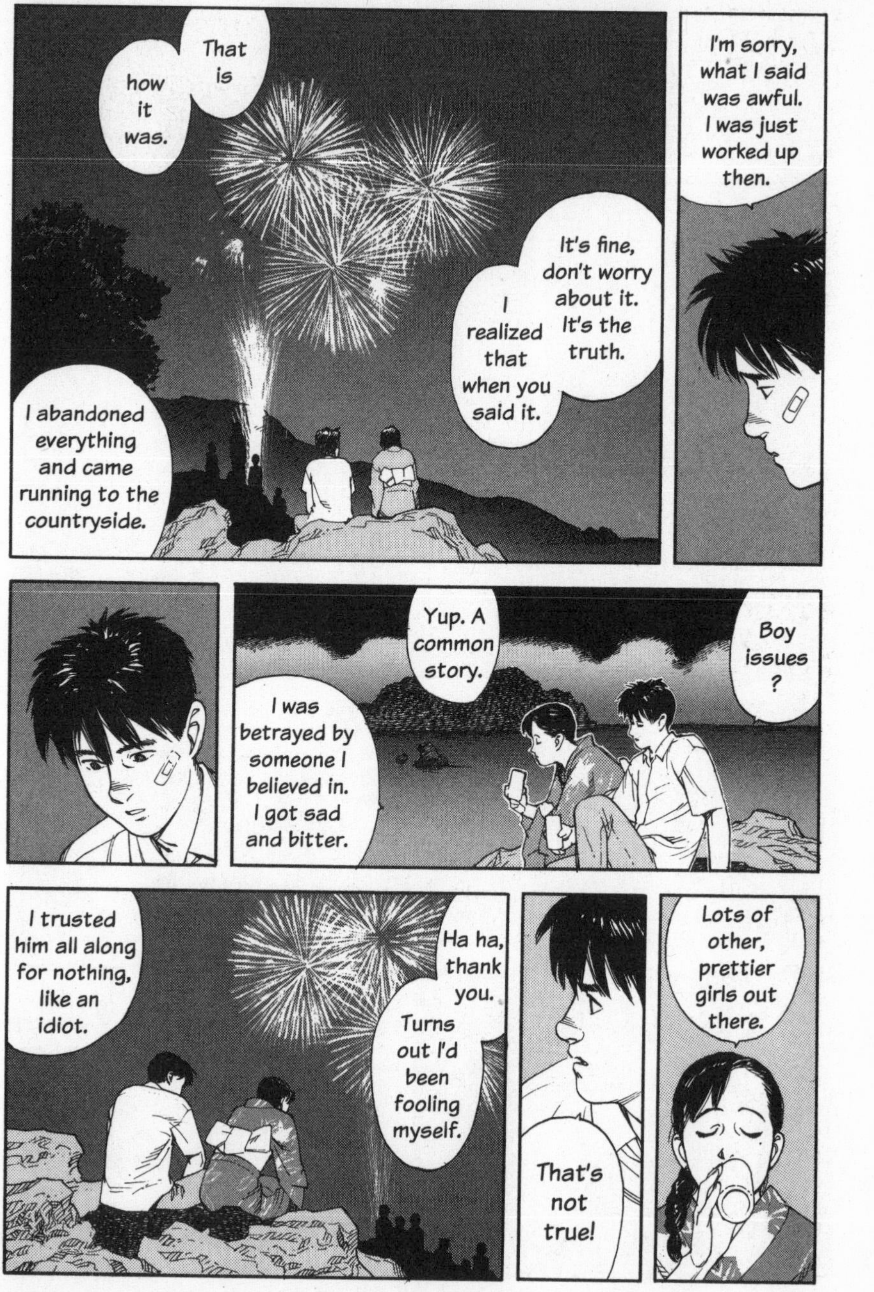
I'm sorry, what I said was awful. I was just worked up then.
It's fine, don't worry about it. It's the truth.
I realized that when you said it.
That is
how it was.
I abandoned everything and came running to the countryside.
Boy issues?
Yup. A common story.
I was betrayed by someone I believed in. I got sad and bitter.
Lots of other, prettier girls out there.
That's not true!
Ha ha, thank you.
Turns out I'd been fooling myself.
I trusted him all along for nothing, like an idiot.

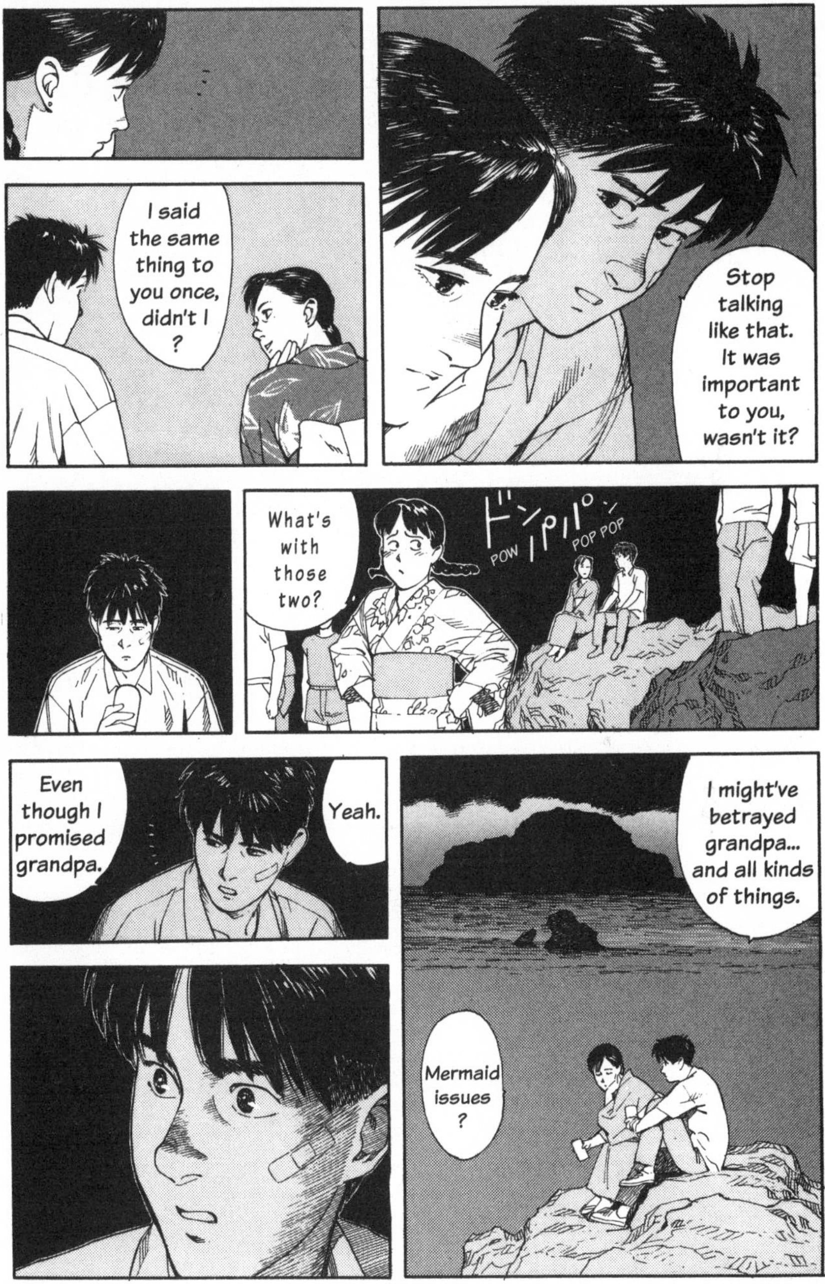
Stop talking like that. It was important to you, wasn't it?
I said the same thing to you once, didn't I ?
ドンパパ
POW
POP POP
What's with those two?
I might've betrayed grandpa... and all kinds of things.
Mermaid issues ?
Yeah.
Even though I promised grandpa.

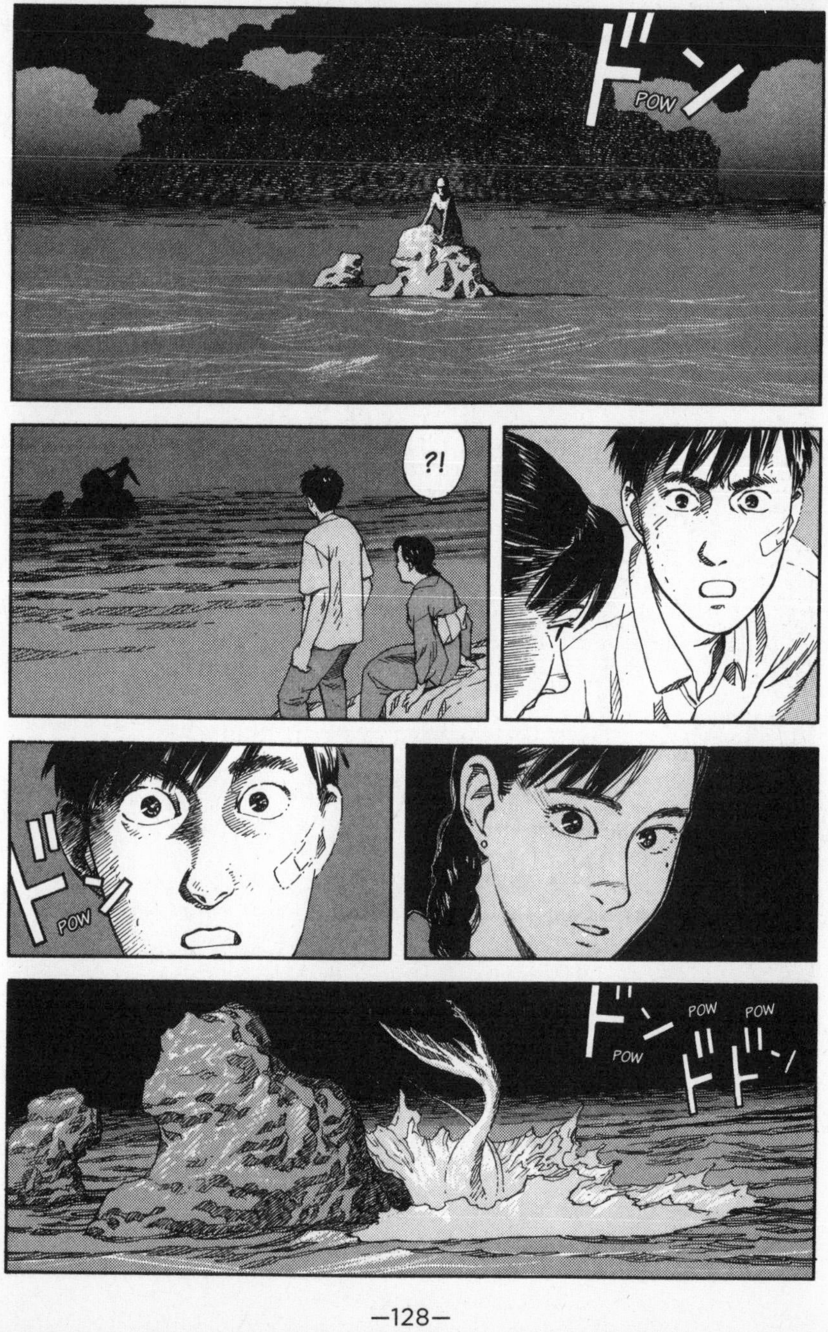
ドン
POW
?!
ドーン
POW
ドン
POW
ドドーン
POW
POW

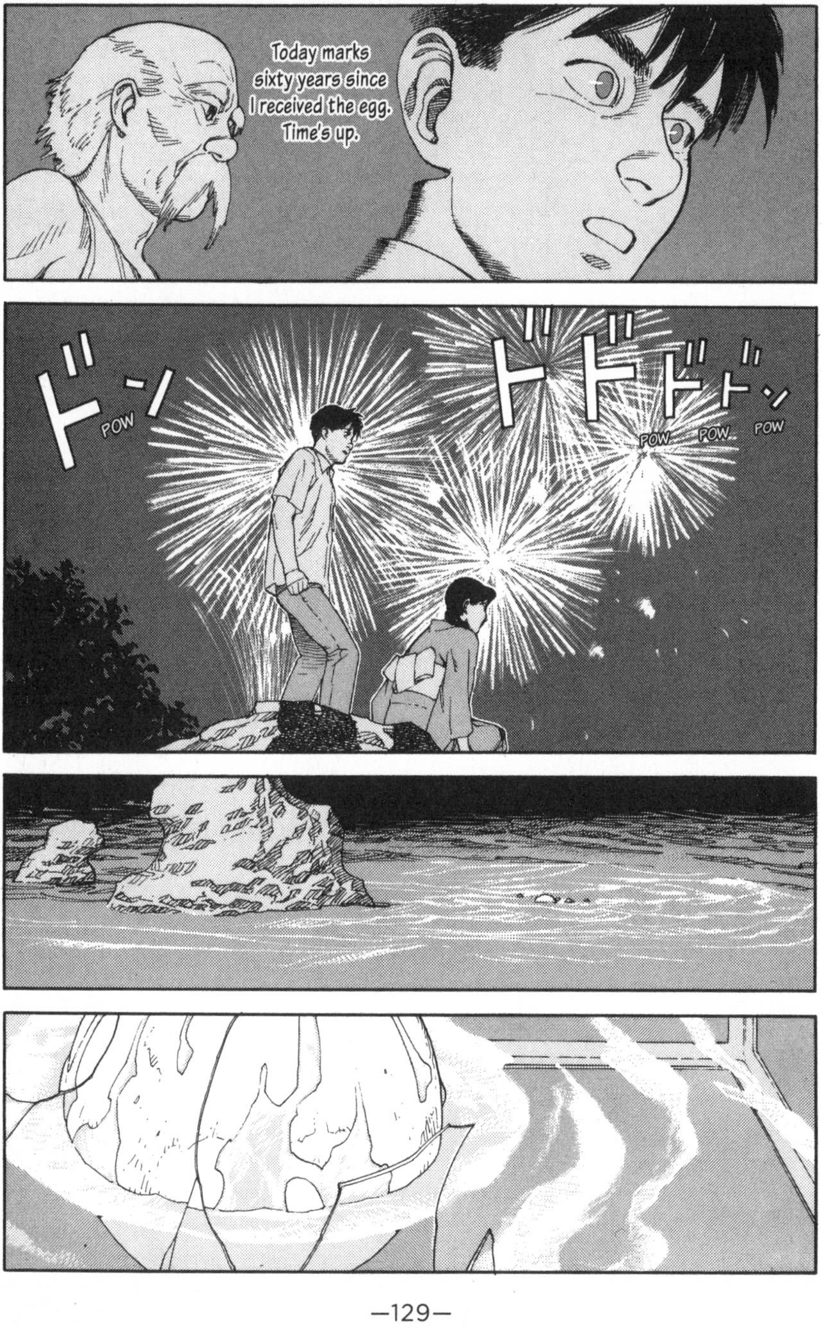
Today marks sixty years since I received the egg. Time's up.
ドドドドン
POW POW POW
ドーン
POW

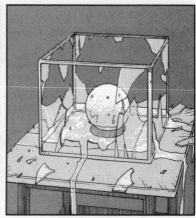

Did
you...
see
that?

SPLASH

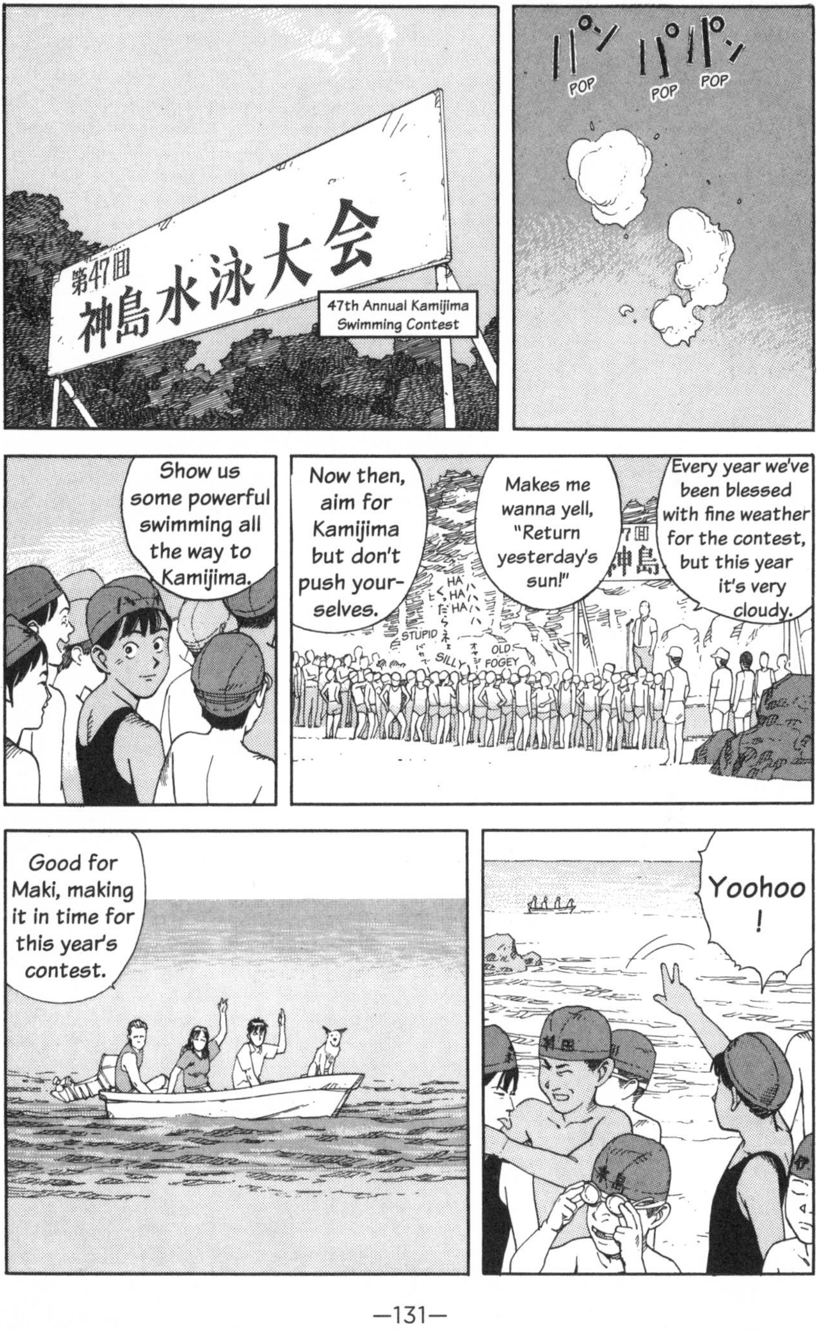
パンパンパン
POP
POP
POP
第47回 神島水泳大会
47th Annual Kamijima Swimming Contest
Every year we've been blessed with fine weather for the contest, but this year it's very cloudy.
Makes me wanna yell, "Return yesterday's sun!"
Now then, aim for Kamijima but don't push yourselves.
HA HA HA
STUPID
SILLY
OLD FOGEY
Show us some powerful swimming all the way to Kamijima.
Yoohoo !
Good for Maki, making it in time for this year's contest.

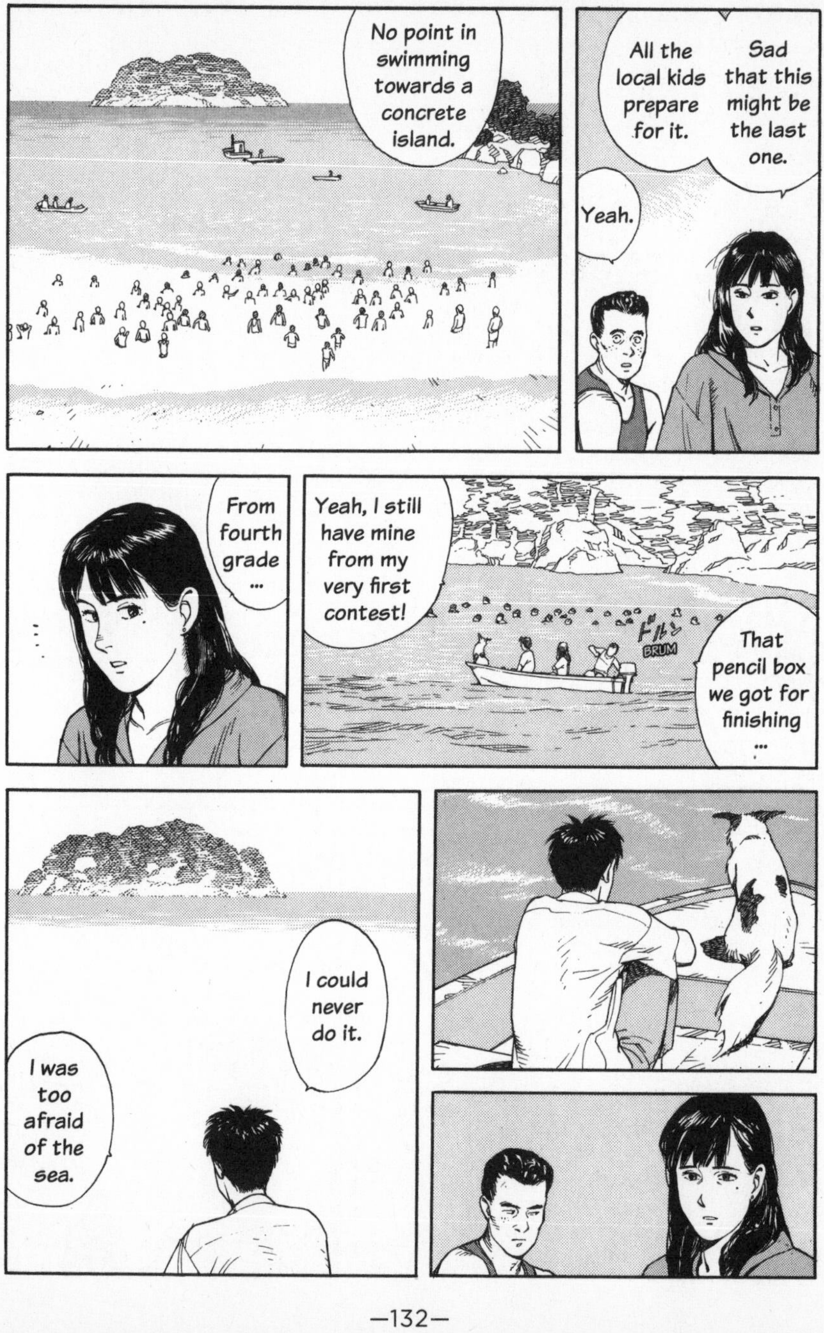
Sad that this might be the last one.
All the local kids prepare for it.
Yeah.
No point in swimming towards a concrete island.
That pencil box we got for finishing ...
Yeah, I still have mine from my very first contest!
BRUM
From fourth grade ...
I could never do it.
I was too afraid of the sea.

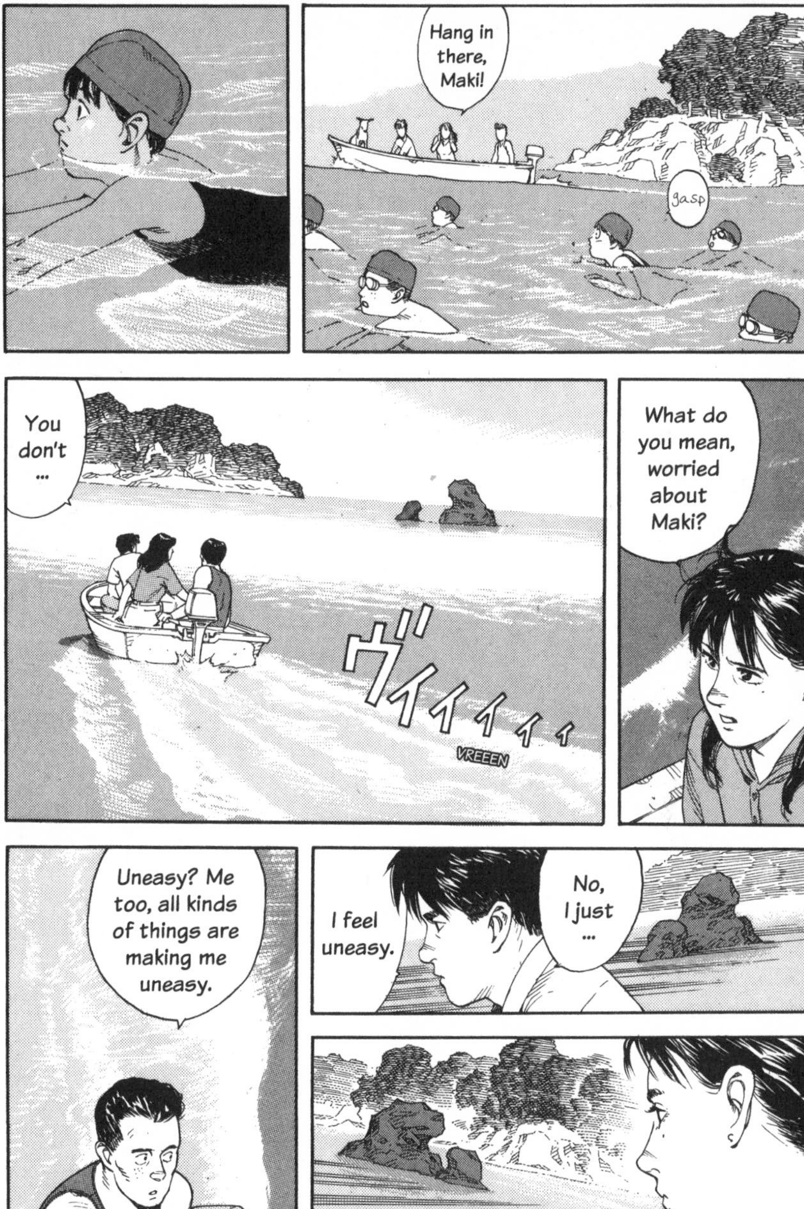
Hang in there, Maki!
gasp
What do you mean, worried about Maki?
You don't ...
ヴィィィィィ
VREEEN
No, I just ...
I feel uneasy.
Uneasy? Me too, all kinds of things are making me uneasy.

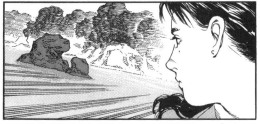

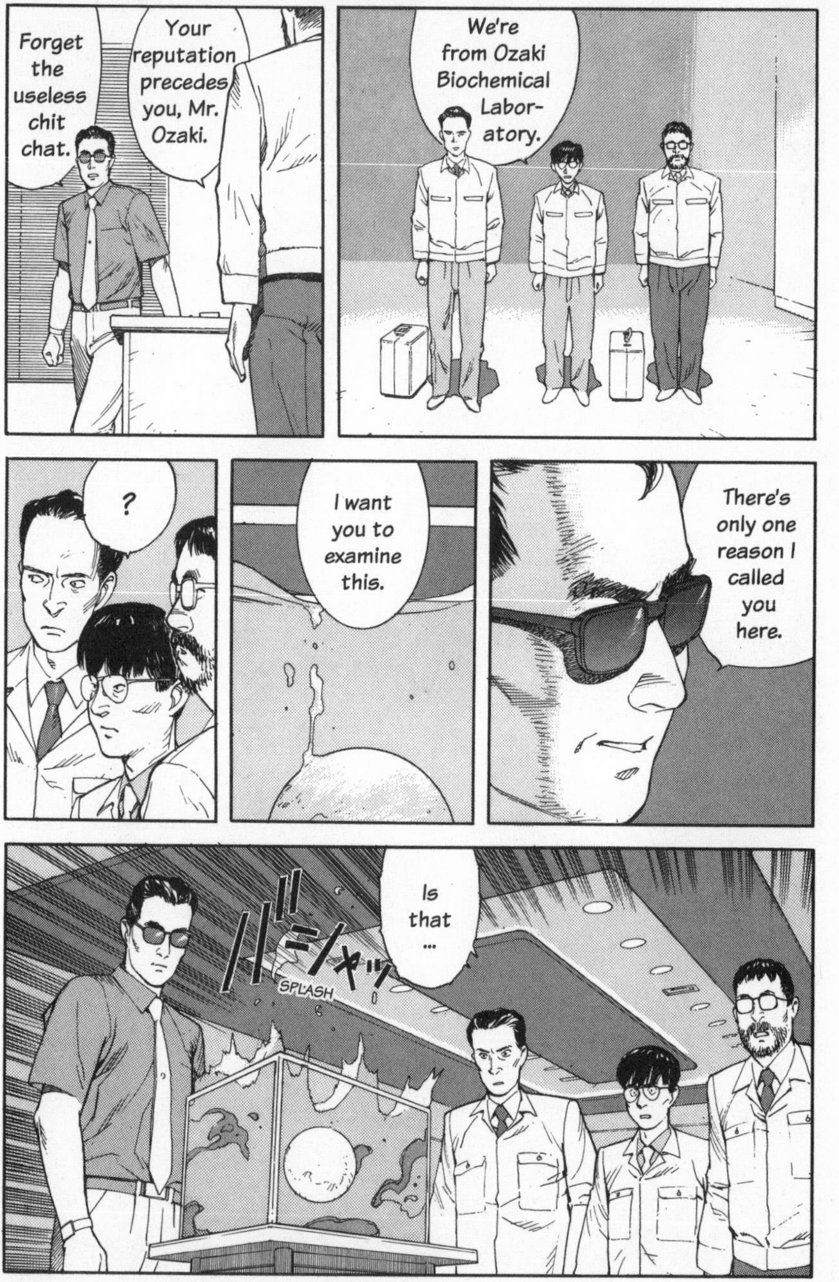
We're from Ozaki Biochemical Laboratory.
Your reputation precedes you, Mr. Ozaki.
Forget the useless chit chat.
There's only one reason I called you here.
I want you to examine this.
?
Is that ...
バシャッ
SPLASH

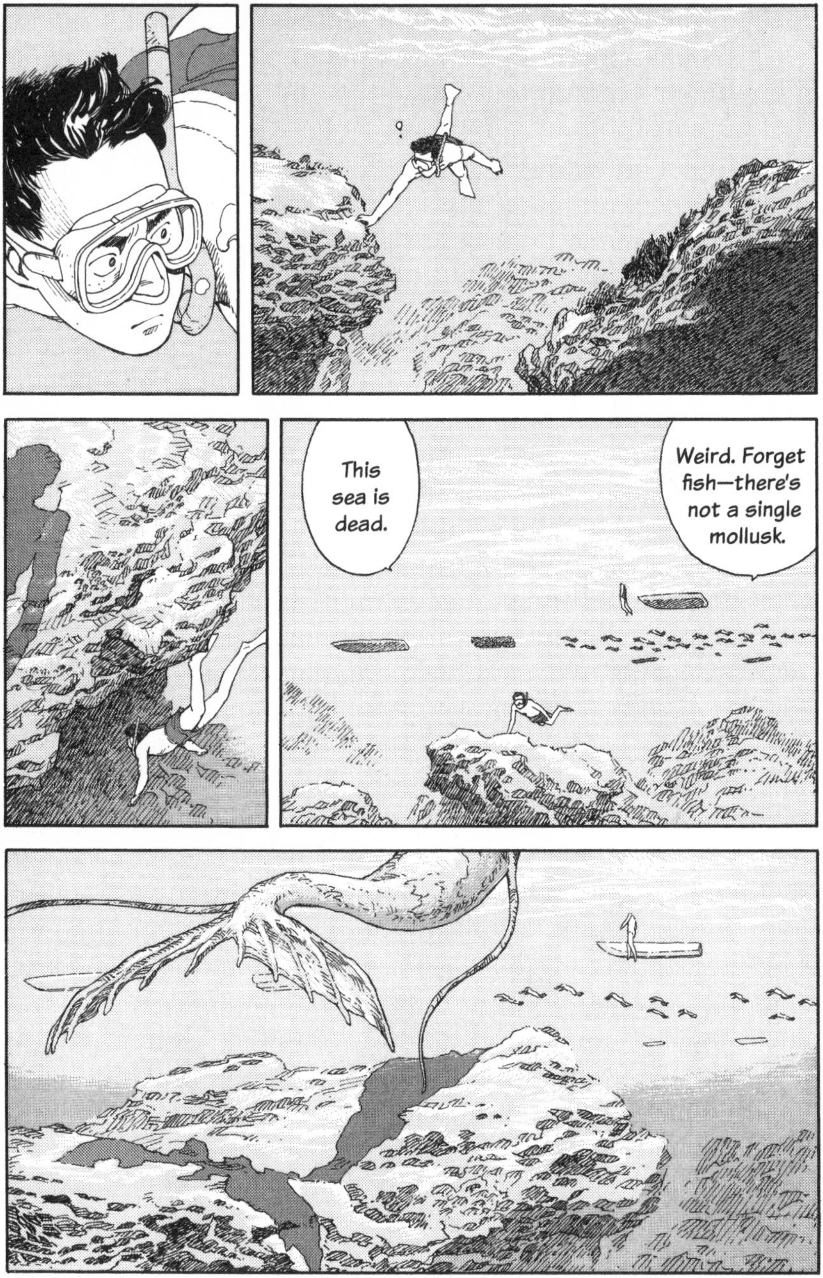
Weird. Forget fish—there's not a single mollusk.
This sea is dead.

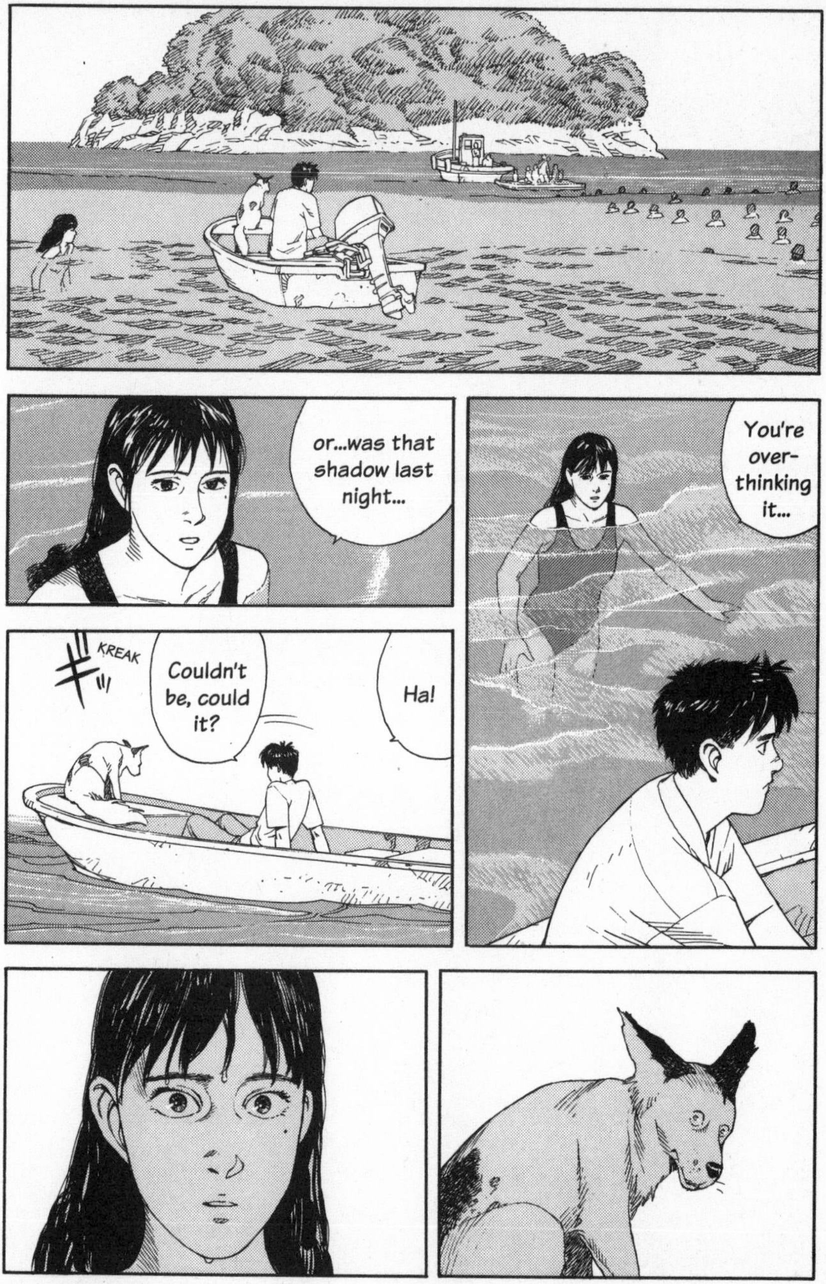
You're over-thinking it...
or...was that shadow last night...
Ha!
Couldn't be, could it?
KREAK

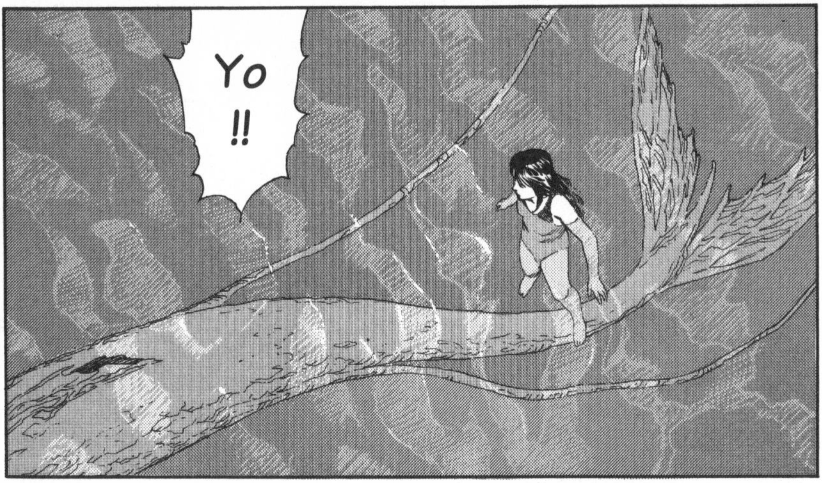
Yo !!

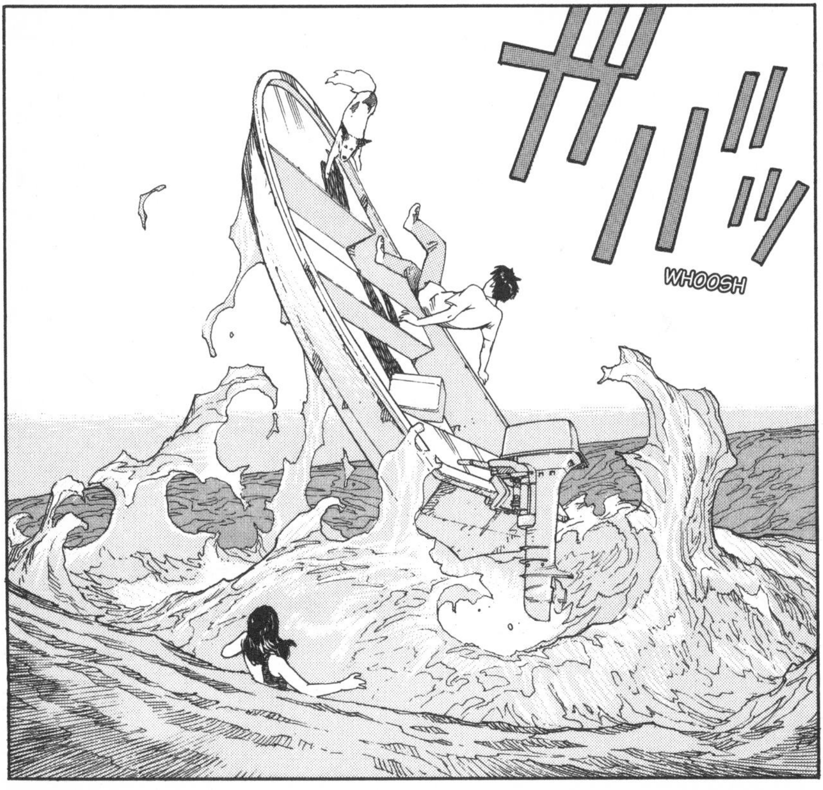
ザバッ
WHOOSH

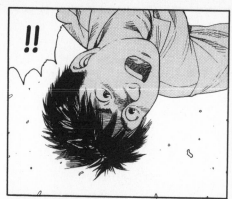

!!

Aaah !!

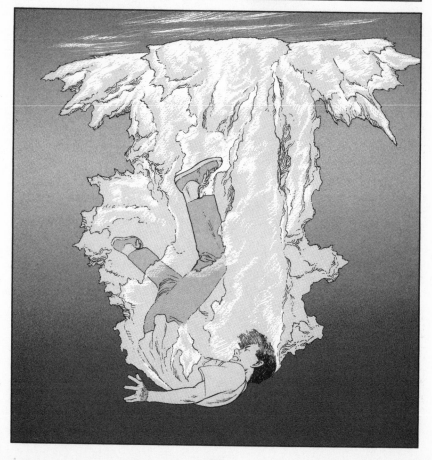

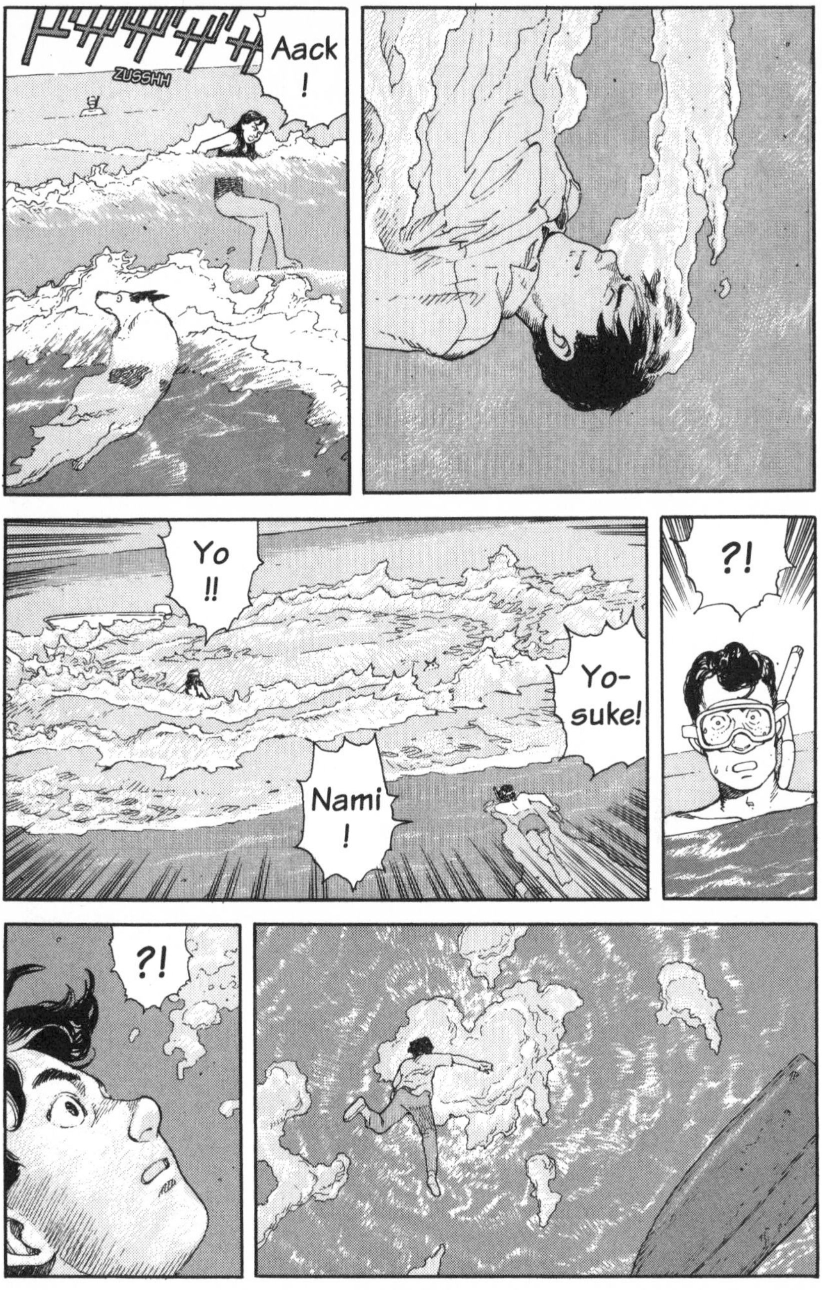
ZUSSHH
Aack !
?!
Yo !!
Yo-suke!
Nami !
?!

Yo
!!

Ah
!!

Mother
...

Help
me...

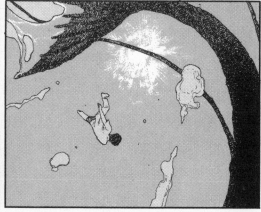

Mother!
Mo—

Gah
!

Yosuke
!

Yosuke
!

Ah...

Mother
....?

?

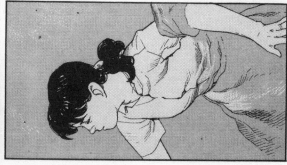

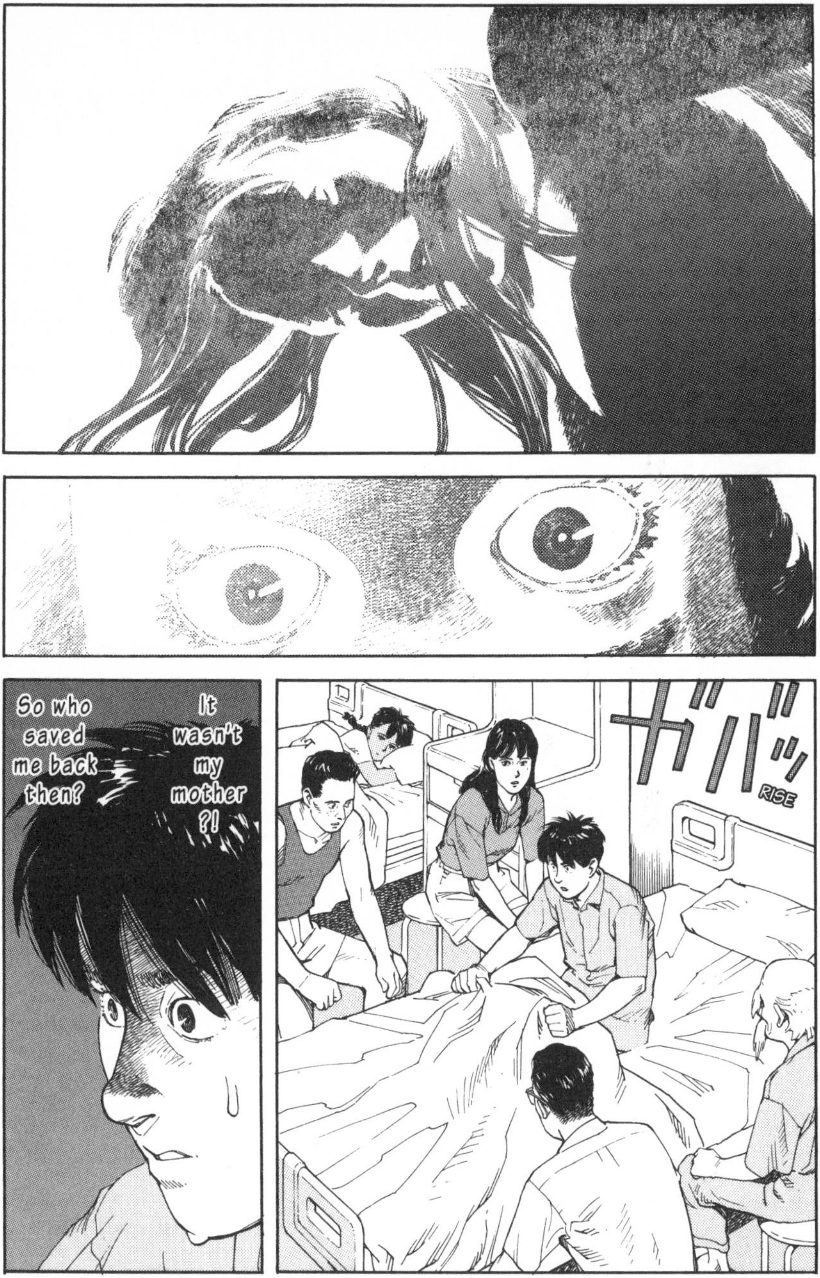
ガバッ
RISE
It wasn't my mother ?!
So who saved me back then?

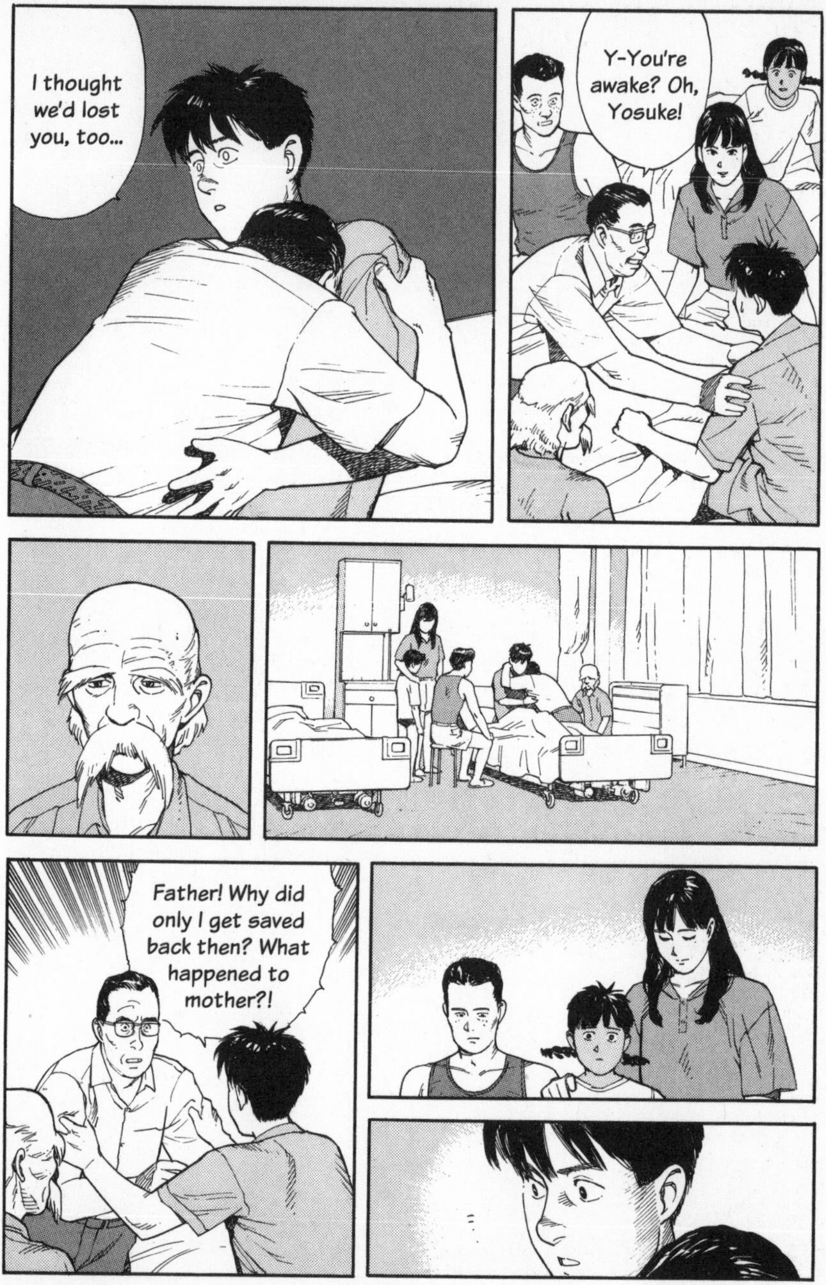
Y-You're awake? Oh, Yosuke!
I thought we'd lost you, too...
Father! Why did only I get saved back then? What happened to mother?!

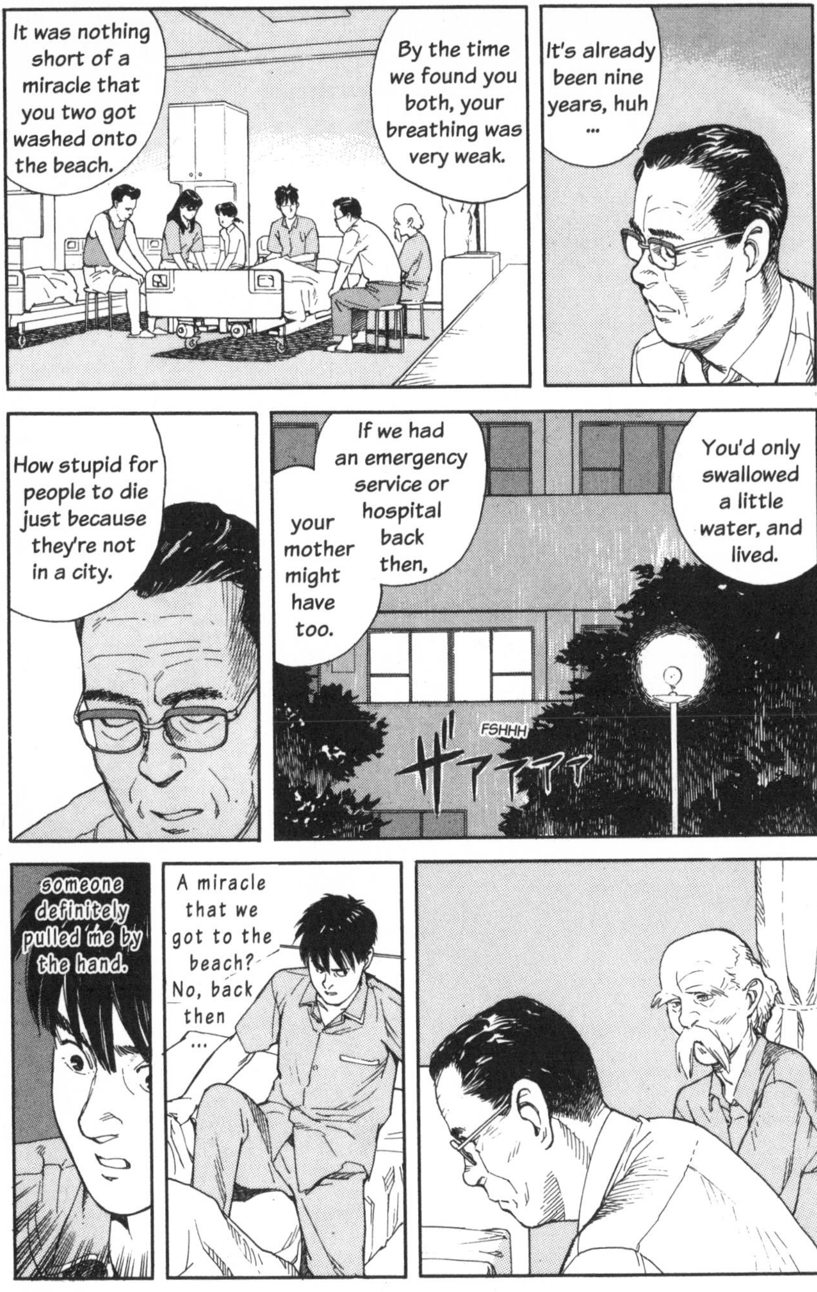
It's already been nine years, huh ...
By the time we found you both, your breathing was very weak.
It was nothing short of a miracle that you two got washed onto the beach.
You'd only swallowed a little water, and lived.
If we had an emergency service or hospital back then,
your mother might have too.
FSHHH
How stupid for people to die just because they're not in a city.
A miracle that we got to the beach? No, back then ...
someone definitely pulled me by the hand.

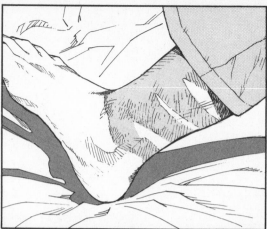

ドドォン
ZUSSHH

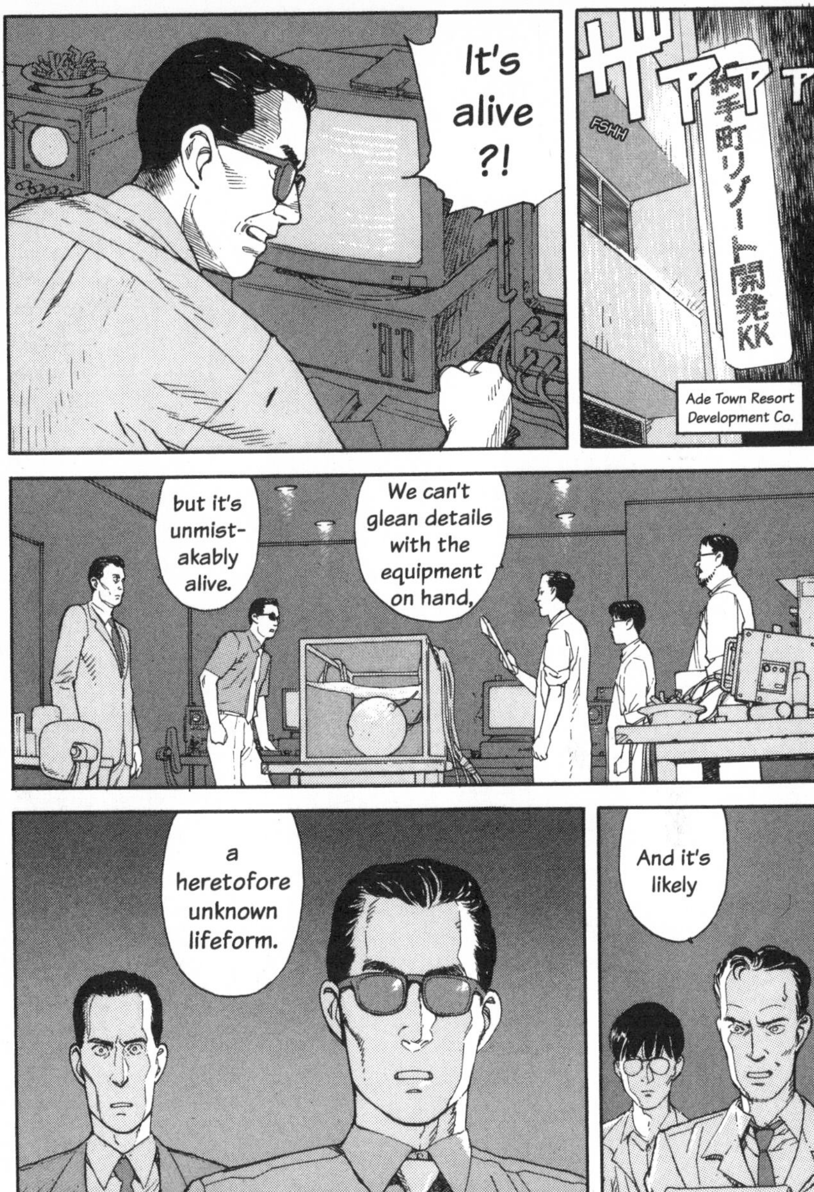
ザァァァ
FSHH
手町リゾート開発KK
Ade Town Resort Development Co.
It's alive ?!
We can't glean details with the equipment on hand,
but it's unmist-akably alive.
And it's likely
a heretofore unknown lifeform.

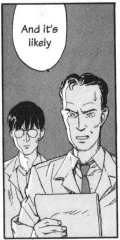

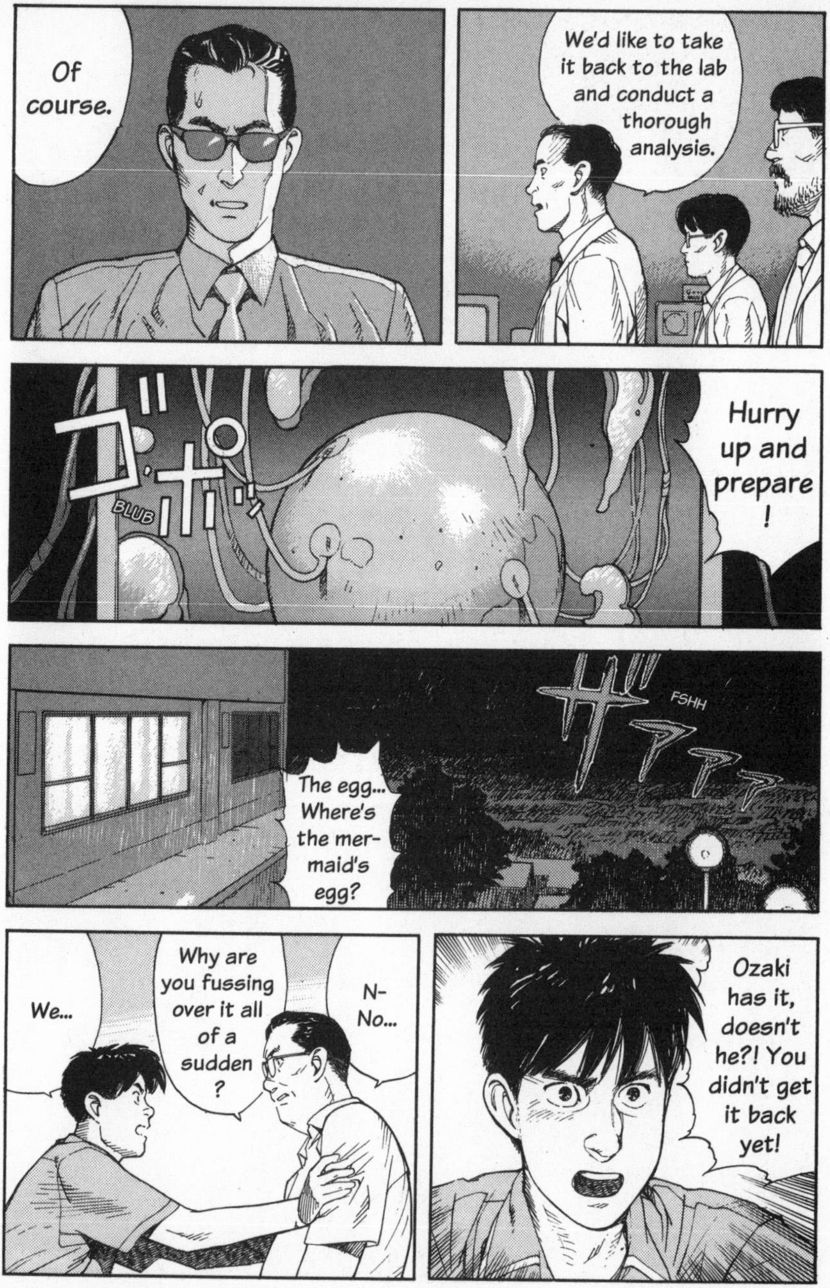
We'd like to take it back to the lab and conduct a thorough analysis.
Of course.
Hurry up and prepare!
BLUB
FSHH
The egg... Where's the mermaid's egg?
Ozaki has it, doesn't he?! You didn't get it back yet!
N- No...
Why are you fussing over it all of a sudden?
We...

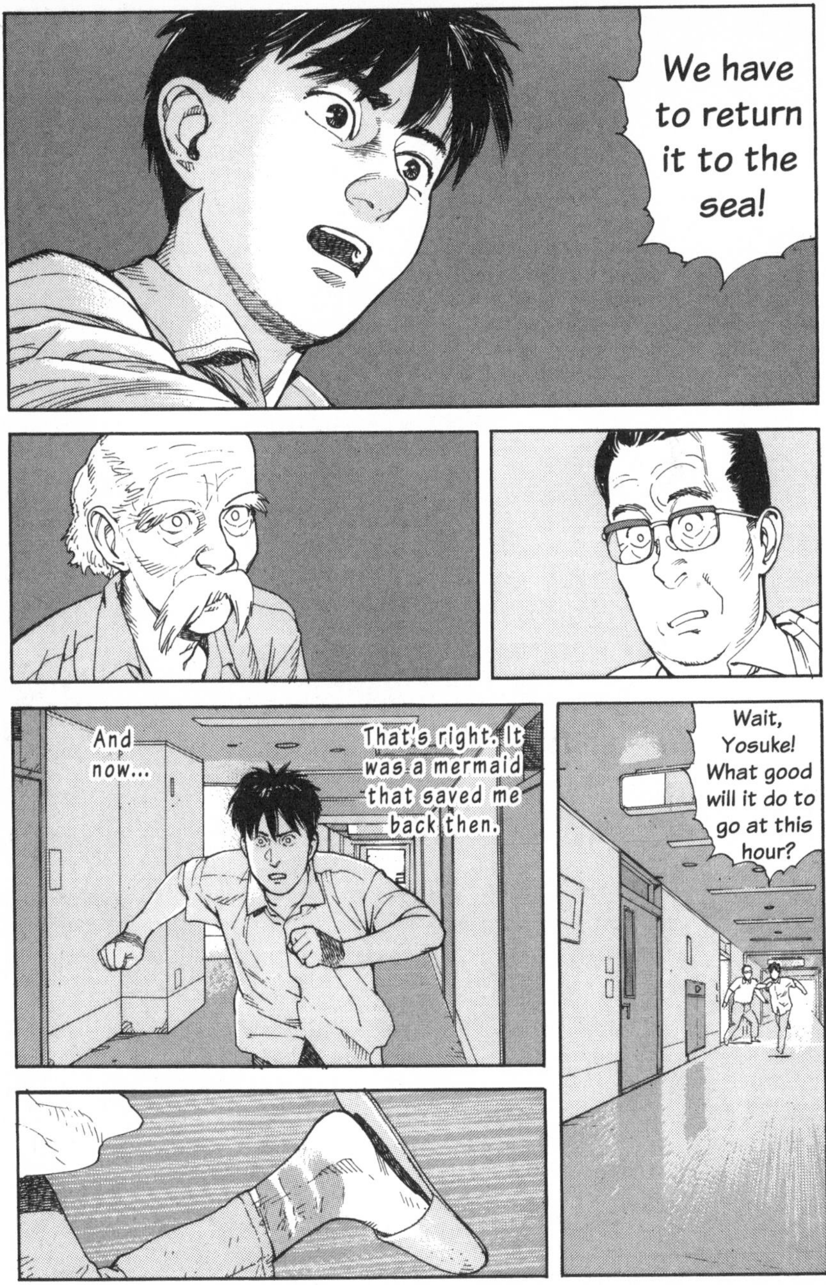
We have to return it to the sea!
Wait, Yosuke! What good will it do to go at this hour?
That's right. It was a mermaid that saved me back then.
And now...

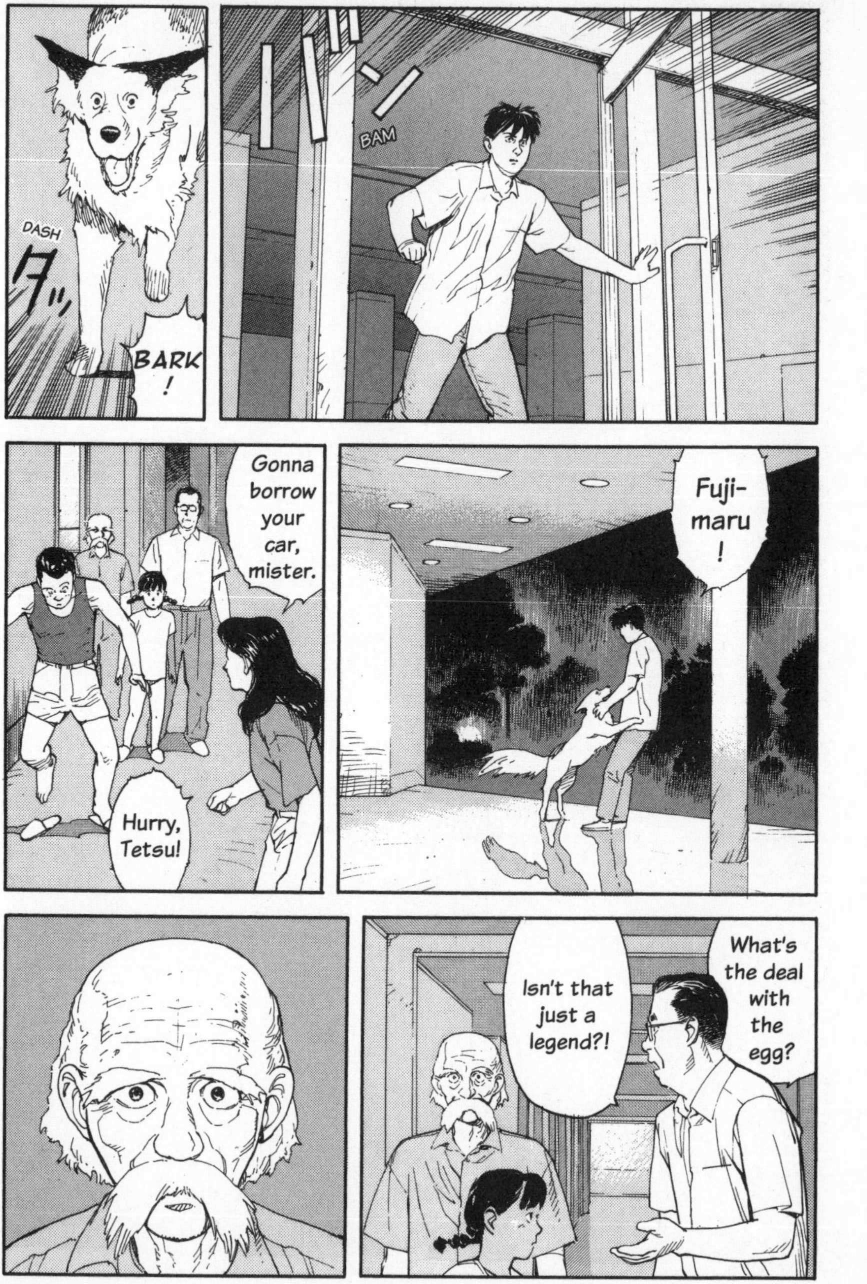
BAM
DASH
タッ
BARK!
Fuji-maru!
Gonna borrow your car, mister.
Hurry, Tetsu!
What's the deal with the egg?
Isn't that just a legend?!

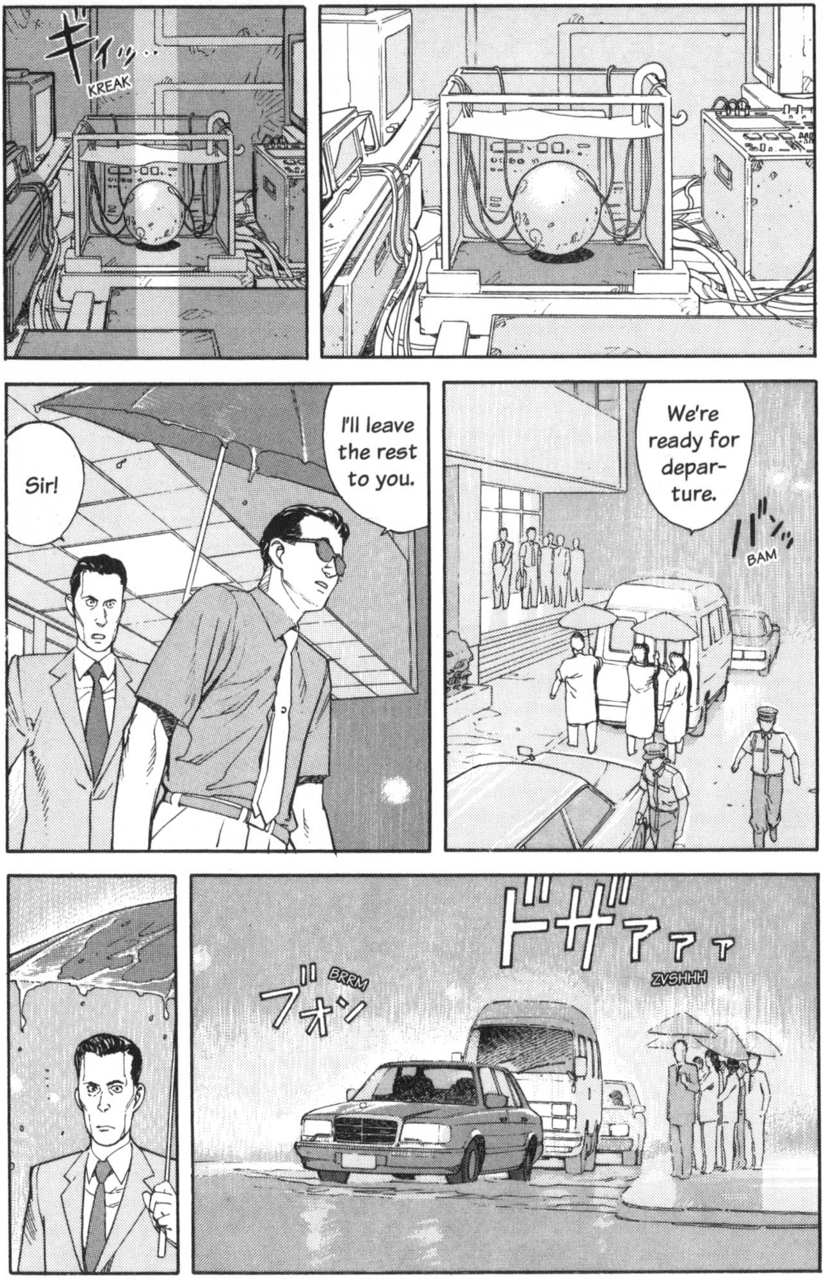
ギィッ..
KREAK
We're ready for depar- ture.
バンッ
BAM
I'll leave the rest to you.
Sir!
ドザァァァ
ZVSHHH
ブォン
BRRM

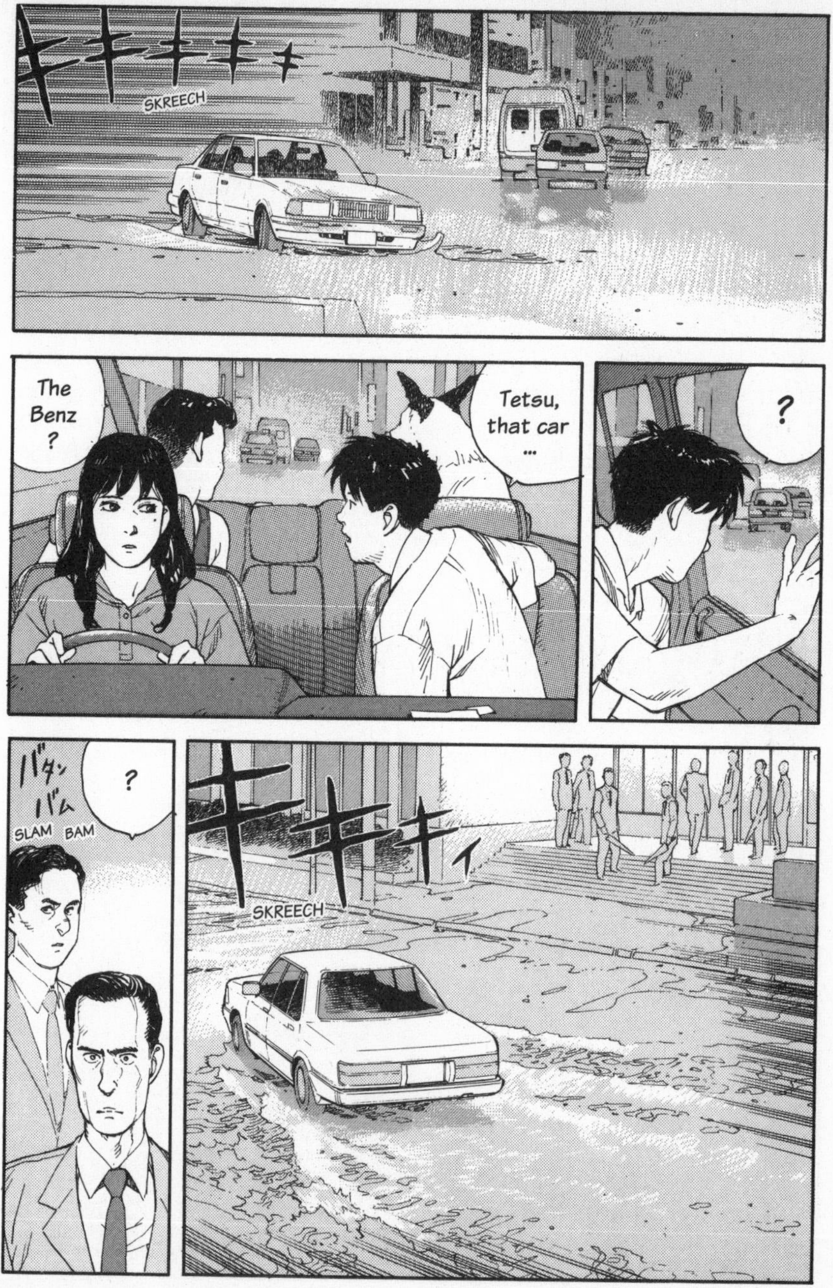
キキキキキ
SKREECH
?
Tetsu, that car ...
The Benz ?
キキィ
SKREECH
バタン バム
SLAM BAM
?

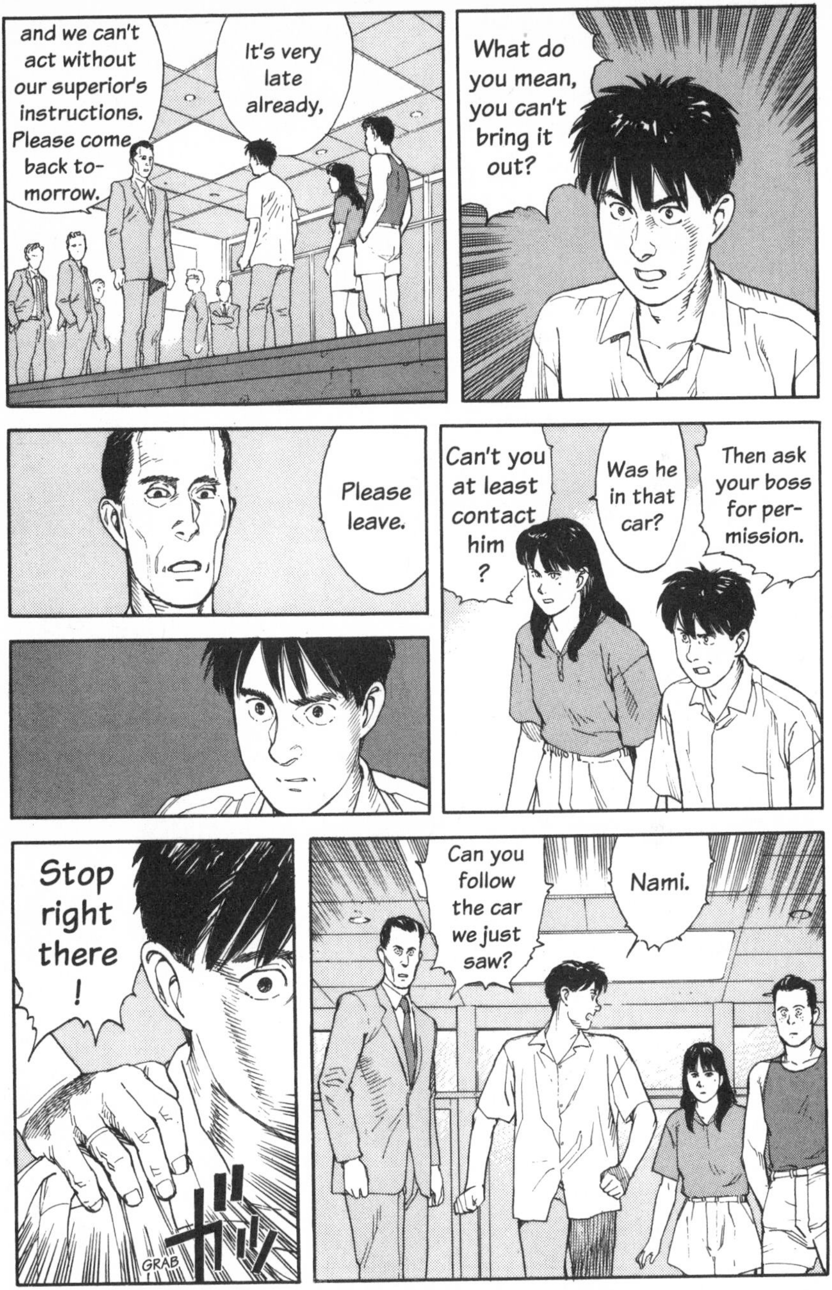
What do you mean, you can't bring it out?
It's very late already,
and we can't act without our superior's instructions. Please come back to-morrow.
Then ask your boss for per-mission.
Was he in that car?
Can't you at least contact him?
Please leave.
Nami.
Can you follow the car we just saw?
Stop right there!
ガッ
GRAB

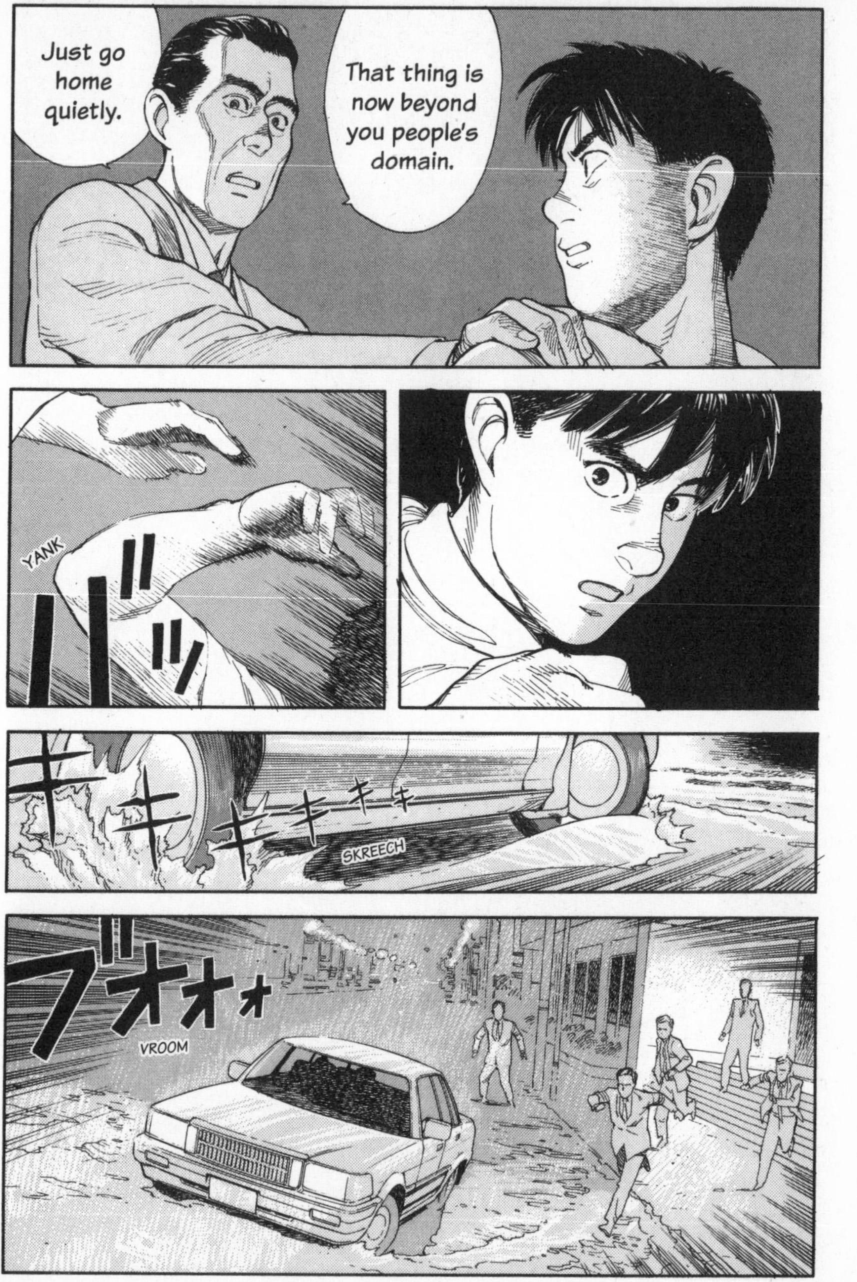
That thing is now beyond you people's domain.
Just go home quietly.
YANK
SKREECH
VROOM

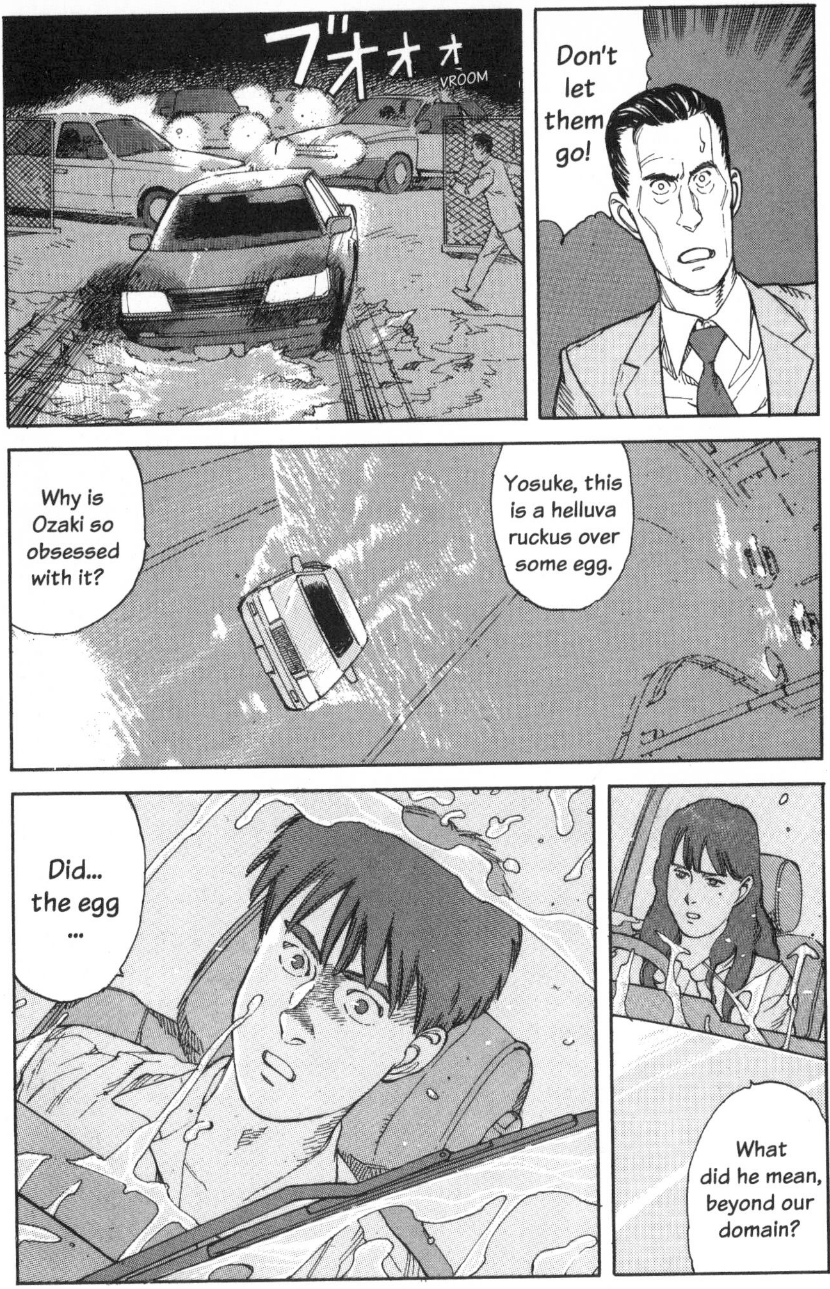
Don't let them go!
ブオオオ
VROOM
Yosuke, this is a helluva ruckus over some egg.
Why is Ozaki so obsessed with it?
What did he mean, beyond our domain?
Did... the egg ...

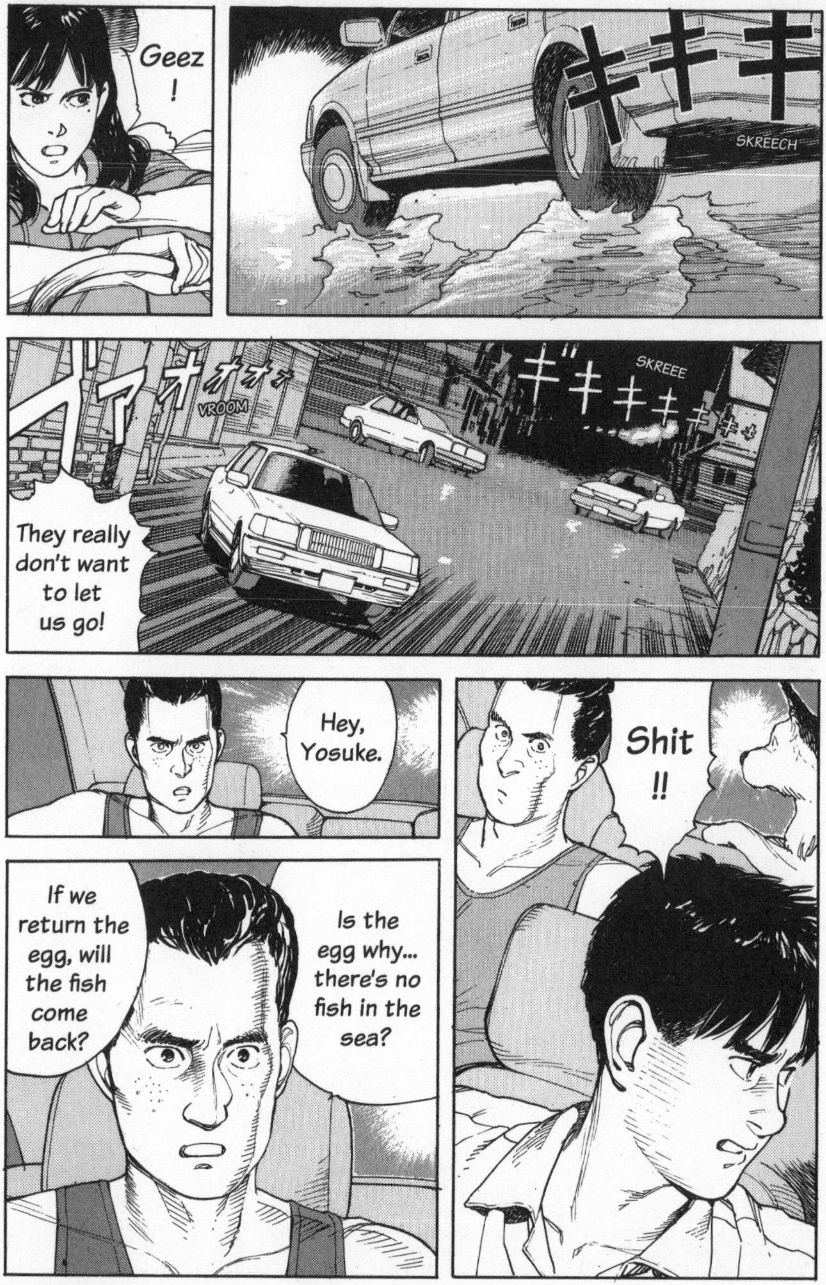
キキキ
SKREECH
Geez !
SKREEE
VROOM
They really don't want to let us go!
Shit !!
Hey, Yosuke.
Is the egg why... there's no fish in the sea?
If we return the egg, will the fish come back?

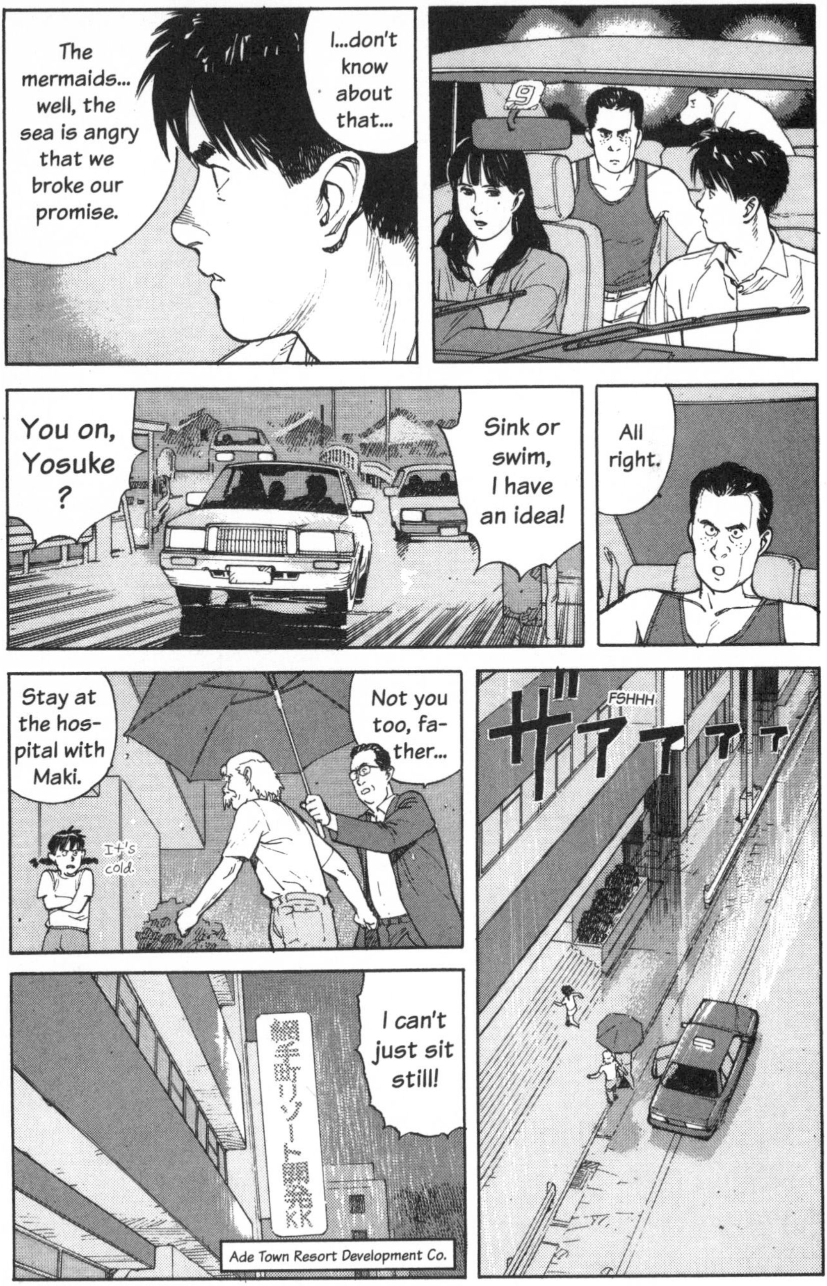
I...don't know about that...
The mermaids... well, the sea is angry that we broke our promise.
All right.
Sink or swim, I have an idea!
You on, Yosuke?
FSHHH
ザァァァァ
Not you too, father...
Stay at the hospital with Maki.
It's cold.
I can't just sit still!
網手町リゾート開発KK
Ade Town Resort Development Co.

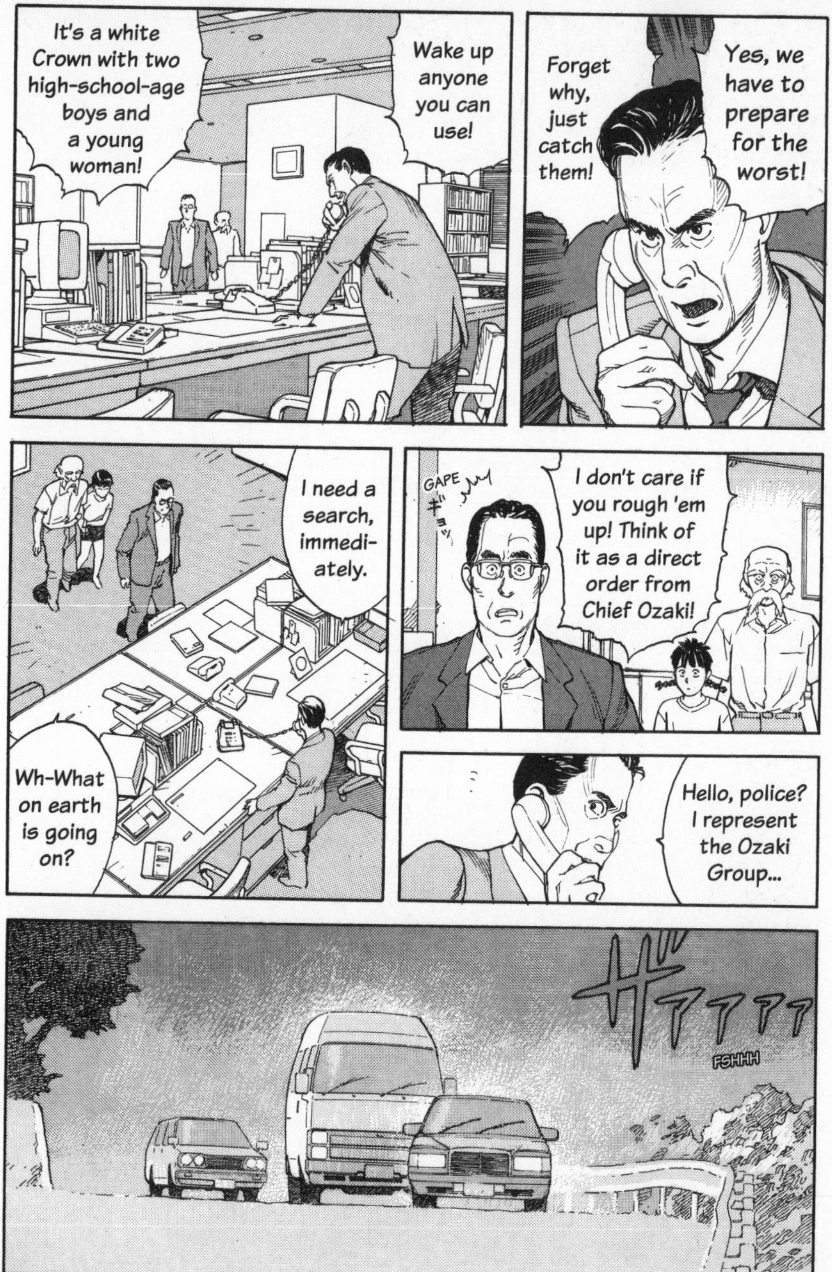

Yes, we have to prepare for the worst!
Forget why, just catch them!
Wake up anyone you can use!
It's a white Crown with two high-school-age boys and a young woman!
I don't care if you rough 'em up! Think of it as a direct order from Chief Ozaki!
GAPE
Hello, police? I represent the Ozaki Group...
I need a search, immedi-ately.
Wh-What on earth is going on?
FSHHH

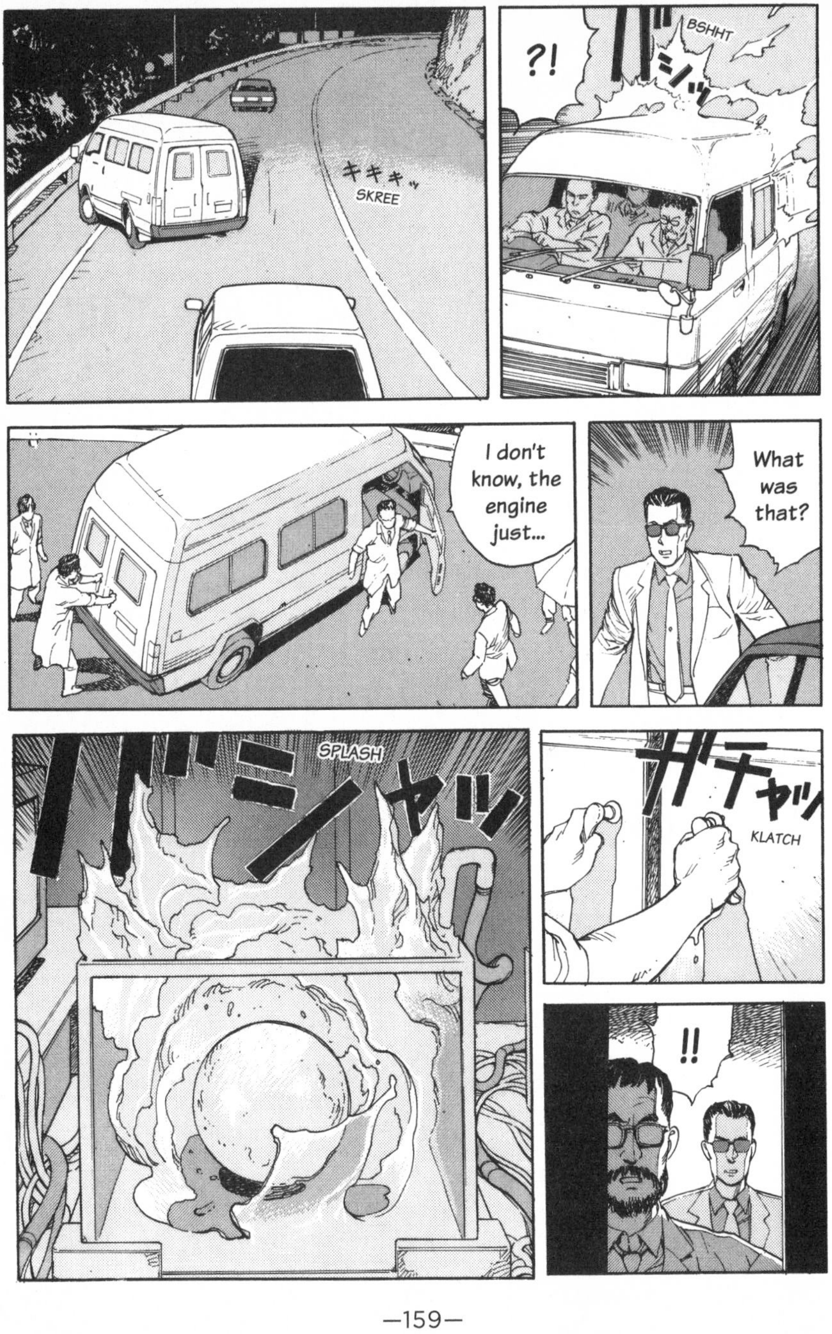
?!
バシッ
BSHHT
キキキッ
SKREE
What was that?
I don't know, the engine just...
ガチャッ
KLATCH
!!
バシャッ
SPLASH

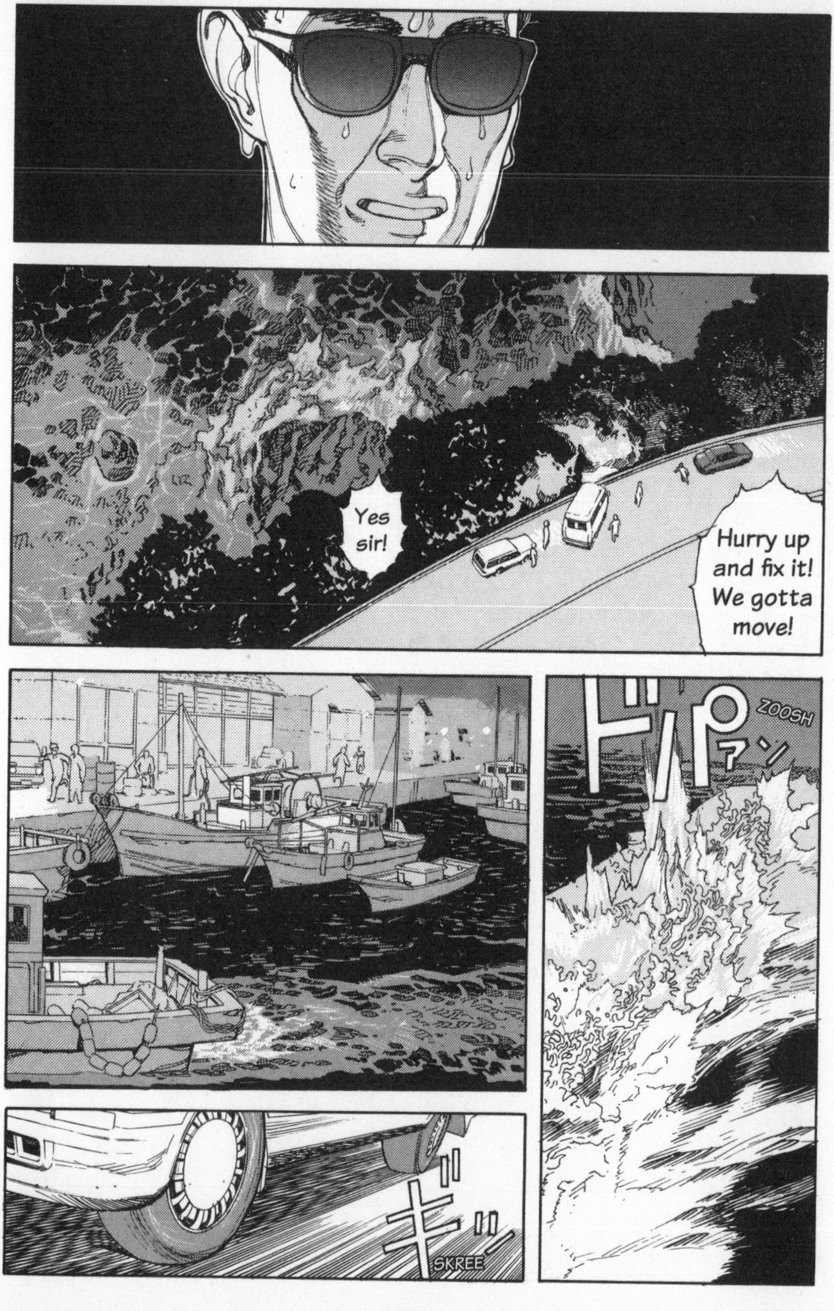
Hurry up and fix it! We gotta move!
Yes sir!
ドパァン
ZOOSH
SKREE

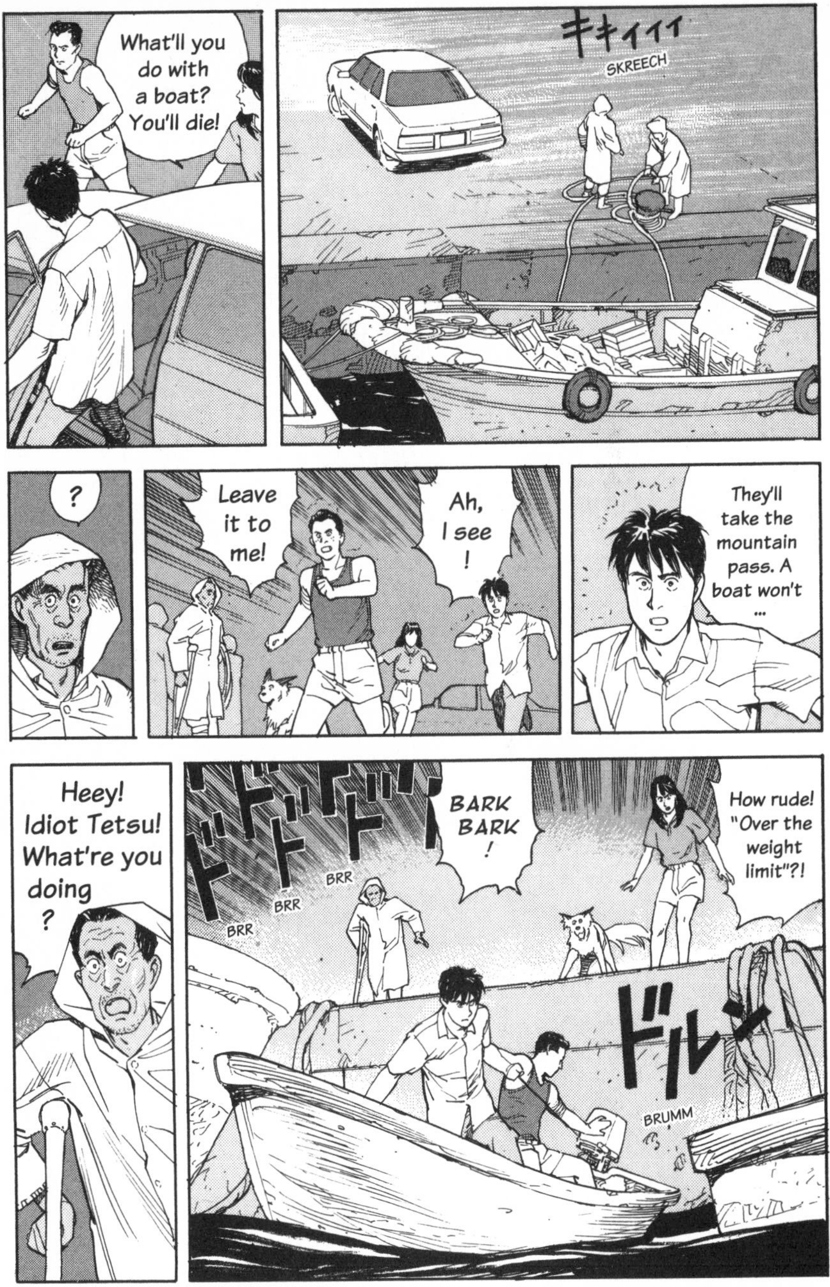

キキイイイ
SKREECH
What'll you do with a boat? You'll die!
They'll take the mountain pass. A boat won't ...
Ah, I see !
Leave it to me!
?
How rude! "Over the weight limit"?!
BARK BARK !
BRR
BRR
BRR
BRUMM
Heey! Idiot Tetsu! What're you doing ?

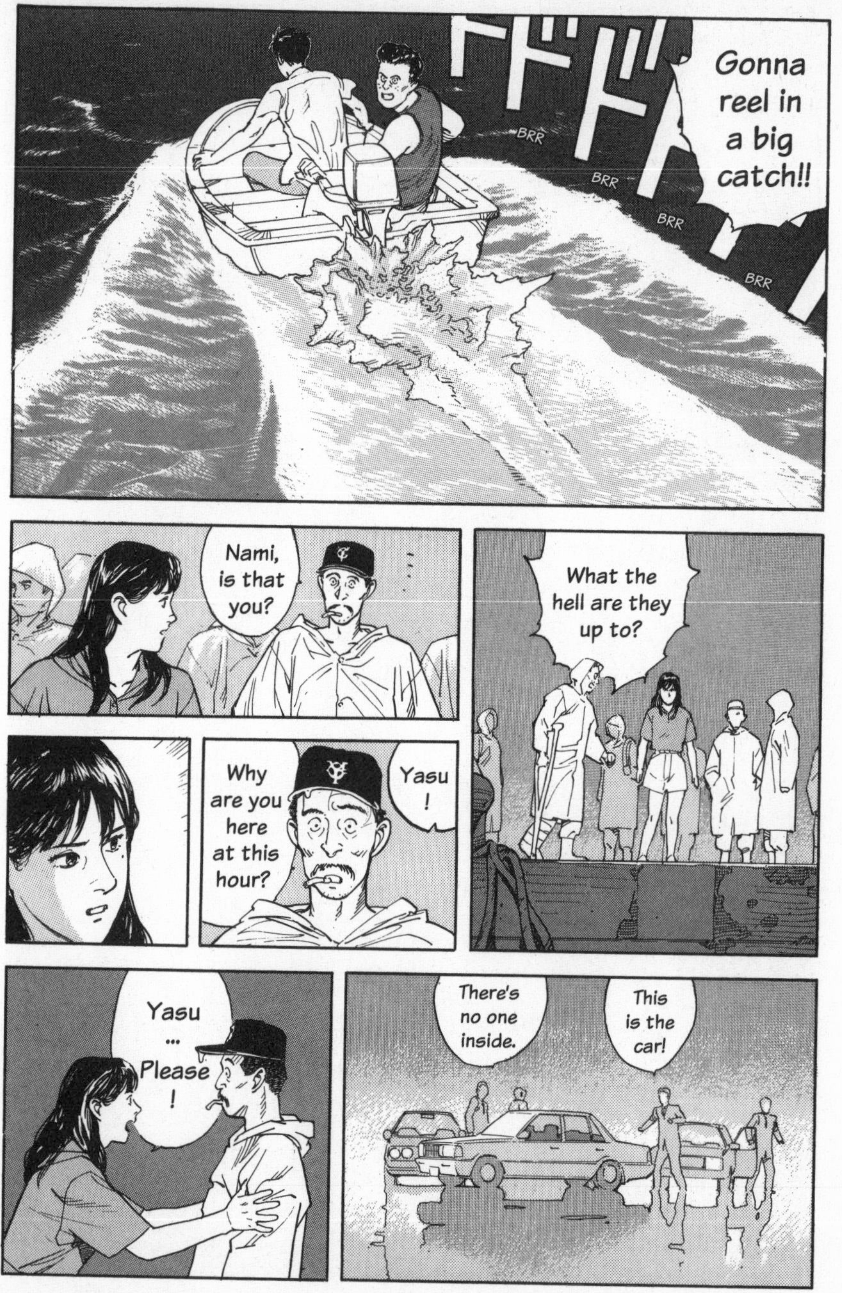
Gonna reel in a big catch!!
BRR
BRR
BRR
BRR
What the hell are they up to?
Nami, is that you?
Yasu !
Why are you here at this hour?
This is the car!
There's no one inside.
Yasu ... Please !

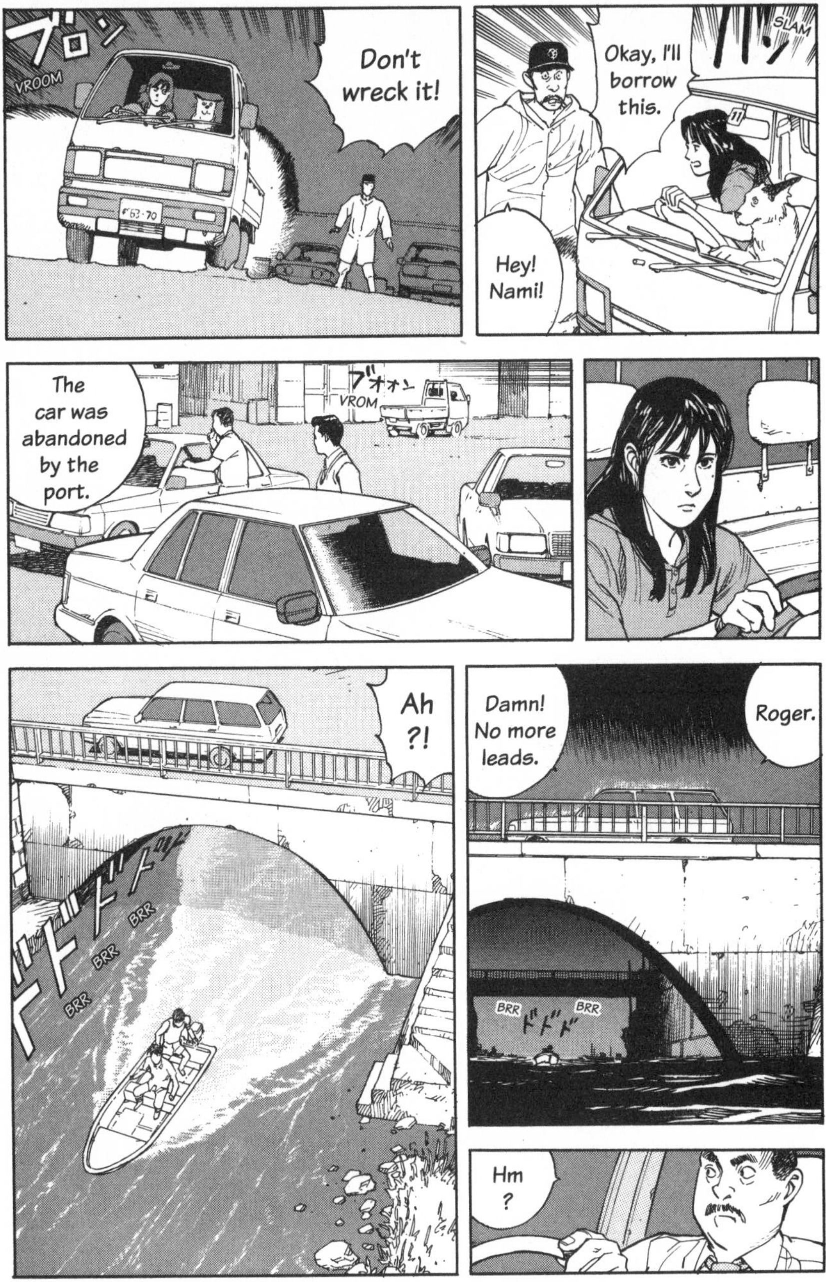
SLAM
Okay, I'll borrow this.
Hey! Nami!
ブロン
VROOM
Don't wreck it!
VROM
The car was abandoned by the port.
Roger.
Damn! No more leads.
BRR
ドドド
BRR
Hm ?
Ah ?!
BRR
BRR
BRR
BRR

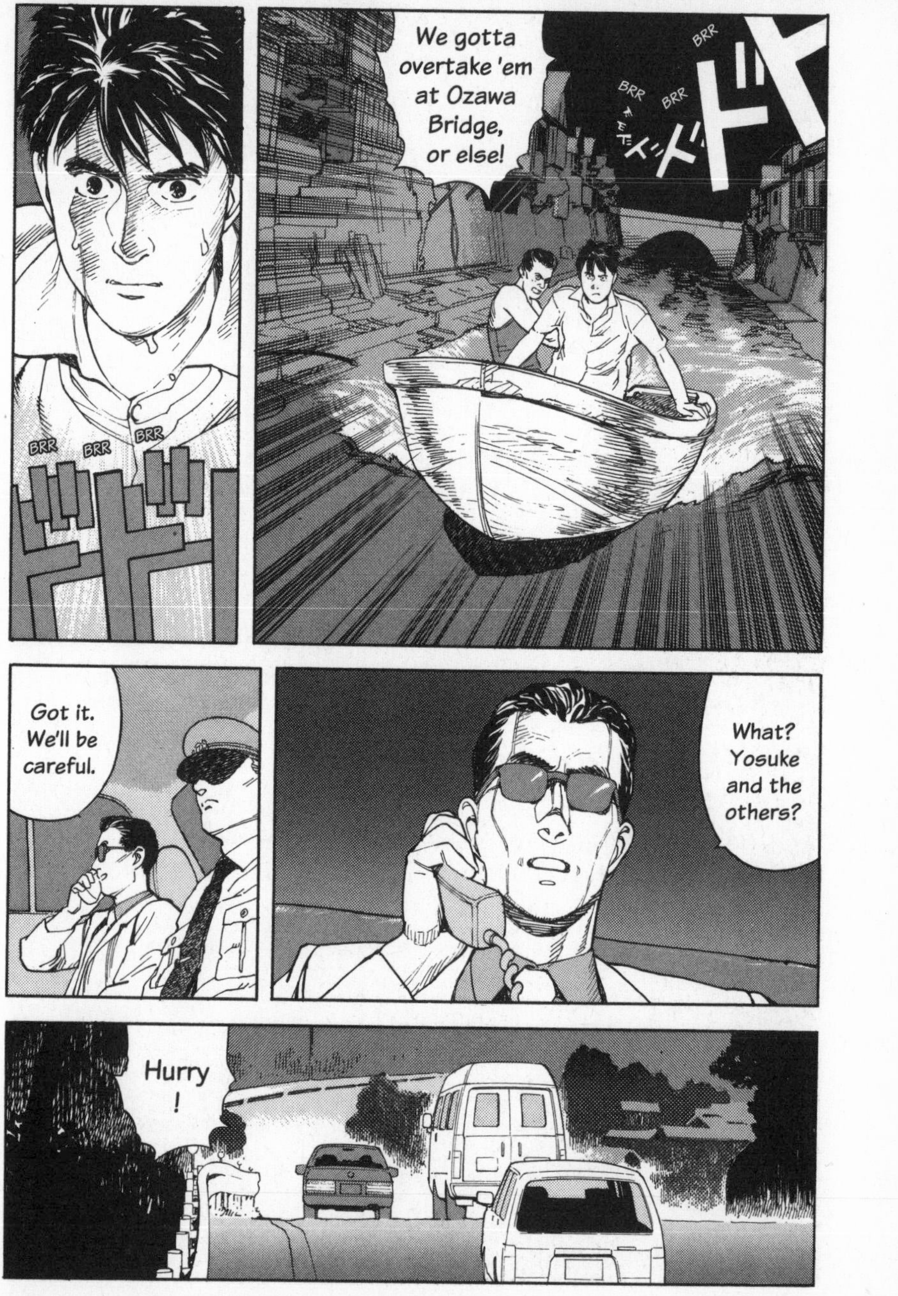
We gotta overtake 'em at Ozawa Bridge, or else!
BRR BRR BRR
BRR BRR BRR
What? Yosuke and the others?
Got it. We'll be careful.
Hurry !

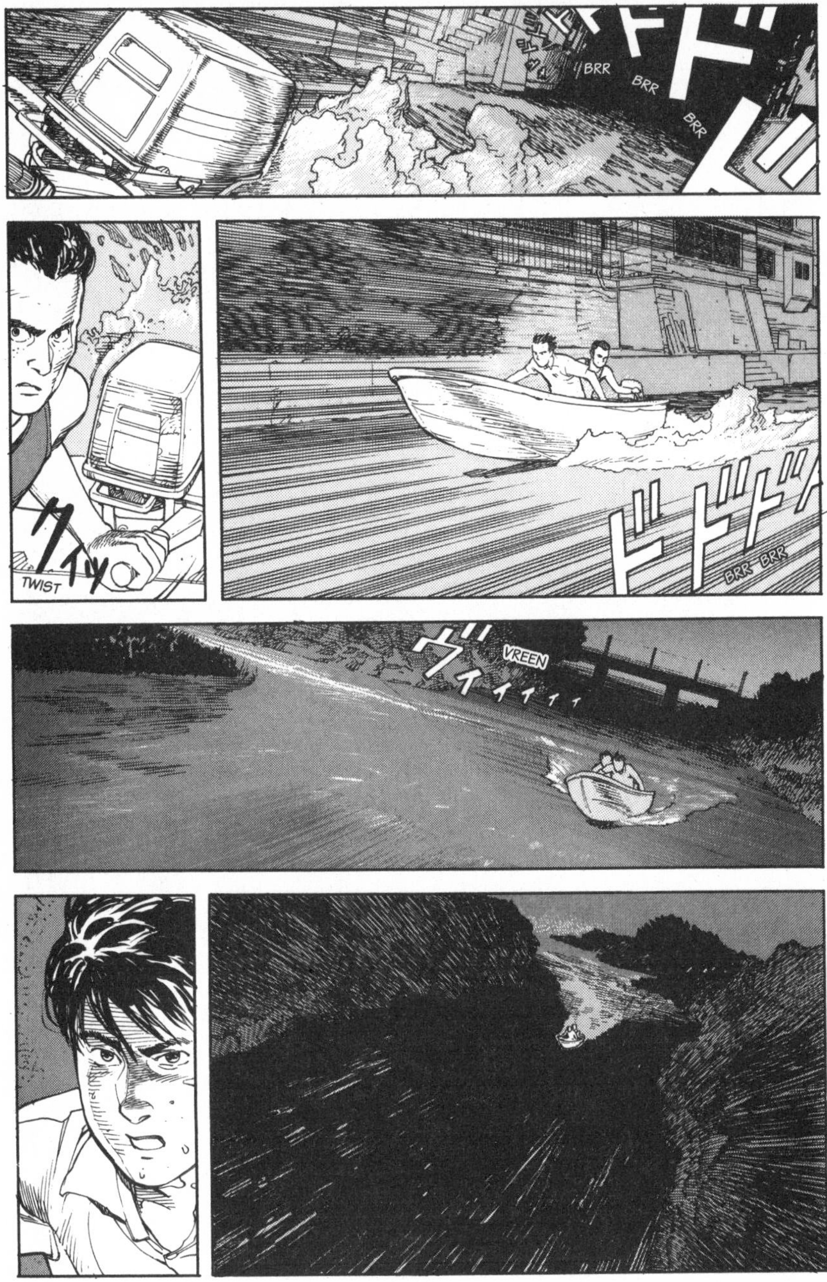
BRR BRR BRR
BRR BRR
ウイッ
TWIST
ヴィイイイイ
VREEN

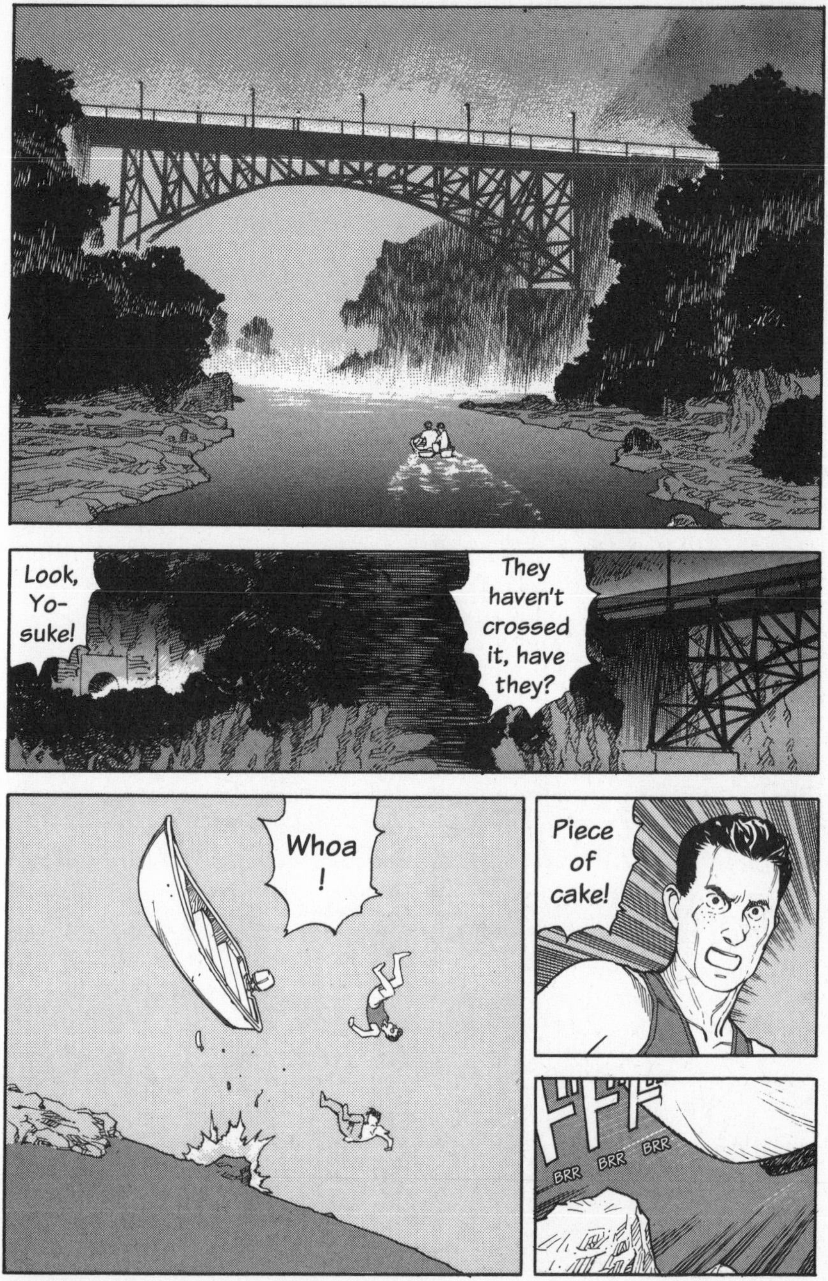
They haven't crossed it, have they?
Look, Yo-suke!
Piece of cake!
BRR BRR BRR
Whoa !

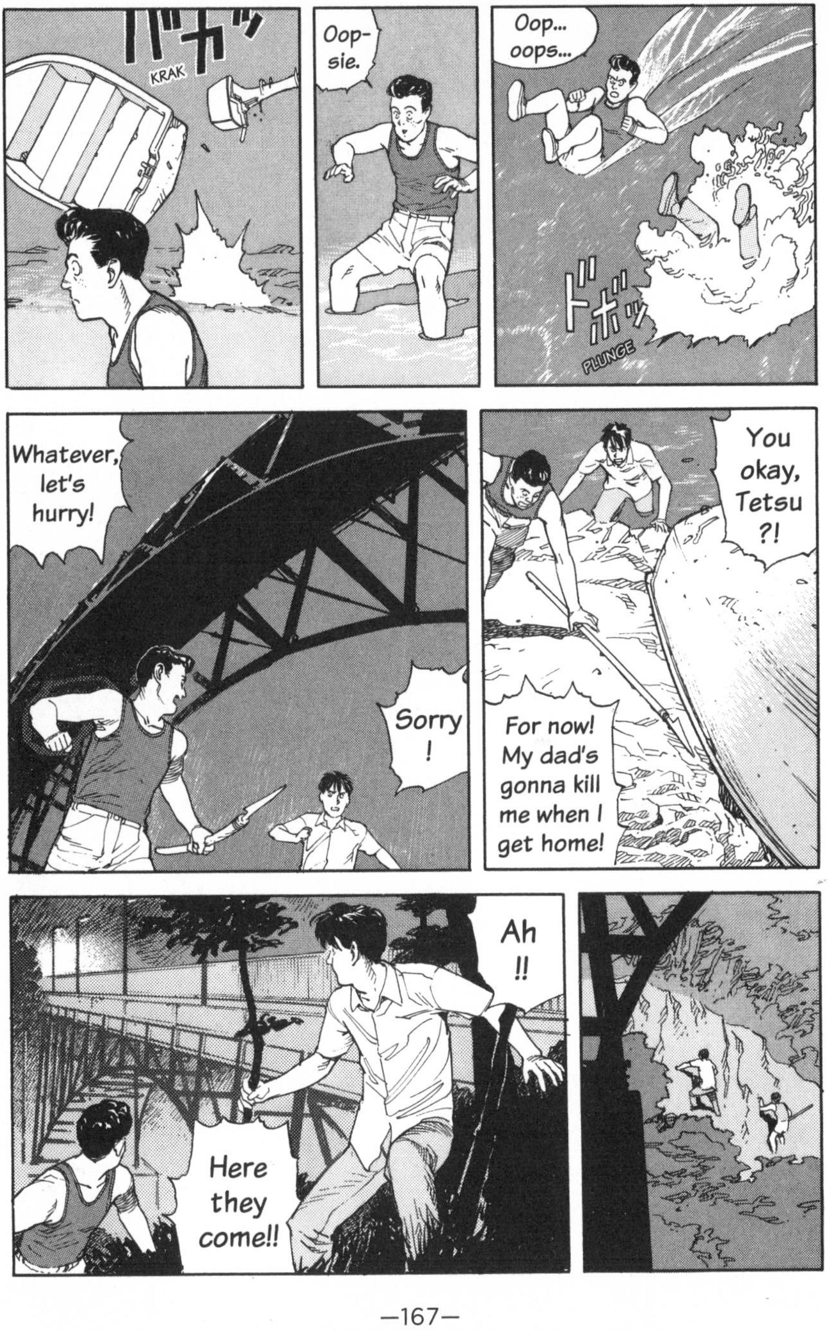
Oop... oops...
ドボッ
PLUNGE
Oop- sie.
バカッ
KRAK
You okay, Tetsu ?!
For now! My dad's gonna kill me when I get home!
Whatever, let's hurry!
Sorry !
Ah !!
Here they come!!

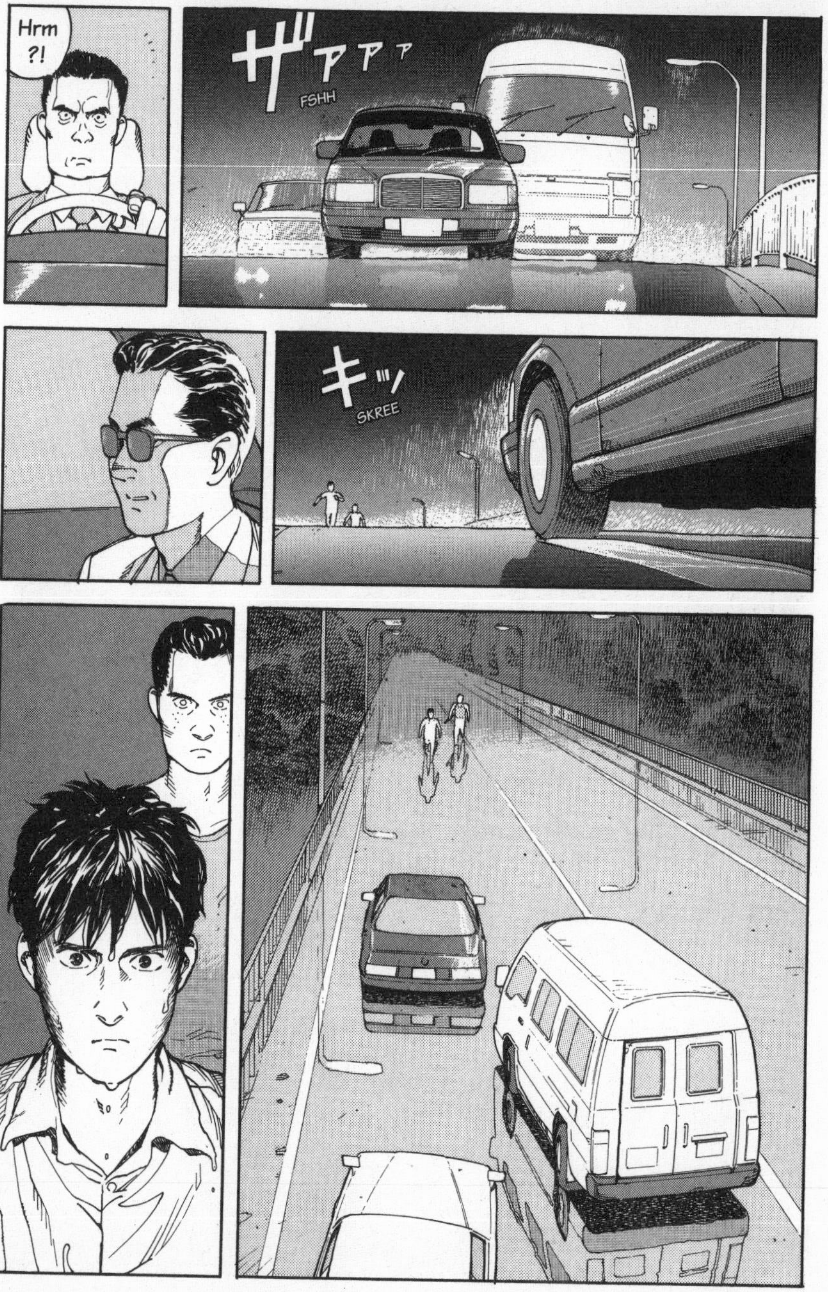
ザァァァ
FSHH
Hrm ?!
キッ
SKREE

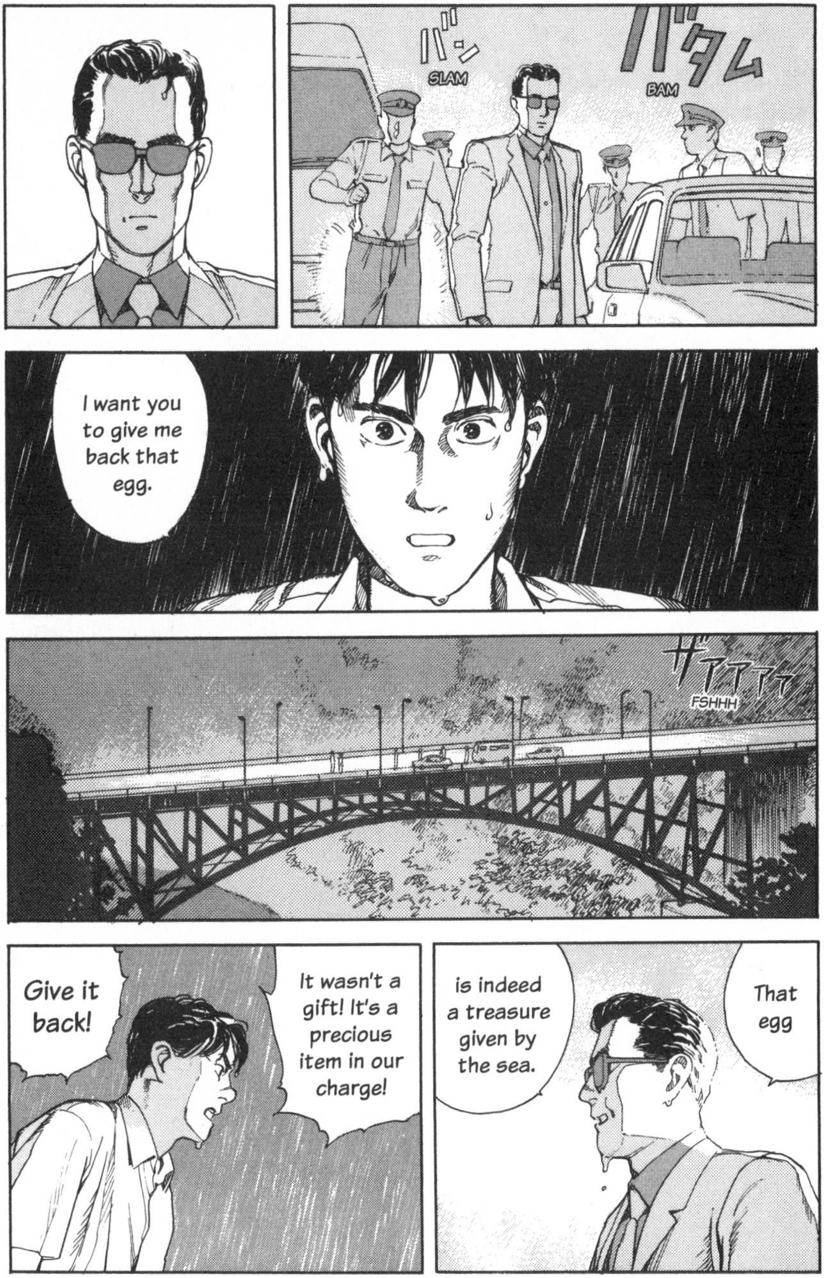

バタム
BAM
SLAM
I want you to give me back that egg.
ザアアアア
FSHHH
That egg
is indeed a treasure given by the sea.
It wasn't a gift! It's a precious item in our charge!
Give it back!

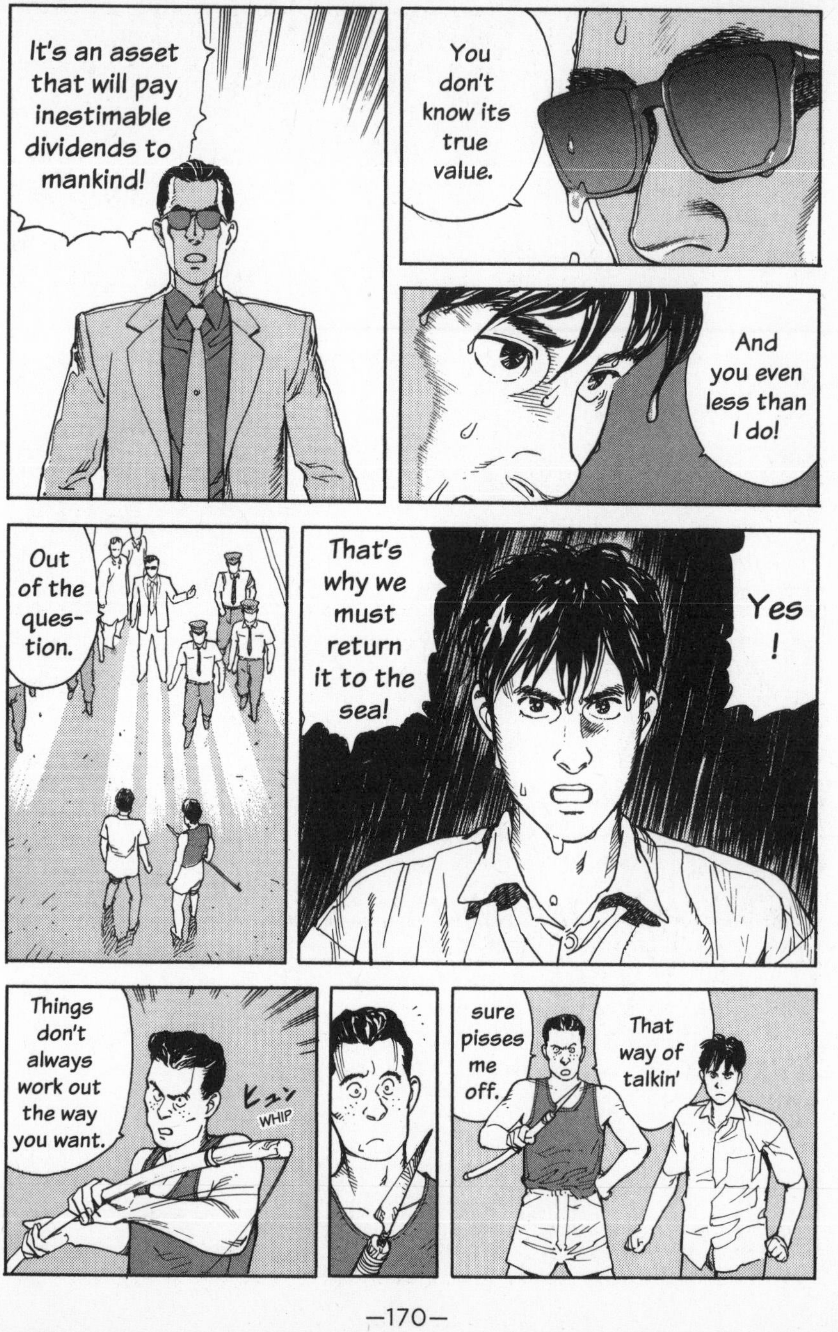

You don't know its true value.
And you even less than I do!
It's an asset that will pay inestimable dividends to mankind!
That's why we must return it to the sea!
Yes !
Out of the question.
That way of talkin'
sure pisses me off.
Things don't always work out the way you want.
ヒュン
WHIP

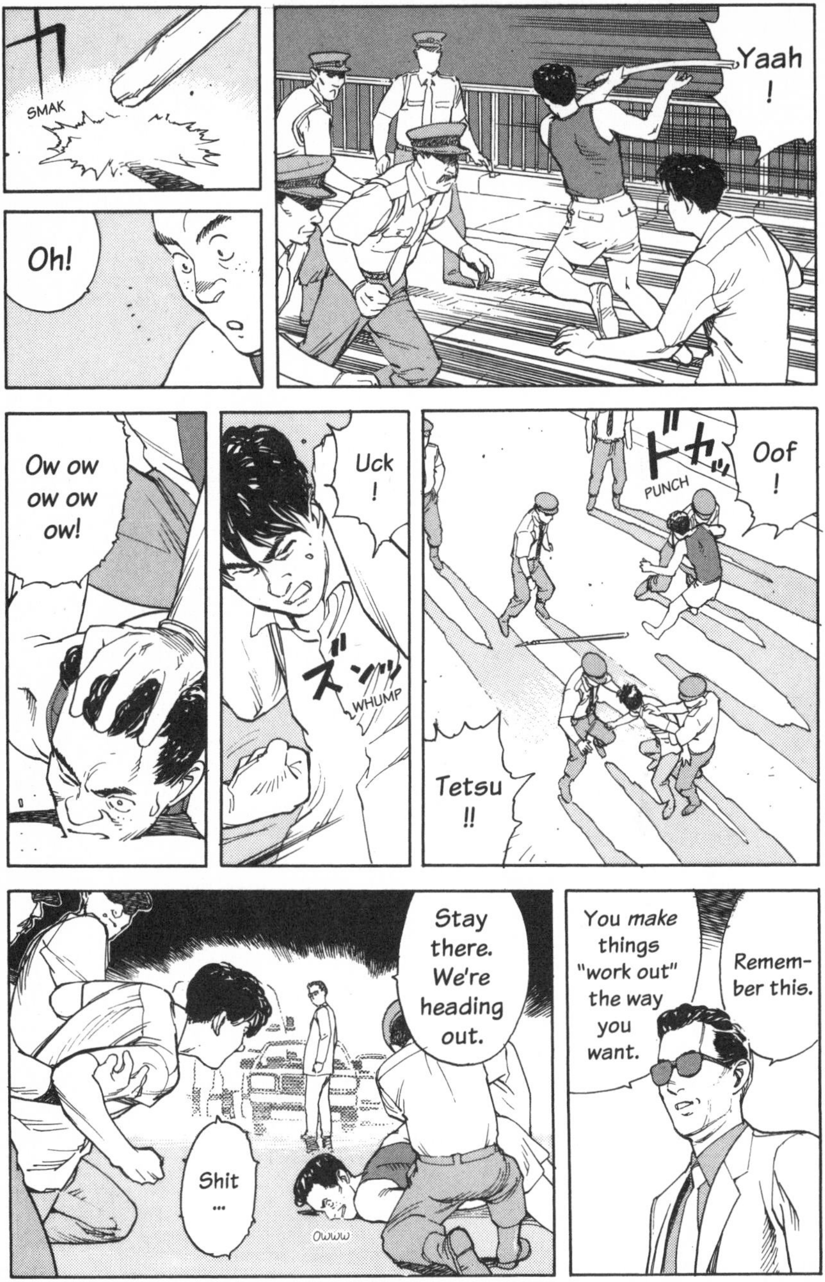
Yaah !
SMAK
Oh!
Oof !
PUNCH
Tetsu !!
Uck !
WHUMP
Ow ow ow ow ow!
You make things "work out" the way you want.
Remem-ber this.
Stay there. We're heading out.
Shit ...
owww

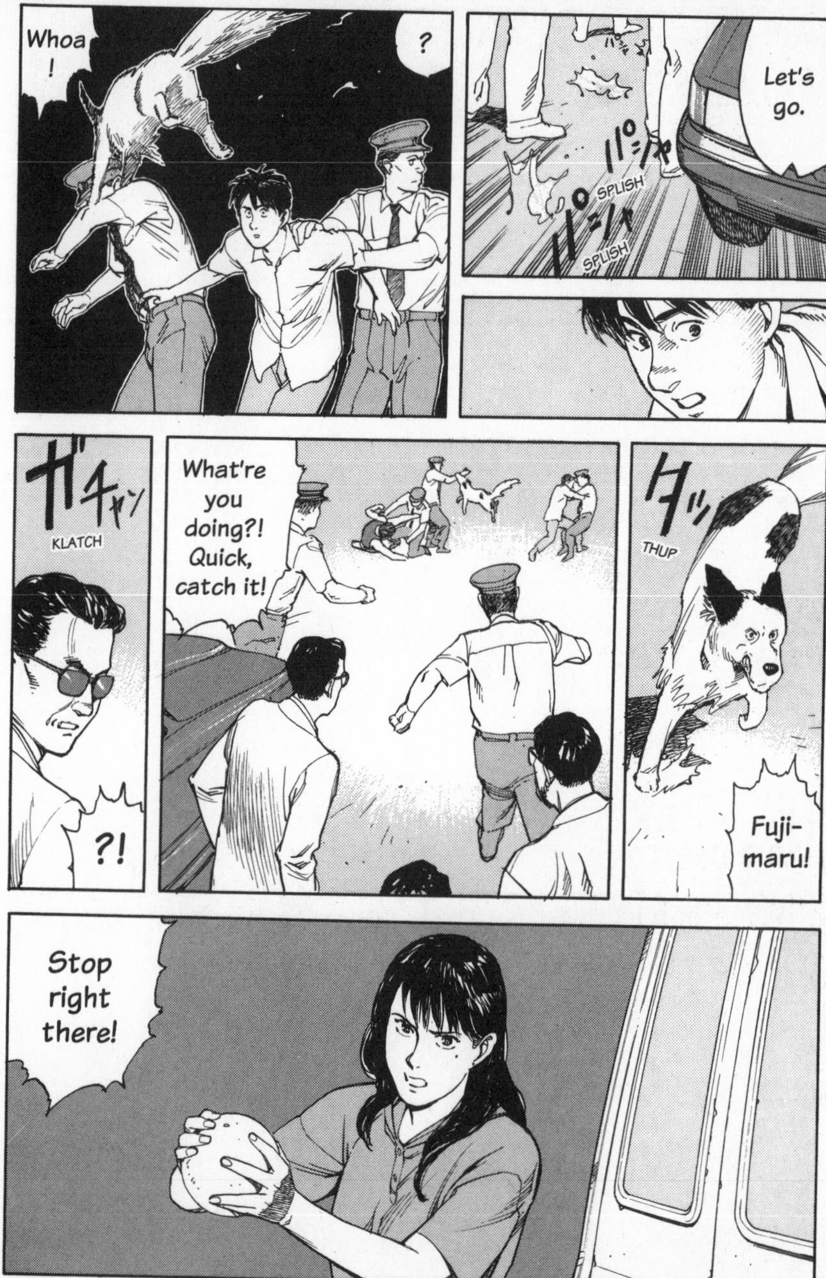
Let's go.
パシャ
SPLISH
パシャ
SPLISH
?
Whoa !
タッ
THUP
Fuji-maru!
What're you doing?! Quick, catch it!
ガチャン
KLATCH
?!
Stop right there!

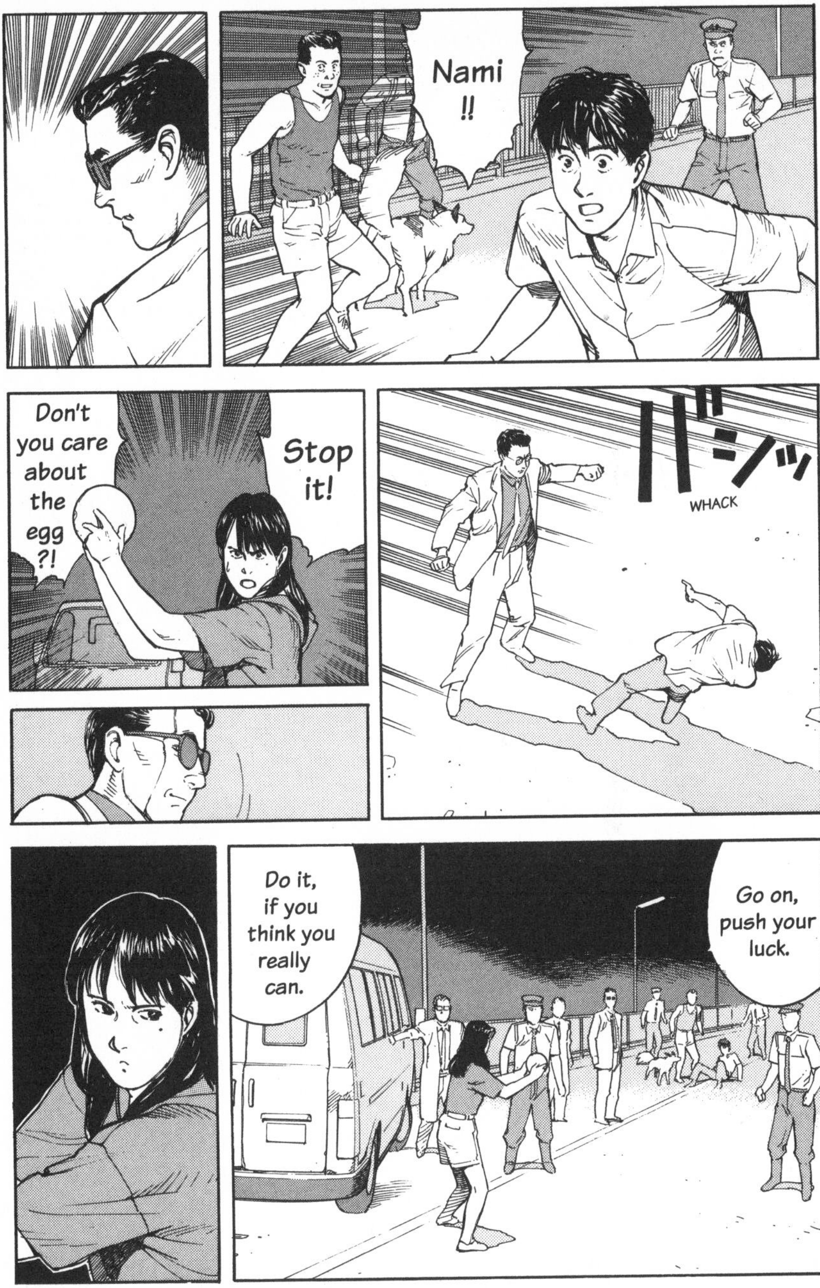

Nami !!
バシッ
WHACK
Stop it!
Don't you care about the egg ?!
Go on, push your luck.
Do it, if you think you really can.

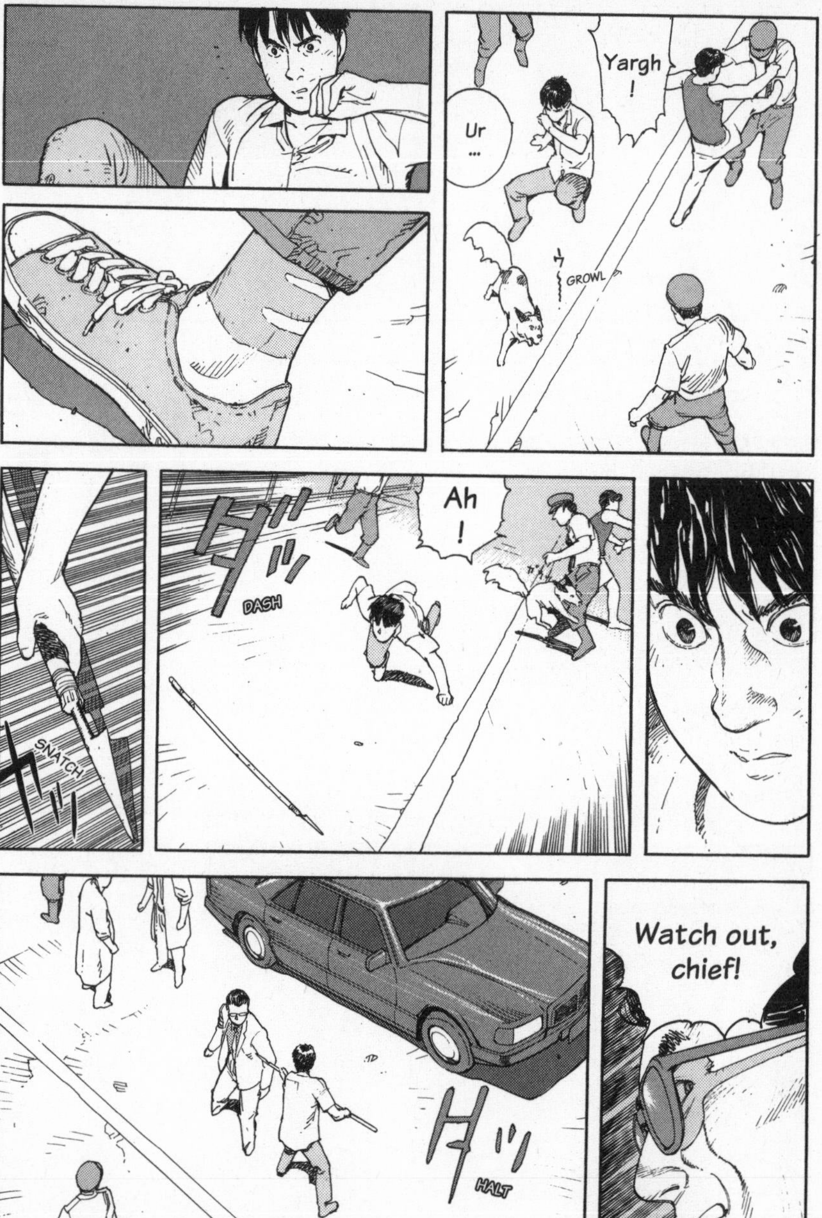
Yargh
!
Ur
...
GROWL
Ah
!
DASH
SNATCH
Watch out, chief!
HALT

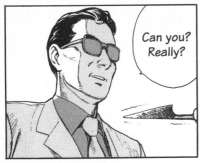

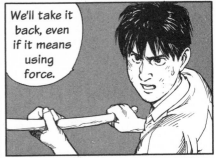

We'll take it back, even if it means using force.
Can you? Really?
I have to return it to the sea.
ドスッ
ZOK
ドスッ
POW
ドン
POP

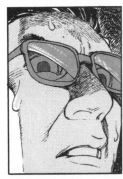

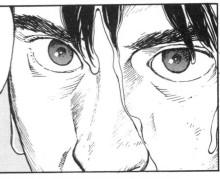

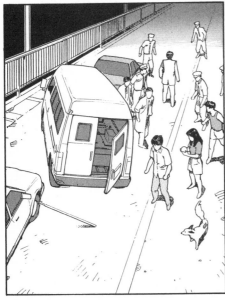

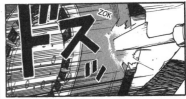

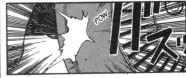

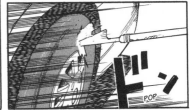

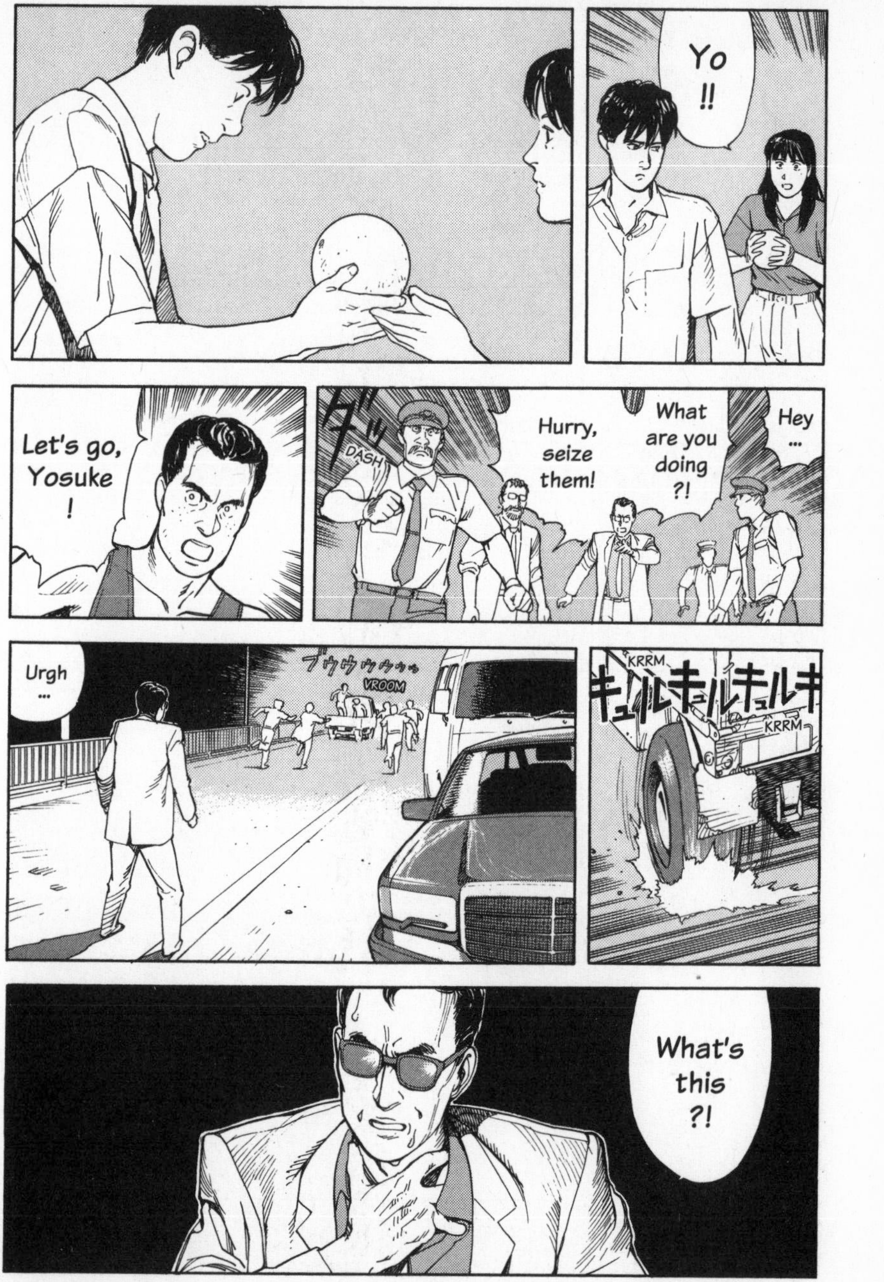
Yo !!
Hey ...
What are you doing ?!
Hurry, seize them!
ダッ
DASH
Let's go, Yosuke !
KRRM
キュルキュルキュルキ
KRRM
VROOM
Urgh ...
What's this ?!

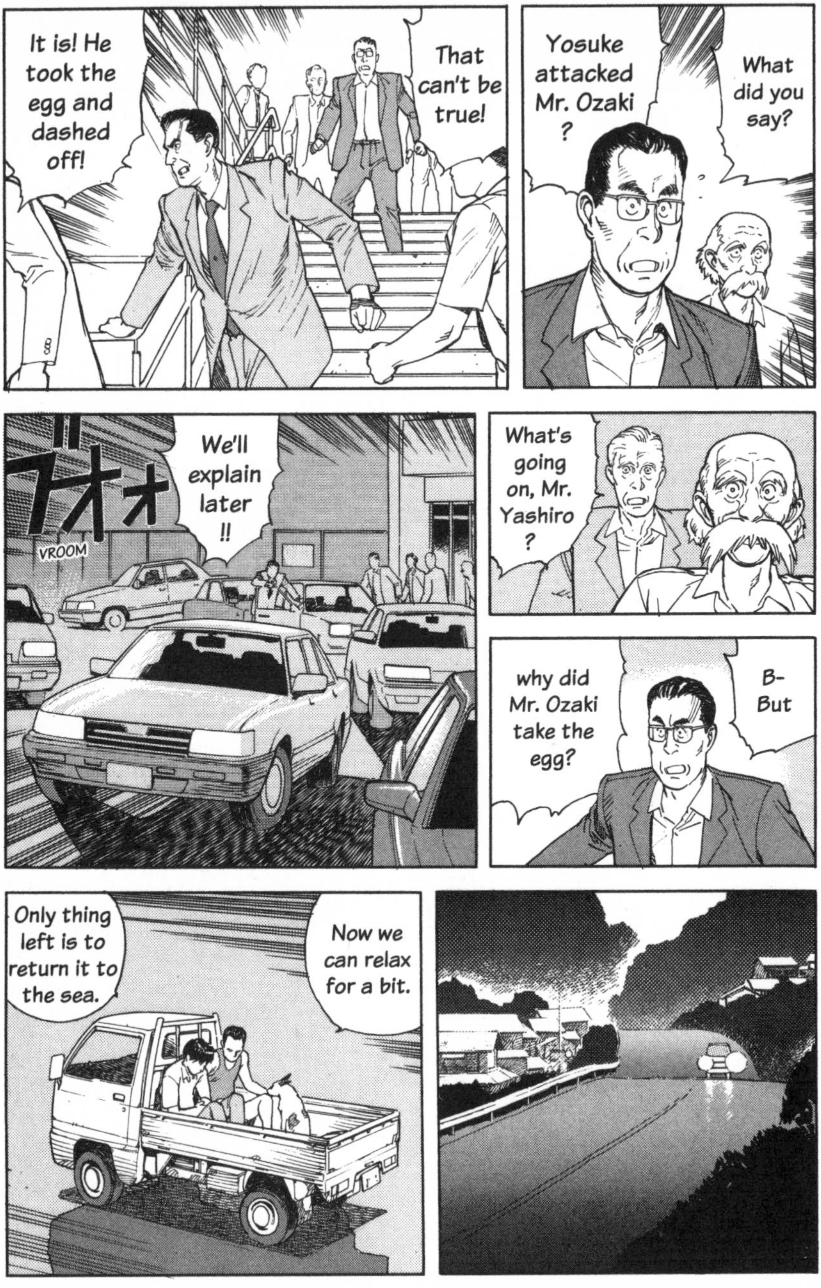
What did you say?
Yosuke attacked Mr. Ozaki?
That can't be true!
It is! He took the egg and dashed off!
What's going on, Mr. Yashiro?
B-But
why did Mr. Ozaki take the egg?
We'll explain later!!
ブオォ
VROOM
Now we can relax for a bit.
Only thing left is to return it to the sea.

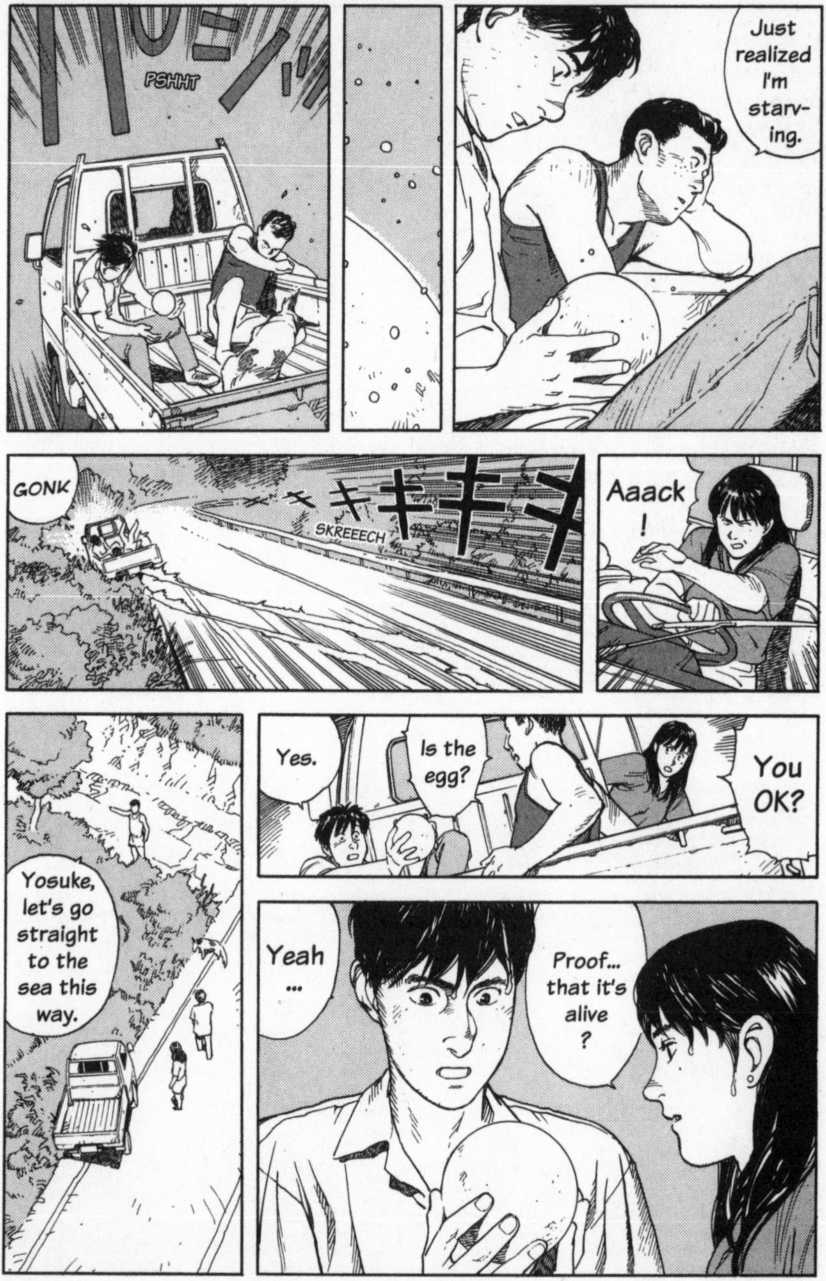
Just realized I'm starv-ing.
PSHHT
Aaack !
GONK
SKREEECH
You OK?
Is the egg?
Yes.
Proof... that it's alive ?
Yeah ...
Yosuke, let's go straight to the sea this way.

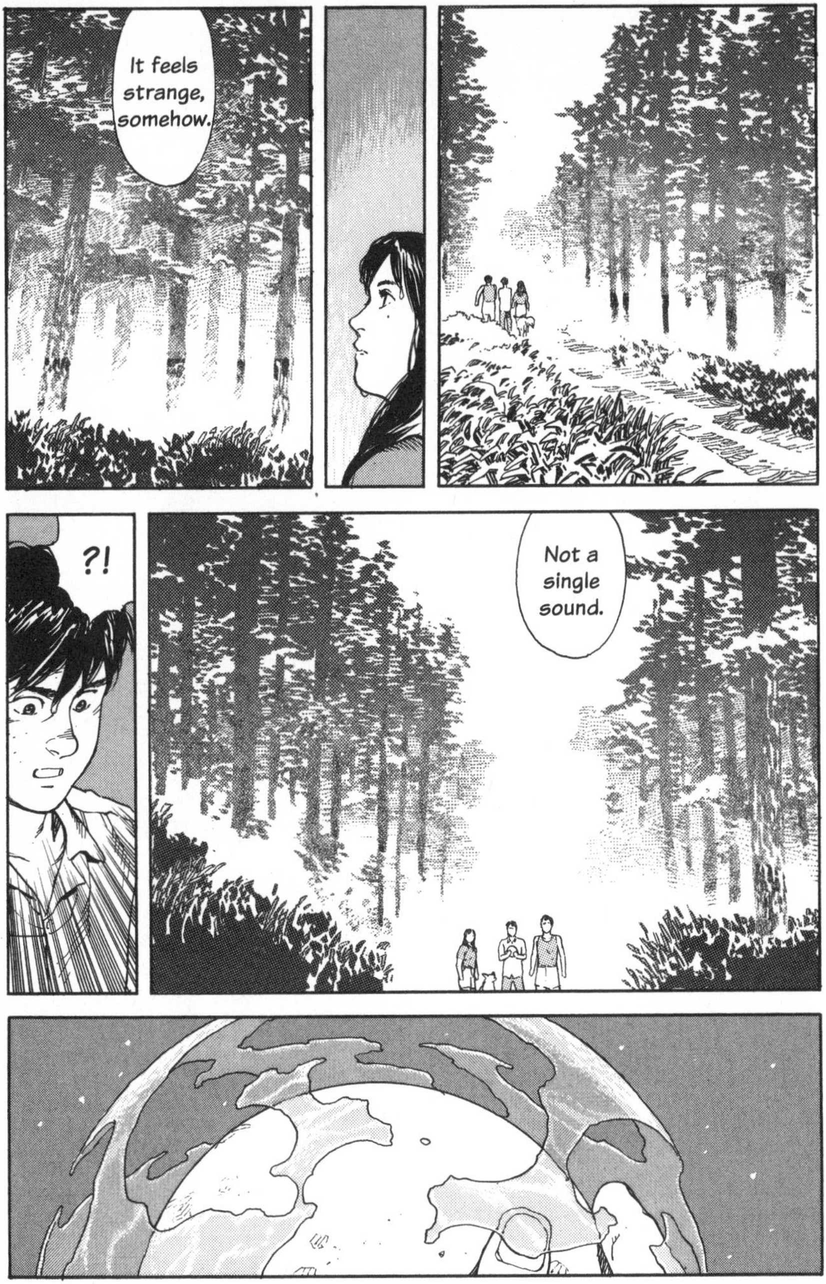
It feels strange, somehow.
Not a single sound.
?!

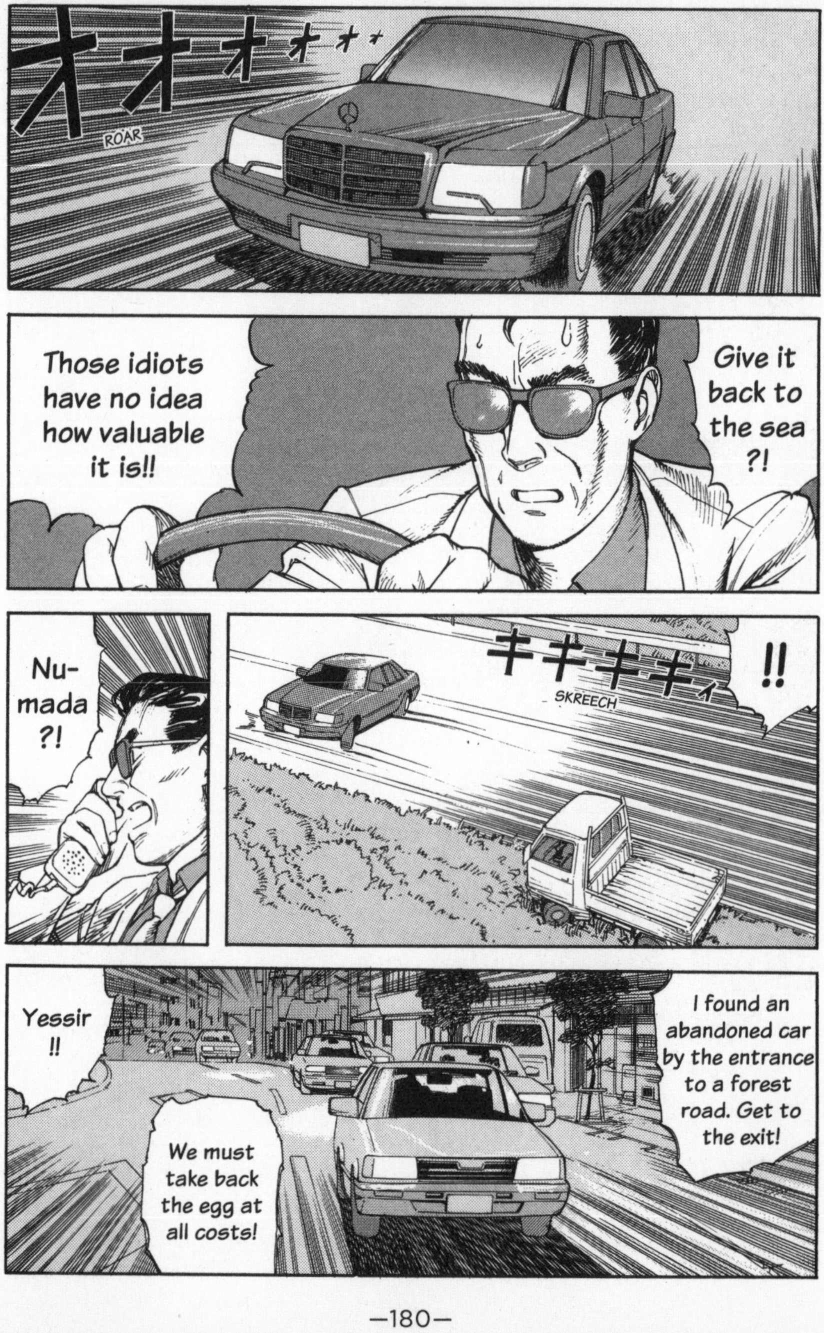

オオオオォォ
ROAR
Give it back to the sea ?!
Those idiots have no idea how valuable it is!!
キキキキィ !!
SKREECH
Nu-mada ?!
I found an abandoned car by the entrance to a forest road. Get to the exit!
Yessir !!
We must take back the egg at all costs!

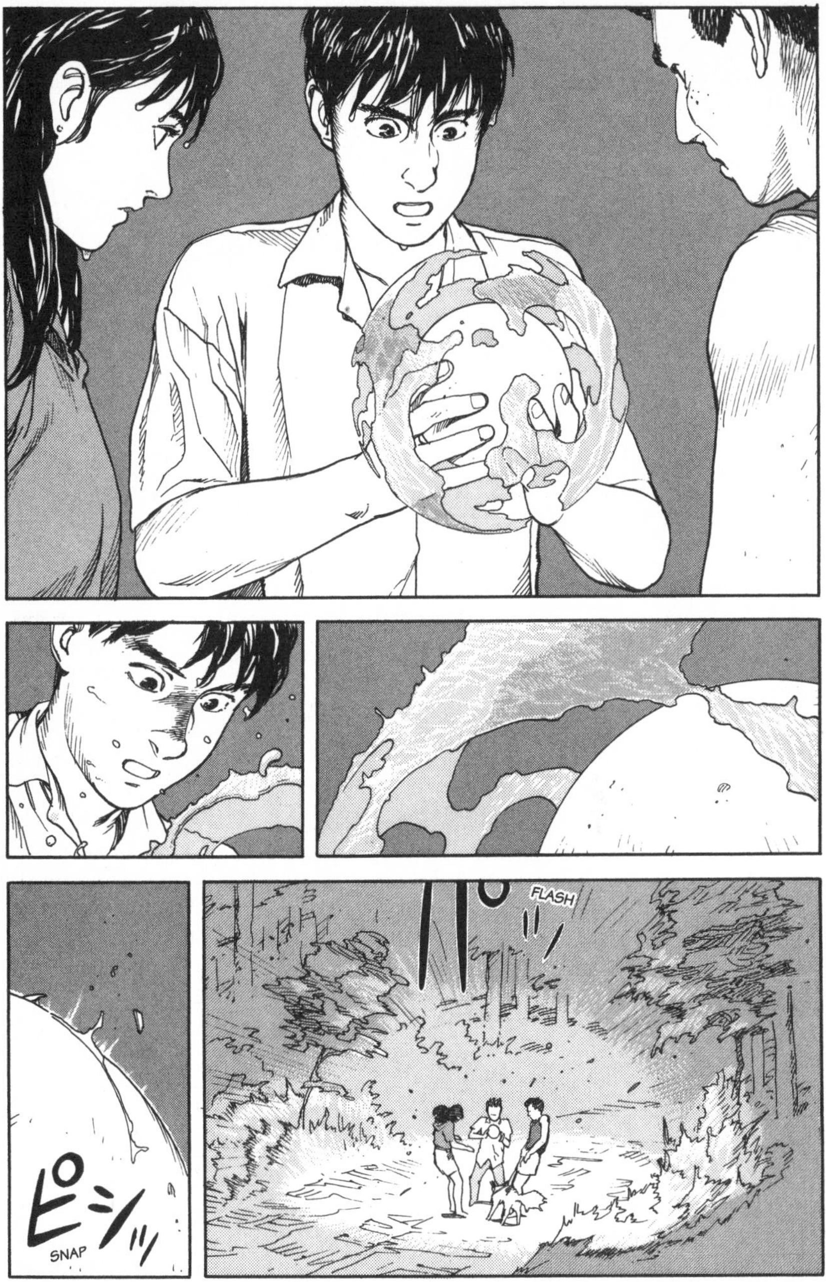
FLASH
ピシッ
SNAP

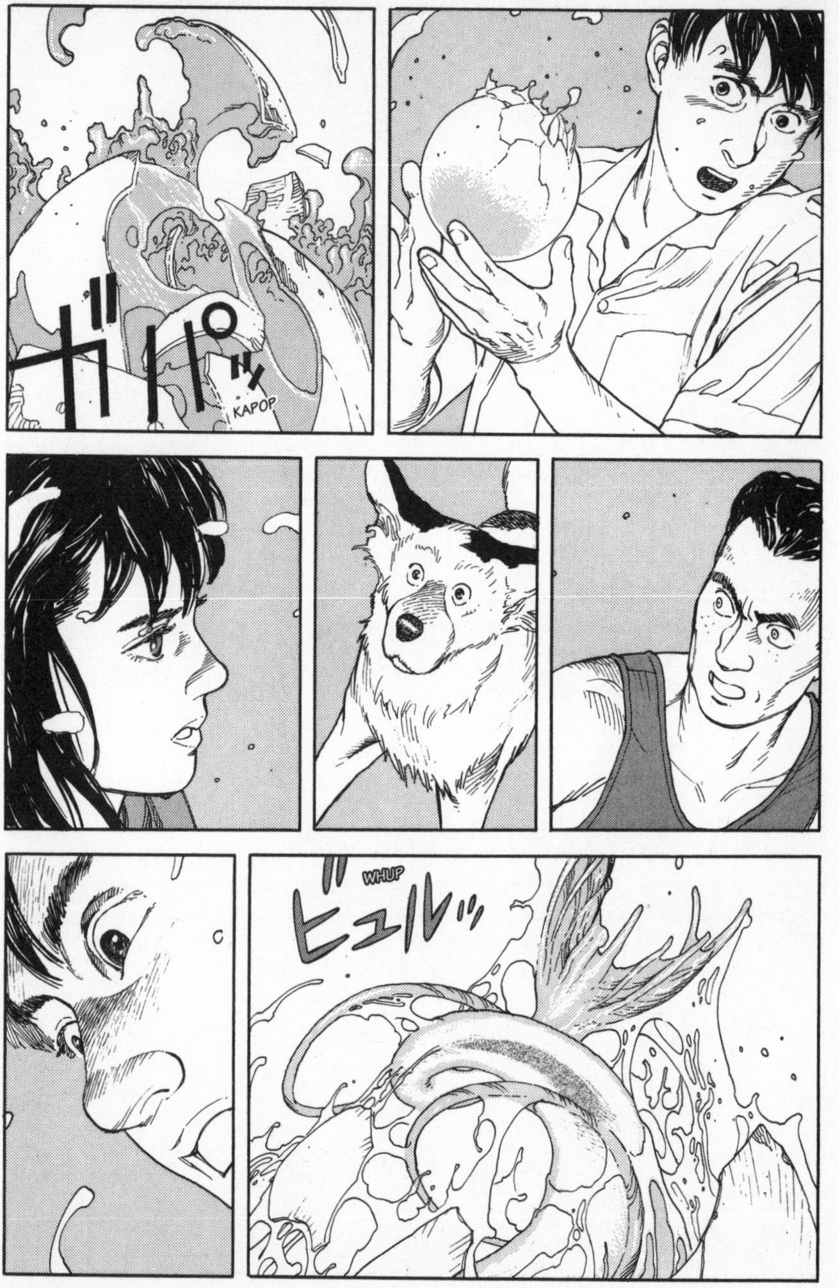
ガパッ
KAPOP
ビュルッ
WHUP

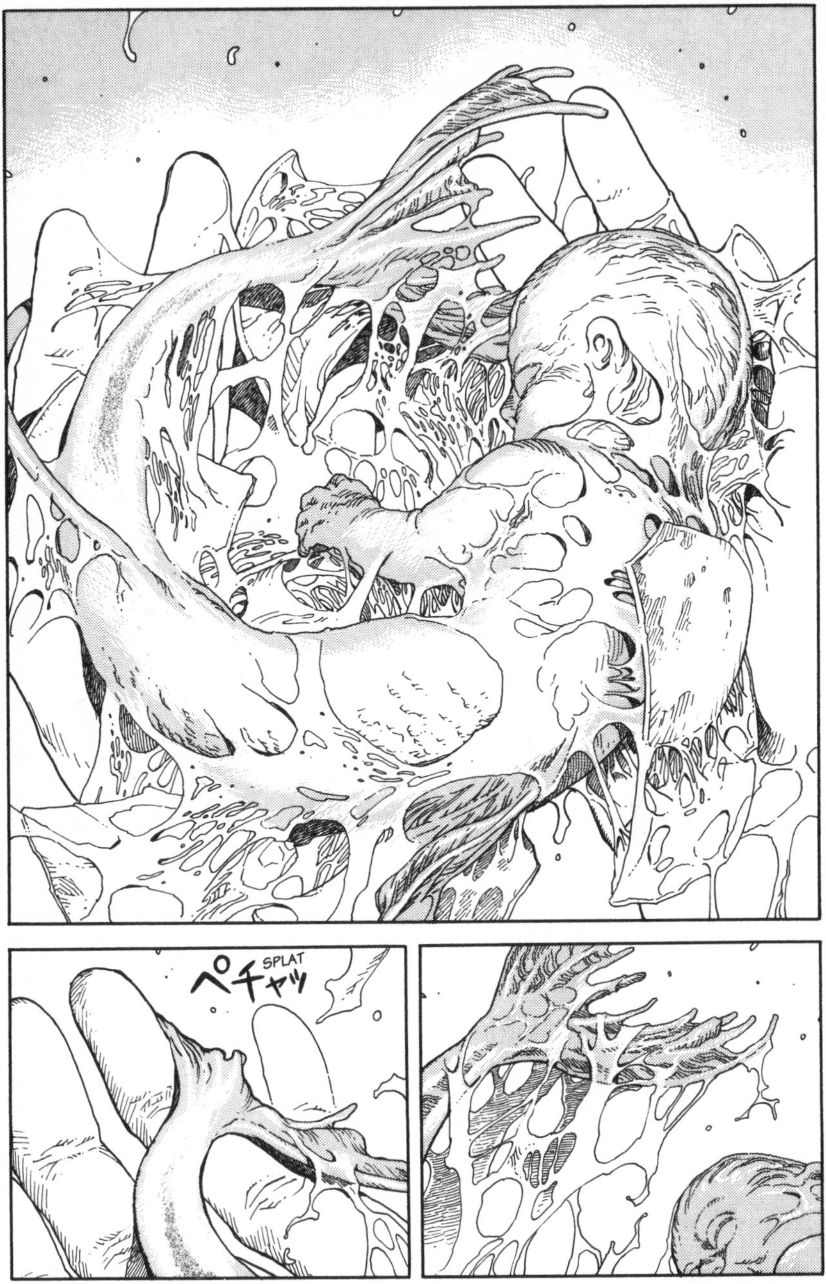
ペチャッ
SPLAT

Ah
!!

Uh!

?!

ゴポポポ
BURBLE

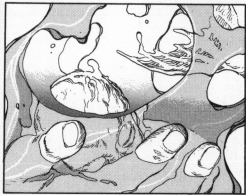

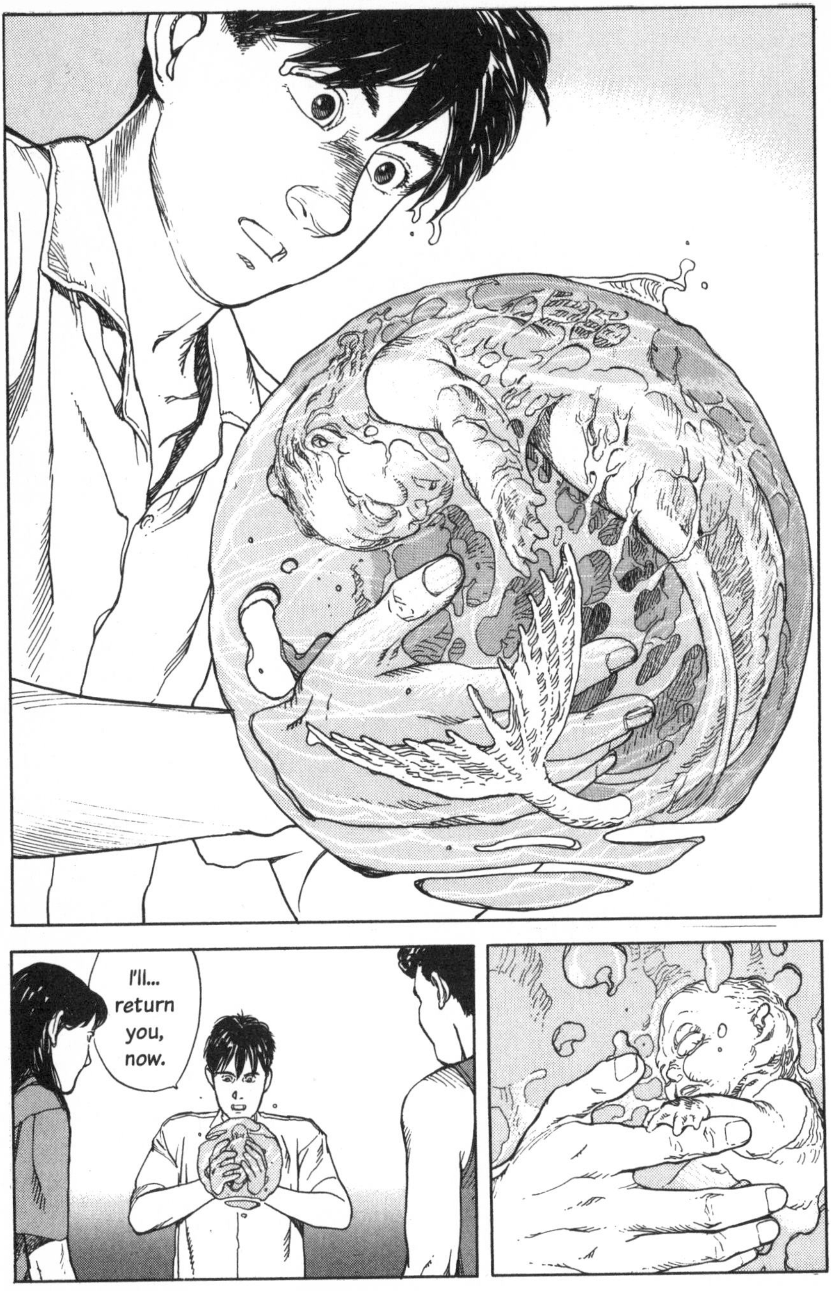
I'll... return you, now.

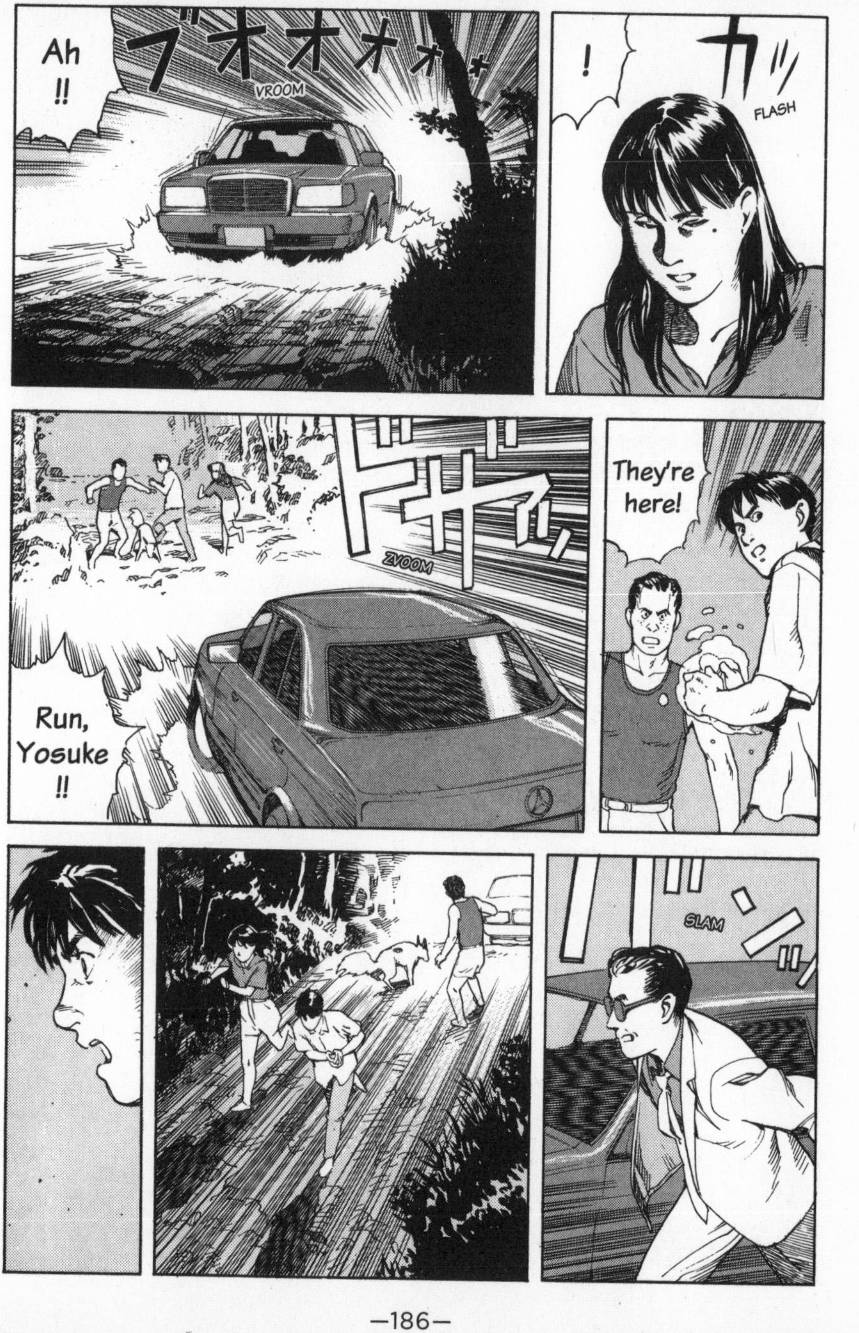
!
FLASH
Ah !!
VROOM
They're here!
Run, Yosuke !!
ZVOOM
SLAM

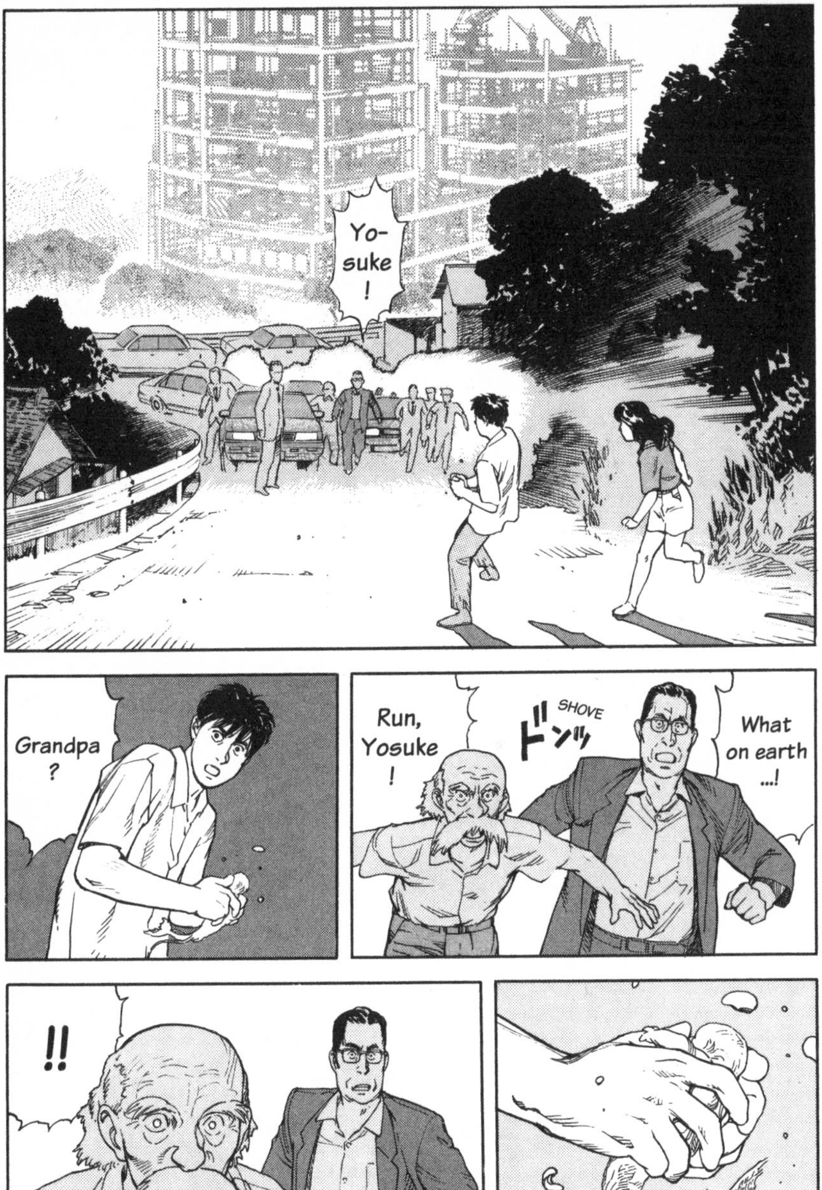
Yo-suke!
What on earth ...!
SHOVE
ドンッ
Run, Yosuke!
Grandpa?
!!

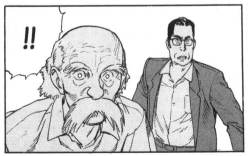

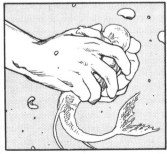

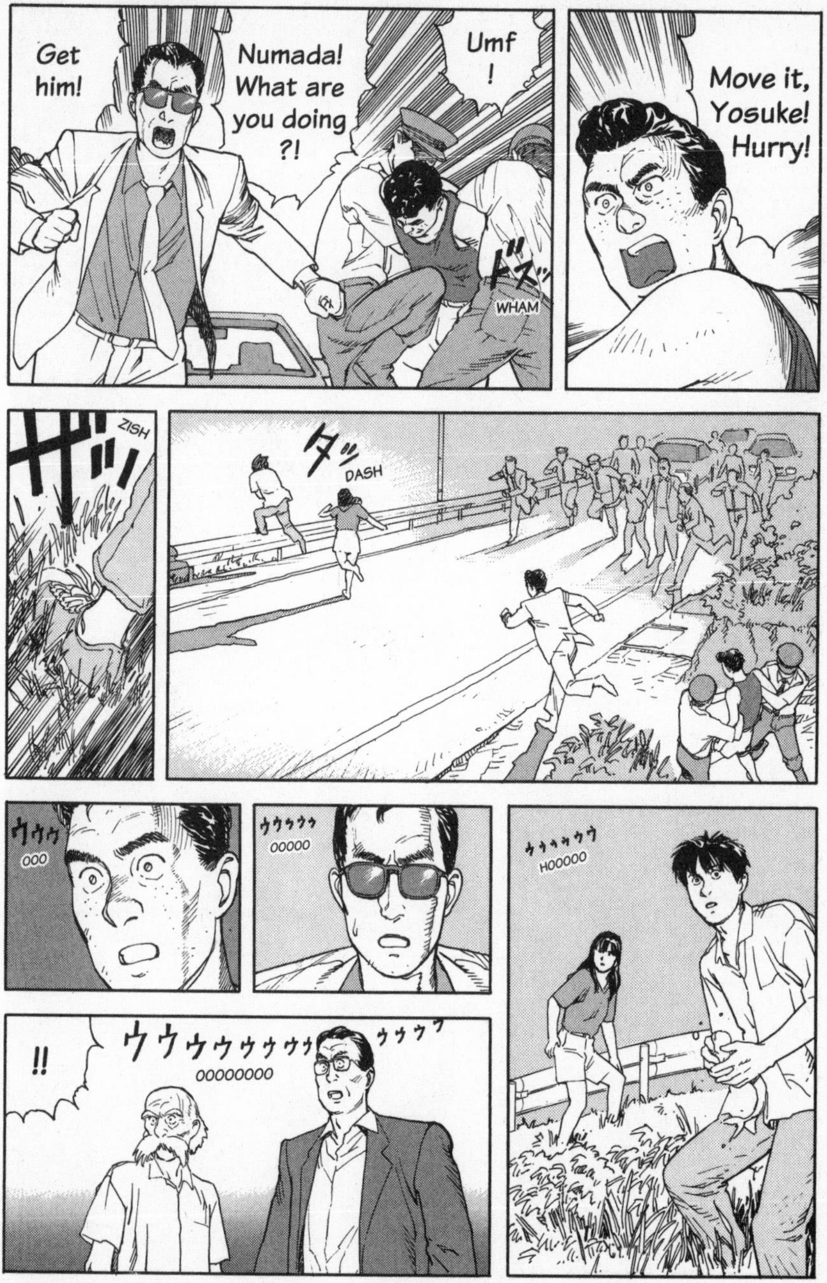

Move it, Yosuke! Hurry!
Umf !
ドスッ
WHAM
Numada! What are you doing ?!
Get him!
タッ
DASH
ザッ
ZISH
ウゥゥゥゥウ
HOOOOO
ウゥゥゥゥ
OOOOO
ウゥゥ
OOO
ウゥゥウ
ウゥゥゥゥゥゥゥ
OOOOOOOO
!!

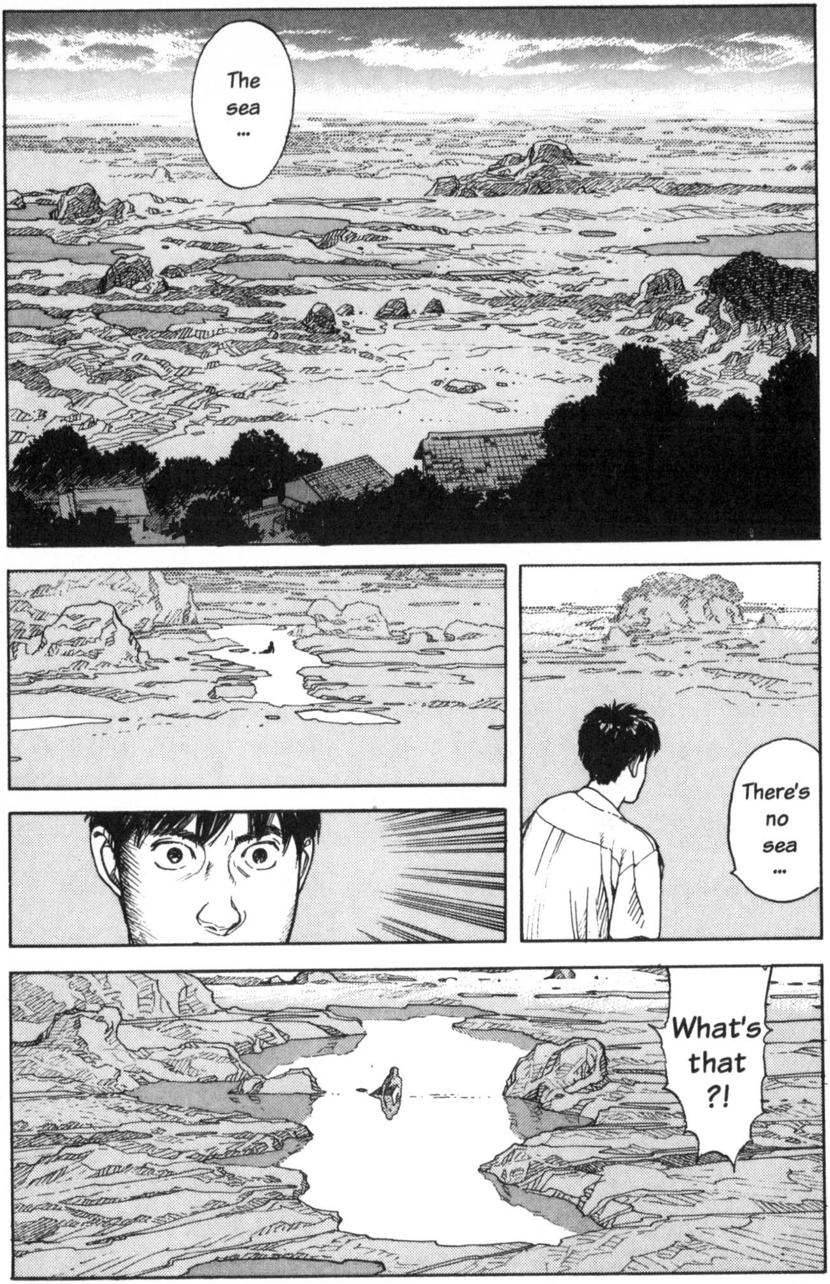
The sea ...
There's no sea ...
What's that ?!

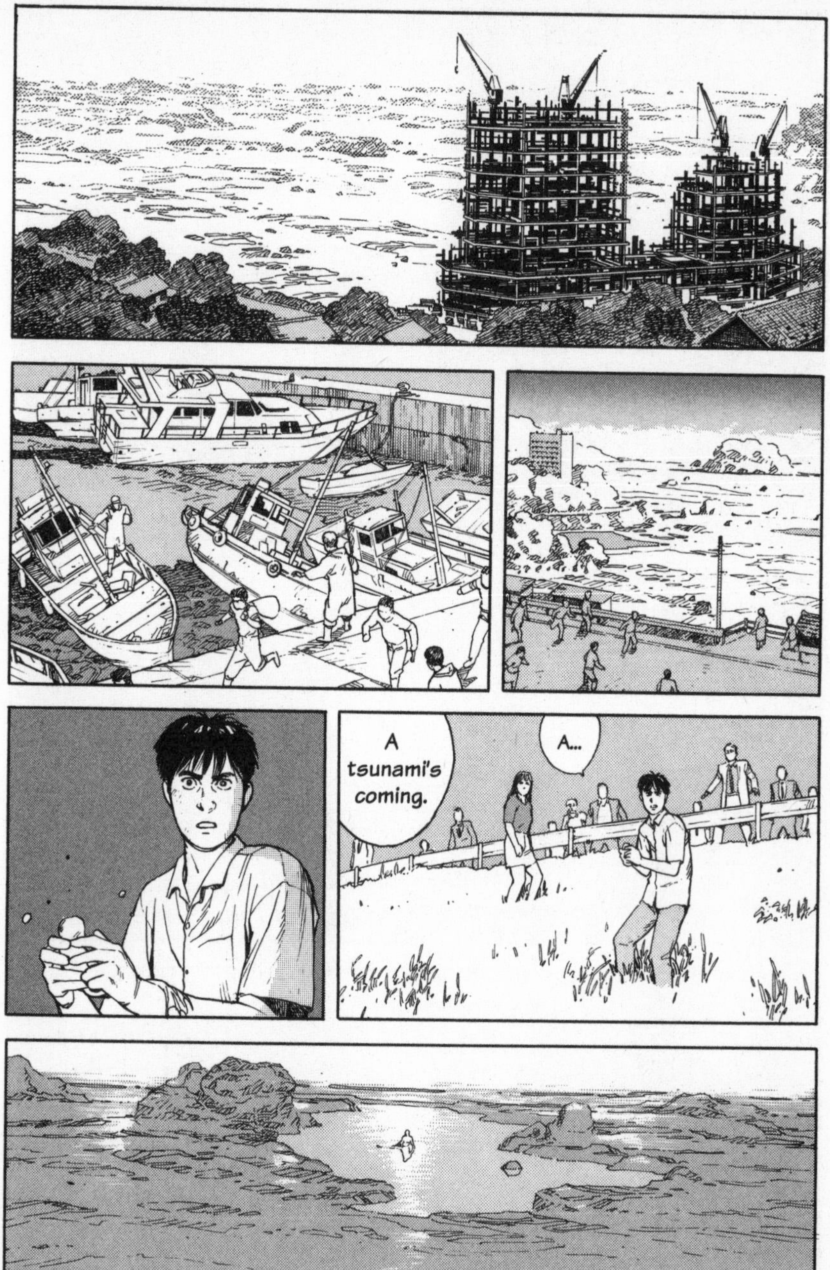
A...
A tsunami's coming.

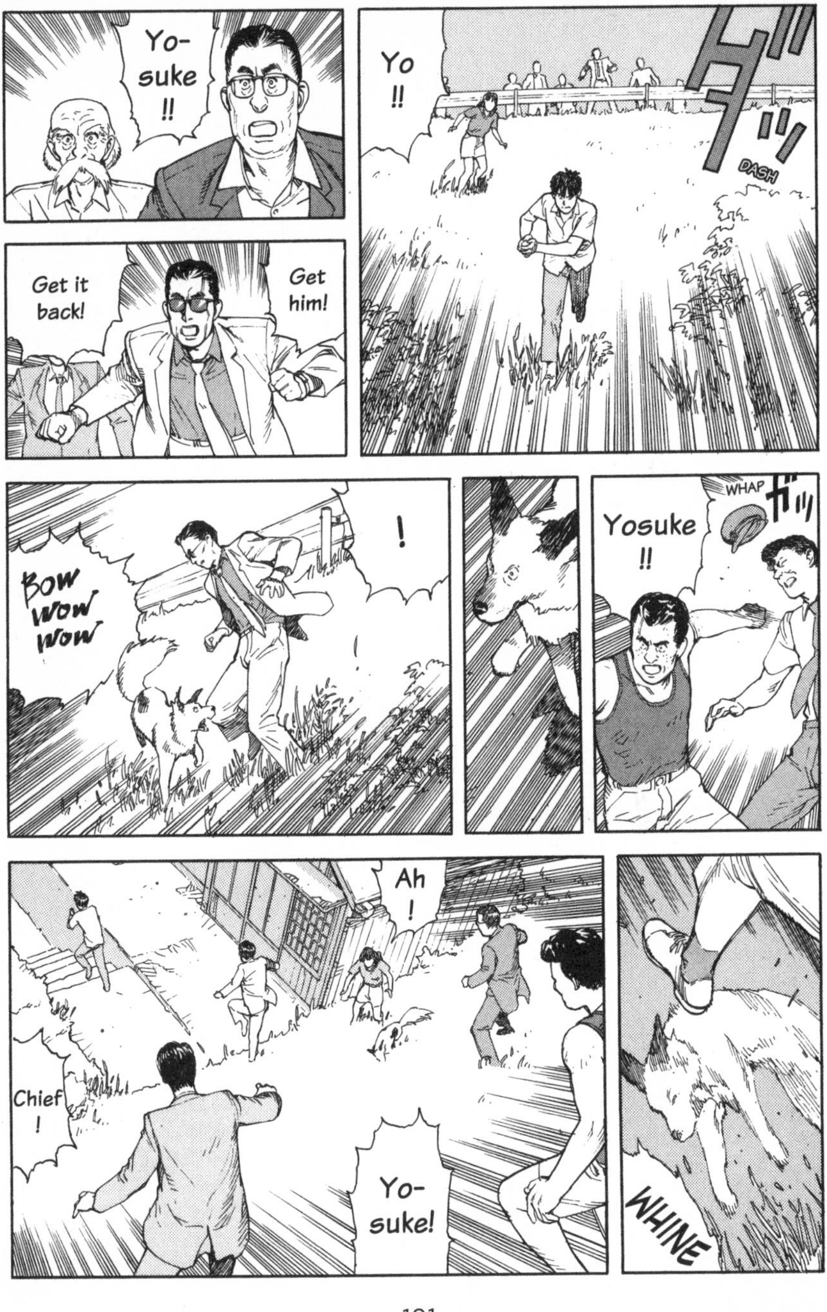

DASH
Yo !!
Yo- suke !!
Get him!
Get it back!
WHAP
Yosuke !!
!
Bow wow wow
WHINE
Ah !
Yo- suke!
Chief !

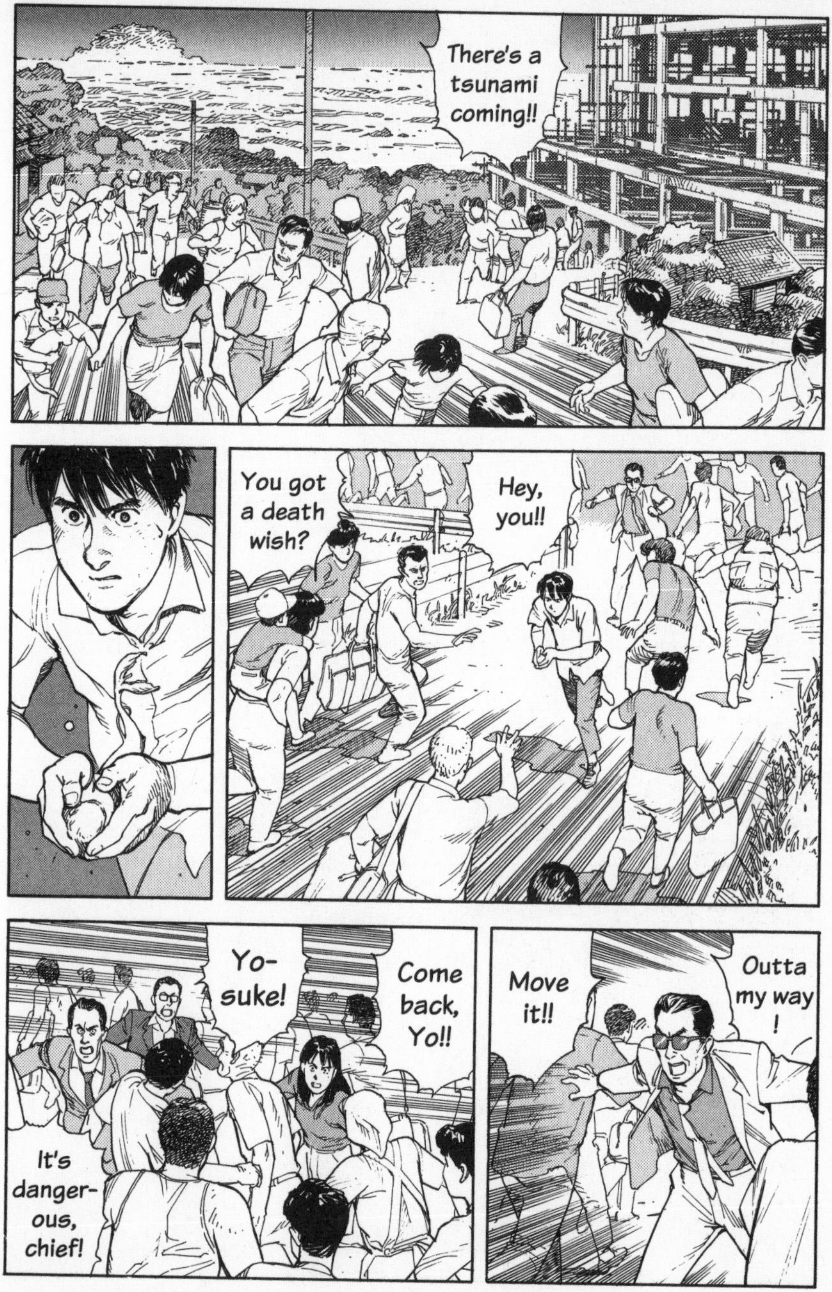
There's a tsunami coming!!
Hey, you!!
You got a death wish?
Outta my way !
Move it!!
Come back, Yo!!
Yo-suke!
It's danger-ous, chief!

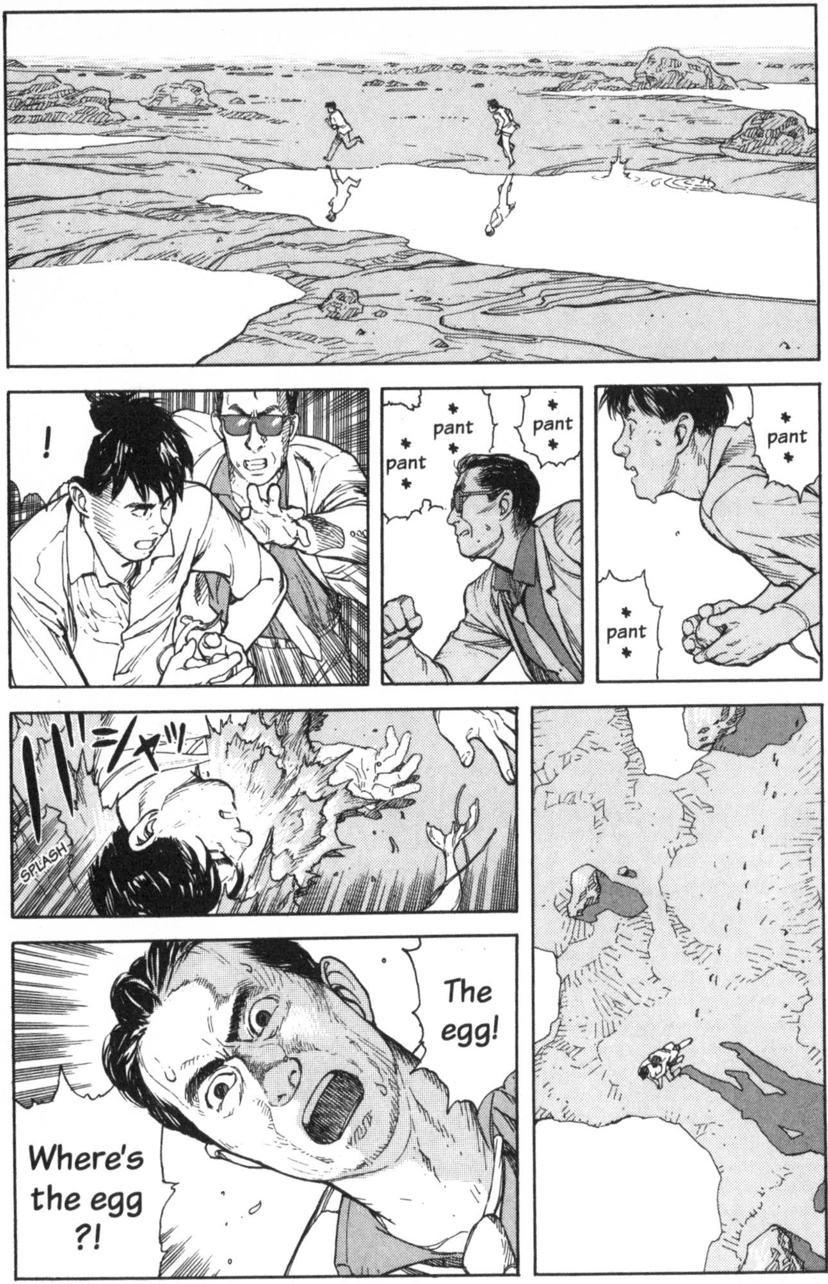

pant
pant
pant
pant
pant
!
SPLASH
The egg!
Where's the egg ?!

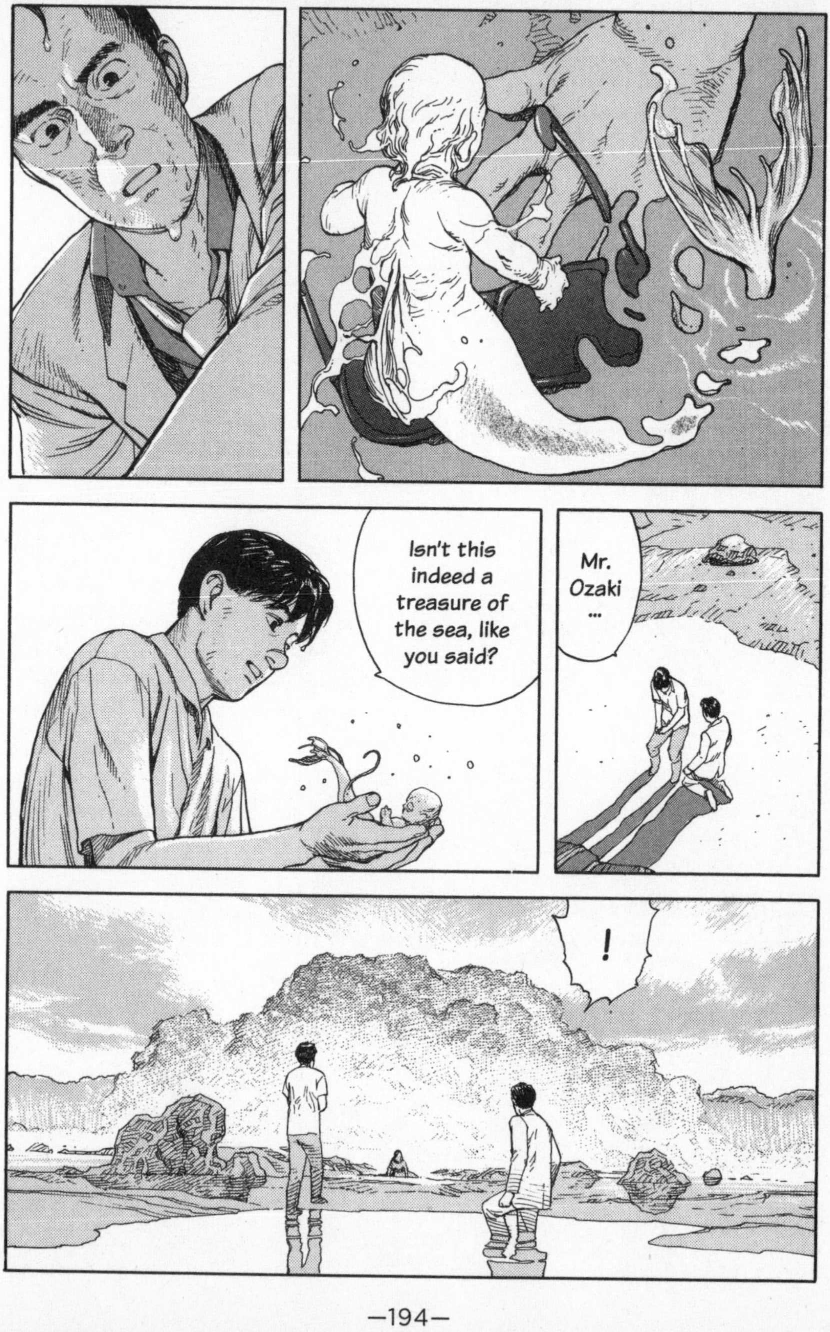
Mr. Ozaki ...
Isn't this indeed a treasure of the sea, like you said?
!

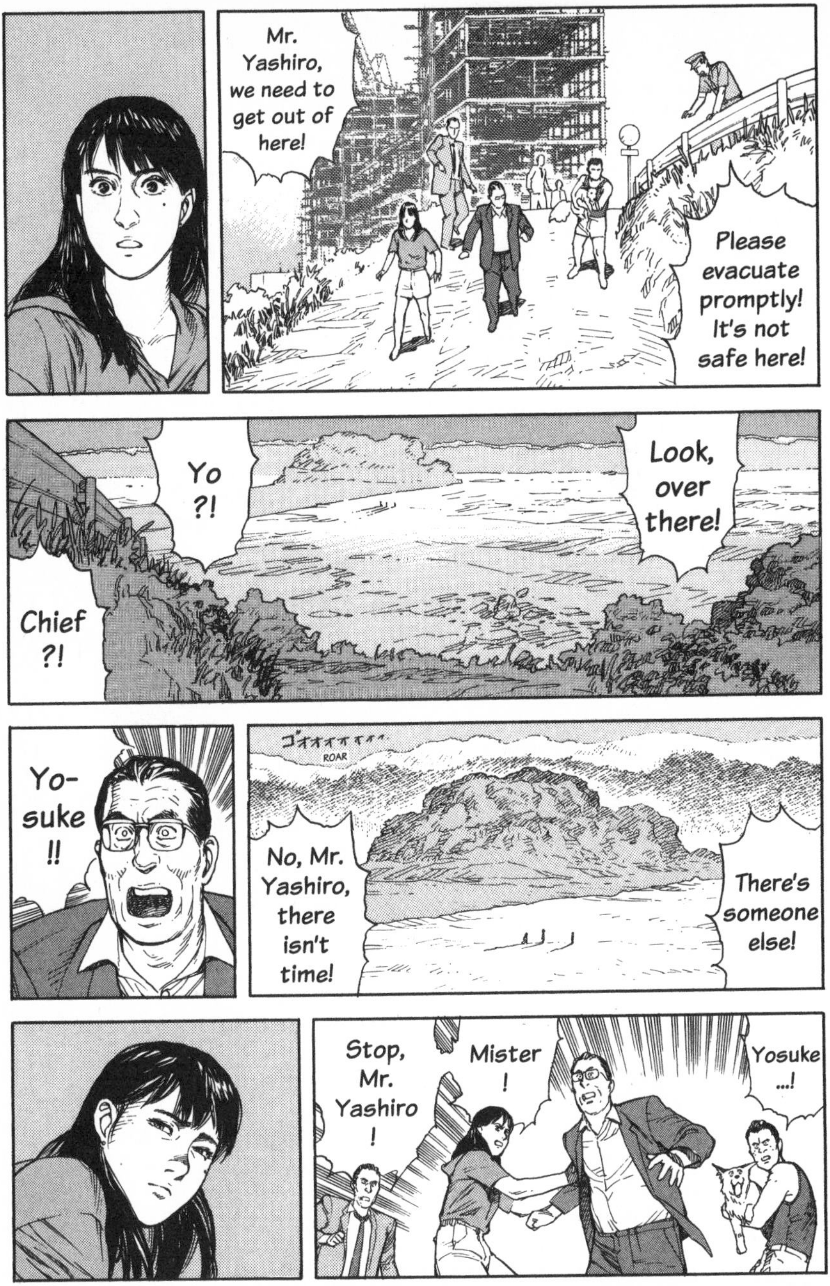
Please evacuate promptly! It's not safe here!
Mr. Yashiro, we need to get out of here!
Look, over there!
Yo ?!
Chief ?!
ROAR
There's someone else!
No, Mr. Yashiro, there isn't time!
Yo- suke !!
Yosuke ...!
Mister !
Stop, Mr. Yashiro !

ゴゴゴゴ
ROAR

ゴゴゴゴ
ROAR

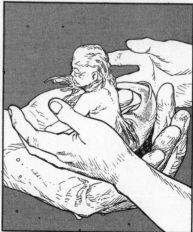

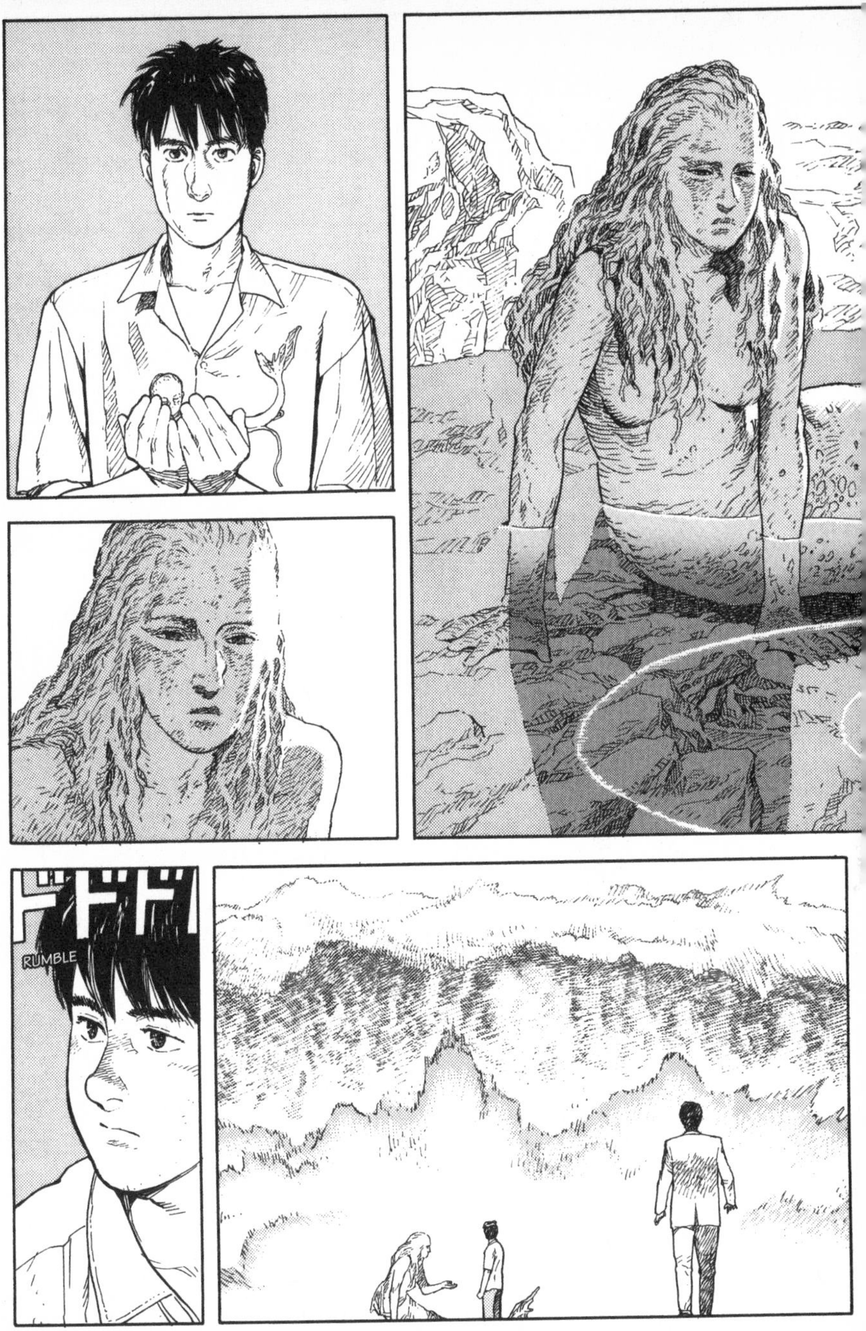
ドドド
RUMBLE

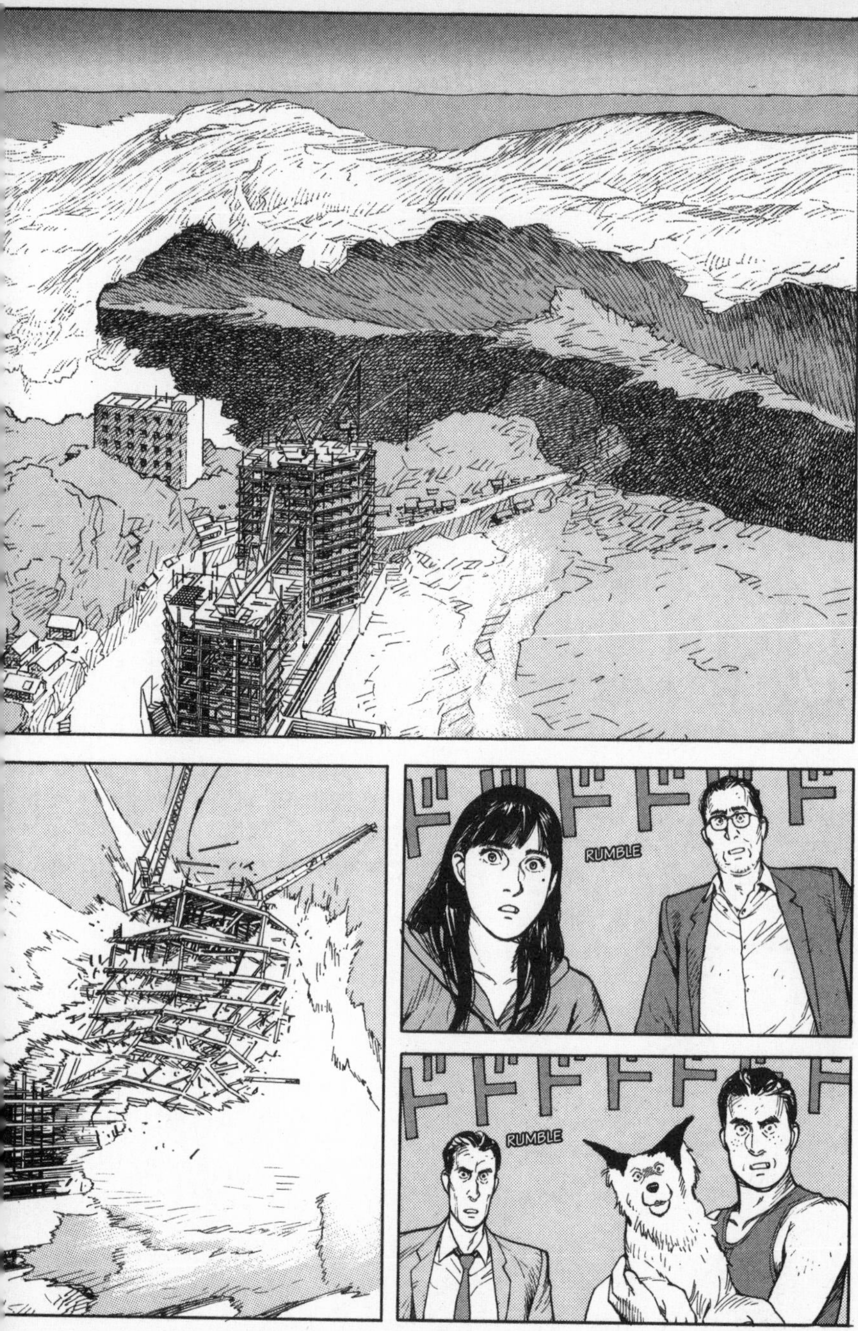
RUMBLE
RUMBLE

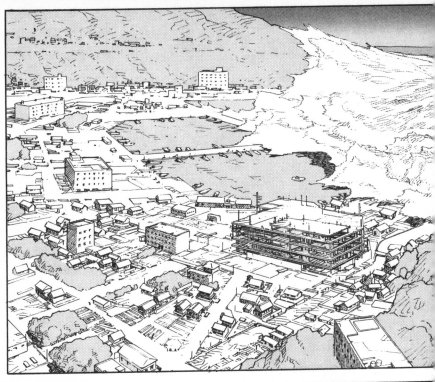

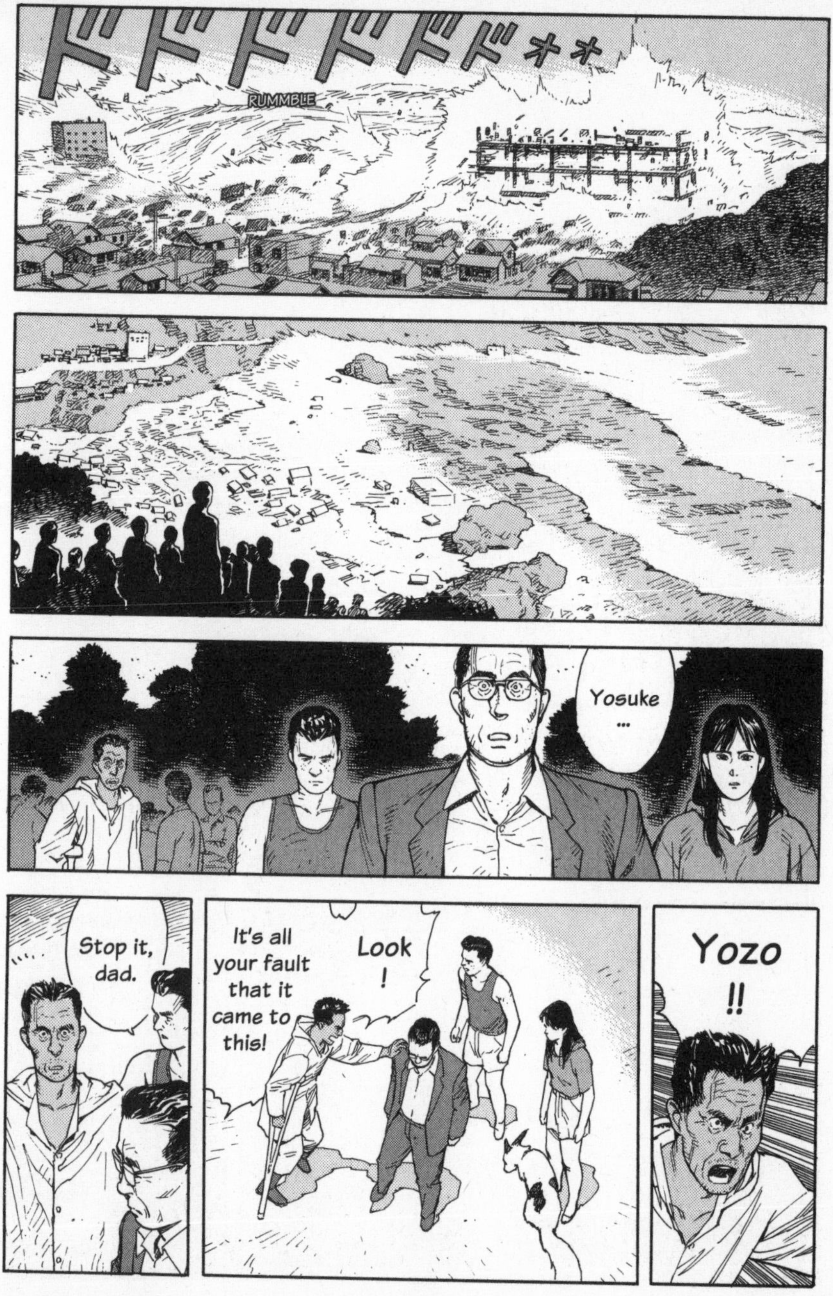
ドドドドドドォォ
RUMMBLE
Yosuke ...
Yozo !!
Look !
It's all your fault that it came to this!
Stop it, dad.

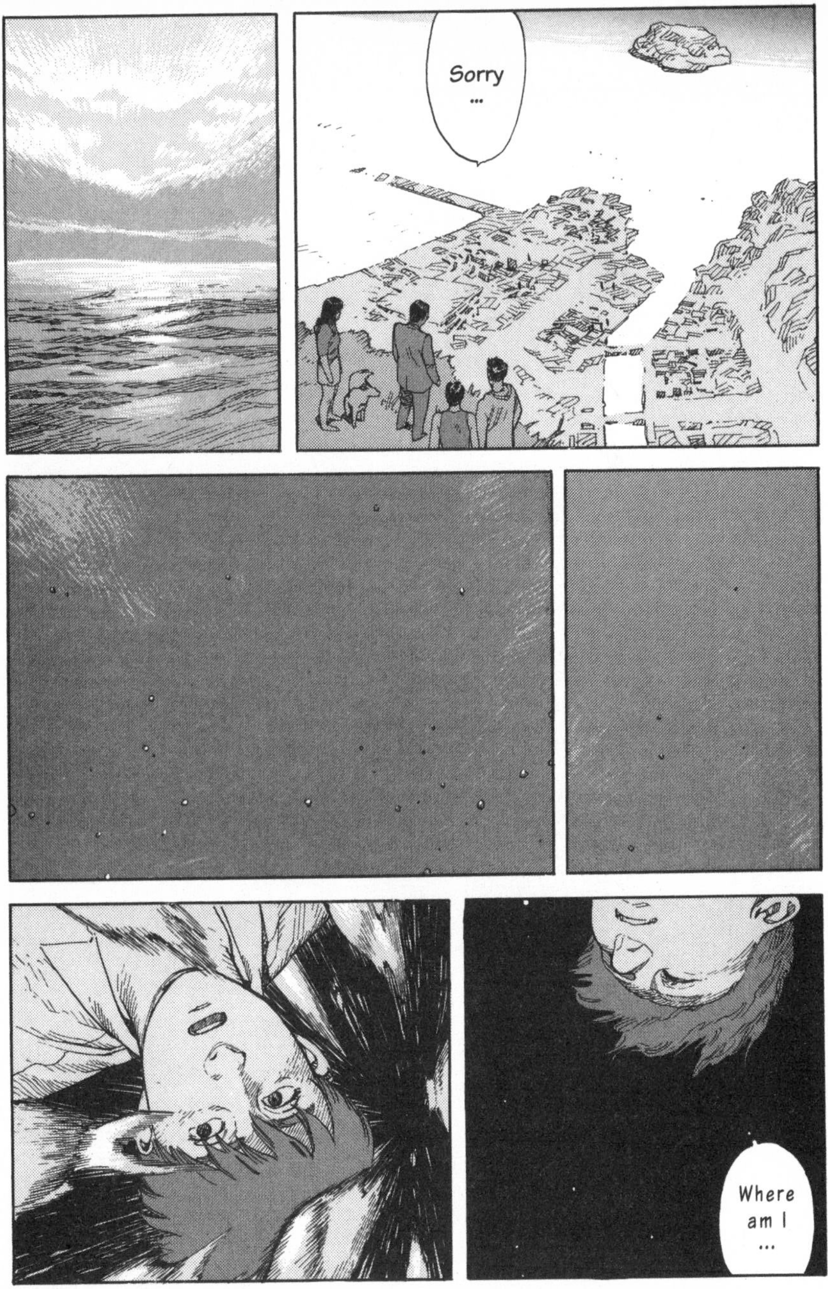
Sorry ...
Where am I ...

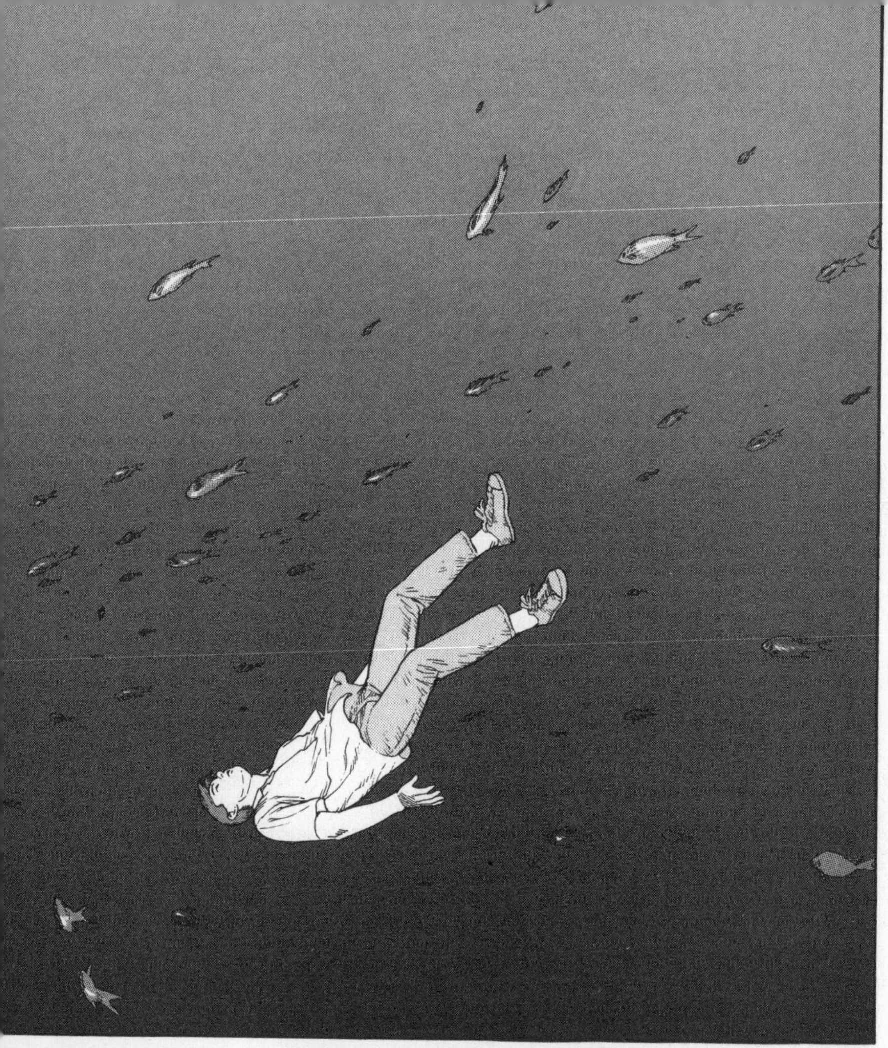
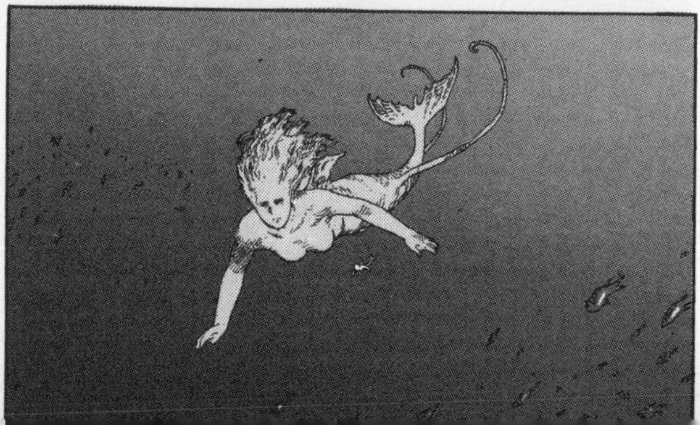
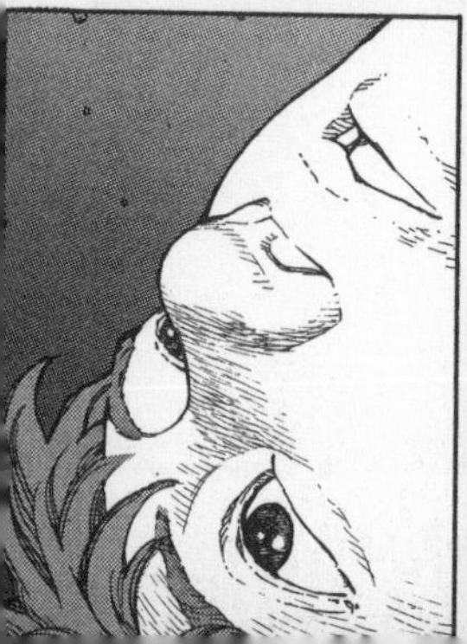

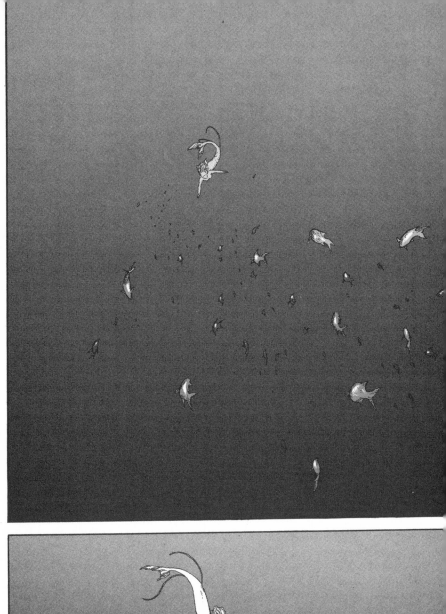

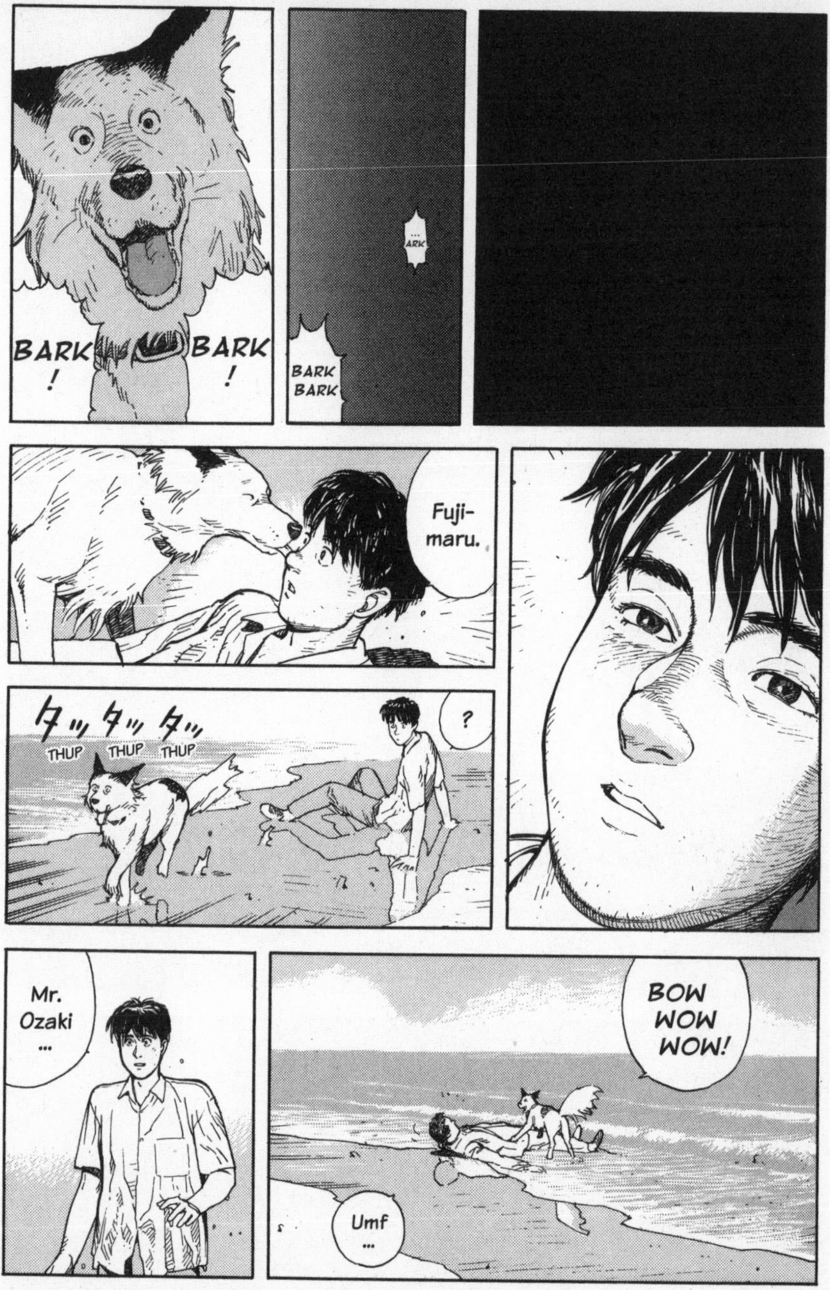
...ARK
BARK BARK
BARK! BARK!
Fuji-maru.
?
タッ タッ タッ
THUP THUP THUP
BOW WOW WOW!
Umf ...
Mr. Ozaki ...

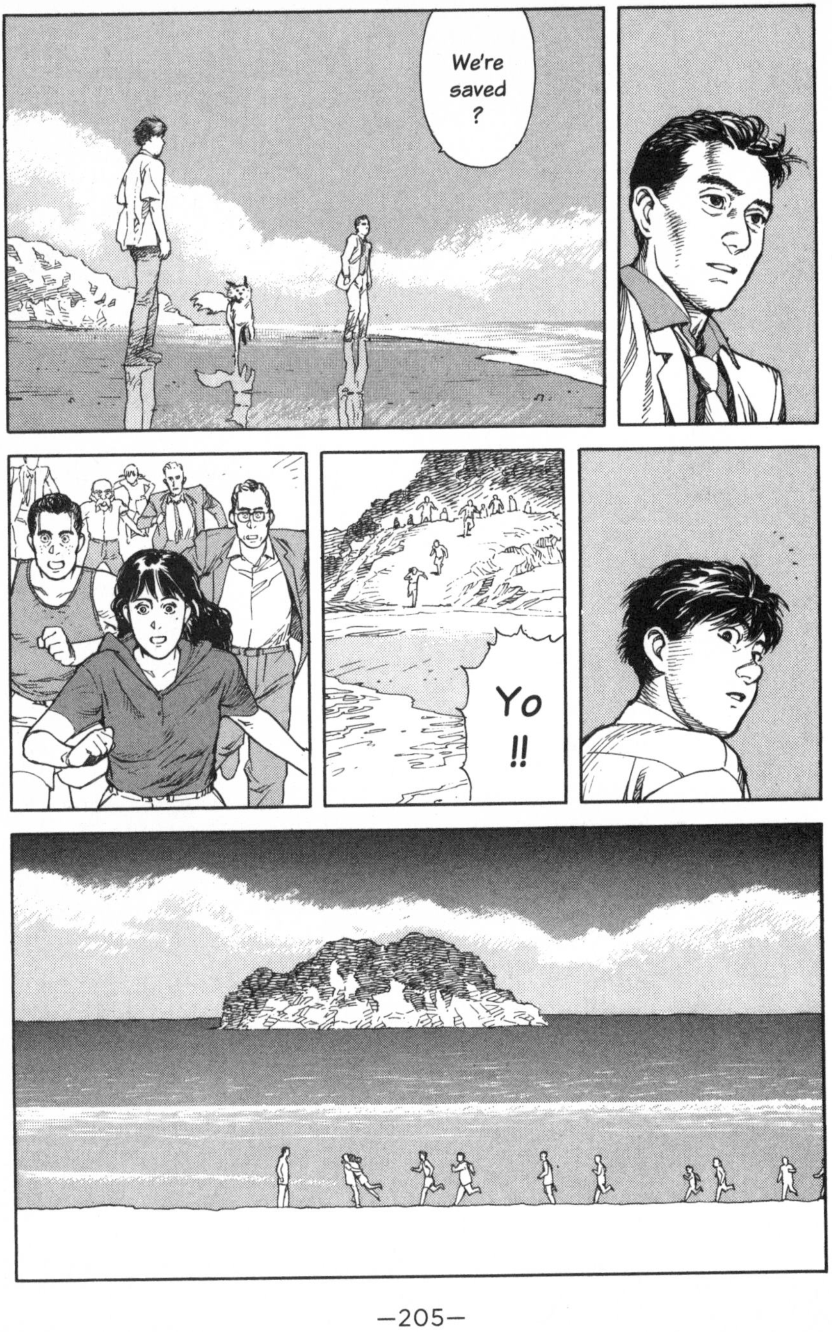
We're saved ?
Yo !!

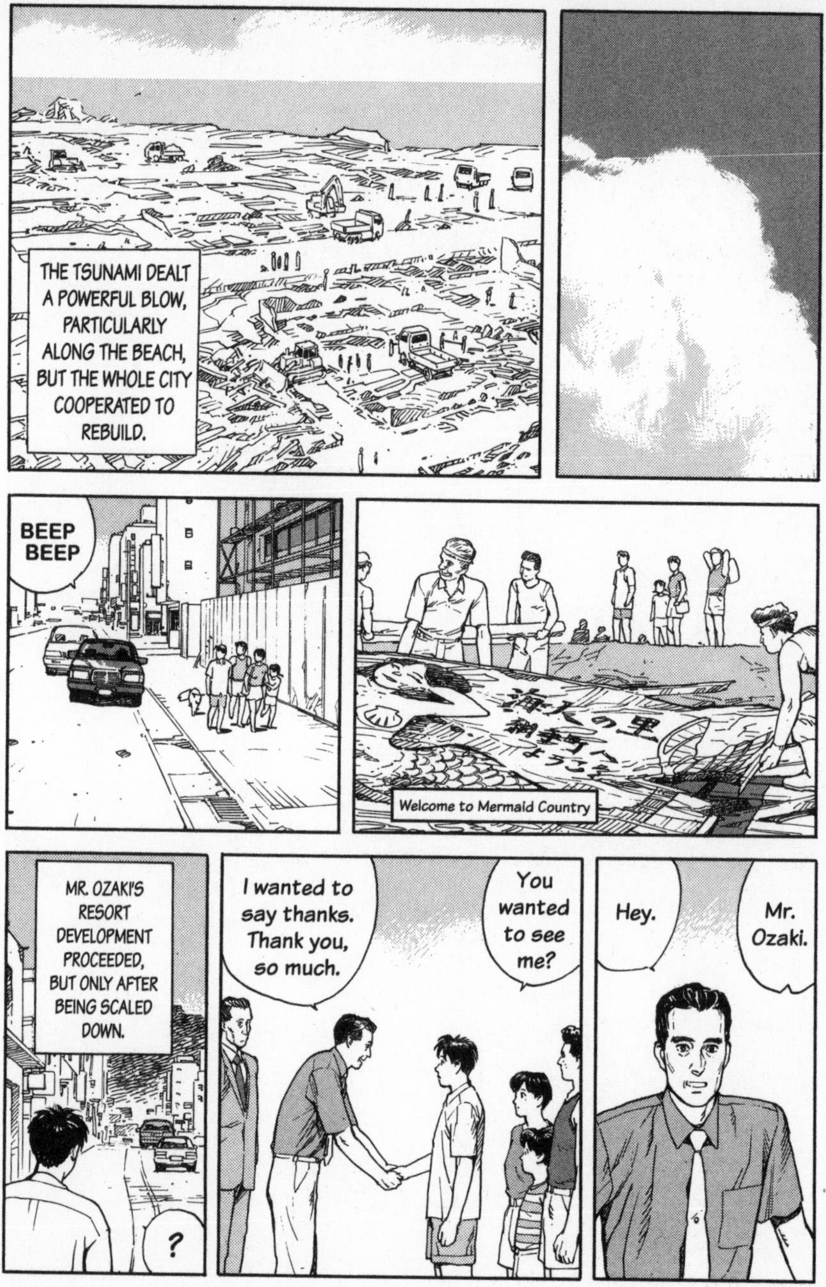
THE TSUNAMI DEALT A POWERFUL BLOW, PARTICULARLY ALONG THE BEACH, BUT THE WHOLE CITY COOPERATED TO REBUILD.
Welcome to Mermaid Country
BEEP BEEP
Mr. Ozaki.
Hey.
You wanted to see me?
I wanted to say thanks. Thank you, so much.
MR. OZAKI'S RESORT DEVELOPMENT PROCEEDED, BUT ONLY AFTER BEING SCALED DOWN.
?

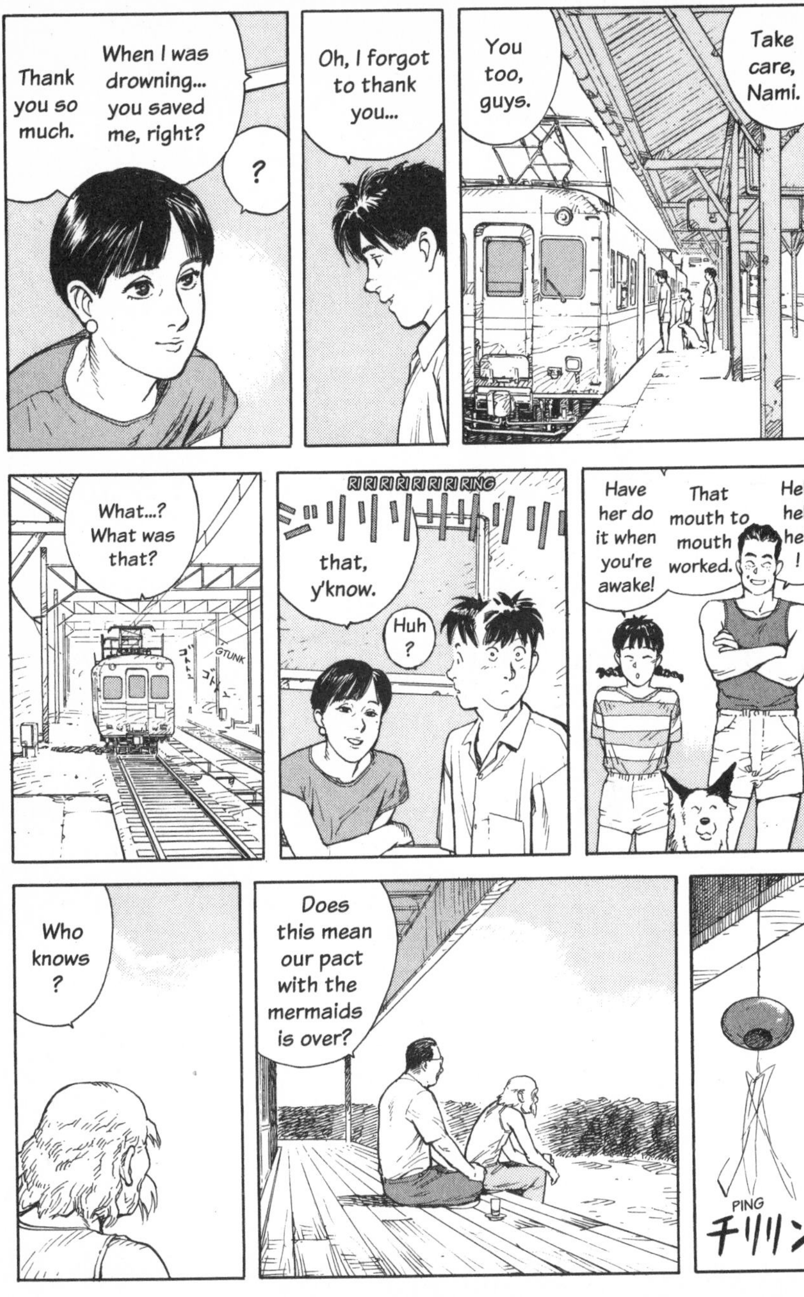
Take care, Nami.
You too, guys.
Oh, I forgot to thank you...
When I was drowning... you saved me, right?
Thank you so much.
?
Heh heh heh!
That mouth to mouth worked.
Have her do it when you're awake!
RIRIRIRIRIRIRIRING
that, y'know.
Huh?
What...? What was that?
GTUNK
PING
チリリン
Does this mean our pact with the mermaids is over?
Who knows?

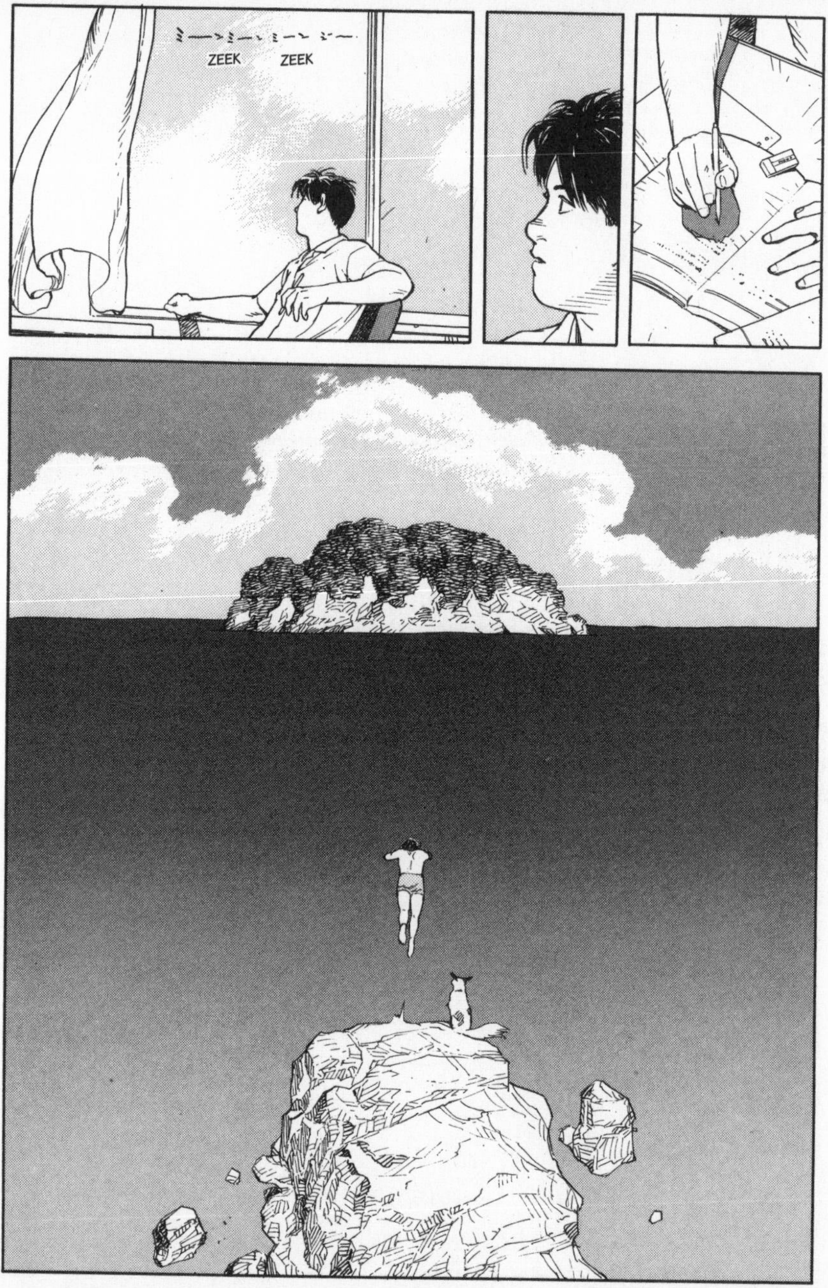
ミーンミーンミーン ジー
ZEEK ZEEK

THE END

Selected
Title Pages

Young Magazine 1990
Issues 17-29

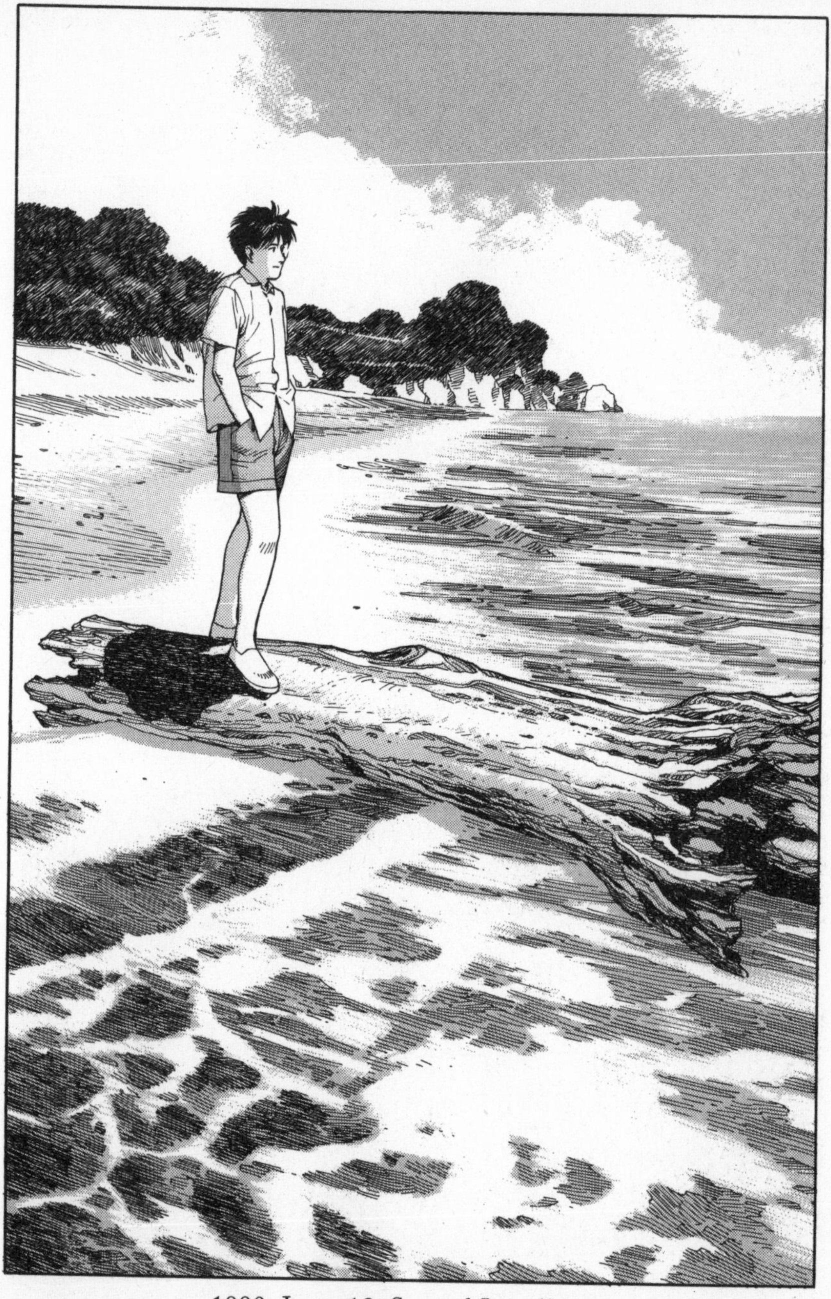

1990: Issue 18, Second Installment

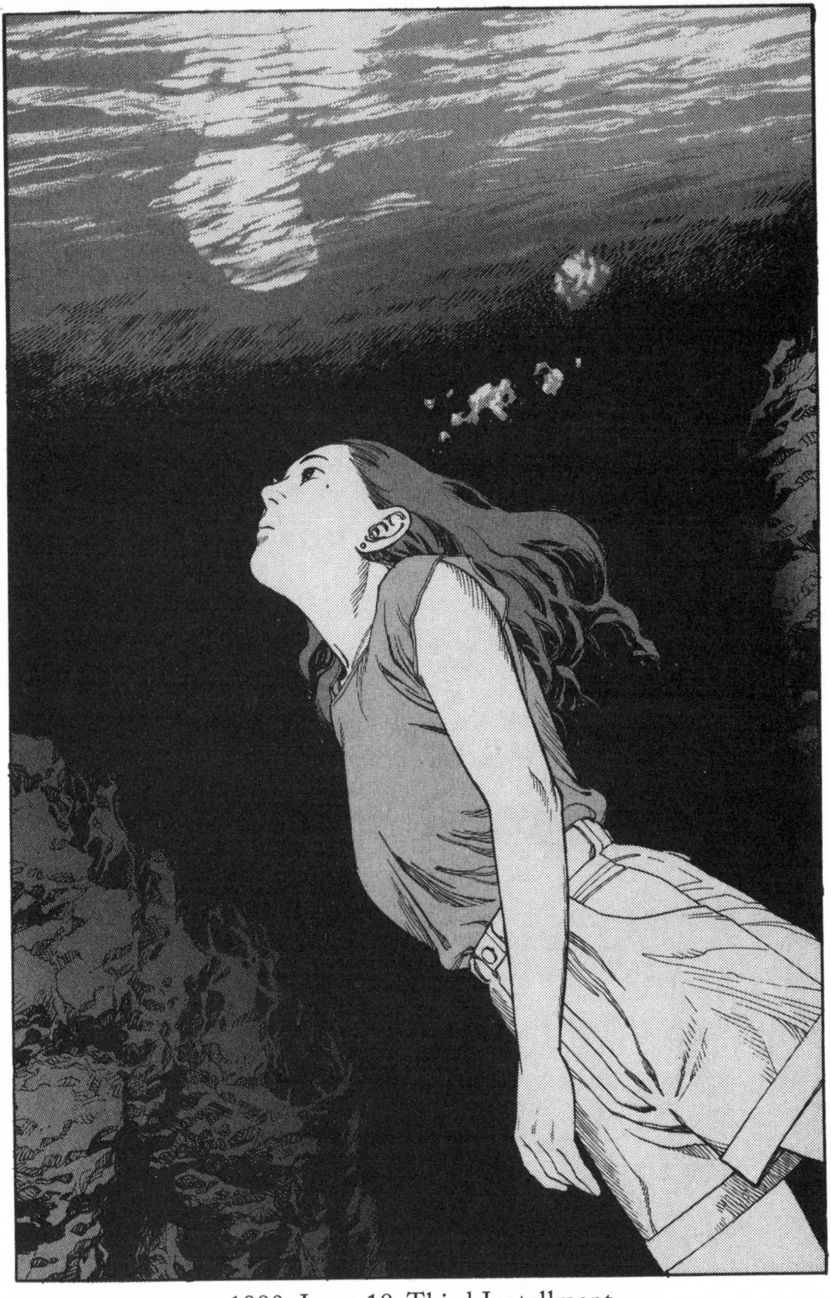

1990: Issue 19, Third Installment

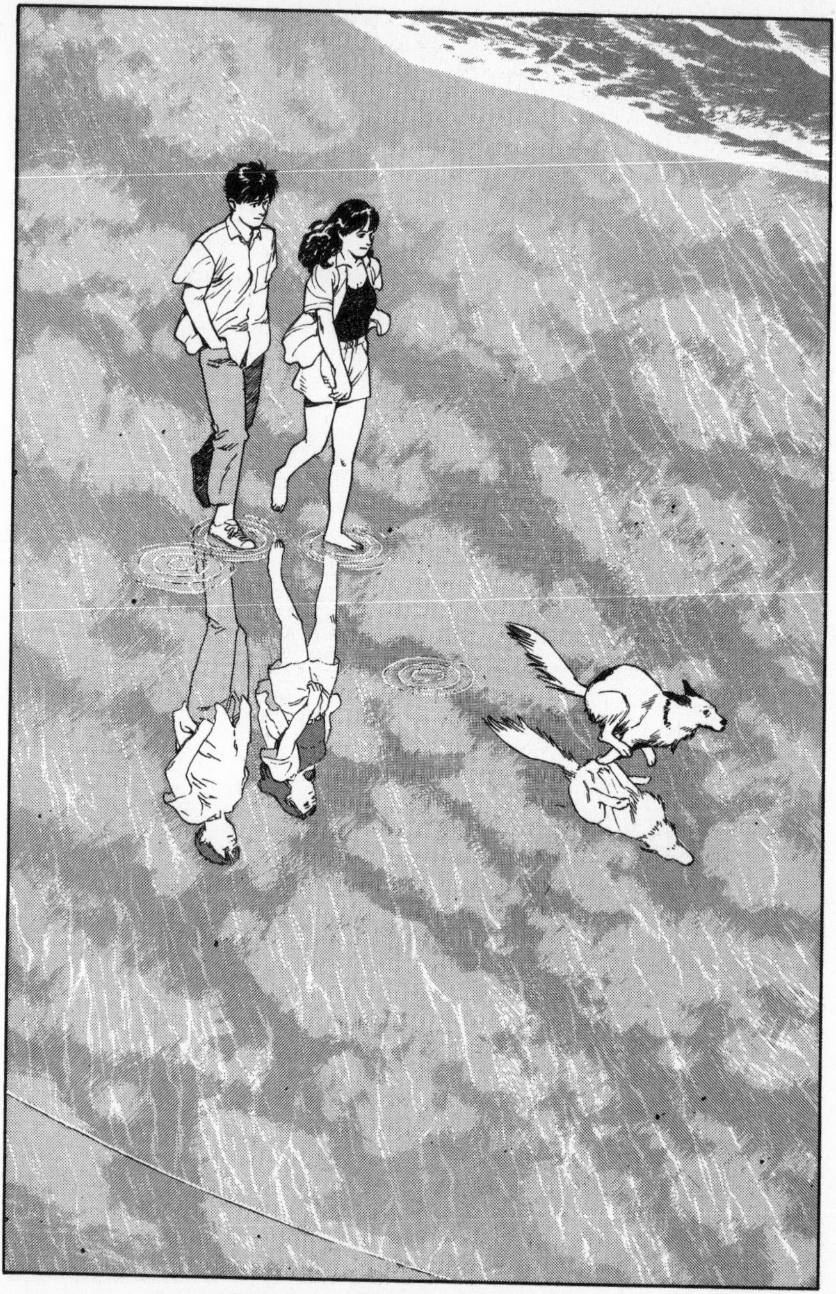

1990: Issue 20, Fourth Installment

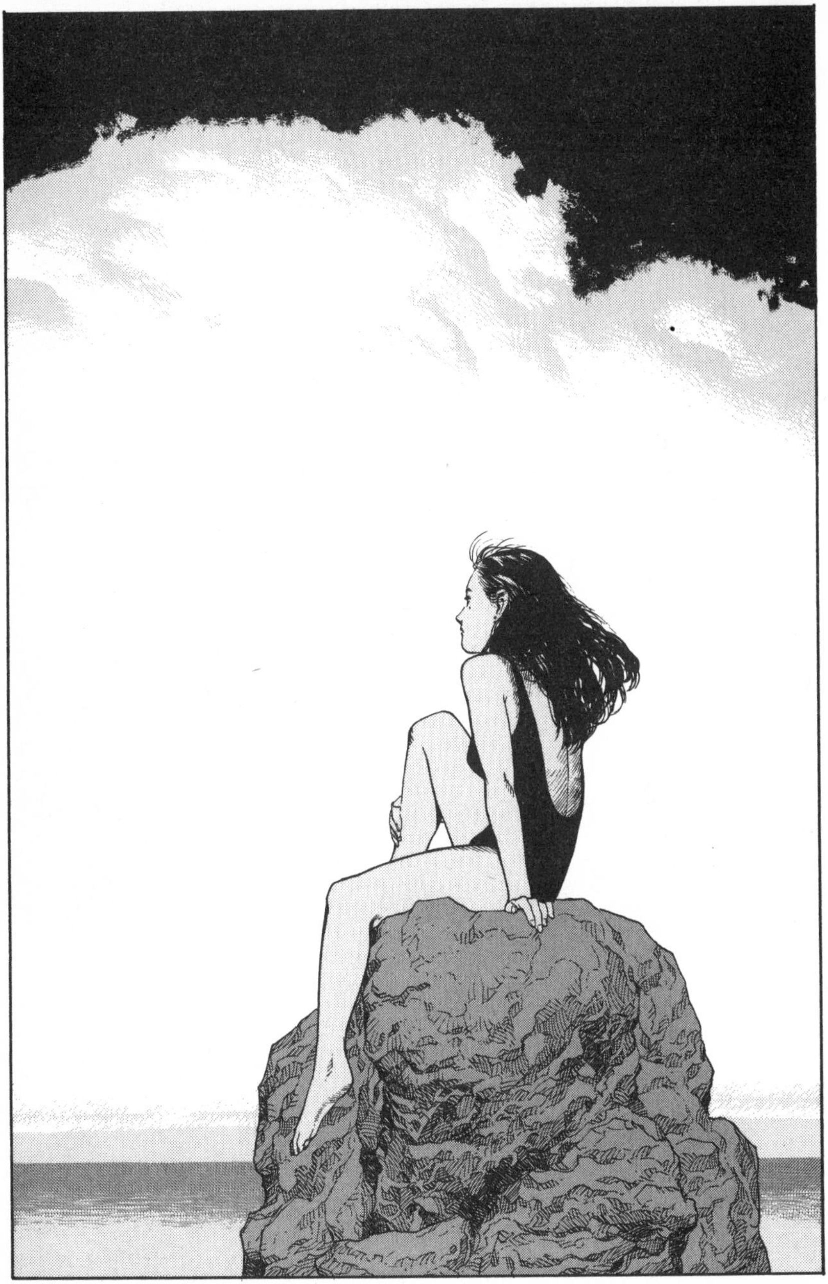

1990: Combined Issue 21 & 22 Fifth Installment

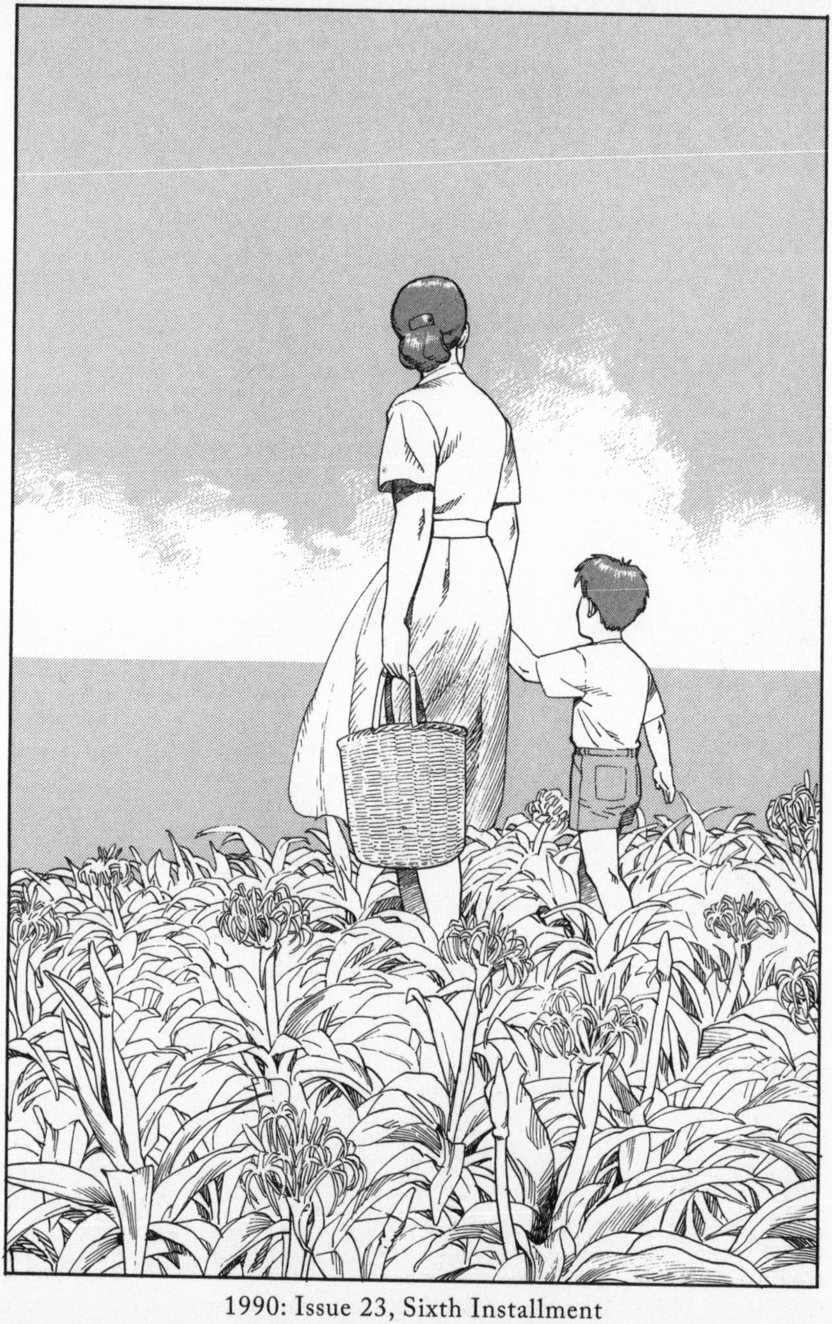

1990: Issue 23, Sixth Installment

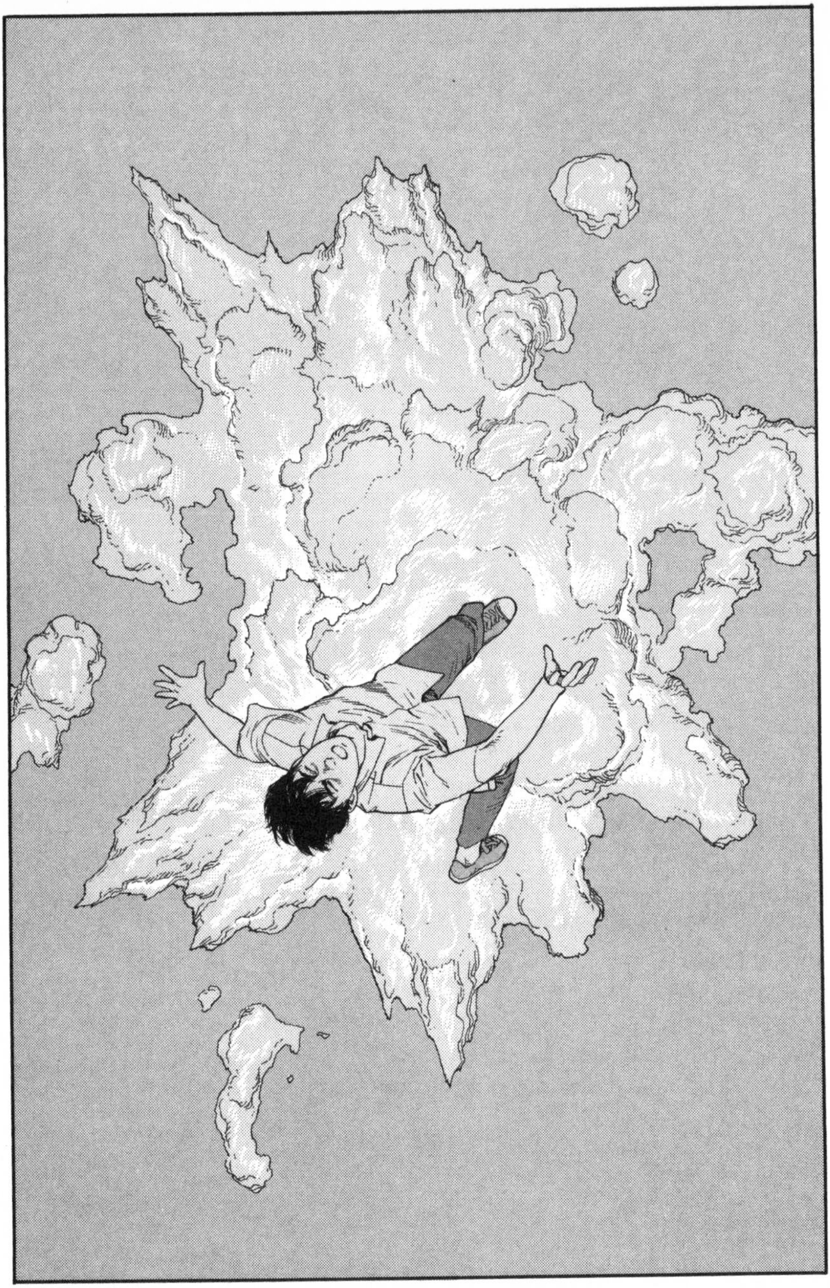

1990: Issue 26, Eighth Installment

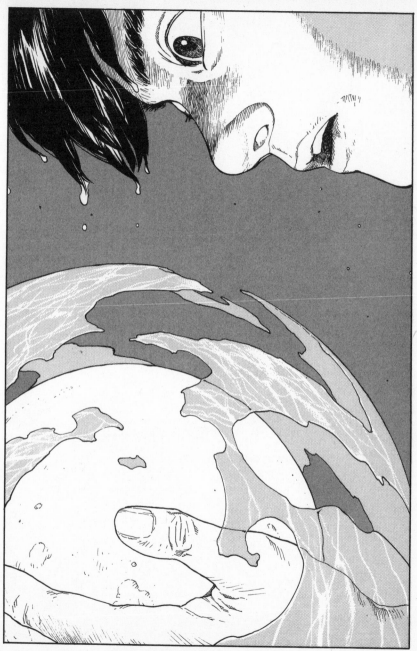

1990: Issue 28, Tenth Installment

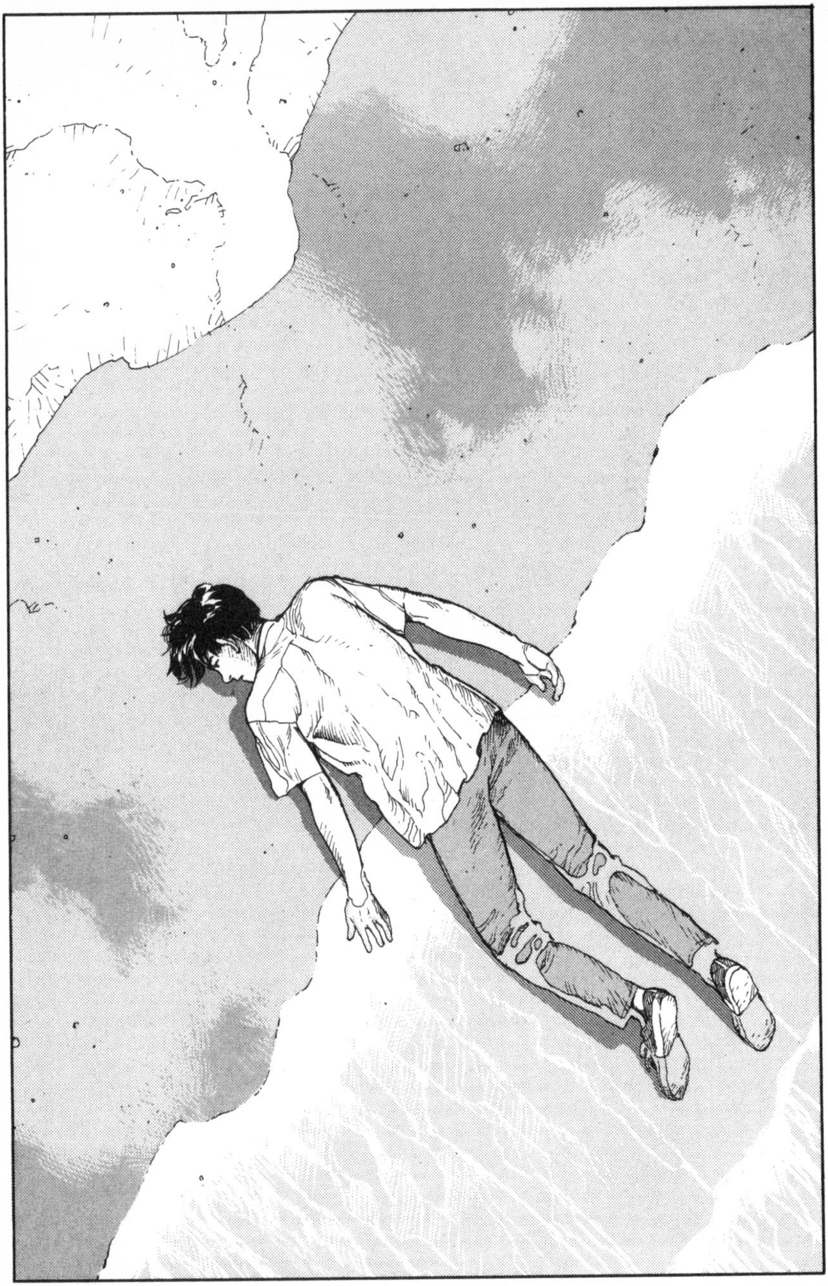

1990: Issue 29, Final Installment

Ninth Anniversary Revival

In the nine years since my first serialized manga, surprisingly many layers have formed into a sort of geological stratum. I put out another manga in book form, *World Apartment Horror*, while two series met the misfortunes of falling apart mid-story and a magazine folding. I also participated in a number of anime projects in various capacities. In 1998 my directorial debut, *Perfect Blue*, was hysterically repented—er, theatrically released and also made available the same year on VHS and LD, thankfully garnering many positive reviews.

"Satoshi Kon, who works in a wide variety of fields including manga, illustration and animation" sounds good on the face of it, but perhaps I just lack the patience to stay in one place.

In my own view I've been wearing the hats of both manga artist and animator, but when I'm introduced in magazines and such they refer to me as "anime director," with my "manga artist" hat consigned to oblivion. I don't recall ever tossing that hat away or shuttering that business, but I can't fight society's objective valuation. These days I myself self-deprecatingly settle for "manga artist in my previous incarnation."

**END
OF
AFTERWORD**

the intense stint, as expected my physical and mental stocks were drastically depleted. Wrapping rationalizations with spoiling kindness ("I did my utmost during serialization after all," "This bit could stay, I'll let you, little bit"), the manuscript returned to my editor, and thus the book found its way to store shelves.

It was summer. On a clear sunny day, my first book was there stacked face-up in my local bookstore. I felt joy like a powerful ray of sunshine, shyness like Tokyo's own creeping humidity, and inadequacy like a shimmering haze, all of which made the day feel hotter.

A Parting Gift

I think this was right after the book went on sale. I already did animation work back then, and around dawn at a studio I suddenly sensed an anomaly.

"Is the Earth's gravity getting stronger?!"

No joke, that was the thought that crossed my mind, but the anomaly was in my own body. Extreme fatigue seized me out of the blue. My body felt so heavy I could barely stay seated on the train home. When I finally reached my apartment and took my temperature, the mercury rose past the 104° mark.

I lay in bed, groaning, for half a month. After that I had to be hospitalized. Come to think of it, that was my first time, so *Tropic of the Sea* indeed inundated me with all sorts of new experiences.

Hepatitis A. Such an impressive-sounding illness was also a first for me. By the time I was hospitalized, I wasn't pale, I was dyed thoroughly yellow. I was jaundiced.

Today, I can see that having been weakened body and soul by work on the series, I shouldn't have engaged in sustained heavy drinking exuberant that I was done. Days of booze and folly. I believe it was a result of excessive alcohol consumption further chipping away at my constitution and the virus gaily going to town in my body. Yet I recovered faster than anticipated, and after just a month of burdening a hospital bed and nurses I was discharged.

My royalty payments covered the costs of my hospitalization, luckily... Wait, no!

would stay up all night finishing the manuscript, immediately collapse and wander through unconscious limbo, then wake up only to find time was running out for the next storyboard. Oh what fun. At the time it wasn't a part of my vocabulary, but looking back now maybe those instants of waking up were precisely "perfect blue." Because the first thought that would pop into my head on waking was: "I've got no time left..."

With each new installment, my body weight and that of my manuscripts fell. That isn't some metaphor. The manuscripts must have gotten physically lighter. In other words, I would run out of time for adding touches and end up with fewer and fewer pen strokes. Frustration and shame raced from the right side of my brain to the left, and seasonal changes crept past me out my window. Neither the first signs of spring, the fragrant breezes of May, nor the sunshine of early summer knocked on the door of my sad little apartment, and by the time the serialization ended it was nearing the gloomy rainy season of June.

Only the bits of screentone floating in the foam in the washing machine granted me a seeping sense of accomplishment, tinged with faint numbed regret.

"Ah... So it's over."

After I was done, I felt distant, screened by a milky white film, like the whole thing had happened to another person. But when it rains it shines. The fun part for the manga artist comes after serialization. The Good News is called "tankobon" (the book form). Yes, the El Dorado that so many people dream of—royalties. They say manga sells dreams, but the manga artist's waking dream is none other than that book form.

A book, with my own name printed on the cover—my first book did make me immensely happy.

I did a cover image in color for the occasion.

Since it was my first collected volume, I went back and retouched some of the manuscript a little as well. I wanted to do what I could to fix the art which had gotten rough to meet deadlines, and I also added a few pages. Remembering my harried days, what it was like at this or that point, or for that panel, and fixing it, I tried to bring the work a little closer to my original intentions.

Even though I'd only just completed the work a couple of months before, I thought it looked astonishingly terrible and, as I revised here and there and there too, found myself wanting to redo the entire thing. But after with, my normally sharp tongue must have been finely honed. I'd like to take this opportunity to apologize. I'm sorry.

This tsunami-like experience made me painfully aware of my own shallow thinking and immature technique and added no small sum to my stores of experience and craft as well as a pretty small sum to my bank account.

To spell it out, I'm not joking when I say I didn't have the time to leave my apartment. As I recall, it took me two days to come up with a storyboard (basically a scenario), three days to do the rough sketching, and another two to ink the pages. Unless you're extremely bad at arithmetic, you see it took me a total of seven days. *Young Magazine* is published weekly. A new issue comes out every seven days, which is a happy system for the readers but a woefully unhappy one for the creators.

Yet I couldn't resort to the mass-production method of buying time and quality by mobilizing an army of assistants. There simply wasn't enough room in the shabby apartment I lived in at the time, and I guess if nothing else I had my little pride and wanted to draw as much as possible with my own hands. This is a terrible way to put it, but maybe I was conceited enough to "ruin it by my own hand" if it had to come to that. To the reader, the customer, there is no greater arrogance, but I'm an honest fellow who can't do what I cannot do. Yeah, right.

At the most, I had three assistants. I usually relied on just two.

Toward the beginning, even though I bemoaned my lack of time I had pages I'd finished in advance and was able to deliver the manuscript to the editorial department in person. I engaged in this fanciful behavior with an eye to being "entertained" by my editor, in Ikebukuro or thereabouts. Entertained, entertained, gleefully entertained. Naturally, I don't mean some unsexy tête-à-tête over drinks with my editor but a visit to an establishment filled with young women believed to be paid splendid hourly rates.

There is no liquor more delicious or richly-hued than that tasted after the workday is done, you see.

"This is the life of a manga artist! Ha ha ha!"

Halfwit.

That dream was, of course, ephemeral, and by the middle of the serialization my lifestyle was as dark as could be, my sole source of pleasure the nightcap I'd have before getting the little sleep I could.

In the days leading up to the deadline, that nemesis of manga artists, I

AFTERWORD
by Satoshi Kon

(Excerpted from the 1999 Bijutsu Shuppan edition of *Tropic of the Sea*)

The neologism "Tropic of the Sea" was my own doing. [Note: the original Japanese title, "Kaikisen," is phonetically equivalent to the Japanese word for "tropic" as in Tropic of Cancer; however, the character for "kai," meaning "turn," was replaced with a homophone meaning "sea."]

This work whose title is quite embarrassing in hindsight ran in Kodansha's *Young Magazine* in eleven installments between March and June of 1990. As of this writing, that was nine years ago. They say "a decade is an age ago," and it's a span of time an artist still in a growth spurt dare not underestimate and a sufficient tally of months and years for the water behind his ears to begin to dry. Since then both my art and I have seen changes. One's innate abilities don't ever increase, but technique must be something that's cultivated through repetition and practice since I seem to have made a little progress. Going back over the manuscript on the occasion of this reprint made me blush incessantly.

Back Then

Since I'm already embarrassed, let me reminisce about those times.

Tropic of the Sea was my first long-form manga, serialization an unfamiliar experience. Ignorance and inexperience are formidable things. My half-hearted preparations prior to serialization were blown away by the third installment, and for a few turbulent months, on a stormy sea, I blindly rowed and rowed with the none-too-smart oars called Youth and was done before I knew it. Perhaps it wasn't the fictitious town of Ade that provides the setting for this work that was beset by a tsunami, but me.

During the serialization I caused much trouble for my editor and all my assistants. Having rapidly used up what little composure I have to begin